Empowering the White House

Empowering
the White House

Governance under Nixon, Ford, and Carter

Karen M. Hult and Charles E. Walcott

 University Press of Kansas

Published by the University Press of Kansas (Lawrence, Kansas 66049), which was organized by the Kansas Board of Regents and is operated and funded by Emporia State University, Fort Hays State University, Kansas State University, Pittsburg State University, the University of Kansas, and Wichita State University

Library of Congress Cataloging-in-Publication Data

Hult, Karen Marie.
    Empowering the White House : governance under Nixon, Ford, and Carter / Karen M. Hult and Charles E. Walcott.
        p.   cm. — (Studies in government and public policy)
Includes bibliographical references (p.   ) and index.
    ISBN 0-7006-1298-X (cloth : alk. paper) — ISBN 0-7006-1299-8 (pbk. : alk. paper)
    1. United States—Politics and government—1969–1974.   2. United States—Politics and government—1974–1977.   3. United States—Politics and government—1977–1981.   4. Nixon, Richard M. (Richard Milhous), 1913– —Influence.   5. Presidents—United States—Staff—History—20th century.   6. Ford, Gerald R., 1913–   7. Carter, Jimmy, 1924– 8. Executive power—United States—Case studies.   I. Walcott, Charles Eliot, 1943–   II. Title.   III. Series.

E855   .H84   2004
973.92—dc22   2003017059

British Library Cataloguing in Publication Data is available.

Printed in the United States of America

10 9 8 7 6 5 4 3 2 1

The paper used in this publication meets the minimum requirements of the American National Standard for Permanence of Paper for Printed Library Materials Z39.48-1984.

Contents

Preface

This book represents the culmination—at least to this point—of a research program we have been pursuing for almost twenty years. Working at the intersection of organization theory and presidency research, we set the goal of constructing a theoretically informed account of the organizational evolution of the White House over much of the course of the modern presidency. In one sense, this volume extends the analysis we presented in *Governing the White House: From Hoover through LBJ*. Yet in a second—and in our view more important—sense, this is a very different book.

The current study began with two expectations. First, in moving from the first, or early modern, era of the modern presidency to the second era, White House aides both continued the tasks (and kept many of the structures) of the first era and pursued additional presidential goals. Although LBJ anticipated these changes in how presidents use their staffs, Nixon was the key break point. Unlike Johnson, he *systematically* pursued the enhanced use of his staff to, for example, cultivate public and interest group support for his political and policy objectives. Second, like other scholars,* we believe that the Nixon presidency introduced discontinuous changes into the evolution of staff structuring, which have had longer-term effects.

To probe these expectations, we decided to focus on the Nixon, Ford, and Carter administrations. This comparison permitted us to explore possible changes and continuities in presidencies occupied by both political parties. It also provided what seemed to be a "hard test" of predictions of continuity: reactions to the Nixon presidency in general, and to the misdeeds and abuses for which "Watergate" has become shorthand in particular, might well have impelled Nixon's successors to rid their own White Houses of anything even remotely "Nixonian."

In addition, the Nixon through Carter comparison gave us the opportunity to focus on only three administrations, each of which has far more, and far richer, materials documenting its organization and activities than was the case for earlier presidencies. As a result, our ability to identify and describe governance structures in detail was enhanced. Moreover, by viewing the Nixon administration as a "tipping point" of sorts in the scope and orientation of presidential staffing, we made

---

*For example, John H. Kessel, *Presidents, the Presidency, and the Political Environment* (Washington, D.C.: CQ Press, 2001), 9ff; George A. Krause and Jeffrey E. Cohen, "Opportunity, Constraints, and the Development of the Institutional Presidency: The Issuance of Executive Orders," *Journal of Politics* 62 (February 2000): 88–114; Lyn Ragsdale and John J. Theis III, "The Institutionalization of the American Presidency, 1924–92," *American Journal of Political Science* 41 (October 1997): 1314–15.

theoretical contact with historical institutionalist accounts of the development of the presidency. At the same time, we sought to clarify the connection between our theorizing and the approach of so-called rational-choice institutionalists. We have come to view these sometimes competing perspectives as potentially complementary, although to do so requires pushing beyond the usual boundaries of each.*

The White Houses we explore here, plus or minus a few details (such as a National Economic Council or an Office of Homeland Security), generally resemble the White House of today. Experience has demonstrated that a general approach—which we call (borrowing shamelessly from physics) the standard model—is most effective at allowing presidents to pursue their policy and political objectives amid the myriad constraints they confront. Certainly, that appears to be the current consensus among both practitioners and scholars. Indeed, the term *standard* has certain normative implications that we acknowledge. Yet we do not claim that there is one best way to organize the White House or that seeming enhancements of presidential capacity are always desirable. Instead, we hope that our exploration of the failings as well as the accomplishments of the presidents of the 1970s will encourage creative thought about alternatives.

We are grateful for research support from the American Political Science Association, the Ford Library Foundation, and the travel grants program and Department of Political Science at Virginia Tech. We are especially grateful to Dr. Joan S. Hult for loaning us her condo in Greenbelt, Maryland, for several months while we worked with the Nixon Papers at the National Archives II facility in College Park. We had only to water the plants while Joan was off climbing mountains.

As always, we profited immensely from interactions with colleagues. Notable among them were those who worked with us on the White House Interview Project: Martha Joynt Kumar, Terry Sullivan, Peri Arnold, MaryAnne Borrelli, Nancy Kassop, Bradley Patterson, Kathryn Dunn Tenpas, Shirley Anne Warshaw, and Stephen Wayne. George Edwards was helpful in many ways, including his gracious hosting of gatherings of the "presidency research" clan in College Station.

We owe a great deal as well to the helpful and efficient staffs at the Carter and Ford Presidential Libraries and the Nixon Presidential Materials Project. One cannot do archival research without archivists, and we had the assistance of some of the best.

The book would have been significantly weaker without the constructive and careful comments and suggestions of Joseph Pika. His own work on interest group liaison proved to be a useful resource as well.

Perhaps our greatest debt is to our publisher, Fred Woodward. Not only did he believe in and encourage the project, but he also had confidence that someday it would be finished. At times, he probably thought that he was the only one. We deeply appreciate his patience, good humor, and clear commitment to scholarship.

---

*Cf. Kathleen Thelen, "Historical Institutionalism in Comparative Politics," *Annual Review of Political Science* 2 (1999): 369–404.

Introduction

The aftermath of the September 11, 2001, terrorist attacks on the Pentagon and the World Trade Center has cast into sharp relief some of the continuing puzzles confronting scholars of the U.S. presidency. To what extent, for example, have the responses of the George W. Bush administration been shaped primarily by the president's personality, experiences, or leadership style? Would virtually any president confronting such a catastrophe have responded in a similar way? How much influence has been exerted by the organizational infrastructure of the presidency or by the larger political and policy environments (both inside and outside the United States) in which the modern White House is embedded?

Questions persist about the relative impact on presidential decision making of factors such as the idiosyncratic characteristics of individual chief executives, the strategic choices of presidents behaving as rational (i.e., purposive) actors, the growth and specialization of the "institutional presidency," and the opportunities and constraints imposed by external actors and forces. Increasingly, it seems, presidential scholars are resisting dichotomous distinctions—for instance, between the "person" and the "institution" or between the presidency and the environment.[1] Still, debate continues over how best to identify and untangle such influences.

Although myriad factors affect presidential performance, attention frequently focuses on the influence of White House structuring and operations. At least since Herbert Hoover, presidents have relied on plural professional staffs. Several years later, the Brownlow Committee, created by FDR after his first reelection, declared, "the president needs help." One of the committee's recommendations that Roosevelt implemented was the creation of the White House Office (WHO) within the larger Executive Office of the President. Since then, even as the White House staff has grown in size and become more specialized, the presidency and the staff often receive attention only after serious problems arise in which the White House or the president is implicated (e.g., the Bay of Pigs, Watergate, Iran-contra, the failed nominations of Zoe Baird and Kimba Wood). It is telling as well that one of the Bush administration's initial responses to September 11 was the creation of the Office of Homeland Security in the Executive Office of the President, headed by an assistant to the president. Meanwhile, as Burke notes, "Since the Kennedy administration, presidents have received, solicited and unsolicited, a range of advice on organizing their White House staffs."[2] Yet, despite all these efforts, Burke finds scant evidence of either "an upward learning curve" in drawing on the institutional resources of the presidency "or as much stock-taking from the mistakes or difficulties (or, in some

1

cases, successes) of predecessors as might make the task easier and more effective."[3] Moreover, as already mentioned, disagreements often arise over the value added (or subtracted) by staffing.

The study that follows begins from the premise that the structure and operation of contemporary White Houses *can* make a difference in presidential politics, policy, and performance. At the same time, White House organization and activities are endogenous, variably shaped by presidential preferences and strategies, policy and political settings, and past structures and operations. We contend that it is critical to locate White House staffing both longitudinally and within varying problem contexts.

Here, we seek to build on our work on the Herbert Hoover through Lyndon Johnson White Houses,[4] exploring how staffing evolved from these first-era (or early modern) administrations to those of the second era of the modern presidency. Other presidential scholars agree that the late 1960s marked a key juncture in the evolution of the presidency. According to Krause and Cohen, for example, this is the point at which a model that emphasizes constraints on presidential behavior becomes more useful.[5] Similarly, Ragsdale and Theis conclude that "the 1970s was a pivotal decade for the presidency as an institution"; not only had the institution "acquired a full range of policy responsibilities it had not held before," but the presidency also had assumed "value independent of presidents themselves."[6]

STREAMS OF CHANGE

Our major concerns are tracing and explaining White House staff structuring over time, with an eye toward exploring the possible implications for presidential governance. In particular, we see several streams of change, which may vary in importance between the two eras of the modern presidency.

The First Era

The early modern presidency was a time of considerable change in U.S. politics, in the presidency, and in the White House. This period encompassed, for example, the Great Depression and the New Deal, the Second World War, the use of atomic bombs, the Cold War, the end of de jure racial segregation, a presidential assassination, and the War on Poverty. As the era drew to a close, public discord over U.S. foreign policy in Vietnam mounted, and divisions based on race, gender, age, and lifestyle deepened.

Over the forty years from the Hoover through the Johnson presidencies, considerable structural change also took place in the White House.[7] One evident stream of change reflected *partisan learning*. Partisan learning involves the replication of structural features of previous same-party White Houses: presidents tend to follow the organizing strategies of presidents of their own political party, while rejecting those of predecessors from the other party. Typically, partisan learning is transmitted by transition advisers with experience from previous White Houses, such as Truman aides Clark Clifford and Richard Neustadt counseling Presidents John Kennedy and Lyndon Johnson. Often, it is grounded as well in exaggerated perceptions of problems experienced by opposition-party White Houses (e.g., the alleged difficulties produced by Dwight Eisenhower's formal processes for national security decision making).

A second kind of change involved the influences of *environmental expectations*. Frequently, these can dampen the degree and smooth the flow of change. Some staff structuring persisted and was elaborated across administrations as external actors came to consider tasks such as press relations or congressional liaison to be part of "normal" White House operations. To some extent, this type of change can be viewed as reflecting environmentally driven strategic choice, a kind of "nonpartisan learning" as administrations imitate the evident successes of their predecessors. It also is consistent with the notion of strategic presidents protecting their political stakes by adjusting to changing circumstances.[8]

More gradual, continuous change may be reinforced by *organizational dynamics* other than partisan learning within the WHO. For example, in most complex organizations, there is a tendency for the division of labor to increase incrementally. In addition, such specialization may trigger a *differentiation dynamic,* as new structures and activities create the need for additional coordinating structures. Organizational politics can generate structural change in response to uncertainties or disputes that arise within the White House. Meanwhile, inertia may limit the extent of change, since satisfactory structuring may persist due to the apparent costs of change.

Finally, the *preferences, objectives, and strategies* of individual presidents may induce change. The varying policy agendas, campaign promises, and political experiences of particular presidents influenced structuring for (in order of declining impact) supervision and coordination, policy processing, and outreach of first-era presidents.

Although these kinds of change also appear in second-era White Houses, their relative significance remains a question for empirical examination. We hypothesize in the next chapter, for example, that partisan learning would become less influential as the WHO further institutionalized and structuring was driven more by organizational dynamics and often inertial environmental expectations.

Nonetheless, chapter 2 explores one important instance of partisan learning that has shaped White Houses since the Nixon administration (and thus has been transformed into an example of nonpartisan learning): Richard Nixon's adoption of Eisenhower's approach to overall staff management, including a staff secretariat and a chief of staff. Efforts to avoid using either (as Gerald Ford and Jimmy Carter both attempted) typically fail, as White Houses try to cope with high expectations and an enormous workload. At the same time, as Nixon himself discovered, when these innovations operate ineffectively (as they arguably did under Mack McLarty, the first Clinton chief of staff) or are used inappropriately (as in the decision clearance process during Reagan's second term), they can have serious implications for presidential governance.

The Second Era

The second era began with a period of more *discontinuous* change. In addition to continuing most of the tasks of first-era White Houses, presidents started to use their staffs for a broader range of purposes, such as public relations, legal advice, and policy formulation. To be sure, LBJ anticipated some of these changes, but Nixon pursued these efforts, and pursued them far more systematically.

The most significant Nixon-era shifts were those involving staff complexity and tasks, which showed ratchet effects.[9] Such changes constituted "tipping points"[10] that have had lasting effects not only on White House staffing but also on the expectations of presidents and on the values and goals of those with whom the presidency interacts. These latter changes, in turn, have further constrained the structural and behavioral options open to individual presidents.[11]

In more concrete terms, for instance, the number of subunits in the WHO doubled from its first-era high of fifteen under Eisenhower to more than thirty, where it has stayed since the Nixon years. More important, contemporary White Houses routinely have staffers and units dedicated to, for example, interest group liaison, economic policy, and contact with the non-Washington media. The offices of communications and White House counsel that Nixon introduced have appeared in one form or another in all subsequent White Houses, as has what Ford called a unit for public liaison.

Why did this kind of discontinuous change in the presidency occur during the Nixon years? One possible reason involves what Skowronek has called "secular" and "political" time and what we have labeled environmental and presidential choice factors. In secular (or chronological) time, the political and policy *environments* in which White House occupants found themselves during the 1960s and early 1970s were quite volatile, with exploding numbers of interest groups, weakening political parties, an increasingly hostile media, and wrenching policy controversies over issues such as Vietnam and civil rights.[12]

Yet much of this turbulence was present in the final years of the Johnson administration. A consideration of political time and the influence of presidential choices may shed some light on why it was Nixon and not LBJ who ushered in the second era of the modern presidency. In Skowronek's framework, Nixon was an "opposition leader in a resilient regime," which led him to pursue a "politics of preemption." During such periods, presidents seek "to build new, personal bases of political support outside of regular political alliances," to repudiate current arrangements, and to challenge the still resilient establishment.[13] Although these preemptive presidencies often trigger "governing crises," they also can foster longer-term enhancements of presidential power.

That Nixon was a preemptive president is difficult to challenge. Clearly, he was an opposition leader. Elected by a narrow margin by fewer than half the voters, he confronted a Congress and a majority of statehouses controlled by opposition Democrats. Nixon also struggled against what he saw as an elitist and increasingly discredited "Eastern Establishment" that dominated the two political parties and the mass media.[14] The implications for his presidency, however, are less clear. Skowronek has not fully examined the dynamics of preemptive presidencies, calling them the wild cards of his analysis.[15] We suggest that such presidencies are especially likely to be associated with discontinuous change, since they are free from established commitments and pursue "programs designed to aggravate interest cleavages and factional discontent within the dominant coalition."[16] Viewed from this perspective, Nixon's association with the first period of marked discontinuous change in White House staffing in the modern presidency is not surprising: he was the first clearly preemptive president since Woodrow Wilson.

Skowronek contends that few of the accomplishments of preemptive presidents survive their terms in office.[17] Whether such expectations apply to alterations of governance structuring is questionable, however, especially given the influence of organizational inertia and environmental expectations that can help structural innovations take root. Indeed, many of the staffing changes that Nixon introduced to the White House have persisted into the twenty-first century.

SCOPE OF THE ANALYSIS: WHY NIXON, FORD, AND CARTER?

In any longitudinal study, the span of time covered is an important issue. Here, the starting point was relatively straightforward. Since we had already examined the Hoover through Johnson administrations, the Nixon presidency came next chronologically, permitting further tracing and comparison of continuity and change.

Moreover, as the author of what we believe was discontinuous change in the White House, Nixon is a pivotal figure in the organizational evolution of the staff and the presidency. Moving on to the Ford administration provides a clearer end to the official Nixon years, since many Nixon staffers remained in Washington after the disgraced president boarded *Air Force One* for exile in California. At the same time, the specter of the Nixon presidency haunted the Ford White House. Comparing White House staffing under Nixon and Ford allows an initial assessment of the lasting effects of the Nixon administration's changes. Such a comparison arguably presents a more difficult test of the tipping-point idea than it might seem to initially. Given the intense reactions to Watergate and the congressional investigations of the size and activities of the White House staff that began as early as 1970, one might have expected the Ford administration to dismantle most of the Nixon operation.

Of course, a stronger test of the longer-run impact of Nixon's staffing innovations is examining their fate under an opposing-party president. Examining the Carter White House extends the exploration of the Nixon years as a tipping point.

More important, discovering continuities in a Democratic administration should strengthen our inferences about staff dynamics during second-era presidencies. In addition, inclusion of the Carter presidency permits another comparison: between Carter and JFK-LBJ. The similarities and differences in these Democratic presidents' staffs allow another test of the partisan-learning proposition.

Thus, in what follows, the most in-depth documentation and analysis focus on the Nixon, Ford, and Carter presidencies. Where relevant, we also consider prior and subsequent White Houses, looking for evidence of further change or continuity.

OUTLINE OF THE BOOK

As in the analysis of first-era White Houses, our examination of the Nixon, Ford, and Carter staffs examines three primary clusters of tasks: outreach, policy processing, and internal coordination and supervision. Here, however, we emphasize activities and structures that were new or different from those in most early modern White Houses.

After we review in chapter 1 the theoretical framework for the study and lay out the main theoretical propositions, several empirical chapters sketch some of the innovative elements that appeared in the Nixon, Ford, and Carter White Houses and that allow initial testing of our theoretical expectations. Chapter 2 explores how Nixon adapted Eisenhower's staffing approach to his own objectives and priorities and to the increasing demands on U.S. presidents. Since then, reliance on similar structuring has become the standard model for organizing White Houses.

Attention turns next to some of the innovations in White House staffing that Nixon introduced. Chapter 3 traces the emergence and evolution of structuring to support what has come to be called the "public relations presidency," paying particular attention to the Office of Communications that first appeared in the WHO under Nixon. Similarly, chapter 4 examines how cultivating relations with interest groups increasingly became the responsibility of specialized aides lodged in what came to be called public liaison units, and chapter 5 follows the creation and early evolution of the White House counsel's office.

In contrast, chapter 6's look at congressional relations uncovers less innovation as well as considerable continuity with first-era White Houses dating back to Eisenhower. At the same time, it underscores the waning of partisan learning, as Carter was pushed to return to some of the specific strategies that his two Republican predecessors had relied on.

Chapter 7 turns to policy processing, both highlighting the emergence and stabilization of White House staffing to handle domestic and economic policy and looking at the continuities and shifts in national security staffing. Chapter 8 then examines speechwriting, concentrating on the early links that Nixon forged between policy decision making and speechwriting, and speculating about explanations for the general demise of his approach.

Finally, chapter 9 evaluates the performance of the theoretical propositions and returns to the questions with which the analysis began. Although our findings do not depict a presidency fully transformed from that of the first era, they do highlight the impact of the Nixon presidency, of the diverse environments that contemporary presidents confront, and of the intraorganizational dynamics of the White House.

1
Setting the Stage

Before tracing the paths of structural change and continuity in the initial second-era presidencies, we briefly review the analytical framework that animated our examination of first-era White Houses. With that as a foundation, the discussion turns to a more explicit delineation of our theoretical expectations for the Nixon, Ford, and Carter administrations.

ANALYTICAL FRAMEWORK

As in *Governing the White House,* the emphasis here is on *governance structures.* *Governance* "refers to politics within a relatively orderly, rule-bound setting." Working within an organizational governance approach permits us to focus on how organizations such as the White House Office "work continually to establish and define their orienting goals and to discover and choose means for achieving them."[1]

At the outset, it should be underscored that our use of the term organizational *structure* differs from that of some presidency scholars. Here (as in much of organization theory), a structure refers to a set of recurring interactions within and between organizations (and their subunits); structures can be formal or informal, permanent or temporary.[2] From this perspective, the WHO encompasses numerous governance structures.[3] Such arrangements may be contained within individual units (e.g., the office of the press secretary), they may connect units (e.g., the National Security Council staff and the White House counsel's office), or they may be ad hoc groups of officials that assemble to address a particular problem (e.g., task forces to push for the passage of legislation, war rooms).

Structuring: Dimensions and Influences

We explore three distinct dimensions of governance structures: emergence, stability, and nature.[4] Structures *emerge* when relationships and decision processes become repetitive and routinized.[5] The *stability* of any particular structure can vary both within and between presidential terms. We consider a structure to be *institutionalized* when it persists across at least two presidencies.[6] Arguably, evidence of institutionalization is strongest when two or more of those administrations are of different political parties. Finally, since structural form may vary, the *nature* of a governance structure is also examined. In previous work, we identified seven types of structure, ranging from hierarchical through market structures (see Table 1.1).

What influences these structural dimensions? We examine three clusters of variables that may help shape the emergence, stability, and nature of White House governance structures: environmental, presidential choice, and organizational factors. First, the structuring of the WHO is subject to myriad external influences, including the demands and expectations of interest groups, political parties, the U.S. public, members of Congress, executive branch officials, leaders of other nation-states, and the national and international media. Important, too, may be the constraints and opportunities presented by global, regional, national, and local economic dynamics; information, communication, and weapons technologies; and persistent, cyclical, and emergent policy problems.

The second cluster of variables focuses on the influence of presidents themselves. As in *Governing the White House,* we focus on presidential choice, that is, on the possible effects of both presidential preferences (e.g., policy objectives, desired ways of receiving advice) and presidential strategies (e.g., coping with interest groups, dealing with staff conflict).

Third are the organizational variables, which tap the dynamics within the WHO. Of interest is the possibility of particular kinds of path dependence: whether and how "structures designed at one [time] affect later organizational patterns."[7] First-era White Houses, for instance, exhibited several instances of partisan learning, in which new presidents established structures used by predecessors of the same party (while rejecting those of other-party presidents). Similarly, Republican Richard Nixon included several arrangements that Dwight Eisenhower had introduced, such as a chief of staff, cabinet secretary, and staff secretary.

Sometimes, particular structures become more institutionalized, persisting across several administrations of both political parties. In part, this may be a sort of "'non-partisan learning' that reflects an understanding of successful experience on the part of the preceding administration," as evidently happened with press relations and the handling of various constituency groups by the end of Lyndon Johnson's administration.[8] External expectations of appropriate White House tasks and structures may well reinforce the tendency of new presidents to follow precedent.

Meanwhile, complex organizations of all kinds involve other dynamics as well. As demands and the structures for coping with them escalate, for example, the need for additional structuring to provide coordination (and perhaps resolution of disputes over organizational turf) may arise. This lies at the heart of what the introduction called a *differentiation dynamic.*[9]

Thus, we expect three clusters of factors to help account for changes and continuities in the emergence, stabilization, and nature of White House structuring. Our analysis also distinguishes among several kinds of tasks undertaken by con-

Table 1.1. Characteristics of Selected Governance Structures

Governance Structure	Participation	Expertise	Decision Rule	Conflict Management	Uncertainty Management
Hierarchy	Giving or following orders	Organizational position, technical knowledge	Preference of top decision maker	Resolution, avoidance	Resolution, avoidance
Collegial-competitive	Advocacy of interests, perspective	Political expertise, skills in persuasion and bargaining	Majority vote (or provision for extraordinary majority)	Competition, collaboration, compromise	Competition, collaboration, compromise
Collegial-mediative	Argument before neutral third party	Skills in argumentation, mediation	Parties' acceptance or rejection of mediator's advice, proposed settlement	Guided compromise	Guided compromise
Collegial-consensual	Cooperative search	Skills in collaboration, persuasion	Consensus	Collaboration, avoidance (groupthink)	Collaboration, avoidance
Adjudicative	Two parties advocating opposing views	Skills in persuasion, marshaling evidence	Burden of proof	Competition between two parties	Reduction: issues cast as right-wrong, correct-incorrect
Adversarial	Multiparty advocacy	Skills in persuasion, marshaling evidence	Judgment of decision maker (not an advocate)	Multiparty competition	Competition; may exacerbate uncertainty
Market	Pursuit of individual objectives, interests	Varies by party, situation	Epiphenomenal coordination	Competition, avoidance	Acceptance as inevitable

SOURCES: Charles E. Walcott and Karen M. Hult, *Governing the White House: From Hoover through LBJ* (Lawrence: University Press of Kansas, 1995), 15; cf. Karen M. Hult and Charles E. Walcott, *Governing Public Organizations: Politics, Structures, and Institutional Design* (Pacific Grove, Calif.: Brooks/Cole, 1990).

temporary White Houses: outreach, policy processing, and coordination and supervision. Later, we introduce several propositions about the relevant influences of the three clusters on the structuring of tasks in the Nixon, Ford, and Carter staffs. First, though, we provide a brief overview of the theoretical links among governance structuring, the influences on such structuring, and the decision settings that contemporary presidencies confront.

A Problem-Contingency Perspective

Our analysis is grounded in what we term a problem-contingency logic. Building on the work of structural contingency scholars in organization theory, a problem-contingency approach to decision making[10] predicts that the type of governance structure used in an organization will be congruent with ("fit") the prevailing decision setting. It is expected that more congruent structures will emerge, and as the congruence between the decision setting and the nature of the structure increases, so will the stability of the structure.

Of special concern when identifying the nature of congruent governance structures are the levels of goal consensus, uncertainty, and controversy and of technical (i.e., focused on "means") certainty, uncertainty, and controversy that actors perceive to be present in the relevant decision setting. Clearly, environmental factors are likely to be key influences on the prevailing levels of uncertainty and controversy. Yet a problem-contingency approach need not involve environmental determinism. As in *Governing the White House,* our analysis begins with the premise that much staff structuring emerges as a result of the strategic responses of presidents (and their most senior aides) to environmental demands. Like Moe and other so-called rational-choice institutionalists,[11] we view presidents as purposive actors who strive to attain their political and policy objectives within the incentives and constraints of given problem contexts and the institution of the U.S. presidency. Our main focus, then, is not on the idiosyncratic characteristics of particular chief executives but on the likely responses of presidents as strategic actors with sets of political commitments and policy goals.[12]

Further, we have argued that the extent of congruence between such responses and the prevailing decision setting rises as structuring encourages the incorporation of relevant expertise and information into discussion, improves the capacity to take action or reach decision closure, heightens accountability to the president, and increases representation of relevant interests.[13] Figure 1.1 summarizes the types of governance structure predicted for various decision settings.

Several additional points about these predictions should be made. First, characterizations of White House decision settings may change over time (e.g., as new information is examined, presidential aides are replaced, party balances shift) and may vary among decision participants (and observers). Based in part on actors' perceptions (or "constructions") of the situation, the classification of decision settings also may be influenced by existing governance structures. Thus, we view

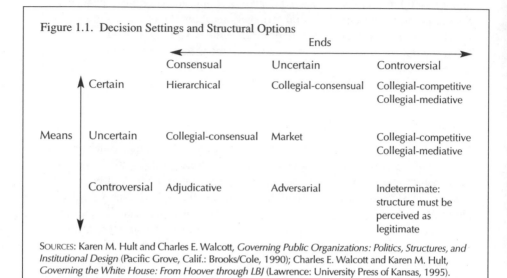

Figure 1.1. Decision Settings and Structural Options

		Ends		
		Consensual	Uncertain	Controversial
	Certain	Hierarchical	Collegial-consensual	Collegial-competitive Collegial-mediative
Means	Uncertain	Collegial-consensual	Market	Collegial-competitive Collegial-mediative
	Controversial	Adjudicative	Adversarial	Indeterminate: structure must be perceived as legitimate

SOURCES: Karen M. Hult and Charles E. Walcott, *Governing Public Organizations: Politics, Structures, and Institutional Design* (Pacific Grove, Calif.: Brooks/Cole, 1990); Charles E. Walcott and Karen M. Hult, *Governing the White House: From Hoover through LBJ* (Lawrence: University Press of Kansas, 1995).

structure as an independent as well as a dependent variable. That is, existing structures may shape how individuals recognize and define problems and solutions and how they assess information and alternatives; structures also may influence the degree and the nature of the uncertainty or conflict they perceive in the larger decision setting, as well as the range of options for action they consider.

Second, governance structures themselves cannot guarantee specific results or desirable outcomes. Yet, as we discovered in examining the Hoover through Johnson presidencies, structuring often affects the likelihood of better or worse performance when it comes to tasks such as foreign policy advising, staff supervision, and congressional liaison.[14] In general, too, we expect more successful elements of the White House to include more extensive informal structures that augment and interconnect formal structures.

Third, as structural dynamics under these earlier presidencies suggested, multipurpose structures may appear. That is, existing governance structures may adjust to cope with changing decision settings. For example, a structure that typically operates as a collegial-consensual unit (e.g., some first-era speechwriting operations) may shift to a more collegial-competitive or collegial-mediative operation as the issues change from those characterized by considerable uncertainty over ends or means to those engendering disagreement over goals or the strategies for pursuing them.[15] This highlights that adaptability and flexibility need not be inconsistent with formal structuring.[16]

ASSEMBLING THE PIECES: PROPOSITIONS ABOUT CONTINUITY AND CHANGE

With this sketch of the conceptual grounding of our examination of White House structuring in place, we turn to our initial expectations with regard to the dynamics of White House structuring at the beginning of the second era of the modern presidency. In general, we expected to see second-era White Houses continuing many of the activities and much of the structuring of first-era administrations. At the same time, we anticipated that there would be increasing evidence of the staff being used for broader purposes. Five specific propositions framed our empirical investigation of the structuring of the White House staff under Presidents Richard Nixon, Gerald Ford, and Jimmy Carter.

First, structuring for outreach tasks would be influenced by presidential choice factors (in addition to environmental and organizational variables) more during the Nixon presidency than it had been in first-era administrations or would be in the Ford and Carter administrations. Looking at structuring for outreach tasks (forging and maintaining presidential links with, e.g., interest groups or the public) was especially important when examining the argument that Nixon was a catalyst of discontinuous change. During the first era, structuring for outreach tasks was influenced most by environmental factors and least by presidential choice. Structuring for outreach tasks, then, became the "hardest," or least likely, setting in which presidential influence would appear. If presidential effects *did* surface in the Nixon White House, one could more confidently argue that the president's involvement was critical.

Second, we anticipated that significantly more change would appear in structuring for public relations and interest group outreach than for congressional liaison as one moved from the Johnson to the Nixon administrations. A comparison of staffing under Johnson and Nixon allowed us to hold much of the environment roughly constant. (Again, a key intervening variable was likely to be presidential and White House staffers' perceptions of the environment.) Evidence of the emergence of new structures, changes in the stability of existing ones, or shifts in the range of tasks staffers pursued would suggest the influence of presidential preferences and strategy. We could also conclude that there was greater presidential influence if structures that involved active presidential participation (e.g., hierarchical, adversarial, adjudicative) were used more frequently. We expected that structuring for congressional liaison would show little drastic change, because this operation had become an institutionalized part of the WHO; its continued stability was likely based on both environmental expectations and organizational inertia. In contrast, such structural stability did not exist in the areas of public relations and interest group outreach in the midst of ongoing environmental volatility.

Third, we predicted that little change would take place in staff structuring between the Nixon and Ford administrations, particularly in positions below the level of visible senior staff. Comparing the Nixon and Ford administrations allowed an initial assessment of the lasting effects of the Nixon administration's changes, although it arguably presented a more difficult test of the tipping-point notion introduced in the introduction. Given the response to Watergate and the congressional investigations into the size and activities of the White House staff, one might have expected the Ford administration to dismantle much of the Nixon operation. We, however, anticipated considerable continuity, especially among the less senior ranks, as a result of the lack of sufficient time for a genuine transition and the relative (perceived) success of most existing White House structures for staff governance.

More provocatively, perhaps, the fourth proposition predicted that there would be little change in staff structuring with the shift from the Nixon-Ford to the Carter administrations. Like Ford's staff, Carter's evolved in the shadow of Richard Nixon. Like Ford, we expected Carter to attempt to reverse Nixon's staffing practices but to ultimately fail, providing additional support for the impact of Nixon's innovations as well as the environmental expectations and organizational momentum they created. Thus, examining the Carter White House extended the exploration of the Nixon years as a tipping point. More important, discovering continuities in a Democratic administration would strengthen confidence in our inferences about staff dynamics during second-era presidencies.

Fifth, other than Nixon's adoption of Eisenhower's overall strategy of staff supervision and coordination, partisan learning would become less influential as White House staff structuring became more institutionalized and increasingly driven by organizational dynamics and inertial environmental expectations. We expected to find similarities in formal structuring, and dissimilarities in informal structuring, between the Eisenhower and Nixon administrations, reflecting in large part the more expansive way Nixon hoped to use the White House staff. Initial evidence of partisan learning appeared in Nixon's reliance on a chief of staff, in his return to Eisenhower's failed public relations operation, and in his resurrection of a White House counsel's office to handle legal affairs. Yet the Nixon White House's general neglect of cabinet members and its systematic efforts to forge links with interest groups were at odds with Eisenhower's practices.

Looking at Nixon and Eisenhower also allowed us to compare the staffing influences of a clearly preemptive president (Nixon) with the one other president since Woodrow Wilson who might be so classified. Skowronek has called Eisenhower a "hard case." Although Ike's political identity was opposed to the established regime (which was "resilient"), he was "reluctant to employ presidential power aggressively in the service of political innovation" and only "pruned the radical edge of New Deal liberalism."[17] Nixon had far broader objectives, was more of a policy and political activist, and confronted a more hostile and volatile environment. Such differences led us to anticipate many formal similarities in White House structuring but quite different uses of the staff.

Meanwhile, we expected to find fewer similarities in staff structuring between

Democrats Carter and Johnson than between Carter and his immediate Republican predecessors, Nixon and Ford. In effect, Carter's structuring modified the experience base of Democrats and nearly eliminated differences in partisan "ideal-type" governance models. It is well to recall that, despite initial difficulties, the Clinton administration started with a chief of staff.

CONCLUSION

The five propositions summarized below guided our examination of White House staff structuring under Presidents Nixon, Ford, and Carter:

1. Structuring for outreach tasks will be influenced by presidential preferences and strategies (in addition to environmental and organizational variables) more during the Nixon presidency than it was in first-era administrations or than it will be in the Ford and Carter administrations.
2. Comparing the Nixon and Johnson presidencies, significantly more change will appear in structuring for public relations and interest group outreach than for congressional liaison.
3. Little change in staff structuring will take place between the Nixon and Ford administrations, particularly below the ranks of visible senior staff.
4. There will be little change in staff structuring from the Nixon-Ford to the Carter administrations.
5. Other than Nixon's adoption of Eisenhower's overall strategy of staff coordination and supervision, partisan learning will be less influential as White House staff structuring further institutionalizes and becomes driven more by organizational dynamics and inertial environmental expectations.
    a. When there are similarities in formal structuring between the Eisenhower and Nixon administrations, there will be dissimilarities in informal structuring.
    b. There will be fewer similarities in staff structuring between Democrats Carter and Johnson than between Carter and his immediate Republican predecessors, Nixon and Ford.

In informally testing these propositions, we drew primarily from evidence in Nixon's presidential papers (currently housed at the National Archives and Records Administration facility in College Park, Maryland) and from materials in the Ford and Carter presidential libraries. In addition, we consulted the memoirs of the presidents and their staffers, contemporary newspapers and periodicals, interviews and oral histories, and scholarly studies of these three administrations.[18] The chapters that follow form a narrative in which we "present the results of [our] empirical analysis . . . to provide empirical support for a theoretical argument" about governance structuring in the White House.[19] Although we attempt to signal our degree of confidence in particular inferences through the use of "verbal evaluations,"[20] the tentative, exploratory nature of the enterprise should be underscored.

Our examination starts by probing an area of initial partisan continuity: Nixon's reliance on his experience as Eisenhower's vice president in organizing his own White House.

2

Staff Organization and Governance

The problem of creating structures and processes for governing the White House staff has challenged presidents since at least 1929, when Herbert Hoover introduced multiple professional staffers. In a sense, the basic structuring of presidential decision making is inherently adversarial, with multiple advisers competing for influence but only one with the final authority to decide. But how to channel this advice and persuasion, and whether to formalize the process, was a matter of contention during the early modern era of the institutional presidency. During this time, two basic models emerged, each associated in practice with one of the major political parties. Both acknowledged that, overall, the presidency is a hierarchy, since the president has no organizational equal. Both likewise accepted that structuring for presidential decision processes is frequently adversarial or adjudicative. Yet they differed on the shape of the hierarchy and the degree of formality of the structuring. The Democrats' preferred model, in large part owing to Franklin Roosevelt and Harry Truman, featured small, flexible staffs with fluid job descriptions and little concern for hierarchy or routinized process.[1] Often referred to by such labels as "spokes of the wheel," this approach gave top aides, as well as selected cabinet members, routine, unmediated access to the president, effectively leaving it to the chief executive to coordinate activities. Although sometimes led manipulatively and plagued by staff rivalries, Democratic White Houses also displayed, at their best, an admirable collegiality.[2]

The "spokes" approach to governance found favor in academe, largely through the writings of such scholars as political scientist (and Truman White House aide) Richard Neustadt.[3] It tended to be endorsed and passed on to newly elected Democratic presidents by scholars and veterans of prior administrations. This pattern exemplifies the process we call partisan learning.

An alternative model was developed by Dwight Eisenhower. Owing in part to Eisenhower's experience with military organization, his White House featured a clear hierarchy and job definitions, along with an emphasis on orderly, if often lengthy, decision processes.[4] In lieu of the peer-group informality and collegiality of Democratic White Houses, the Eisenhower model stressed careful attention to process and supplemented hierarchical relationships with an array of more collegial governance structures.[5] Access to the president was controlled by a strong chief of staff. Although frequently derided as "rigid" or "formalistic" by critics, this approach ultimately proved to be the more enduring of the two, as White House staffs grew too large and complex to be governed on an ad hoc basis and presidents no longer had the time to cope personally with staff management.

The problems associated with governing a large, segmented staff through informal structures became clear in the early 1960s. By the time of Lyndon Johnson's presidency, with the White House bulging with over 300 staffers, turf claims, infighting, and lack of coordination became apparent. LBJ struggled vainly to bring some order to his staff, attempting to institute regular staff meetings and repeatedly asking aides to undertake organizational analyses of the staff.[6] But LBJ, struggling with far greater problems than staff governance, never made much headway.

When Richard Nixon assumed the presidency in 1969, the Republican model returned with a vengeance. In his two terms as vice president under Eisenhower, Nixon had come to believe in the basic principles of organization that Ike espoused. Nixon's newly appointed chief of staff was H. R. (Bob) Haldeman, an executive with the J. Walter Thompson advertising agency, a Nixon campaigner as far back as 1956, and a designer of Nixon's successful 1968 strategy. Haldeman shared his boss's conviction that organization mattered greatly. Haldeman reported that "I gave it a lot of thought during the transition period, as we were setting up our White House staff structure and procedures. I studied everything I could get my hands on regarding the operations of earlier White House staffs, but I recognized from the outset that we had to develop our own approach, adapted to the particular needs and demands of this particular president."[7]

Nevertheless, the White House organization that Haldeman and Nixon developed closely resembled Eisenhower's in almost all important organizational respects. Most obviously, it closely emulated Eisenhower's structures for staff governance. That it would not function identically was, as Haldeman suggested, due to the differences between the presidents, as well as in the circumstances under which they governed. Still, it was clear that in 1968 partisan learning was alive and well on the Republican side. Any possible decline in its influence (see Proposition 5 in chapter 1) would come later.

The Nixon White House worked well in many respects. It was effective in guarding the president's time, planning and executing political strategy, and managing the ever-increasing flow of paper through the White House.[8] However, when the criminal excesses known as "Watergate" implicated White House staff members, critics suggested that the staff system itself was partly to blame, especially as it required a larger White House staff than ever before.[9] Such criticisms tended to be accepted by Nixon's successors, Gerald Ford and Jimmy Carter, and their advisers. Their arrangements for White House governance have to be understood partly in terms of the reaction against the Nixon system.

In examining the design and operation of the Nixon staff system, therefore, one must ask questions not only about structural congruence with decision settings, effectiveness, and efficiency but also about pathologies of a deeper sort. Likewise, one must consider the costs of rejecting Nixon's innovations.

THE NIXON MODEL: FORMAL STRUCTURING

The influence of the Eisenhower model could be seen most clearly on organizational charts, of which both the Eisenhower and the Nixon White Houses produced many. Like Eisenhower, but unlike his other predecessors, Nixon chose to run the White House through a chief of staff, aided by staff and cabinet secretariats as well as an appointments secretary. To this, at the outset, was added the position of deputy chief of staff.

Chief of Staff

The chief of staff, initially Haldeman, was responsible for the overall coordination of White House decision making and follow-up, as well as myriad administrative details involved in running the presidential office. Haldeman's own description of his job gives an idea of the scope of his responsibility and an intimation of the power that went with it. In his memoir *The Ends of Power,* Haldeman summarized the general purpose of his job as "to enable the President to function most effectively." He then enumerated the specific responsibilities of his office:

- ensure than when an issue came before the President, all points of view were represented;
- review all paperwork going to the president, and most coming from him;
- follow up all decisions;
- plan and execute the President's schedule, including trips both foreign and domestic;
- travel with the President on all trips;
- be available to the President at all times.[10]

All that, however, is a bit too antiseptic to fully capture the role of the man who was variously called "the abominable 'no' man" and "Nixon's son-of-a-bitch."

Haldeman's control of both the president's daily schedule and the paper flow in and out of the Oval Office meant, in effect, that nobody (except those Nixon designated) could see Nixon without approval from Haldeman or his staff; nor would any paper go into the Oval Office without Haldeman's scrutiny. He or one of his staff wrote covering memos on all decision papers. His proximity and availability meant that he had more of that most precious commodity—access—than anyone else in or out of the White House. In fact, he was the only aide authorized to awaken Nixon at night. The importance of this gatekeeping role was amplified by the president's reclusive habits. As Rather and Gates put it, "What gave Haldeman such overwhelming power was that he served as sentinel for a President who chose to sequester himself behind 'Do Not Disturb' signs."[11] Haldeman took his responsibilities more than seriously: "I pushed for a 'zero defects' operation, for which I have been soundly ridiculed in the press. But I felt that there was no margin for error in the operation of the Office of the President of the United States."[12]

Haldeman's control of the staff was enhanced by his placement of loyal aides in key positions on his own staff. The core of this group was a set of young men, connected through common experience at the J. Walter Thompson advertising firm: Haldeman aides Dwight Chapin, Larry Higby, Ken Cole, and John Brown, plus Press Secretary Ron Ziegler and his assistant, Tim Elbourne. Collectively, this group would come to be known as the "Beaver Patrol," in part a reference to Haldeman's Eagle Scout background, and in part to "the heel-clicking, busy way they scurried about the White House."[13] These young men, wholly loyal to Haldeman, extended the reach of his oversight and discipline.[14] Even Haldeman, in retrospect, understood that he may have gone too far in that regard. He speculated on the implications: "I can see now that I substantially over-reached in this approach. I put on too much pressure, and in the process laid the groundwork for the mental attitude that 'the job must be done' which badly disserved the cause when Watergate struck. By then, our whole crew was so strongly indoctrinated in the principle that there were to be results, not alibis, that they simply once again swung into action—doing what they felt was expected of them."[15] Thus, the origin of the mentality that led to the excesses of Watergate (and related events) can be traced to the atmosphere of coercion and compliance fostered under Haldeman. It is useful to note, however, that this is less an indictment of the Haldeman-Nixon system than of those who operated it—beginning at the top.

As a consequence of his prior experience in the advertising business, Haldeman also became, de facto, "the President's top image man."[16] He oversaw constant efforts to present Nixon to the public in the most favorable light possible. To this end, he instituted a variety of groups that met regularly—collegial governance structures—and tended to focus on politics and public relations. These, in a sense, put flesh on the bones of the White House hierarchy. Haldeman himself tended not to join such groups, preferring to be represented by members of his staff.[17] Nonetheless, he not only gave such efforts their impetus but also controlled their results when he needed to.

Haldeman left the White House in May 1973, fired as part of Nixon's attempt to distance himself from cover-up charges in connection with Watergate. The former White House martinet would later serve time in federal prison, essentially for following the orders of his superior in the same way he expected obedience from his subordinates. He was replaced by General Alexander Haig, a professional soldier and former deputy to Henry Kissinger on the National Security Council staff.

Haig was resolved to keep the staff system working. In a memo to "Senior Staff" dated May 23, he stated that "recent staff changes should not affect in any way the established staffing patterns and follow-up on Presidential requests."[18] Along the same lines, in an interview with journalist Dom Bonafede, he stressed the "honest broker" role, insisting that Nixon wanted all viewpoints on policy questions "not waffled, not mushed into consensus-type recommendations but rather in sharp, clear, conceptually pure, philosophically pure options."[19]

Nonetheless, Haldeman's demise and Haig's arrival did result in a temporary lapse in discipline. Congressional liaison head William Timmons, for instance, had to ask Haig to put out a memo to senior staff reminding them to clear congressional contacts through him. Some, Timmons complained, "may now take a more free-wheeling approach to Congress, making commitments and trade-offs without proper staffing."[20] Similarly, Staff Secretary Bruce Kehrli was at pains to restore order to White House administrative processes (discussed later). Although Haig maintained the system, his personality was not Haldeman's, and the crisp discipline of prior years tended to slip.[21] Ultimately, however, the administration's plunge into the morass of the Watergate investigations had consequences for the operation of the White House and the administration as a whole, placing the chief of staff in a role that was, if anything, more crucial than that of his predecessor.

Since domestic policy adviser John Ehrlichman had been dismissed along with Haldeman and not replaced (though his assistant, Ken Cole, now nominally headed the Domestic Council [DC]), Haig also took on a greater role in that area than Haldeman had played.[22] Office of Management and Budget (OMB) head Roy Ash later recalled that, unlike his predecessors at OMB, he (Ash) did not report to the DC head (Cole). Rather, Ash and Kissinger divided up the substance of policy and relied on Haig to keep things "stuck together."[23] With Nixon preoccupied with his own defense, Haig's responsibility grew to the point that in 1974, according to Ash, the three of them "pretty much were responsible for the sum total of everything, between us."[24]

Deputy Chief of Staff

Like Sherman Adams, his predecessor under Eisenhower, Haldeman had the assistance of a relatively small staff. As his principal deputy, Alex Butterfield had a broad array of duties, ranging from serving as Haldeman's alter ego in guarding the Oval Office through maintaining a "current inventory of the President's personal wines" to attending to "special classified and/or highly sensitive projects of particular interest to the President."[25] Most conspicuously, Butterfield was responsible for detailed supervision of the rest of the staff secretariat and allied offices,[26] overseeing the staffing (i.e., circulating for comment) and timing of papers going to the president, and serving as principal liaison with an array of White House offices, including the Secret Service, the Military Office, and the First Lady's staff.

As befitted a highly organized White House, Nixon's had a penchant for record keeping, and Butterfield stood squarely in the middle of important elements of it. Most Nixon meetings with individuals or groups, whether of a ceremonial or a business nature, included a member or members of the White House staff who took notes of the proceedings. Sometimes this was Haldeman, but often Butterfield attended such meetings. When he did not, the aide who did so was required to report in writing to Butterfield.[27] This staff presence in Oval Office meetings not only facilitated the creation of a record but also protected the president against offhand decisions in response to unexpected requests—what James Baker III has called "oh, by the way" decisions.[28]

Even when Nixon met alone with important persons such as George Shultz or George Meany, Butterfield would collar them afterward to inquire what had transpired. In keeping with another Nixon White House emphasis—public relations—Butterfield and the others recorded not only the substance of meetings but also any "color" they could glean from them.[29]

Such efforts at recording color did not satisfy the president for long. By early 1971, an "anecdotalist" system was established, whereby a second staffer, often a speechwriter, would also sit in on Nixon meetings for the express purpose of collecting (and ultimately publicizing) colorful or humanizing anecdotes about the president. Appointments Secretary Dwight Chapin assigned the anecdotalists (William Safire was a favorite), but it fell to Butterfield to collect their reports.

Butterfield was more than a nuts-and-bolts administrator. He had at least one try at being a political operative when he was given responsibility for coordinating the administration's campaign for the Safeguard ABM (antiballistic missile) system. Butterfield also participated in a series of more collegial governance structures, including a steering committee created for the Safeguard effort.[30] Beginning in the spring of 1969, he met twice weekly with Communications Director Herb Klein, Press Secretary Ron Ziegler, and Chapin to prepare and update news "game plans" for the coming week. His reports were directed to either Haldeman or Nixon, though it was clear that he was Haldeman's representative to the group.[31] Butterfield also participated in preparing game plans for publicizing Nixon's speeches.

Butterfield became part of the "presidential objectives planning group," another ad hoc collegial-consensual structure that met weekly between the fall of 1969 and the spring of 1970 to develop "programmed approaches" to "long term objectives that the President has decided upon" and create game plans for them.[32] He also participated in at least two efforts at weekly "political" meetings that Haldeman set up in 1969 and 1970.[33] In July 1970, at Chapin's suggestion, Butterfield began meeting daily with Chapin, Personal Aide Steve Bull, and Staff Secretary John Brown to go over the planning of all events scheduled for the following day.[34]

In perhaps his most unusual assignment, Butterfield served for a time as White House liaison to the "Tell It to Hanoi" Committee, an example of what would now be called an "astroturf" (emulating the "grass roots," but without much real popular participation) lobbying effort on behalf of U.S. Vietnam policy, chaired by William Casey.[35] In addition, Butterfield was often used by Nixon to convey his views, including statements of gratitude, to other staffers.[36]

Butterfield's job as liaison to the White House security forces (Security Office, Secret Service, Executive Protection Service) was serious work in the era of anti–Vietnam War protests and radical political activism. He was the person in the White House to be notified in case of threats to the president,[37] and he was involved early in the first term in planning responses to "summer violence in colleges and high schools."[38] More routinely, Butterfield's job included monitoring guest lists and White House security guards, especially to ensure that nobody on the administration's "Do Not Admit" list was inadvertently let in for a special event.[39]

Over time, Butterfield's formal responsibilities grew. When the title of cabinet secretary was abolished in November 1969, Butterfield assumed the now-diminished duties of that office.[40] Then, in early 1971, the staff secretary was officially made a subunit of Butterfield's office.[41]

Butterfield, like his colleagues in the Haldeman office, was a loyal assistant to the chief of staff. But the potential for Haldeman's disapproval always loomed in the background. A memo from Butterfield to Haldeman, written June 9, 1970, reveals both the severity of Haldeman's wrath (toward Chapin as well as Butterfield) and his subordinate's reaction: "This is just a quickie to thank you for having me into your office this morning. The fact that I was dangling there with Dwight on the receiving end of a well-deserved reprimand mattered not. It was just a 'really great thrill' to be a part of the action again, for as you may or may not know I've spent the last several months in relative isolation—feeling much like the guy who brought his oboe to the party . . . and wasn't asked to play."[42]

Haldeman's demands were continuous, from insisting that briefing papers for Nixon's meetings with visitors be shortened to no more than one page[43] to demands that staffers do more careful preliminary preparation for such meetings. On the latter, Haldeman sent Butterfield a note stressing "the importance of productivity," prompting Butterfield to promise to take the matter up with Staff Secretary Jon Huntsman.[44]

Butterfield left the White House in early 1973 to become administrator of the Federal Aviation Administration. Some of his duties were assumed by Steve Bull, Nixon's longtime personal assistant, now promoted to special assistant to the president. Butterfield would come to public prominence a few months later when he revealed, during Senator Sam Ervin's Watergate hearings, the existence of the White House taping system.

With the departure of Haldeman and the arrival of Haig, John Bennett became the new deputy chief of staff, taking on many of Butterfield's administrative tasks. Bull remained in the White House as Nixon's personal assistant and political adviser. Bennett did not inherit the cabinet secretary duties, which fell to David Parker as appointments secretary.

Cabinet Secretary

Nixon and Haldeman also borrowed from the Eisenhower White House model when they established the position of secretary to the cabinet. Under Ike, the cabinet secretariat had been an important tool for monitoring the activities of the rest of the executive branch.[45] Although the job had continued to exist through the Kennedy and Johnson administrations, its importance had waned, largely because of the presidents' inattention to the cabinet per se. Nixon's appointment of campaign veteran John Whitaker as cabinet secretary may have signaled the new president's interest in monitoring and coordinating the departments and agencies of the executive branch. However, the inherited structure soon proved inadequate to the task.

Nixon, like his immediate predecessors but unlike Eisenhower, had little use for the cabinet as a deliberative body. As a result, the job of the cabinet secretary, which involved mainly liaison and meeting preparation, quickly became, in Whitaker's words, a "hokey job, a non-job. Once the White House got organized, it didn't amount to much."[46] Nixon's primary concern was the implementation of presidential decisions by the executive branch. The cabinet secretary, in Whitaker's view, had the potential to be a "soother" but lacked the authority to oversee implementation.[47]

Whitaker established a system of "political coordinators," one per department at first, who were concerned mainly with filling job vacancies with Republicans. They reported to political aide Harry Dent.[48] Whitaker also brought back former Eisenhower aide Albert Toner to reprise "staff notes," a sort of early-warning system that tracked potential problems in the departments.[49] Although these actions may have presaged later Nixon efforts to plant loyalists throughout the executive branch, they by no means amounted to a tool of an "administrative presidency."[50] Although Staff Secretary Ken Cole did ask Whitaker in January 1969 to find "a key aide to use as my contact to get things done within each agency,"[51] this request evidently was not fulfilled. Nor did Whitaker respond to another Cole request to filter informal reports from the departments and agencies to the staff secretary for circulation in the White House.[52]

Whitaker was able to act as something of a liaison between cabinet members and the White House, and he accompanied them during meetings with the president, at least when John Ehrlichman was unavailable.[53] He likewise carried departmental requests for information to the White House. Still, the job became dispensable. When Whitaker went with Ehrlichman to the newly formed DC staff, his job was simply added to Butterfield's portfolio.

By the end of Nixon's first term, the only cabinet-related activities Butterfield spent time on were related to preparations for formal meetings of the cabinet and recommendations concerning presidential calls to cabinet members.[54] Nevertheless, Butterfield thought the job was at least potentially important. Upon leaving, he recommended that it be passed to Steve Bull and that the title of cabinet secretary be revived. "We owe it," he wrote, "to the Cabinet members."[55] In fact, most of this work, including setting up cabinet meetings, went to David Parker.[56]

Appointments Secretary

As in the Eisenhower White House, Nixon's chief of staff had overall control of scheduling the president's time. Like his predecessor, Sherman Adams, Haldeman kept a close eye on this. Also like Adams, Haldeman named an appointments secretary with whom he worked closely.[57] At the outset, this aide was Dwight Chapin, special assistant to the president. As a former protégé of Haldeman's at J. Walter Thompson, Chapin was a logical choice for the job.

Chapin's primary responsibilities were first to plan the schedule, and then to make sure the plans were implemented. He supervised the advance staff, which Nixon had put on the White House payroll for the first time, and served as a liaison to White House media consultants. Although initially charged with both planning and implementation, after a few months, Chapin began to focus on planning, leaving operational matters largely to his assistants—Steve Bull and Hugh Sloan, then David Parker.[58] Ronald Walker took primary responsibility for the advance staff.[59]

Planning priorities began, of course, with the president, who made it clear to Haldeman that he wanted his appointments prioritized. In one 1969 memo, Nixon admonished his chief of staff: "The general rule should be to put at top priority subjects of substance that need to be discussed and have in those people, whether they be from the Cabinet, staff, Congress, politics, personal, or press, who have something to say on those subjects. After we have completed those items we then should go to the therapy appointments."[60]

Nixon went on to indicate the order in which "therapy" appointments should be prioritized, beginning with members of Congress and the cabinet and ending with personal friends and staff. Haldeman passed this information on to Chapin with a note urging more schedule planning and less reaction to requests.[61]

As the administration wore on, Chapin moved more into the center of the politics and planning structures of the White House. From the beginning, he took a strong interest in public relations, often representing Haldeman at the Five O'Clock Group, a PR planning body led by speechwriter William Safire.[62] So important to the group was Chapin that once, when he missed a meeting, Safire chided him, "The Five O'Clock Group meetings would be much more valuable with you in attendance. . . . When you are absent, the meetings will feature captious and unfeeling criticism of the bumbling in the Office of the Appointments Secretary."[63]

This group eventually disbanded but was reformed as the Saturday "communications" group in the fall of 1970, with Chapin still a regular. Also in 1970, Chapin became a member of a "political" group initially organized by Harry Dent—a group that included Haldeman.[64]

Chapin left the White House for the private sector after Nixon's reelection.[65] He was replaced by his deputy, David Parker, who had also begun to be involved in PR and event planning. Although not as central a figure in the White House as Chapin had been, Parker continued in Chapin's role as a key point of intersection between the administrative routines surrounding the president and the political planning that Nixon loved so well. He also assumed elements of the cabinet secretary job that Butterfield left behind.

Staff Secretary

Also reporting to Haldeman in the early Nixon White House, holding the rank of special assistant, was Kenneth Cole, a former advertising executive at J. Walter Thompson and a Nixon staffer since 1966. As staff secretary, a post carried over from the Eisenhower model, Cole's job was to organize and monitor the paper flow in and out of the chief of staff's office and the Oval Office. John R. Brown III was designated as Cole's deputy.

In the Haldeman scheme of things, the staff secretary was a key position. It was not fully in accord with the Eisenhower model, since some of the responsibility for paper flow and record keeping that had been the staff secretary's under Ike was now handled by the deputy chief of staff or in other parts of the White House, such as the National Security Council or (after November 1970) the Domestic Council staffs.[66] But two core duties were clear. One of Cole's primary responsibilities was to serve as a channel for all incoming communications to the president.[67] In this capacity, he not only screened documents but also oversaw their circulation to relevant members of the administration for comment before they were deemed ready for presentation as proposals to the president.[68] This staffing process was the essence of the "honest broker" function of the chief of staff's office, as it sought to guarantee input to all relevant advisers on matters of potential concern. It also exemplified the adaptations in decision making necessitated by Nixon's preference for paper over face-to-face interaction.

The second key responsibility of the staff secretary and his assistant was to "record and follow implementation of Presidential decisions, actions."[69] This was the well-known Haldeman "tickler" system, whereby the chief's office not only tracked implementation but also aggressively prodded it.

Beyond that, staff secretaries and their deputies were responsible for record keeping and for maintaining communications with, for example, the cabinet, the Secret Service, and the Military Office, always at the behest of the chief or deputy chief of staff.[70]

When Cole moved in late 1969 to Ehrlichman's newly formed DC staff, he was replaced as staff secretary by his assistant, John R. Brown III. The high-pressure job would produce further turnover during the Haldeman years. Brown left in March 1971, replaced by Jon M. Huntsman. After a year, Huntsman, too, moved on, giving way to Haldeman assistant Bruce Kehrli.[71] Huntsman and Kehrli were backed up by an assistant, David Hoopes; in mid-1973, still another assistant, Charles Wardell, was added to the office.[72] The larger staff secretariat took some of the pressure off the staff secretary, which was no doubt partly responsible for the fact that Hoopes and Wardell stayed to the end of Nixon's administration. The shift from Haldeman's intensity to the less demanding style of Haig may have contributed as well, even though Kehrli was another of Haldeman's J. Walter Thompson protégés.

The staff secretary's job required not only the ability to perform under pressure but also, on occasion, the ability to exercise delicate administrative judgment. Kehrli, for example, found himself in the middle of demands by Counselor Anne Armstrong for access by women to the White House health unit.[73] Haig had resisted, but Kehrli evidently talked him into it, arguing, "let's try it for a while— I'm sure interest will fade!"[74] Still, despite the sensitivity of the position, staff secretaries were not close to the reclusive Nixon. Indeed, after Kehrli had been in the

White House about eighteen months, Butterfield was still trying to get his staff an audience with the president, noting that most of them, including Kehrli, had never even met Nixon.[75]

The departure of Haldeman and the accession of Haig brought initial confusion over White House practices and the duties of the chief's assistants. Most critically, the orderly control of the tickler process and the decision memo system by the staff secretariat broke down. Kehrli sought to restore order, pointing out in a memo to Bennett that "it was this office's responsibility to make sure that directions were passed along to the people responsible for implementing the requests and that the projects were completed on time based on the President's, not the individual's priorities. . . . I can understand the tendency to keep information close, however, the people responsible for implementing the President's requests need to know what's going on to be sure the project is coordinated and staffed well."[76] On the issue of decision memos, Kehrli added that the staff secretary's office had provided the president with "unbiased papers on major decisions" and that "while, initially, a number of people were disturbed by the fact that they could not send something 'direct' to the President, they found that it worked both ways and they would receive anything initiated by another staff member that touched on their area of responsibility."[77] Kehrli's suggested return to the system Haldeman had built was partially successful, although it was never implemented with quite the rigor that had characterized Nixon's first term.

Kehrli left the White House in May 1974. He was succeeded by Jerry Jones, who moved from the personnel office. Jones would stay through the end of Nixon's administration and into that of Gerald Ford.

Administrative Assistant

From the outset of the administration, Haldeman had several young staff assistants[78] who largely had their roles defined as the administration progressed. These included John Brown, Stephen Bull (who became Nixon's personal assistant), and Jay Wilkinson (who left after a few months to run unsuccessfully for Congress). The member of this group who was closest to his boss was Larry Higby, like Haldeman, an alumnus of both UCLA and the J. Walter Thompson advertising firm. From the beginning, Higby was Haldeman's primary assistant for administrative (as opposed to political) matters. He made his mark attending to such things as White House personnel and staff budgets. His zeal in this role earned him the nickname "Haldeman's Haldeman."

Higby spent more time "covering" (accompanying, taking notes for) Haldeman than anyone else, and he often served as the initial recipient of staff memos meant for the chief of staff. He acted in Haldeman's stead in some matters, including prodding staffers to complete their assignments (i.e., being the "tickler").[79] He also became involved early on in the allocation of personnel to the various White House offices.[80]

By virtue of his position close to Haldeman, Higby often functioned as a go-between. Charles Colson, for instance, cultivated Higby and sent his written communications for Haldeman through Higby. He regarded Higby as a "key player" in the White House, along with Chapin, and he instructed his assistant, Patrick O'Donnell, to get to know them better in order to understand Nixon's wishes on certain matters.[81]

Higby was sometimes called on to coordinate, or restore coordination, among various parts of the White House. For instance, he tried to work with, and calm relations between, Colson's office and Cole's DC staff over such things as the timing of the release of presidential messages.[82]

Higby's involvement in partisan politics tended to come as a result of his role as Haldeman's stand-in. Along with Chapin and Bull, he helped develop, at Haldeman's behest, a procedure for developing lists of individuals who would receive phone calls from the president.[83] He likewise became involved in the development of "action" or (later) "game" plans after major events, and he transmitted political instructions from Haldeman to other staffers. As an example, he conveyed Haldeman's instructions to Gordon Strachan, who ran the White House–Republican National Committee "surrogate letter writing" operation, whereby White House–written letters would be sent to the editors of publications under the names of Republican volunteers.[84]

Although Higby remained in the White House as a special assistant after Haldeman's departure, the job of administrative assistant to the chief of staff was given to a Haig recruit, General George Joulwan.

Political Assistant

Several of Haldeman's aides were involved in public relations and political activities, and as the White House matured during the first term, and as the 1970 and 1972 elections impended, more attention was devoted to these activities. The structuring of the White House reflected this, as Haldeman moved to extend the reach of his discretion by adding hierarchy. The arrival of Charles Colson and his multifaceted interest in public outreach (see chapter 3) moved Haldeman to install his own man, Jeb Magruder, in Herb Klein's office, both to interface with Colson and to ensure Haldeman's overall control. Magruder, in turn, was given an assistant, Gordon Strachan, who had been a USC classmate of Dwight Chapin's and was clearly part of Haldeman's group of young White House loyalists. In March 1971, Strachan moved on to Haldeman's staff with the primary responsibility to "implement political directives" relative to campaigning.[85] In that capacity, Strachan was the main White House contact for Magruder after the latter moved to the Committee to Reelect the President.

In December 1972, Strachan left the White House to become general counsel of the U.S. Information Agency. He did not recommend a replacement. "The President," he wrote, "has decided to remove politics from the White House. That decision means that Bob Haldeman does not need a Staff Assistant who spends three-fourths of his time on political matters."[86]

Personal Assistant to the President

Stephen Bull was one of the young aides in Haldeman's office from the beginning. He was assigned to Chapin, working on the "implementation" aspect of the president's schedule with both Chapin and Butterfield. His duties included covering Haldeman, taking notes at staff meetings, drafting memos, and prioritizing presidential phone call opportunities. He also developed "scenarios" for meetings involving Nixon,[87] as well as "meeting folders" covering all meetings and scheduled events, including those in San Clemente.[88]

Bull's job brought him into regular contact with Nixon, which pleased the president. Gradually, Bull (and, to some extent, Chapin) became such a fixture in the president's company that the military aides began to feel slighted, since having "the body" in crowds had traditionally been their responsibility. By late 1969, though, Nixon had made it clear that he preferred Bull in this capacity.[89] Thus was born a staff job that would persist thereafter—the personal assistant.

Bull's role expanded as Nixon entered his second term and Butterfield left the White House, transferring some of his duties, as noted earlier, to Bull. Never accused of a Watergate-related crime, Bull remained in the White House until the end of the Nixon administration.

Appraisal of the Nixon Model

In adopting the basic logic of the Eisenhower model, Haldeman and Nixon created a staff organization whose backbone was hierarchy and whose fundamental purposes were to achieve administrative control and to structure decision making. The former was most clearly compatible with hierarchy in its simplest form. Haldeman's assistants acted persistently on his (and ultimately Nixon's) behalf to gather information and convey orders, incidentally creating the kind of dysfunctional tensions that can accompany a rigid hierarchy, but nonetheless succeeding in placing Nixon and Haldeman in control of their variegated staff. In this respect, the system succeeded and represented a major improvement over its predecessor.

Of course, the zeal of Haldeman and his Beaver Patrol had a downside. The problem did not lie in the idea of centralized control. After all, the White House staff's raison d'etre is to serve as an extension of the president. Without control, that cannot happen. Hierarchy is an entirely appropriate means to that end. As we have written elsewhere, "for those who view organizations as control systems, hierarchy becomes almost synonymous with formal organization."[90]

The problem with the Nixon-Haldeman system was that it worked *too* well. Pure hierarchy is effective when goals are clear and authoritative, when it can be assumed that no serious controversy exists about either means or ends. Yet, when value and empirical judgments are in play, hierarchical structuring not supplemented by alternative governance structures thwarts the kind of full deliberation that ought to occur. In the Nixon administration, this was manifested in the willingness of subordinates (including, perhaps, Haldeman himself) to accept and carry out orders that should have been vetted and questioned. Haldeman has famously noted that he did not implement some of Nixon's worst, least-considered ideas,[91] but this was not always the case. And when Nixon's and Haldeman's judgments failed to stop a bad idea, the response from below was to carry it out.

The decision structures and processes in the Nixon White House also have been criticized. Most commonly, the complaints have been that Nixon's preference for paper as opposed to personal give-and-take resulted in his "isolation," and that the decision memos the president received were inadequate, attempting to reduce complex issues to a couple of paragraphs with "yes" and "no" checkoffs.[92] If one sees the system as an application of the hierarchical principle to complex choices among different combinations of ends and means, it seems clearly incongruent.

In defense of the decision memo system, however, it can be pointed out that as long as the top managers—the chief of staff, his deputy, and the staff secretary—were both competent and honest brokers, the system was operationally less hierarchical than it seemed. In fact, it represented a form of collegial decision making in which all—or at least many—relevant views (in contrast to the views of those who happened to be in the Oval Office at a particular time) were collected and brought to bear on a problem. Thus, the decision memo system is the basis for Haldeman's claim that Nixon "was really the most *un*isolated President in history."[93] Not only did the system expose the president to a diversity of views, but it also freed his time, because reading is more efficient than group discussion.

The truth appears to lie somewhere between these two points of view. Abbreviated issue summaries and brief comments are not the equivalent of thorough, face-to-face discussion. Yet they were not the tools of isolation and manipulation that critics thought they were. In fact, it is clear that many—probably most—decisions do not require much deliberation, so, on the one hand, the memo system might have been preferable, at least some of the time. On the other hand, to the extent that strong pleas on important matters were condensed to impersonal notes, one could conclude that the system had its limitations and needed to be supplemented. It is questionable whether Nixon was always willing to do that, or Haldeman to advise it.

Perhaps a more telling limitation of the staffing system is its relative complexity. To ensure full participation and a wide range of opinion, Haldeman had to be prepared to endure high transaction costs in collecting information, not to mention monitoring decision outcomes. The result was a system that sought to maximize thoroughness, not quickness or flexibility. This may have been accentuated by Haldeman's "zero defects" approach, because if all matters are utterly important, it is hard to recognize and set priorities. That was less of a problem under Haig, because priorities tended to impose themselves unmistakably.

A final point about Watergate should be addressed. Critics at the time typically suggested that the Nixon-Haldeman approach to decision making, because of the claimed isolation of the president, was a causal factor in the break-ins, wiretapping, and cover-ups that brought Nixon down. There is a serious problem with this kind of argument: the scheming that led to criminal acts did *not* pass through the staffing system. If it had, it would have been exposed and almost certainly rejected. That, after all, is what happened to the notorious "Huston Plan," an earlier attempt to expand domestic intelligence-gathering activities.[94] Such decisions had to be made in back channels, if they were to be made at all. As Haldeman has argued, the decision making surrounding the events of Watergate constituted an exception to normal procedures: "The problem was not the White House staff system . . . but the failure to handle this particular problem in the usual way. . . . [It] was handled differently because either the President did not know, or did not choose to tell us, what it was really all about and what he wanted done about it."[95] One need not accept all of Haldeman's claims about his own involvement to credit this analysis. In all phases of the extended story called Watergate, from Henry Kissinger's wiretappings to the final cover-up, the problem lay mainly with the decision makers, not the overall decision system.[96]

THE FORD MODEL: LESS CHANGE THAN MET THE EYE

Richard Nixon's abrupt departure from the presidency in the wake of the "smoking gun" Watergate tape left Vice President Gerald R. Ford with almost no time to make the transition to the presidency. On his first day as president, Ford had an extensive memo prepared for him by a small, informal team of Washington veterans headed by Ford's longtime friend Philip Buchen, who became counsel to the president. In fifty pages, the report outlined objectives for the new administration. With respect to White House staffing, the report proceeded from a doubtful premise: "The old White House staff will submit their resignations. . . . But they should be asked to stay on for a time to help with the transition. It will be clear that most of the political types will be expected to leave within a reasonable time."[97] Buchen's team, according to Ford adviser Robert Hartmann, "saw clearly the necessity of a thoroughgoing housecleaning as soon as the transition period was over."[98] The only exception was Al Haig, whom they recommended be retained for the sake of continuity, albeit not in the position of chief of staff.[99] The informal transition advisers then disbanded, to be replaced by a more formally constituted transition team consisting of William Scranton, John Marsh, Rogers Morton, and Donald Rumsfeld.

Many of the Nixon people were willing to stay on at least for a while, which was made clear in a memo to Ford on his first day as president, August 9, 1974.[100] Meanwhile, the erstwhile Nixon staff began to serve President Ford in the manner they knew best, including the operation of the White House according to the routines first laid down for Nixon by Haldeman. Into this mix, in short order, were injected Ford's own advisers, including Marsh, Hartmann, and Buchen. Most important, Ford brought his own legislative and personal experience, which predisposed him to prefer more collegial decision making in face-to-face settings. Ford's preferred model was the spokes of the wheel.

Problems swiftly arose. As Greene has observed, "it was the decision to keep Haig on that caused the most immediate trouble," in part because it enraged Hartmann, who had been Ford's vice presidential chief of staff.[101] Haig's attempt to resume the Nixon routines exacerbated tensions, especially in light of Ford's initial decision to be his own chief of staff. The resulting tension bred confusion. On the one hand, Hartmann and other Ford loyalists distrusted the Nixon holdovers; on the other hand, they had to acquiesce in some form of structuring for routine decision making.[102] Hartmann also has argued that Haig, accustomed to acting in place of the beleaguered Nixon, tried to treat Ford the same way—initialing certain decision memos on behalf of the president. When Patrick Buchanan's nomination for an ambassadorship almost went through without the president's approval, Ford was forced to crack down.[103] As a result of such problems, "staff meetings continued to be poorly attended; key personnel were not getting information needed for proper decision making. By the end of his first month, a disappointed Ford had given up on the 'spokes in a wheel' and was searching the market for his own Haldeman."[104]

On September 15, Donald Rumsfeld, a member of the transition team and former counselor to Nixon, was called back from his position as ambassador to the North Atlantic Treaty Organization (NATO) and installed in the White House as "staff coordinator." Haig, in turn, assumed the NATO portfolio.

Staff Coordinator

Although Ford conceded the need for someone to replace Haig, he still clung to his determination not to have a chief of staff. He ordered a McKinsey & Co. study of staff leadership predicated on the assumption that the White House staff would be smaller and that there would be no chief of staff.[105] The study resulted mainly in a recitation of platitudes, such as the need for a staff coordinator with experience, ability, and "a willingness to serve unobtrusively and without personal ambition." At the same time, Ted Beal, consultant to the White House Personnel Office, compiled a list of potential candidates for "chief of administration," grouped into "political types" and "business types." Among the former was Rumsfeld.[106]

Rumsfeld had served in the House with Ford and in the Nixon administration as both head of the Office of Economic Opportunity and counselor to the president, where his main job was to head the Cost of Living Council. In Rumsfeld, Ford got experience, including familiarity with the Nixon staff system, as well as political savvy. As his career clearly suggested, Rumsfeld also brought considerable personal ambition to the job.

As if to emphasize that Rumsfeld would be something less than a chief of staff, one of his first assignments was to produce an organizational chart for a spokes-of-the-wheel system. It showed nine "spokes" who would have direct, unmediated access to Ford: Marsh, Hartmann, Buchen, and Rumsfeld (all of whom held cabinet rank); Press Secretary Ron Nessen; Henry Kissinger; DC staff chief Ken Cole; OMB Director Roy Ash; and Economic Policy Board head William Seidman.[107] Each of the top staff members would have operational responsibilities, including Marsh (legislative liaison) and Hartmann (speechwriting and politics).

Within that framework, however, Rumsfeld retained a significant share of what had been the chief of staff's responsibility. The job had two main aspects, according to his deputy and later successor, Dick Cheney. The first was to "coordinate" the other eight spokes who had access to the president. This included overseeing the staffing of decisions.[108] The other was to manage the part of the White House operation that had to do with the president's time, including scheduling and advance. Thus, the other eight spokes still generally needed to make appointments through Rumsfeld's office to see Ford, although Hartmann, at least, had a meeting scheduled daily, and Ford left open the possibility of untrammeled access, at least sometimes.[109] Rumsfeld or Cheney also presided over senior staff meetings.

At Rumsfeld's first staff meeting, Ford urged all the senior staff to work through the staff coordinator and keep him informed of their activities. But he also reiterated his invitation for senior staff to bring "significant" matters directly to him. According to Hartmann, at this time, most Ford confidants perceived Rumsfeld as a threat.[110] More generally, Hartmann in particular perceived the large collection of Nixon holdovers that Ford had invited to stay on (the "praetorians," he called them) as a threat to a genuine Ford presidency. The ex-Nixonites, including Rumsfeld, Cheney, and most of their staff, saw their purpose as ensuring a modicum of orderly process, thus serving the president.[111]

In the beginning, the new arrangement did not function smoothly. Staffing, for instance, was less than reliable. At one point, Rumsfeld complained to Ford that inadequate staffing of speeches had led to "errors of fact and conflicts with previous Presidential statements."[112] Senior staff meetings were also a problem. Press Secretary Ron Nessen, for instance, complained that they were "pretty loose and formless, and some of the people attending don't seem to understand what the purpose is."[113] Such problems, plus a mandate from Ford to reduce the size of the staff, led Rumsfeld to undertake a staff reorganization in December 1974. For the most part, it confirmed existing arrangements while cutting the overall staff by 10 percent, changing some titles, and requiring that key staff members have deputies.[114] The staff coordinator, as head of the operations office, emerged with a mandate to coordinate all White House operations as well as to control the offices of staff secretary, cabinet secretary, White House personnel (slots and salaries), and the military aides.

Jerry Jones, the staff secretary at the time, recalled that the system Rumsfeld and Ford had created was essentially the same as Haldeman's, although it ran with the kind of relatively loose discipline characteristic of Haig's staff. He attributed the difference in large part to the presidents themselves, noting that Ford, with his legislative background, was "not nearly as sensitive to management matters as Nixon was."[115] Ford did not want an aggressive staff management system, and as a result, in Jones's view, "the place, as a managed organization, did not work nearly as well as the Haldeman White House did."[116] As evidence, as late as mid-1975, Rumsfeld was still trying to arrange for staff follow-up of presidential directives,[117] attempting to keep uninvited staff members from attending Ford's meetings with congressional leaders,[118] and continuing his efforts to keep attendance at senior staff meetings limited to one person from each office.[119]

Not all White House officials fully agreed, however, at least with respect to decision processes. Philip Buchen, Ford's counsel and longtime friend, argued that "the collegial system worked" and that Rumsfeld's staffing did not get in the way of anyone's access to the president.[120] Staff and Cabinet Secretary James Connor likewise noted that by the latter part of the administration, the flow of paper through the staffing process had become smooth, although Kissinger still had a tendency to circumvent it.[121]

Despite falling short of Haldeman in span and penetration of hierarchical control, Rumsfeld appeared to many of his contemporaries to be, in effect, a full-fledged chief of staff.[122] Nevertheless, Rumsfeld was perceived by some (in addition to Hartmann) as being frustrated by his lack of authority over the total staff, which limited him.[123] Part of his problem was the factional nature of the hastily assembled Ford White House. Several distinct groups could be identified: the Nixon holdovers, Ford's Grand Rapids friends and congressional associates, and those who owed primary allegiance to Vice President Nelson Rockefeller. Suspicion and backbiting among these groups were practically inevitable. The staff, Cheney assistant Foster Chanock observed, was not cohesive, but rather "a sort of fluid, floating bunch of people who are getting settled, learning to work with each other, what their responsibilities were."[124]

Rumsfeld left the White House, as many had predicted he would, in November 1975 to become secretary of defense. He was replaced by his deputy, Dick Cheney. In most respects, Cheney's job was the same as Rumsfeld's, the most important part being to control the paper flow surrounding the decision process.[125] However, Cheney's ascent coincided with the start of the campaign year of 1976. In a reelection campaign year, White House priorities and activities change substantially.[126]

Cheney moved quickly to equip his office to be the nerve center of the campaign. He brought James Cavanaugh, another old Nixon hand, to his staff from the DC; formally, Cavanaugh was Cheney's deputy, but mainly he was supposed to work on policy and political matters. Cheney likewise moved Nixon veteran Michael Raoul-Duval from Marsh's staff to his own, along with David Gergen, who had been head of the White House editorial office at the end of Nixon's administration. Duval was to handle special political projects, while Gergen worked on campaign strategy and (to Hartmann's dismay) wrote some speeches. Chanock also worked out of Cheney's office doing a variety of things, but mostly political tasks during the campaign.[127] In sum, as Stephen Wayne has suggested, Cheney created a "subterranean advisory system" that was able to circumvent senior staff, especially in matters related to the campaign.[128]

Beyond the political operation, Cheney's White House ran much like Rumsfeld's, albeit with less direction from the staff coordinator, since Cheney was deeply involved in campaign planning. In the words of journalist Dom Bonafede, White House operations in midcampaign were "running on momentum."[129] Cheney enjoyed better relations with Hartmann than his predecessor had, but his distance from operational nuts and bolts led some to see him as something less than a full chief of staff.[130]

Operations Office

Directly below the staff coordinator, in what came to be called the operations office, was additional hierarchical structuring that closely resembled Nixon's. As Rumsfeld's deputy, Cheney did work that was similar to that done by Butterfield for Haldeman and Bennett for Haig. As noted earlier, however, when Cheney became coordinator, he assembled more of a campaign team, no single member of which functioned as he had, as a true deputy.

The heart of the operations office, as it had been under Haldeman, was the staff secretary. The duties were much the same: supervision of the majority of the paper flow that constituted the staffing process, plus follow-up on behalf of the staff coordinator. Jerry Jones, Nixon's last staff secretary, continued in that role for the first half of the Ford presidency. In mid-1975, Jones moved over to head scheduling and advance. He was succeeded by James Connor, who had come to the White House in late 1974 and, since January 1975, had been (and continued to be) the cabinet secretary.

As had been the case under Nixon, the DC staff, the National Security Council staff, and others had responsibility for staffing policy papers in their own areas (and occasionally beyond), although at times the staff secretary might restaff a paper if he believed that something was missing. Jones, in fact, became somewhat more aggressive in reviewing DC staffing after Cole left the White House in early 1975, sensing a heightened need to ensure "that the President's political interests were safeguarded."[131] Both Jones and Connor continued in the tradition of the honest broker, with Connor, at the administration's end, relating that his greatest satisfaction in the White House was "the basic sense of running what has been a damnably good, objective staffing system for the President" without injecting his own "strong" policy views.[132]

Under Ford's coordinators, the job of monitoring implementation on behalf of the staff coordinator was not the task it had been under Haldeman. The Ford White House, of course, was not run like a "tight ship," because the president did not want it that way.[133] Nevertheless, the staff secretaries did become involved in follow-up activities as necessary. For instance, Rumsfeld, concerned about sluggish White

House responses to congressional mail, ordered Connor to identify the glitches and fix them.[134]

The staff secretary was also an administrative officer and thus was sometimes caught in the middle of conflicts between the staff coordinator and other staff members over such things as staff positions, salaries, and offices. For instance, Connor was the go-between and immediate target of Hartmann's wrath in a drawn-out dispute with Cheney over hiring and salary levels for the counselor's staff.[135] In this area, at least, the staff secretary could get results. As Connor noted in an interview, if people did not return his calls, he could take their phones away.[136]

The Ford White House also resuscitated the position of cabinet secretary as a primary task, bestowing it on Connor in January 1975.[137] Prior to that, Director of Scheduling Warren Rustand (David Parker's replacement) had handled the work; Connor had been brought in initially to help him. Ultimately, however, cabinet secretary again proved not to be a full-time job, and Connor simply kept it when he took on the larger duties of staff secretary. Nonetheless, it signaled that the care and feeding of cabinet officers was a priority in the Ford White House. Connor arranged cabinet meetings and their follow-up and generally served as a liaison to cabinet members.[138]

The erstwhile Chapin-Parker position of appointments secretary was redubbed director of scheduling. The main elements of the job did not change, and its first occupant, Warren Rustand, although not the political force Chapin had been, took the initiative in long-range schedule planning.[139] Rustand was forced to leave the job in mid-1975 in the wake of allegations of ethical problems surrounding a business deal. He was replaced by Jerry Jones, whose role in strategic decision making during the 1976 campaign made him one of the major White House players. Jones's staff included assistants for scheduling (William Nicholson) and advance (James "Red" Cavaney), as well as Terry O'Donnell, who took on the personal assistant role that Steve Bull had played for Nixon.

Appraisal of the Ford Model

Gerald Ford and his longtime associates aspired to a White House constructed on principles different from those of Richard Nixon. Instead of a clear hierarchy running from the president through the chief of staff, the central principle would be collegiality, at least among the nine top advisers. Advocacy of divergent interests or points of view among the nine spokes of the wheel would be structured in a collegial-competitive fashion, with the one inevitable hierarch, the president, in the middle, directing traffic. Instead of communication with the president largely through the surrogate collegiality of decision memoranda, the emphasis would be on face-to-face contact and discussion between President Ford and his top staff, as well as cabinet members.

The Ford staff would be more led than managed. Instead of dogged efforts to enforce presidential directives, there would be trust in the goodwill and competence of the top staff. Not only would structuring be different but, following from that, so would the atmosphere of the White House. Openness rather than a closed defensiveness would be the order of the day.

Just about the only aspect of the Nixon model that Ford did not propose to change was the clear division of labor among the various offices in the White House, which marked a substantial change from the reliance on "generalists" favored by Democrats. Here, in fact, the Ford people took matters one step further, formally naming the offices and listing them in the *Government Manual*. If one were not aware that these structures emulated Nixon's almost perfectly, one might think that Ford had presided over this development. In fact, a particular kind of partisan learning was taking place, passing the Eisenhower-Nixon staff design principles on to Ford despite the skepticism of the president and his closest advisers.

The new Ford model was hardly out of the showroom, so to speak, when certain limitations became apparent. Since there was no time for a true transition, Ford had no choice but to rely on a large number of Nixon holdovers (Hartmann's "praetorians") to perform essential White House tasks, with the result that the staffing system quickly became entrenched. Moreover, Ford quickly came to see that a chief of staff (even if called a staff coordinator) was indispensable in a White House as large and diverse as his. Much later, he explicitly acknowledged this: "I started out in effect not having an effective chief of staff and it didn't work. . . . You need a filter, a person that you have total confidence in who works so closely with you that in effect his is almost an alter ego. I just can't imagine a President not having an effective chief of staff."[140] Ford, as befitted his legislative background, continued to prefer people to paper in his own decision-making process. Yet the staff system saw to it that he got the paper as well.

Thus, the Ford White House structures looked and operated much like Nixon's. But that does not mean that nothing had changed. Access to Ford was far easier, because he wanted it to be. The atmosphere was more open and less defensive toward, for example, the press, and management from the top—especially in the area of chasing down implementation problems—was looser. Perhaps ironically, the greatest internal problem Ford's staff faced stemmed from organizational politics: the persistent suspicion and sporadic conflict that arose out of the hostility of the hard-line proponents of openness (notably, Hartmann) toward the quasi-Nixonian governance structures that finally prevailed.[141]

Even though Ford was unable to fully redesign the White House staff and move it away from the Nixon model, the ideas that motivated his effort remained current. Among Democrats, especially, it was common to blame Nixon's staffing, at least in part, for the president's downfall. Of course, the Democrats had their own, very different conception of desirable White House governance. Thus, when Jimmy Carter was elected in 1976, it was no surprise that he made connections to his own partisan roots and sought to take the anti-Nixon reaction much further than Ford had.

THE CARTER MODEL: REORGANIZATION AND REINVENTION

Jimmy Carter took his transition to the presidency with unprecedented seriousness, long before he was even elected. Beginning in June 1976, a transition staff working under Jack Watson prepared documents on matters ranging from selecting the cabinet to organizing the White House staff, and it developed a talent bank of potential appointees.[142] Watson's team met with a wide array of former cabinet officers, White House staffers, and academics. Most were Democrats, including such luminaries as Richard Neustadt, Ted Sorensen (John Kennedy's counsel), and Joseph Califano (who led the domestic policy staff under Lyndon Johnson). These were the sort of advisers who in the past would have urged adoption of the Democratic "model" of the White House staff. But Watson was hesitant to recommend such structuring because, he said, "I knew it to be wrong. . . . Not because I'm a genius, but because everybody I had ever talked to said 'It won't work.' "[143] Partisan learning was not what it used to be.

Nevertheless, Watson did recommend a "spokes" design with no chief of staff, in deference to Carter's own declared preference. Carter stated his affection for the spokes-of-the-wheel system strongly: "I never have wanted to have a major chief of staff between me and the people who worked for me. I have always wanted to have a multiple like seven or eight, or maybe as many as ten people who had direct access to me all of the time without having to go through an interim boss. And I appreciate working that way. I don't even mind if those ten or twelve people are incompatible with each other."[144] The president's preference for this kind of structuring had, in the view of his former aide Peter Bourne, several sources.[145] One, consistent with the idea of partisan learning, was admiration for the presidency of John F. Kennedy. Another, which Carter shared with Kennedy, was experience with the team concept in the navy. Mostly, Bourne concluded, it was, as with JFK, "a manifestation of their personalities." Beyond that, Carter evidenced a kind of "learning" that echoed Ford: "What Carter did not appreciate was the vital role played by the White House chief of staff in organizing the president's time, helping him set priorities, managing the paper flow, and limiting access to those officials who needed decisions only the president could make. Carter did not want a repetition of the excesses of Ehrlichman and Haldeman that occurred under Richard Nixon."[146]

Nonetheless, the president did accept another key element of the Nixon model: the clear division of labor. Studies of the Ford White House done by the Carter transition team recommended some reorganization and the elimination of some offices, such as public liaison.[147] For the most part, however, the key formal structures of the Ford White House remained intact. The new president saw an important virtue in specialization. Unlike Kennedy's White House of (more or less) generalists, "Carter wanted everyone working for him in a functionally limited pigeonhole" to ensure that only the Oval Office would be the nexus of policy, politics, and strategy.[148]

Staff Organization and Governance: The First Phase

Although the Carter administration began without a chief of staff, it was widely agreed that there was nonetheless a hierarchy among the president's top advisers. First among equals, having won his transition battle with Watson, was campaign chief Hamilton Jordan. Avowedly innocent of any enthusiasm for administration, Jordan did not want the duties of a chief of staff and, for the most part, was able to avoid them. Also close to the president was a collection of longtime associates popularly known as the "Georgians." These included such high-profile advisers as Press Secretary Jody Powell and Counsel Robert Lipshutz.

On the administrative side, Watson was given the consolation prize of the cabinet secretary job, with additional responsibility for intergovernmental relations. Hugh Carter Jr., the president's first cousin once removed, was placed in charge of the details of day-to-day administration, including such potentially controversial duties as the allocation of detailed personnel from elsewhere in the government to White House offices. His frugality soon earned him the nickname "Cousin Cheap." Young Jordan protégés Rick Hutcheson (staff secretary) and Tim Kraft (appointments secretary) were placed in key positions. Richard Harden, who had presided over executive branch reorganization for Carter in Georgia, came to Washington to perform the same task in the White House.[149] Overall guidance would be provided by a collegial-consensual management committee that consisted of Lipshutz, Jordan, domestic policy chief Stuart Eizenstat, Powell, and other top aides and included Harden, Hutcheson, and Hugh Carter.[150]

The most successful among these may well have been Watson, who took on both his cabinet and his intergovernmental duties with energy. In the former, he experimented with cabinet clusters, subsets of the cabinet that held regular meetings. This idea had arisen out of the transition, but it proved less than successful. Watson ultimately concluded that cabinet members were better used on issue-focused task forces, where the cabinet secretariat acted as a go-between.[151] Watson also chaired interagency groups,[152] coordinated cabinet members' travel and speaking schedules,[153] helped cabinet secretaries with outreach activities,[154] and served as a liaison between the cabinet and the president. What he did not do initially, at Carter's behest, was to admonish cabinet members to follow the administration's line. Eventually, he persuaded Carter that this was necessary, but too late to help with mavericks such as Joseph Califano.[155] Watson was further limited by the fact that involvement in foreign policy was "off limits."[156]

The additional responsibility for intergovernmental relations fleshed out Watson's job—cabinet secretary was still not a full-time occupation. In this aspect of his work, Watson was White House liaison with governors and mayors, as well as with organizations such as the National Association of Counties and the Conference of Mayors. Sometimes his roles interacted fruitfully, such as when he and his staff were able to discover communication problems between federal agencies and state and local officials.[157]

Philosophically, and as a matter of campaign promises, President Carter was committed to shrinking the White House and Executive Office staffs along with the rest of the executive branch, similar to his accomplishments as governor of Georgia. In addition, he was a believer in the power of contemporary techniques of business management, another of Richard Harden's specialties. Thus, the Carter White House soon featured "responsibility centers" and "key actors" who would compile "responsibility matrixes" to track who did what and for what proportion of the time.[158] White House budgeting would now be "zero based" and decentralized to the "centers."[159] All this was supposed to lay the groundwork for reorganization and staff reduction.

The reorganization effort was the focus of attention at the outset of the administration. It played to dubious reviews in some quarters, including the business press and parts of the Executive Office of the President (EOP). "Like fleas exploring an elephant, little bands of Carter researchers are fanning out into the vast bureaucracy, starting with the 18 agencies that make up the Executive Office of the President. . . . 'They're handling this like a research project for first-year students at a third-rate business school,' fume[d] one upper-level bureaucrat."[160] Nevertheless, Harden (whose main responsibility was the White House Office), A. D. Frazier (responsible for the rest of the EOP), and Harrison Wellford (responsible for the governmentwide aspect of the project) pushed ahead. They scored some clear successes. For instance, they identified a serious deficit in the area of information management (e.g., data processing) to support decisions.[161] Harden also worked with the congressional liaison staff to improve their ability to track legislation and develop plans for new bills.[162] These efforts culminated in a major reorganization of the White House and the EOP, announced in July of Carter's first year.[163]

Perhaps the key Carter goal in the reorganization was to reduce the White House staff to 351 people, roughly 100 fewer than Ford had at the end. A primary result, anticipated from the beginning, was to transfer Harden's entire staff out of the White House Office and into the EOP, as the Office of Administration. Other notable changes involved eliminating some holdover Ford offices, such as the Council on International Economic Policy and the Energy Research Council, and reconstituting the Domestic Council as the Domestic Policy Staff (DPS), no longer a "cabinet council."[164] All in all, as far as the White House itself was concerned, the main effect was staff reduction. Although a priority of the president's all along, the staff cuts were also motivated by demands from Congress.[165] Although the cuts were to some extent illusory—such as sending staff from the White House to the EOP and then declaring the White House staff to be shrunken—they were real in several White House offices.[166]

Some personnel and process changes in the White House also accompanied the reorganization. Greg Schneiders, a freewheeling political adviser, was now assigned to Watson, in the intergovernmental relations area. Staff Secretary Rick Hutcheson was given control of the paper flow between cabinet officials and the president— previously Watson's responsibility. These changes addressed a situation that was becoming a problem for the administration: the perception that the White House was disorganized and staffed by people who were in over their heads. To that end, the remedies did not go far enough.

Problems in the White House

Jimmy Carter's first year as president did not go smoothly. In part, his problems stemmed from policy choices, such as his initial opposition to public works projects cherished by members of Congress. Still, the White House came in for its share of criticism. Part of the problem stemmed from the youth or lack of government experience of some of Carter's aides. Staff Secretary Rick Hutcheson, for instance, was twenty-five years old when he began the job. These were mostly Jordan's people, selected for their loyalty. Carter aide Peter Bourne stated the problem most bluntly: "Carter gave him (Jordan) free rein in the White House to place loyalty and submissiveness above competence."[167]

Hutcheson faced circumstances that might have been daunting even for an experienced person. He struggled initially with a system in which he was only one of several channels through which paper could reach Carter.[168] Although the first Carter reorganization moved Hutcheson from Watson's office to Jordan's, in part to avoid confusion, the problems persisted. By October 1977, it was still necessary for Watson to send a memo to the departments and agencies stating, "effective immediately, memoranda sent by Department and Agency heads to the President . . . except those dealing with national security and foreign policy" must go through Hutcheson.[169]

Hutcheson himself was seen as a "neutral conveyor" in the staffing process, which was essential to his role.[170] Few suspected him of exercising the kind of discretion that Nixon's and Ford's chiefs of staff had over paper flow. At the same time, he explicitly did not engage in any tickler-style follow-up activities—the aversion to Haldeman's system (as it was perceived by Democrats such as Carter) was too strong. A memo from Hutcheson to senior staff in January 1977 made that clear: "It is the responsibility of the author of the memorandum to communicate the President's decision to other involved parties."[171] Thus, to initial confusion was added uncertainty about staff implementation of the president's decisions.

Appointments Secretary Tim Kraft also experienced a certain amount of disarray in his area of responsibility. A thirty-five-year-old campaign worker from New Mexico, Kraft, like Hutcheson, had little relevant experience and was a non-Georgian besides. From the beginning, there were problems of end runs, whereby staff or cabinet members sent appointment requests directly to Carter, evidently with success.[172] Nor was Kraft particularly successful in getting senior staff to attend or send a representative to his Wednesday morning scheduling meetings, where proposals for the president's schedule were discussed. In November 1977, Kraft admonished his colleagues: "Unfortunately, there is a recurring phenomenon (which we hope will cease to reoccur) of certain offices not sending a representative to the meeting, and then calling us Thursday or Friday with their own requests, submitted more or less in a vacuum."[173] He threatened that late requests would henceforth be considered only if they were emergencies.

Some saw Kraft and his assistants as the problem. Frank Moore, head of congressional liaison, recalled that when it came to members of Congress, "the attitude was, why does the President have to see these people, they're not important to the operation of the country."[174] He noted that things changed in 1978, when Kraft was replaced.

Problems in such areas as appointments and staffing (not to mention others, such as congressional relations) were exacerbated by a lack of hierarchical direction of the staff. Jordan, though first among equals, was admittedly no manager, and he did little to strengthen the hands of his subordinates as they tried to effect orderly processes. Carter, already immersed in the details of policy, had no time to be a staff leader either. This led to a situation in which the various White House offices displayed a tendency to act autonomously, with little communication among them. As Bourne put it: "The White House became increasingly compartmentalized with little or no lateral communication. Phone calls from one 'spoke' to another were often deliberately never returned. Except through Carter, coordination was minimal. This led to destructive competition and undercutting through leaks to the press that served Carter poorly."[175]

The absence of a chief of staff was increasingly singled out as a central problem in the Carter White House. The compartmentalized staff lacked the point of intersection between politics and policy that the chief's (or coordinator's) office had become for Nixon and Ford. As a result, "policy recommendations were forwarded independently to Carter without assessment for their political implications and political advice was given by people who often had little grasp of the issues involved."[176]

Another limited staff reorganization in April 1978 had little impact on White House governance, other than the replacement of Appointments Secretary Kraft by Phillip Wise, whose performance proved more satisfactory. Otherwise, the main impact was to bring in political veteran Anne Wexler and grease the skids under controversial public liaison head Midge Costanza (see chapter 4). Not until the following year would the governance problem finally be addressed.

A New Regime

The persistence of organizational problems in the White House finally led President Carter to appoint Jordan chief of staff in July 1979, following a several-day sojourn to Camp David, where Carter decided to redefine his presidency; this process resulted in the resignation of five cabinet members.[177] By this time, Jordan had acquired more liabilities than merely his lack of management skill. He was widely disliked on Capitol Hill (Speaker Tip O'Neill called him "Hannibal Jerkin") and lacked the respect of some in the administration itself. National Security Assistant Zbigniew Brzezinski, for instance, reacted to Jordan's appointment by sending a note to Carter stating that "he was hired to work for the President, not for Hamilton Jordan, and he subsequently ignored Jordan's role."[178] Bourne's take on Jordan was likewise dark: "Having spent two years fostering the conflict and compartmentalization within the White House staff, Jordan faced an impossible task in trying to build a cohesive team."[179] Nevertheless, if there was to be a chief, it could be none other than Jordan due to his closeness to Carter.[180]

Carter and Jordan undertook changes in White House personnel, designed in part "to calm the semi-hysteria that [Press Secretary] Jody Powell said his cabinet changes had caused."[181] Washington stalwart Lloyd Cutler became counsel to the president, and *Time* magazine executive Hedley Donovan was brought in as a media expert. Most important for the operation of the White House, though, was the addition of Alonzo McDonald, a former managing director of the consulting firm McKinsey & Co., which had worked with the Ford White House. Placed under Jordan on the organizational chart but given the title "staff director" and the rank of assistant to the president, McDonald was to devise and carry out the reforms that all agreed were needed. Jordan would actually have little role in that project, and as Jack Watson noted, McDonald's role was precisely tailored to Jordan's limitations.[182] Jordan eventually became preoccupied with the Iranian hostage crisis, gladly leaving the governance of the White House to McDonald.

McDonald in some ways was an upgraded version of Harden, whose involvement in White House affairs had faded since his move to the Executive Office.[183] The mandate given McDonald, though, was not to cut and reorganize but to rationalize the policy decision processes of the White House. Unlike Jordan, McDonald was uninterested in influencing the content of those decisions, seeing himself—in the tradition of chiefs of staff—as an "honest broker."[184] Rather than instituting responsibility centers and other techniques, McDonald brought a belief in orderly organizational charts and collegial governance structures reminiscent of the practice under Nixon and Haldeman. Indeed, it would be fair to say that McDonald in part reinvented the Nixon system for Jimmy Carter.

McDonald's reforms were many, but his basic task was to install himself at the same apex of the information flow, the nexus of policy and politics, that had been occupied by Haldeman, Haig, Rumsfeld, and Cheney before him (not to mention Sherman Adams). He stood near the top of a hierarchy, but he understood that hierarchy in the White House was not about command and control but about information and expected relationships. As he put it, "hierarchy does not mean the same in the White House as it means in government. And government's definition of hierarchy is one notch below what it means in the commercial and private sectors."[185]

McDonald may have been best known for establishing a range of collegial governance structures designed to overcome the compartmentalization that handicapped the White House. He instituted a series of senior staff meetings every morning, plus expanded staff meetings on one or two days a week. McDonald chaired the meetings when the chief of staff was absent.[186] He also set up a variety of regular meetings for particular purposes, such as speech planning,[187] trip planning,[188] and issues planning for the 1980 campaign,[189] and he organized meetings of deputies in the various White House offices chaired by his own deputy, Michael Rowny.[190] Like Rumsfeld before him, he insisted that the White House principals have deputies. Often, McDonald would pick the deputy, with the intent of using that person to rationalize administration of the unit.[191] On a grander scale, he and Wexler were the prime movers behind the task forces that were organized around policy and legislative initiatives (see chapter 6). Despite these efforts, however, McDonald never quite overcame the tendency of some units to remain aloof. He did not succeed, for instance, in getting the DPS involved in consultation with the rest of the White House on a regular basis.[192]

McDonald did not, by and large, redefine jobs or try to exert complete dominion over the staff system. For instance, decision memoranda could still be staffed outside the offices of the chief and staff secretary—by the DPS, for instance. Nor was there any sustained attempt to follow up on the implementation of Carter's decisions.[193] The basic notion of the spokes-of-the-wheel system—direct access to the president by senior staff—remained, albeit slightly circumscribed. On a November 1979 White House organizational chart, a box conspicuously states: "Note: All Senior White House Staff have direct access to the President on major policy issues in their areas of responsibility."[194]

In June 1980, Hamilton Jordan left the White House to work full-time on the campaign. He was succeeded by his onetime rival Jack Watson, who proved to be more of a hands-on chief of staff than Jordan had been.[195] Watson did not undertake yet another organizational fix—in fact, he believed that too much energy had already been expended on that.[196] However, he did cut back a bit on the calling of meetings and the production of organizational charts, which had become a hallmark of McDonald's leadership. McDonald fit well enough under Watson's leadership, however, and their work convinced some, such as Anne Wexler, that the White House was working well during the last six months.[197] Congressional liaison head Frank Moore concurred.[198] Not everyone agreed. David Rubenstein of the DPS agreed that with Watson there was, for the first time, a true chief of staff. But "by that time it was too late and too much of the power had been diffused and the major problems that Carter faced . . . were not related to the government."[199]

Appraisal of the Carter Model

The administration of Jimmy Carter represented the high-water mark of reaction against Richard Nixon. Whereas Gerald Ford had been unable (and unwilling) to fully shake off the tentacles of Haldeman's system, Carter did so. He would have no chief of staff, and he would shrink the staff—each a reaction to the alleged excesses of Nixon and to Watergate. Yet the result was not good, and in time, he knew it. After more limited reorganizations failed to bring order and effectiveness to the White House, he finally relented and appointed a chief.

At that point, Carter's White House did change, not because of Hamilton Jordan—the chief who was not really a chief—but because of Al McDonald. Still working within the constraints of a spokes-of-the-wheel design, McDonald in essence resurrected as much of Haldeman as he could. He sought to regularize the staffing system, a surrogate "multiple advocacy" paper process. He recognized, as Haldeman had, that division of labor causes problems and that collegial governance structuring is needed to bridge the gaps that arise. He understood his place in the White House hierarchy as a nexus of information and advice. A mature executive from the same business culture as Haldeman, McDonald applied a similar organizational philosophy. He was partially successful.

With the arrival of Jack Watson as chief of staff, the Carter White House was finally beginning, in most respects, to look like a well-designed organization. But by then, it was the middle of 1980. The hostage crisis and the presidential campaign dominated all other considerations. A well-oiled White House was still important, but in much narrower ways than a year or two before. Whatever Watson and McDonald could do, it was ultimately not enough.

Nonetheless, the Carter experience is crucial for understanding the impact of the Eisenhower-Nixon model of White House governance. Simply put, despite his best efforts, Carter could not get away from it because it worked better than the alternative he tried. The fact that it was a Democrat who learned this lesson is important. It became the basis for a new era in organizational learning among presidents-elect and their advisers. Learning would henceforth be bipartisan. Subsequent presidents, drawing on the experiences and insights of veterans from both parties, would come to accept at least the basic wisdom that a chief of staff and a staffing system are necessary in the contemporary White House. Even Bill Clinton's effort to make do with a "weak" chief of staff (Mack McLarty) was abandoned after a year and a half, and Leon Panetta was brought in to restore order and implement what can now be called the "standard model" of White House organization. Clinton's subsequent choices and George W. Bush's selection of White House veteran Andrew Card as chief of staff confirm the institutionalization not only of the chief's office but also of the "strong" version of it. Advice to new presidents from White House veterans, now readily available in seminars and in print, confirms the strong consensus that the Nixon-Eisenhower model of White House governance is here to stay.[200]

3
Public Outreach

By 1968, the environment that the new U.S. president would confront included fragmenting political parties, multiplying interests, a Washington press corps distrustful of government pronouncements, and citizens divided by age, class, race, view of the Vietnam conflict, and myriad other issues. It seems probable that any of the men running for president would have chosen to focus on boosting public support for both the president and his policy initiatives. That the candidate elected that November was Republican Richard Nixon only reinforced the appeal of such a strategy. The new president emerged from a close race that yielded little mandate, and he faced a Congress controlled by the Democrats. Moreover, Nixon's more idiosyncratic characteristics—for example, his deep disdain for the media and his resentment of the "Eastern Establishment"[1]—likely bolstered his emphasis on reaching out to "ordinary" Americans.

This chapter first explores the Nixon administration's efforts at public outreach, highlighting its relentless attention to public relations and examining the structuring for a variety of publicity-related tasks. Although Nixon's efforts broke new ground in the area of presidential public relations, they also became entangled in the web of scandal that became Watergate. In consequence, Presidents Ford and Carter struggled to distance themselves from such activities, in part by dismantling or downgrading some of Nixon's structural innovations. Here again, as in the case of overall staff structuring, environmental demands constrained these efforts and helped reduce the degree of separation from the tainted Nixon initiatives.

PUBLIC RELATIONS IN THE NIXON WHITE HOUSE

It is not novel to observe that public relations permeated the Nixon White House.[2] Indeed, in the 1953 edition of their public administration text, Dimock and Dimock could have been describing the Nixon White House: "The public relations program of any organization must be broadly conceived, formulated with the help of everyone in the institution, carried out by every employee, focused on the public, and largely directed from the office of the top executive."[3] At the same time, it should be acknowledged that the very definition of public relations is unclear and frequently contested.[4] Even so, James Hutton has proposed three dimensions that, taken together, define distinct models of "public relations practice."[5] These ideas can be used to compare presidencies by their placement on Hutton's continua: extent of presidential focus on image versus substance, on proactive versus reactive action, and on public versus presidential interests. One of his models—"image/reputation management"—is especially relevant to the Nixon administration. This perspective "looks primarily to publicity, spin control and the creation and manipulation of symbols" as main tactics.[6]

Nixon devoted considerable time to discussing and thinking about ways of advancing himself and his administration. In an oft-quoted estimate, John Ehrlichman recalled that Nixon "spent half his waking time on the nonsubstantive aspects of the presidency, and probably 40% of that dealing with problems of communications."[7] Deputy Director of Communications Jeb Magruder added that he soon "learned that the President's concept of public relations was a broad one that included intelligence gathering, staging rallies, and prompting hostile letters to our critics."[8]

To help the president with such activities were numerous senior aides who themselves had expertise in public relations. Chief of Staff H. R. Haldeman had worked for the J. Walter Thompson advertising agency, as had his assistants Dwight Chapin and Larry Higby; Ron Ziegler and Kenneth Cole were also Thompson alumni. In addition, William Safire had sold his public-relations firm to join the Nixon staff, and Magruder had worked in retail sales.

The Nixon White House engaged in a number of diverse activities that can be encompassed under the public-relations umbrella. In one form or another, they all sought to influence public sentiment and to mobilize (and sometimes neutralize and demobilize) various publics.

Polls

Part of what made the Nixon White House distinctive for its time was its "voracious appetite" for information from public-opinion polling.[9] Presidents, of course, have used polls since the technology became available in the 1930s. Still, no public-opinion analyst had served in the White House Office (WHO) until Fred Panzer, Lyndon Johnson's "poll cat."[10] Ongoing, systematic attention to polling and opinion data emerged under Nixon.[11] Meanwhile, from the Kennedy through the Nixon administrations, "organizational procedures for public opinion analysis became more centralized, with stronger lines of hierarchical control and more tightly structured procedures and staff systems."[12] Moreover, much like its predecessors dating back to FDR, the Nixon White House did far more than monitor public opinion; it also used it to craft policy rhetoric and identify key constituencies. Although opinion gathering and public-relations efforts are closely related in most administrations,[13] the Nixon White House arguably granted the latter more emphasis than most others.

Indicators of the Nixon administration's preoccupation with polls abound. For example, whereas LBJ commissioned 130 private polls throughout his administration, the Nixon White House had 233 such polls conducted in the first term alone.[14] Hardly surprisingly, Nixon's use of polls appeared to follow a "termcycle"[15] driven by the presidential election calendar. The administration commissioned 7 private polls in 1969, followed by 29, 44, and 153 in each of the next three years.[16] At the same time, Nixon aides amassed, examined, and frequently sought to shape the data collected in public polls done by Gallup, Harris, and Sindlinger; the White House also had access to poll data from state party chairs and Republican members of Congress. Staffers cultivated relationships with the public pollsters, seeking to receive advance information about poll results, to suggest questions and topics for the pollsters to examine, and to influence whether and how particular poll results were reported.[17]

Top-Level Involvement. As noted earlier, the structuring for handling poll data was primarily hierarchical. President Nixon wanted polling done from the outset. Even before the inauguration, he wrote a memo to Haldeman, asking, "What progress has been made in setting up a method where we can do some polling in depth on issues?"[18] Although it evidently "took some persuasion to convince [the president] of the importance of getting this information on a regular continuing basis," by April 1969, he had agreed to the routine collection of data on public issue positions.[19] Further, Nixon and his chief of staff frequently discussed polls; a search for "poll" on the *Haldeman Diaries* CD-ROM, for example, yielded 208 matches in 134 entries.[20] The entries indicate that the conversations ranged from reviewing the findings and interpretations of particular surveys[21] to exploring the need for alternative polls.[22] The president also directed specific polling and analytical activities.[23]

Like much else in the Nixon White House, the collection, analysis, and use of public-opinion data were supervised by the chief of staff. Although Haldeman exercised the greatest control over the private polls, as elaborated later, he instructed specific staffers to serve as contacts with particular public pollsters and received most of the reports about polls.[24] The hierarchical structure generally continued after Haldeman left and Alexander Haig replaced him.

Haig, however, was not as strict about limiting the distribution of poll results. Richard (Dick) Howard, a senior aide in the Office of Communications who served as a channel between pollsters and the president, warned the new chief of staff early on about this increased openness: a Haig memo to the White House staff containing polling data from Sindlinger "is a severe mistake and I hope it doesn't turn into a disaster. These types of memos always seem to end up in the press."[25] Although Howard's primary concern was that Haig's cover memo "implie[d] that Sindlinger is a pawn of the White House who will jump to our orders," he sought to explain the importance of limiting access to opinion data. Not only, Howard claimed, was such an inference about Sindlinger incorrect, but it threatened to close off pollsters' (including Sindlinger's and Harris's) confidential communications to the president. It could be noted as well that such secrecy permitted the White House to push public pollsters to minimize unfavorable data in their published reports; it also allowed the White House to leak more favorable opinion findings from private polls and to plan careful publicity strategies for positive public polls.

Yet, throughout the administration, structuring for public opinion involved numerous staffers and units in the WHO. In exploring these arrangements, we distinguish between the collection and analysis of information, on the one hand, and its use, on the other.

Collecting and Analyzing Information. Haldeman relied on several White House staffers to serve as conduits for public pollsters and their operations. From 1969 until October 1971, for example, Haldeman aide Dwight Chapin was the link between the White House and representatives of the Gallup organization. Chapin typically initiated contact; he reported to Haldeman on things such as results from forthcoming Gallup polls and requests for draft questions and question areas for future polls.[26] Chapin also occasionally analyzed the results of public polls at Haldeman's request. In March 1970, for example, the chief of staff asked him to analyze the "relationship between Presidential activities and status and polls." Haldeman expressed concern that Nixon's rating dropped in the polls after press conferences. "The things that have helped would appear to be events, such as the moon landing, the trips abroad, the November 3rd ["Silent Majority"] speech, the State of the Union address."[27]

In addition, Gallup officials on occasion offered to refrain from publishing particular polls. In October 1969, when the findings from polls on possible resolutions of the Vietnam conflict were favorable, editor John Davies indicated that he and George Gallup Sr. "would be willing to give this poll to the administration for its use and would not publish it."[28] Meanwhile, in March 1970, Chapin reported that Gallup had qualms about the sample in a recent poll showing that the president's popularity was declining. Because Gallup might not release the poll, Davies urged that it be considered "very confidential," prompting Chapin to conclude, "Davies, if properly directed, would urge against publication."[29]

Gallup officials apparently grew uncomfortable about providing the White House with advance information, possibly due to suspected leaks.[30] By mid-September 1971, Haldeman asked Donald Rumsfeld to "assume personal responsibility for weekly calls to George Gallup concerning poll results. The follow through details of weekly contact . . . could be handled by Gordon Strachan and possibly Dick Cheney." Chapin's "success in acquiring timely information has been limited."[31] Rumsfeld evidently took on the task in October.

Meanwhile, Charles Colson served as the White House contact for Louis Harris, again reporting to Haldeman.[32] Dick Howard assumed these responsibilities when Colson left the White House, and hierarchical structuring persisted. Howard also monitored data from Sindlinger and relayed the information to the president through Chief of Staff Haig.[33]

As already mentioned, the White House commissioned numerous private polls as well. For the first part of the administration, this was generally done through David Derge (an Indiana University faculty member) under the direction of Haldeman. Derge also worked with Haldeman and his aides on the wording of questions.

Yet the White House grew dissatisfied with the polling consultant's reports, "because they tended to summarize findings rather than provide criticism and insightful analysis."[34] As the 1972 campaign approached, Robert Teeter emerged as Derge's replacement; Teeter "primarily shared the work with Market Opinion Research and Decision Making Information."[35]

For much of the administration, access to public-opinion data was quite limited. Magruder recalled, for example, that he was "under strict orders from Haldeman that no one but [the chief of staff] should see poll results."[36] In her detailed examination of polling memos, Heith found that Chief of Staff Haldeman personally received 24 percent of all memos, and along with aides Gordon Strachan, Larry Higby, and Bruce Kehrli received 30 percent of all polling memos while sending 57 percent.[37] More generally, polling information was "controlled by and disbursed to a limited membership. Of the 49 people who received at least one memo on public opinion during Nixon's six year administration, only 16 sent and received public opinion information on a regular basis, and five of those ran the polling operation."[38]

Even so, in a White House as preoccupied with public outreach as Nixon's, it is hardly surprising that units beyond the Office of the Chief of Staff had some responsibility for polling. The Domestic Council staff, for instance, commissioned several private surveys on domestic policy. The Republican National Committee (RNC) continued a distinct polling operation, as did the Committee to Reelect the President (CRP).[39]

Moreover, as the president's Watergate-related problems worsened, additional aides transmitted opinion data to Haig, and the range of sources multiplied. By September 1973, Larry Higby was among those relaying Gallup data to Chief of Staff Haig.[40] Speechwriter Patrick Buchanan reported on the Sindlinger findings after Nixon ordered the firing of Special Watergate Prosecutor Archibald Cox, which prompted the resignation of the attorney general and deputy attorney general.[41] Bryce Harlow, the former head of congressional relations who had returned as counselor to the president in July 1973, routinely passed along state and congressional district polls from members of Congress,[42] and RNC officials made available survey information from its members.[43]

Other poll-related initiatives were less stable. Jacobs and Shapiro report, for instance, that political aide Harry Dent had a "temporary polling operation." Although he "set up a 'centralized location'" for collecting data in November 1969, it soon disappeared. "Steve Bull also was rather briefly put in charge of assembling polling data on Nixon's approval ratings."[44]

In sum, although gathering polling information involved various individuals and units at different times, hierarchical structuring dominated, and Nixon and his chief of staff remained at the center. Quite clearly, the numerous polls and the near-constant attention they received gave the president and others considerable information about the views, demands, and characteristics of the U.S. public at a turbulent time.[45] As elaborated later, the Nixon White House did not track public opinion primarily as a source of "democratic" input into political positions or policy design and execution. Rather, it focused on efforts to shape such opinion toward its own ends.

Using Public-Opinion Data. Strategic presidents might use detailed information on public attitudes, perceptions, and preferences in countless ways. They might, for example, refer reluctant members of Congress to polls that highlight agreement with the president's position. Opinion data might help the White House identify areas of weak or shifting support in policy coalitions, or polls could be employed to test reactions (and, presumably, receptivity) to presidential initiatives, image, or speech themes.

Richard Nixon observed that the "results of the polls directly affect[ed] our ability to govern, because of their influence on Congressmen, foreign leaders, etc."[46] Moreover, he and his aides believed that they could use polls to enhance the administration's ability to identify and persuade key publics. Eisinger appears to be largely correct when he includes polls among the "marketing devices" in the Nixon public-relations arsenal.[47]

Not only did White House staffers try to influence whether and how the results of public polls were released and reported; they also sought to amplify the effects of positive results with elaborate publicity and dissemination projects. When a Gallup poll on U.S. intervention in Cambodia yielded—from the White House's perspective—unfavorable results, Communications Director Herbert Klein contacted "a large Chicago paper," which was supposed to get in touch with the Gallup organization. "Our attempt is going to be to try to squelch the Sunday [Cambodia] poll."[48]

When results were more positive, Nixon "pressed his aides to 'merchandise' and 'exploit' the polls."[49] Typically, this meant that ad hoc task forces or project teams took on specific publicity tasks. Such temporary structuring appeared to be mostly collegial-consensual, with hierarchical activation and specification of general goals. For example, with advance information that Gallup poll findings on presidential approval levels before and after the 1970 congressional elections were favorable, Haldeman aide Dwight Chapin and communications staffer Robert Odle directed a "project" to publicize the results. Its objectives were to demonstrate that Democratic charges "that the election represented a defeat for the President and a challenge to his popularity . . . have been proved wrong" and that "despite sustained and unparalleled Democratic attacks on the President during the campaign . . . [his] popularity remained basically unchanged."[50] Members of several White House units were enlisted to help achieve these goals, including the Office of Communications (with Director Klein and staffer Al Snyder working to schedule a "heavy" for the Sunday news shows and Klein asked to talk with "one or two friendly columnists"), speechwriters (to "develop talking papers, lines, etc. for use by Administration spokesmen"), and the Office of Congressional Relations (to provide "attack material to our people on the Hill").[51]

Similarly, the White House sought to publicize public poll results showing support for presidential policy initiatives. Magruder assistant Gordon Strachan, for example, worked on disseminating favorable polls, forwarding such information for use by Republican members of Congress.[52] Later, at Charles Colson's direction, communications staffer Kenneth Clawson "fed" survey results from Sindlinger that suggested a "resurgence of hawkish feeling" to *Newsweek* and to columnists James Kilpatrick and Joseph Alsop.[53] Nixon aides also sought to influence polls while they were being conducted.

Meanwhile, favorable *private* polls soon found their way into the hands of receptive editors, columnists, members of Congress, Republican Party officials, and others.[54] Once more, these efforts involved aides throughout the WHO. In the Office of Communications, Van Shumway worked to place such stories. In addition, he and officials from the Opinion Research Corporation (ORC, which conducted many of the administration's private polls) cooperated on plans to spread the polls "around somewhat more among the press." In July 1971, for example, Shumway sent the ORC lists of "key newspaper bureaus—groups and individual newspapers that have headquarters in Washington," noting that he had selected papers in every state "based on either circulation or general attitude of anticipated cooperation."[55] Included as well were "key television news stations" and Washington columnists.[56] Yet higher-level White House involvement remained. Haldeman and his deputy Higby were "active players in writing the ORC press releases."[57]

The White House itself undertook more targeted dissemination of ORC results. For example, following the 1971 May Day antiwar protests in Washington (and public polls indicating that more than 60 percent of the U.S. public agreed that sending troops to Vietnam had been a mistake),[58] Colson reported that his office had mailed an ORC poll on antiwar demonstrations to approximately 10,000 people (with a cover letter from Senator Robert Dole). Included were members of Congress, governors' press secretaries, editors of party publications, U.S. attorneys, state attorneys general, municipal police chiefs, and AFL-CIO leaders. The same poll results were sent "FYI" under Klein's name to members of the cabinet and White House staff, and the ORC mailed the poll to editorial writers.[59] The writing staff also became involved. Patrick Buchanan, for instance, ghostwrote a "news story" about ORC's findings that revealed a gap between union members and leaders,[60] and he suggested other materials for inclusion in *Monday,* an RNC publication.[61]

Particularly as the 1972 election approached and the pace of polling accelerated, the White House used opinion data to help formulate the "line of the day," hoping to reflect "what issues were most sensitive with the public."[62] Colson evidently received daily poll reports from Sindlinger, which were discussed at the 8 A.M. senior staff meeting that Colson also attended. After the president approved the recommended line, Colson turned to his "attack group" (see below) to discuss execution.

Finally, in addition to White House efforts to use polling data to persuade other political elites to support the president and his policies, Nixon and his staff used the findings to identify and track supporters in the mass public. By all accounts, from the start of his administration, the president paid careful attention to poll results and their interpretations.[63] This focus—combined with more, and better trained, aides and consultants analyzing public opinion[64]—permitted the administration "to identify [a] new, crystallizing pool of supporters," soon labeled the Silent Majority.[65] In turn, it became possible to track the reactions of key members of that group to policy and publicity initiatives, as well as their appraisals of Nixon. Such "diagnostic" capacities, then, permitted the White House to undertake "therapeutic" efforts to address identified weaknesses in governing, not just electoral support.[66]

Polling and Public Outreach: A Summary. Chief of Staff H. R. Haldeman was the pivot around which virtually all public-opinion collection and use revolved. Often acting on the president's express instructions, Haldeman directed most tasks involving poll data. The structuring for contracting private pollsters and receiving poll results changed relatively little over the course of the administration, functioning as a series of closed, shallow, hierarchical relationships among Nixon, Haldeman, aides in the chief of staff's office, polling consultants David Derge and Robert Teeter, and outside organizations such as the ORC and Market Opinion Research (MOR). Somewhat similarly, Haldeman directed individual aides to establish and maintain ties with public pollsters Gallup, Harris, and Sindlinger; again, hierarchical structures with few levels emerged, and they were mostly stable. Structuring for the use of polls was more open, involving more individuals and additional WHO units. Within an overall hierarchy headed by Haldeman, collegial-consensual structuring emerged, with temporary groups of aides taking on particular tasks publicizing favorable poll results.

Additional Measures of Public Opinion

The mountains of data generated by opinion polls were not the only indicators of public sentiment that President Nixon and his aides focused on. As in first-era administrations, the White House included a large operation for receiving, distributing, summarizing, and responding to presidential mail. In addition, communications staffers collected and reported Nielsen ratings of television programming about presidential activities. The administration also initiated a daily "News Summary," with a strictly limited circulation, to provide the president with a sense of the major stories and commentaries being carried in the nation's press and television and radio newscasts. Nixon paid relatively close attention to these indicators, typically stressing their potential public-relations value more than their utility as proxy measures of public sentiment.

Presidential Mail. Like most of his predecessors, Nixon examined samples of the mail sent to the White House. The letters, postcards, and telegrams the president received were counted and categorized based on particular issues or presidential statements.

From the outset, Nixon expressed concern about the mail. At an early staff meeting, the president stressed that he "want[ed] the PR staff to read incoming mail and get a feel for what the people think and what they react to."[67] Initially, Nixon requested a "weekly analysis of the mail, not so much on a statistical basis as on a narrative summary of the nature of the mail, giving him a general idea of the principal areas covered in the letters sent to him."[68] Nonetheless, the correspondence unit sent the president reports of the numbers and form (letter, card, or telegram) of incoming mail, as well as short topic-related summaries; these were routed through, and approved by, the director of the speechwriting unit before going to the Oval Office.[69] In addition, Nixon requested and received reports on particular subjects, ranging from reactions to major speeches and other televised appearances to the publication of the Pentagon Papers and views on possible Vietnam peace agreements.[70] Staff Secretary John Brown supplemented these mostly quantitative reports by sending Nixon weekly or biweekly samplings of incoming correspondence.[71] The writing office participated here as well, selecting samples of letters and transmitting them either to the staff secretary or directly to the president.[72]

By early 1971, Nixon was dissatisfied with the mail samples he received, especially as potential sources of speech and publicity material.[73] Although writer Ray Price's performance of the sampling task proved somewhat more satisfactory,[74] the president still believed that "the greatest deficiency" in handling presidential mail was having letters read "for the purpose of getting some nuggets which I can use from time to time in my informal remarks or even in speeches."[75] According to Haldeman, this remained a persistent irritant for much of the administration.[76]

Meanwhile, other staffers sought to use presidential mail to generate positive publicity. In the center of these efforts was the Office of Communications. Early in the administration, the Klein staff had a "regular program to watch mail which can be turned into public interest features." With Anne Higgins in the staff secretary's office and writer William Gavin working in a mostly collegial-consensual structure, "the program includes tipping off newspaper columnists . . . and television stations."[77] As part of this effort, communications aides (with additional input from Higgins and the writers) looked for mail and other items that "were appropriate for Presidential letters and consequent press coverage." Presidential responses would be drafted, approved by Klein, and sent to the West Wing for Nixon's signature. Again, editors and columnists were notified.[78]

In February 1971, also in response to Nixon's demand for more effective use of presidential mail, Magruder reported to Haldeman on a new procedure worked out among the communications, speechwriting, and correspondence units. At its center was Richard Moore, formally a member of Colson's staff, who would receive presidential mail screened by Noble Melencamp (the head of correspondence), as well as responses from the president and executive branch departments to individual letter writers. Moore was to "select key phrases, themes, etc. for possible use in speeches and provide a copy for [Magruder] for possible public relations use." "Friendly newspaper writers and columnists" also received this information.[79]

Similar efforts continued through the rest of the Nixon presidency.[80] As with public-opinion polls, the White House viewed presidential mail primarily as a resource for marketing the administration.

Nielsen Ratings. Another indicator of the public's assessment of the administration seized on by the Nixon staff was the television ratings for presidential news conferences, interviews, and speeches. Again, communications staffers were central to collecting and reporting this information.[81] Of most interest appears to have been the number of households tuned in for particular events. Colson, for example, found the ratings for a 1971 Nixon interview to be "terribly disappointing" and ruminated about the possibility of a rebroadcast and greater promotion.[82] More positively, Klein passed on ratings data comparing President Nixon's appearances on the televised *Conversation with the President* with those of Kennedy and Johnson.[83] For all the attention communications specialists paid to these ratings, an aide to Ray Price could find few relationships between the Nielsen ratings and either the format of the televised appearances or the volume and nature of mail responses.[84]

"News Summary." Both wary of and obsessed with the media, Nixon "from his first day in office until his last . . . insisted on a 'News Summary' that told him what had been said about him, his administration, and world events over the last 24 hours."[85] This six-day-a-week publication monitored numerous newspapers, magazines, and radio and television newscasts. In early 1971, for example, it summarized fifty-five daily papers, the news wires, the networks, and thirty-five magazines.[86] Responsibility for the summary was lodged in the Editorial Department under speechwriter Patrick Buchanan. Buchanan supervised a shallow hierarchy that included "News Summary" editor Lyndon K. ("Mort") Allin, who had his own staff of four.

Particularly during his first term, the president "avidly"[87] read the "News Summary," declaring it "one of the best things we do on the White House staff."[88] Yet he tinkered with its format, especially during 1969.[89] Nixon evidently sensed that at least some of the material in the summaries was not completely "objective." After returning from his triumphant visit to China, for example, the president talked with Haldeman about the need to "work on the news summary people to make sure they cover positive stuff, so we don't get the staff depressed. . . . We also discussed that Buchanan was very negative on the whole thing."[90] Generally, however, Allin and Buchanan "were playing to their audience; very conservative themselves, they goaded the President with their gibes at the liberals."[91]

Public knowledge of the "News Summary" generated criticism and charges that this "faulty lens" distorted the president's view of the media and the country as a whole.[92] Although some in the White House agreed and tried to balance Nixon's reactions to his treatment in the media, most ended up leaving in frustration or seeing their access to the Oval Office disappear.[93]

At the same time, other staffers used the summaries as grist for their public-relations activities. Allin sent Haldeman regular annotations of the summaries, pointing out material that might be more widely disseminated,[94] and he reported weekly to Alexander Butterfield on the success of staff efforts to get items of "presidential color" placed in columns and news stories.[95] The editor of the "News Summary" also highlighted for Haldeman "negative" stories and reports and either suggested possible responses or explained why no response was necessary.[96] Staffers in both the communications office and the public liaison office examined Allin's reports and the news summaries for their possible public-relations value.[97]

For his part, Nixon "almost always used the News Summary as an agenda for action," dictating or scribbling orders in the margins.[98] Often, the president's reaction was to focus anew on press bias and the need for improved public relations. Relatively early in the administration, Haldeman noted, "the news summary is what gets him going to begin with. It clearly does present all the bad stuff and is the basis for his reactions."[99] Such presidential responses helped generate and sustain a host of additional public-relations activities.

Additional Structuring for Public Relations

Often at the president's insistence, staffers kept trying to boost support for Nixon and the administration's policies. They experimented as well with varying governance arrangements.

Early Efforts. Initially, the Office of Communications was the evident fulcrum for White House public-relations activities. Placed under longtime Nixon friend Herbert Klein, the unit's four additional aides sought to establish and maintain ties with the print and broadcast media, focusing on editorial writers, columnists, and outlets located outside of Washington, and they tried to better harness the entire executive branch in support of the administration. Internally, the office was structured hierarchically, with a relatively clear division of labor. Paul Costello, a former *Boston Herald* reporter, was responsible for relations with the print media. With experience as a television executive, Alvin Snyder served as the contact person for TV news programs and attempted to increase the exposure of administration officials on shows such as *Meet the Press* and *Issues and Answers*. Virginia Savell ran the office's Speakers' Bureau, which arranged and coordinated speeches by cabinet members and other "surrogates" throughout the country. Costello also oversaw relations with department and agency public-information officers (PIOs), and each of the four staffers was responsible for staying in daily contact with designated PIOs.[100] Finally, Margita White coordinated the work of the office. For his part, Klein "was particularly active in lobbying columnists and editorial writers."[101] He also oversaw a fledgling "letters to the editor" effort that Nixon demanded, designed to challenge "misrepresentation" in the press.[102]

At the same time, communications aides participated in collegial-consensual structures with other parts of the WHO. As noted earlier, for example, the unit worked with speechwriters and correspondence staff to coordinate the drafting and publicizing of presidential responses to White House mail. Similarly, communications staffers joined with writers and congressional relations aides to provide "attack" material to supportive House and Senate members to use in floor speeches defending Nixon and administration policies. In July 1969, Klein and OCR Director Bryce Harlow agreed to hire Lyn Nofziger to write these speeches.[103] As we elaborate later, efforts to cooperate and work with the emerging group liaison operation headed by Colson would prove less successful.

In addition to the communications unit, the more informal Five O'clock Group met regularly to "review general PR matters, and make recommendations for action."[104] This collegial-consensual structure brought together senior aides from the press, political affairs, writing, and communications units. On occasion, the president specifically asked the group to take up particular subjects and commented on its activities. Soon after he was inaugurated, for instance, Nixon wrote that he "again emphasize[d] my desire to have someone do an effective job on the RN come-back theme. Some way I just don't feel we have adequately presented this case and that we have generally been too defensive in our whole PR approach."[105] Agenda items for meetings typically included discussions of whether and when presidential press conferences should be held, ongoing policy debates (e.g., "what to do about the ABM issue"), and follow-up on presidential speeches.[106]

Yet, as 1969 wore on, the president's frustration with a persistent environmental annoyance—media coverage of the administration—mounted. Repeatedly, perhaps prodded by entries in the daily "News Summary," he pressed for more vigorous challenges to what he and his senior aides saw as biased reporting. He also expressed frustration with the evident lack of responsiveness of those charged with public-relations tasks. In a lengthy memo to Ehrlichman, for instance, Nixon asked for a "hard-nosed briefing" to see what was being planned "on the ABM counter-offensive. . . . What I want to hear from them is what their specific plans are . . . with regard to newspapers and columnists and others that might be swung in our direction and particularly with regard to what we are doing on a matter I have messaged Klein on several occasions—the approximately 10 to 1 ratio that the networks are following in their news coverage of the ABM debate. . . . I want a report from Klein as to what we are positively doing to the networks to put some of our pro-ABM people on to respond."[107]

By September 1969, Nixon appeared to be considering the need to reinforce hierarchical structuring in the White House, aiming to both promote increased morale and provide clearer direction. He suggested to Haldeman the possibility of scheduling a month's worth of weekly presidential meetings with "our four staffs" (Henry Kissinger's, Daniel Patrick Moynihan's, "Ehrlichman's and Flanigan's domestic staff," and the "Keogh PR group, plus two or three from Klein's office").[108] Dwight Chapin expanded on Nixon's concerns, focusing on the " 'President's Offensive' or PR effort." Chapin observed that in Nixon's memos to Haldeman, the president had indicated the "need for programs or activities . . . on a high priority basis." The items listed provide a sense of what the president was worried about. The first item on the list—a "Game plan to counter the October 15 Anti-Vietnam offensive"— points to the importance of another key environmental catalyst: growing opposition to the administration's Vietnam policy. This and the other items underscore the White House's relentless emphasis on "merchandising" through, among other things, "Appearances, Statements, Speakers, Daily news events, Weekly news highlights, messages, Trips."[109]

Improvisation and Reorganization. The ongoing concern with public relations led Haldeman to hire Jeb Magruder as a special assistant to the president. At the outset, Magruder worked directly for the chief of staff. He became coordinator of an additional interunit gathering, the Presidential Objectives Planning Group, which met weekly to assemble a weekly news calendar (focusing on how "major news stories . . . could be best presented and coordinated") and to assign responsibility for significant White House and presidential activities and events.[110] The "P.O. Group" evidently functioned as a collegial-consensual structure, with representatives from the communications, press, congressional relations, speechwriting, and political affairs offices; however, Haldeman and two other members of his unit (Chapin and Butterfield) were also members, which indicates that the group was firmly ensconced within the overall White House hierarchy. Chapin initially explained to Magruder his views on "what is wrong with our present game plans." As the aide responsible for scheduling, Chapin asked Magruder to ensure that the project officer for each game plan had the task of putting together all phases of the activity, including presidential participation, follow-up, and "rejuvenation."[111]

Soon, Haldeman placed Magruder directly into the Office of Communications, where he became deputy director in January 1970. Klein ultimately "bought the whole deal with few exceptions,"[112] even though Magruder in fact reported directly to Haldeman.[113] Nonetheless, Magruder and Klein worked together with few major problems through 1970. Responsibility for coordinating game plans followed Magruder to communications, where he elevated an existing communications aide, Robert Odle, to project manager and hired two others. Increasingly, according to Klein, the office was used to build support for specific policy initiatives.[114] Magruder also reinvigorated the letters to the editor operation, formally lodging it at the RNC but directing it from the White House.[115] At the same time, he expanded the communications unit's mailings to media representatives and others[116] and "politicized" the fact sheets on administration policy and positions sent to broadcasters and editorial writers.[117] In another effort to bypass the Washington press corps, Klein and Magruder collaborated on arranging a series of regional press briefings. Both men also were members of the administration task force on the nomination of G. Harrold Carswell to the U.S. Supreme Court, with Magruder in charge of following up the group's public-relations decisions.[118]

Despite the changes in the Office of Communications, Haldeman's (and the president's) distrust of the media and dissatisfaction with White House publicity efforts mounted, likely exacerbated by Carswell's defeat and by the virulent and violent reactions to the announcement of U.S. intervention in Cambodia.[119] Even earlier, during the Senate debate on the Carswell nomination, Nixon complained about the lack of quotes in the day's papers "from our side. Lots from the other. . . . [The president] wants one man in charge, and pushes [for] Colson, so it will really be covered."[120] By the end of May 1970, an initially reluctant Haldeman lamented the failure "to come up with a PR guy," and he asked group liaison head Charles Colson to form a task force to find such a person.[121]

Although Colson continued to ascend in Nixon's estimation, he came into conflict with others in the White House. Haldeman, for example, saw Colson as a "living 'end run,' "[122] and Magruder resented his interference in communications activities and disagreed with his negative approach to the 1970 congressional elections.[123] Yet the president evidently encouraged Colson in his efforts to infringe on the activities of the Office of Communications.[124] Nixon seemed to desperately want a new communications director,[125] but he could not bring himself to fire his longtime friend Herbert Klein. Using the ruse of a "management study" conducted by Fred Malek, Haldeman finally pushed Klein and Colson to a minimally acceptable reorganization of the Office of Communications.

The Second Restructuring. Colson was the clear winner, taking charge of "day-to-day public relations activities," as well as department and agency liaison, project management, the mailing operation, the Speakers' Bureau, the scheduling department (for placing officials on television and radio), and the drafting of " 'talking papers' for administration officials" to use with the media.[126] Moreover, he eventually named Magruder's replacement as deputy of communications; although Kenneth Clawson formally reported to Klein, Colson actually supervised him.

The turf battles between the Colson and Klein operations persisted, however. At the outset, Colson attempted to at least appear cooperative. In mid-April 1971, for example, he asked aide Dick Howard (who had headed the Speakers' Bureau under Klein before being transferred to Colson's unit) to be sure that Magruder (and his replacement after Magruder left to join the CRP) received copies of all memo traffic between Van Shumway (still formally in Klein's office) and Colson. Yet the memo concluded, "Actually on the things I ask you to do with Shumway we probably are going to be miles ahead if you just call him."[127] The jockeying for position continued through the summer and fall, even as Colson expanded the reach of his operation. He complained about the lack of cooperation from Klein's office in the White House's "wire service operation," while Klein objected to the way Colson appeared to commandeer communications unit staffers.[128]

By November 1971, Klein clearly had had enough. In a long, unhappy memo to Colson (with a copy to Haldeman), the director of communications flatly stated, "the system [of cooperation between the two units] is not working"; there had been a "steady deterioration of relations." "The problem is a lack of coordination and, I believe, [Colson's] unwillingness to cooperate." In a lengthy list of particulars,

Klein charged that Colson had sent numerous "orders" to members of Klein's staff.[129] Colson's written response was to Haldeman (who had written on the memo, "There is considerable merit in Klein's case"), not to Klein. Colson claimed that Klein's memo "hit me like a lightning bolt" and that he had "gone to enormous lengths to keep Herb happy." Colson concluded by urging Haldeman not to jump to conclusions but added that he would "*not* send [Haldeman] a copy of my memo to Herb answering each point. I am not going to waste your time perpetuating the backbiting."[130]

The difficulties in coordination between the Colson and Klein operations to some extent reflected Klein's evident dislike of Colson, a sentiment shared by others in the Office of Communications, such as Magruder and Margita White.[131] Organizational loyalties and turf protection were relevant as well. Both the reorganization of the Office of Communications and the ascendance of Colson generated considerable resentment; Klein's angry memo observed that Colson was using "techniques—mailings, briefings, calls, TV placements—originated by me and my staff before you [Colson] were at the White House."[132] At the same time, the units operated in a setting of marked technical controversy; the two men strongly disagreed on appropriate public-relations strategies. From Klein's perspective, for example, "If Nixon made a speech on Vietnam, I looked at my job as finding out afterward what people thought; Colson felt it was his job to get everyone to say, 'The President did wonderfully.' "[133] In contrast, Colson found Klein's orientation toward public relations to be too "soft," too unwilling to incorporate pressure and "hardball" tactics. In a White House hierarchy in which both the president and his chief of staff "understood public relations to be the use of techniques to badger, bully, bribe, entice, and persuade people to your 'side,' which could be accomplished only by organizing and orchestrating and hammering away,"[134] Colson's approach typically triumphed. Evident as well were the difficulties spawned by the lack of an adjudicative mechanism for resolving conflicts between two units with overlapping responsibilities.

The Colson Operation. "By 1972, Colson was the major technician for orchestrating administration PR."[135] His office pursued a host of public-relations activities, relying on staffers formally assigned to the unit as well as those in the Office of Communications. Internally, the Colson unit divided tasks among numerous relatively specialized staffers who worked within a three-tiered hierarchy, much like that in the original communications office. Several continued the work they had done in communications. Ron Baukol, for example, designed and coordinated White House–inspired mailings to editorial writers, radio and television news directors, and television commentators, often focusing on economic issues.[136] William Rhatican worked on the various domestic policy "road shows" that administration officials participated in during 1971 and 1972, concentrating on initial and follow-up publicity.[137] Dick Howard, who had run the Speakers' Bureau under Magruder, initially performed similar tasks for Colson but soon became the second in command, monitoring work and passing on Colson's directives to other staffers. Bart Porter from the Klein operation was soon replaced by Patrick O'Donnell, who took over the bulk of the Speakers' Bureau activities. Kenneth Khachigian, who had been a writer under Klein, quickly departed the Colson office for a job under Buchanan in the speechwriting office; he was replaced by Steven Karalekas.

Colson also brought in several additional aides. ABC newsman John Scali joined the unit in April 1971 to advise on public-relations strategies in national security affairs and to pass on information to his "media friends."[138] Desmond Barker took over coordinating "news planning" in mid-1971, charged with working to "shape our domestic messages and political messages in such a way that [they] get across to the media."[139] Besides overseeing the news planning calendar, he participated in the execution and follow-up of events.[140] Finally, as already mentioned, Colson continued to direct the work of some of those still formally lodged in the Office of Communications. Van Shumway, assistant to the director of communications until he left for the CRP in early 1972, took instructions from and reported to Colson on his efforts to pass information and "lines" to columnists and reporters.[141] When Kenneth Clawson finally joined the communications staff in February 1972, Colson had another ally; indeed, according to one journalist, "Clawson took to Colson like a duck to water."[142]

Meanwhile, much like the Office of Communications at the beginning of the administration, Colson's office had generally cooperative relations with other WHO units. In typically collegial-consensual structures, Colson aides worked with those on the writing and domestic policy staffs on activities such as following up presidential events and drafting speeches for presidential surrogates. Similarly, the congressional relations office and Colson staffers joined to provide information and floor statements to supportive members of Congress. On occasion, the relationships in these cross-unit efforts were spelled out rather explicitly. In April 1971, for instance, Colson described a hybrid collegial-consensual/adversarial governance structure in which aides would work on printed material for various domestic policy projects. Colson noted that he had "instructed Rhatican to clear all printed materials coming out of the various [domestic issue] project offices with [writer] Bill Safire for style, content, substance, sex appeal, etc." Once Rhatican had assembled the "creative package," he would clear it with the project manager on the Domestic Council staff. Only if the two disagreed on the final product (usually a booklet or reprint) would Colson and Domestic Council aide Edward Morgan "resolve any disputes."[143]

Nonetheless, concerns about overlapping duties and turf struggles continued. In early 1972, for example, Colson aide Bud Evans reported that domestic staffer James Cavanaugh had "made it *emphatically* clear that I was to stay out of" a visit by the presidential consultant on aging, Arthur S. Flemming, to the site of a Cincinnati nursing home fire; Cavanaugh "would handle it all, including PR." Evans warned his boss, "if we want to keep the PR thing in our ship in the future, then we had better get the word out on who had the PR responsibility."[144] Colson believed that he had worked out a more amicable arrangement with Deputy Assistant for

Domestic Affairs Kenneth Cole, but Cole wrote on Colson's memo of complaint: "All of us spend too much time crying and not enough time getting the job done. . . . What counts is the job got done—more or less." Colson evidently got the last word, responding that, "so far as I can tell, Flemming might just as well have stayed home for all the publicity that he got." He added a postscript to the blind copy he sent Higby, pointing out "these little symptoms of the territorial imperative building once more with the Domestic Council."[145]

To many of his colleagues, of course, Colson was an imperialist extraordinaire, albeit one who often operated with approval from the highest level. John Ehrlichman recalled, "As time passed, each of us—Kissinger, [George] Shultz, and I—found Colson operating in our substantive areas at the President's specific instructions."[146] After the second reorganization of public relations, Colson sought to further expand the scope of his job, frequently claiming a presidential mandate to do so. Among the changes he suggested for a draft statement that adviser Peter Flanigan was writing to Nixon on "economic spokesmen" were that "Colson will see that we get maximum media treatment and that our spokesmen and congressional supporters are fully coordinated, and that our general plans are carried out." This, Colson claimed, broadened his own role only "very slightly," since he had already discussed the idea with the president, who had asked him to assume responsibility for "keep[ing] on track all of the major administration news events, both programming the positive stuff and knocking down the negative stuff."[147] More generally, Colson's apparent understanding of his charge was so broad that it could be rationalized to encompass virtually all WHO activity: "Oftentimes we know of a new initiative that is to be taken in advance. . . . We are trying to gear ourselves up to be in a position to make specific recommendations for all of the public relations activities that should go on in connection with such an initiative and all of the support and follow up various parts of the White House and administration should engage in."[148]

At the same time, Colson frequently called for greater coordination. He complained to Cole, for example, that they needed to do a better job "coordinating messages and news plans," adding to Higby that the "situation is getting utterly preposterous. . . . We cannot leave this thing up in the air subject to 'general understandings.' "[149] Yet Colson contended that "structural" responses were not always appropriate. In response to Fred Malek's proposal for strengthening the Domestic Council staff's "issue management" capabilities, he argued that "the solution to the problem is . . . having someone, somewhere, sometime, someplace make the decision as to the issues we need to pursue, how we are going to pursue them, and then let the troops execute."[150] Tellingly (and arguably contributing to the controversy surrounding his goals and activities), Colson outlined his own view "of the gut issues . . . and the substantive follow-through we need."[151]

The End Game. After the landslide victory in November 1972 and the slowly emerging Watergate revelations, President Nixon sought to shake up the White House staff. The resignations of both Colson and Klein were accepted, although each remained in the White House for several months (Colson until March, Klein until late July). Originally, Haldeman and the president had planned to reduce the size of the Office of Communications and place it under the authority of Press Secretary Ron Ziegler. The latter decision was ultimately reversed, as attention to Watergate and furor over Ziegler's handling of the press mounted. Instead, Clawson—like Klein before him—reported directly to the chief of staff.[152]

Negative congressional and public reactions to some of Clawson's work before the election, as well as Watergate-induced distrust, postponed his being officially named director of communications until early 1974. As director, he supervised a unit with two distinct parts. What Larry Speakes called the "Government as Usual team" undertook activities such as organizing small, informal meetings with reporters and columnists (including the by-invitation-only "Cocktails with Clawson"), maintaining contacts with department and agency PIOs, and distributing op-ed pieces. Meanwhile, the "Watergate team" sought to defend Nixon. Its efforts included scheduling surrogate speakers and harnessing the mail operation in support of the president.[153]

Once again, problems of coordination arose. In March 1973, for example, Ziegler wrote a pointed memo to Clawson to "reemphasize" the need to let the press secretary see "in advance the stories you plan to move. *Particularly, especially,* always, when mail is a topic."[154] For all their efforts, of course, the public-relations project of saving the Nixon presidency failed.

Conclusion: The Nixon Years

The Nixon administration can be viewed as perhaps the first "public-relations presidency."[155] Its efforts included both "merchandising" and "building public prestige."[156]

In pursuing its own policy goals and in responding to emerging or growing problems, the administration frequently engaged in presidential efforts to "define issues and shape the agenda"—in "merchandising."[157] Grossman and Kumar observed that, in doing so, the Nixon White House "ran sophisticated, aggressive, partisan, and successful promotional campaigns for a variety of domestic and foreign policy issues."[158] In 1971 and 1972, for example, staffers sought to shape the public's view of economic performance by using a "coordinated barnstorming operation" of regional briefings of journalists and "opinion leaders"[159] and by sending fact sheets with "more bullish economic statistics" to editorial writers, columnists, and administration spokespeople.[160] Predictably, too, White House game plans set forth the efforts to explain and publicize wage and price controls.[161] National security issues frequently received similar treatment. In March 1971, for instance, Haldeman put Colson in charge of an ad hoc group (composed of White House staffers and Department of Defense officials) to "get the drum beat going in support for the operation in Laos."[162] Through much of the administration, too, the

White House sought to influence the amount of emphasis Vietnam casualty figures received in the media.[163]

At the same time, much White House attention was focused on building support for the president personally. A common view of Richard Nixon is that he was a man almost obsessively concerned about his image. Regardless of the accuracy of such a portrait, considerable evidence suggests that an emphasis on presidential support existed and that it reflected Nixon's directives.[164] One of Magruder's initial tasks was to write a "Talking Paper—Image of the President," which included recommendations for improving how the public viewed Nixon.[165] Somewhat later in the administration, staff energy was devoted to the "anecdotalist program." Operated out of the chief of staff's office, this was a "scheme for picking up and getting to the attention of the public in anecdotal form the humorous, the colorful, and the otherwise interesting and different *extra* things which so often occur during Presidential ceremonies, conferences, and meetings." Such material "must be moved without delay by way of our media outlets . . . to the eyes and ears of the American public."[166] In addition to this initiative, which relied primarily on aides in the communications, group liaison, press, and writing units, presidential correspondence and the news summaries were mined for "presidential color."

The search for effective public-relations strategies sometimes seemed to consume the Nixon White House, including the president himself. From the administration's perspective, efforts to bypass an opposition Congress and a deeply skeptical White House press corps by turning to television, forging relations with non-Washington media officials, and speaking around the country appeared quite reasonable. Yet even when there was general internal agreement on the *goals* of increasing public support for Nixon and his policies, conflict often broke out over the *means,* over how to achieve those objectives. Only rarely was congruent structuring present to permit such technical controversies to be probed and at least quasi-resolved. Nor would Nixon address the breakdown in overall White House hierarchy that he encouraged by permitting Colson to have independent access to the Oval Office and by not dismissing either Klein or Colson earlier.

Most, of course, objected to the public-relations efforts of the Nixon White House on quite different grounds. For a time, the administration's apparent attempts to deceive and manipulate the press and the public kept its immediate successors from including an explicit "communications" unit in the White House. Yet, as we know in retrospect, the public-relations genie would not stay in the bottle for long.

PUBLIC OUTREACH UNDER FORD AND CARTER

The environmental demands and expectations that shaped public outreach activities during first-era presidencies only grew under Richard Nixon. These sorts of external pressures, mixed with a sour post-Watergate, post-Vietnam cynicism, now helped push Nixon's successors to reluctantly follow many of his innovations.

Polls

The Ford and Carter administrations scarcely ignored public-opinion polls. Like their predecessor, each had White House aides who gathered and analyzed poll data, and each commissioned private polls paid for by the national party committees. Moreover, Jimmy Carter relied heavily on the interpretations of pollster Patrick Caddell.

In contrast to the near obsession with polling in the Nixon White House, Ford and Carter staffers paid less attention to polls. In particular, the two later administrations focused less on using poll data for publicity purposes. To a significant extent, this reduced emphasis likely reflected a strategic response to a key environmental influence: the hostility and cynicism generated in the media and among the public by many of the Nixon administration's PR initiatives. Moreover, the Carter staff worked under the constraint of having access to fewer financial resources for polling.

Collecting and Analyzing Information. The Ford White House focused less on the details of polling than had Nixon's, leaving much of the survey design and interpretation of results to the RNC and the President Ford Committee (PFC). Although the papers of staffers such as Robert Hartmann's political affairs assistant Gwen Anderson and Staff Secretary James Connor have folders labeled "Polls," they often contain little more than copies of surveys by Gallup, Harris, and Robert Teeter sent by the RNC.[167] Counselor and speechwriter Hartmann evidently paid more attention; his polling reports from the RNC were underlined and annotated, and early in the administration, he received polling proposals from Richard Wirthlin's Decision Making Information (DMI) firm and memos about the polls needed as the presidential campaign developed.[168] After David Gergen rejoined the White House staff in late 1975, he collected some materials on soon-to-be-published Harris polls and analyses of Gallup findings; he also met with Sindlinger to discuss at least one specially commissioned poll.[169]

Yet, as Eisinger notes, little evidence suggests that "Ford's advisors tried to court media pollsters for poll data." Although aides wrote memos about polling and survey results, they did not "systematically collect, organize, or regularly interpret polls."[170] In contrast to the Nixon administration's reliance on multiple sources of information, most of the private polls and analyses that were routinely available to those in the Ford White House came from Robert Teeter's MOR, although Wirthlin's DMI contributed early on.

Like the Nixon administration, however, control over polling within the White House was lodged relatively high in the overall hierarchy. Dick Cheney, initially the deputy staff coordinator and later the staff coordinator, oversaw polling. Cheney was the primary link with pollster Teeter, playing the "pivotal role as poll reader and interpreter for the Ford presidency and the reelection campaign."[171] Cheney assistant Foster Chanock served as the polling specialist in the office, examining and interpreting the results of both private and public polls; as the 1976 election approached, he also served as the conduit for poll data between the campaign and the White House.[172] For a time, too, Fred Slight—who moved from Staff Secretary Jerry Jones's office in September 1975 to become director of research for the PFC—was the voting and public-opinion expert on the campaign committee.[173]

Unlike Haldeman, Cheney did not keep the results of private polls locked in an office safe. Yet access to poll results was similarly restricted. Senior staffers had to go through Cheney or the RNC to see Teeter's data.[174] Only Rumsfeld, Cheney, Chanock, and Hartmann had direct access to the pollster.[175]

In sum, the differences between the Nixon and Ford administrations' approaches to gathering and analyzing poll data were those of emphasis rather than structure. Both relied on shallow hierarchical structures anchored in the office of the chief of staff or staff coordinator. It was the range of data and analyses sought that varied. To a significant extent, this likely reflected the two presidents' differing interests in poll data; unlike Nixon, Gerald Ford was not an "avid poll reader."[176] However, environmental influences evidently helped temper the latter's indifference. Changes in the electorate, the presidential electoral system, and the larger political arena encouraged both administrations to find out more about the public's views of presidents and policy. The ready availability of financial resources through the RNC was important as well. Ford's position as an unelected president made the need for information even more pressing and the results more challenging to interpret. At the same time, the administration was chary of being perceived as paying too much attention to public-opinion polls, a charge frequently lodged against Nixon. Finally, an organizational factor—staff expertise—probably underlay some of the variation: even if they had wanted to integrate polling data more systematically into major decisions, few if any Ford aides were as sophisticated in the interpretation of polls as their predecessors had been.

Under Jimmy Carter, structuring for gathering and interpreting polling data was less hierarchical. In what resembled a market structure, a variety of staffers directly contacted pollster Patrick Caddell or his firm, Cambridge Survey Research (CSR), and generally had access to his polling data. At the same time, hierarchy clearly remained. The president was far more involved than his immediate predecessor had been. Not only did Caddell send data directly to Carter, but the latter decided how, and to whom, the information should be disseminated.[177] At the same time, pollster Caddell and two senior aides—Director of Communications Gerald Rafshoon and Domestic Policy Staff head Stuart Eizenstat—originated more than half (53 percent) of all polling memos.[178] Arguably, the most significant change from the Nixon and Ford years was the virtual inclusion of the pollster on the White House staff and his elevation in the overall WHO hierarchy. Although Caddell was never officially a member of the staff, he opened a branch of CSR blocks from the White House and frequently participated in meetings with the president and with senior staff; he also was a regular sender and recipient of staff memos.

Meanwhile, even more dramatically than in the Ford administration, officials relied almost entirely on CSR and Caddell for information and interpretation. As under Ford, few challenges came from other aides, who mostly lacked survey expertise; nor were mechanisms (e.g., competing surveys, collegial-competitive assessment structures) available to critically examine or challenge either the pollster's questions or his interpretations.[179] Finally, in contrast to both Republican predecessors, Carter (and the Democratic National Committee [DNC]) had fewer financial resources to devote to regular, systematic polling.[180]

Using Public-Opinion Data. Neither the Ford nor the Carter administration devoted as much attention to using poll data to advance the president or his policy initiatives as did the Nixon White House. Nonetheless, opinion data found their way into a range of activities, including tracking supporters, scheduling, evaluating presidential speeches, and setting priorities.

Both in spite of and because of ongoing efforts to distance President Ford from Nixon, issues of public relations remained salient. Polling data were involved in at least some of these efforts. Scarcely surprising for an unelected president, the Ford White House's use of polls was driven largely by electoral concerns. Heith notes that the staff used "standard, almost stereotypical, Republican measures" to create an "artificial electoral coalition baseline" for comparison with the composition of the president's current support coalition.[181]

Private polls also were employed to assess performance and, presumably, to provide information on possible enhancements and strategies for improving public support. In 1975, for instance, DMI conducted "impact studies" following several presidential trips to U.S. cities, providing overall evaluations of citizens' attitudes toward Ford and their perceptions of him.[182] The RNC also sponsored DMI polls on "national issues" and on reactions to the administration's anti-inflation program.[183] In addition, polls frequently followed presidential speeches to gauge how particular groups responded to the message and "rhetorical style" of an address.[184] Pollster Teeter also advised the White House on "how to market President Ford" following major speeches such as the State of the Union.[185]

At the same time, the information frequently helped particular units make cases for their own significance and favored policy pursuits. For example, polls were conducted before and after the Office of Public Liaison sponsored White House conferences around the country. "The favorable ratings for this Administration jumped between 5 and 9 percentage points," indicating that such meetings were a "very successful tool in garnering confidence and therefore support."[186] Similarly, data from polls helped bolster arguments for particular policy priorities. Thus, internal consumer advocates contended, "The necessity for a strong administration consumer initiative is poignantly illustrated by the recent poll taken by Market Opinion Research, which shows that the majority of the Americans think of the Republican Party as untrustworthy, incompetent, and closely aligned with big business."[187]

Carter, of course, was the first president to have a publicly known pollster clearly working with him and with the White House staff. Although Caddell's visibility sometimes created public-relations problems, it also helped ensure that the president received a steady stream of poll data and analyses.

The Carter administration used public-opinion data in a variety of ways. Most often, polls provided information on areas of shifting or weakening support for particular policy initiatives. As the White House geared up to push for Senate ratification of the Panama Canal treaty, for instance, aide Joseph Aragon not only collected results from a variety of surveys but also sought the advice of independent pollster Roger Seasonwein on the implications of some of his national poll findings.[188] Caddell analyzed several polls and argued that the administration needed to place "high priority" on "giving the people knowledge about the treaties."[189] Meanwhile, the White House–spawned Committee of Americans for the Canal Treaties (COACT) contracted with the Opinion Research Corporation to survey Texans, seeking to better target lobbying efforts.[190]

As noted earlier, Carter and his aides did not routinely draw on opinion data from such a wide variety of sources. Yet poll results were injected into the policy process, typically by Caddell himself. For example, he sent data on citizens' concerns about health care to domestic policy chief Eizenstat and discussed public perceptions of Carter's foreign policy with National Security Council staff director Zbigniew Brzezinski.[191] Especially as the administration wore on, Caddell evidently mixed his own policy and publicity prescriptions into the analyses of poll results. In March 1980, for instance, he wrote the president a lengthy memo on the "substance, timing, and exposure" of addressing the problem of inflation.[192]

As in the Ford administration, opinion data also informed other presidential activities. Before joining the White House staff, for instance, Rafshoon used poll findings to recommend against the continuation of President Carter's practice of meeting with the press informally after press conferences.[193] On occasion, results also shaped the content, style, and scheduling of presidential speeches. Certainly, Caddell's significance in urging Carter to focus on the country's "malaise" instead of on energy policy in a pivotal July 1979 speech has long been highlighted.[194]

More generally, the pollster's interpretations of his and others' data probably helped frame the perceptions of Carter and his senior staff with regard to the degree of electoral threat they faced. Just weeks before the misleadingly labeled malaise speech, for example, Caddell sent the president an analysis of a recent *New York Times*–CBS News poll that had found dropping presidential approval ratings as well as "personal" ratings. *"Yesterday's* Times *result, if accurate, is staggering.* It shows the President's favorable/unfavorable personal rating as a negative. . . . *The significance of this result cannot be over-emphasized. . . . This result tends to suggest that frustration with the President is moving toward personal hostility as opposed to indifference or disappointment. . . .* [Such a] qualitative change can only be viewed with alarm."[195]

Very few in the White House successfully challenged Caddell's readings of opinion. In the view of domestic policy aide Bertram Carp, this was because Caddell "had the data. . . . He would come in and he would harangue the President for two or three hours and just convince the President to do something difficult."[196] Anne Wexler has suggested that Caddell and Rafshoon had "disproportionate influence," because each enjoyed Carter's confidence. She also stressed the need for "a little more balance in the decision-making process."[197] Arguably missing were adversarial or collegial-competitive governance structures to increase the likelihood that differing views would be exchanged and resolved.

Polling and Public Outreach: A Summary. Although public-opinion polling was both less visible and less important in the Ford and Carter White Houses than it had been under Nixon, its systematic collection and use persisted. Moreover, Caddell's proximity to President Carter and his most senior aides was the first appearance of what would soon become a familiar phenomenon.

Highlighted as well were recurring governance challenges. One issue revolved around structuring access to pollsters and to opinion data. The Ford approach in essence followed Nixon's, permitting only a handful of very senior staffers to have contacts with pollsters or to see most opinion data. The Carter White House was more open, in large part because of Caddell's ready presence and its heavy reliance on his polls. Hierarchical structuring reemerged, however, because the president frequently determined who would see specific poll results. A second concern had to do with assessments of the quality of the opinion data being received. Arguably, the Nixon and, to a lesser extent, Ford approach of relying on multiple private polls as well as several public polls provided the White House with better results, since aides could compare sampling strategies, questions, and analytical techniques. The Ford administration relied on fewer pollsters and had less skilled staffers to assess the analyses. The Carter administration suffered from too few resources for polling, overreliance on a single source of data and interpretation, and a lack of adequate structuring for examining poll questions and findings.

Additional Measures of Public Opinion

The Ford and Carter White Houses relied on more than polls to assess the public's views. Like their predecessor, they also systematically tracked mail. Unlike the Nixon administration, however, neither generally used presidential correspondence for publicity purposes. Nor did aides typically follow Nielsen ratings for presidential speeches or televised news conferences.

During the Ford administration, Roland Elliott, who had joined the Nixon staff in 1971 and initially worked under writer Ray Price, continued to handle presidential correspondence. Now formally lodged in the staff secretary's office, Elliott forwarded to the president information on the mail, including totals, comments on major issues, and numbers of "Domestic Policy," "Foreign Policy," and "General (Non-Issue)" letters.[198]

The Carter operation was similar. The president (and members of the senior staff) received weekly summaries of incoming mail from Hugh Carter, special assistant for administration. The reports included totals, primary recipient ("Presidential," "First Lady," "Amy," "Other First Family"), running totals of support and opposition on key issues, and reactions to presidential activities[199]; President Carter also received weekly mail samples. In retrospect, press aide Ray Jenkins believed that the mail summary was not very useful and that few paid attention to it. His boss, Press Secretary Jody Powell, went further, arguing that the White House should quit counting mail, since it only inspired journalists to ask, " 'how's the mail running?' "[200]

Additional Structuring for Public Relations

By the time Gerald Ford was sworn in as president in August 1974, many viewed the Office of Communications as an instrument of illegitimate presidential manipulation of information. In such an environment, it is not surprising that no such unit appeared in the new White House. Yet the office reemerged by mid-1975 and was taken out of the control of the press secretary in 1976, reflecting a response to other environmental demands and expectations and increasing concerns about the approaching election. By the end of the Ford years, virtually all the public-relations activities pursued by the Nixon staff were present.

Communications tasks followed a similar organizational trajectory in the Carter White House. At the outset, these activities were placed in the press secretary's office, and no unit was formally labeled "Communications." Skeptical environmental actors, partisan learning, and presidential indifference likely contributed. Again, however, a distinct Office of Communications appeared in 1978, and throughout Carter's term, aides engaged in activities virtually identical to those of the previous two administrations. Once more, external pressures were central.

The Ford Years. At the outset, after Director of Communications Kenneth Clawson's almost immediate resignation, Press Secretary Jerald terHorst eliminated the Office of Communications. At the president's direction, terHorst placed the unit's "media outreach and public information functions" under him in the press office hierarchy.[201] The press secretary divided the responsibility for these public-relations activities between two assistant press secretaries—Paul Miltich, Ford's House and vice presidential press secretary, and James Holland, deputy director of communications under Clawson.

When the president's unexpected pardon of Richard Nixon prompted terHorst's resignation, Ron Nessen took over the press office. Within weeks, as he moved to restore media confidence and to ease some Nixon holdovers out of his office, Nessen requested Holland's resignation. At the same time, he decided to keep Deputy Press Secretary Gerald Warren but to transfer him to "head a public affairs office" within the press operation. With "no desire to infuse any of the more overt political aspects of the old Director of Communications Office,"[202] Nessen named Warren "Deputy Press Secretary for Information Liaison."[203]

Warren was charged with tasks reminiscent of the responsibilities of Herbert Klein's Office of Communications. Nessen directed Warren to take charge of "internal coordination of public affairs activities within the Executive Branch agencies and the external contact with the press outside of Washington."[204] Margita White rejoined the staff, first as Warren's assistant and then as director of the unit. When she took over in July 1975, White persuaded Nessen to rename the unit the Office of Communications; her title became director of the Office of Communications (a "subtle distinction" from the Nixon-era director of communications).[205] Nonetheless, the newly named unit remained lodged in the larger press office hierarchy.

Under Warren and White, many of the activities performed by the Nixon communications operation reappeared. As in the earlier White House, the unit was structured internally as a shallow hierarchy. Among the now-familiar tasks performed by communications aides were sending regular mailings on key policy issues to broadcasters, editors, and publishers and arranging White House and regional briefings for the non-Washington media.[206] The unit also sought to maintain ties with PIOs in the departments and agencies, holding monthly meetings and circulating material on major issues.[207] It scheduled administration speakers, arranged for television and radio interviews for officials, and handled all requests to interview Ford.[208] As the 1976 election drew nearer, the office, at White's suggestion, received approval to oversee a "presidential surrogates" program, responsible for scheduling presidential spokespeople to speak all over the country.[209]

In addition, the Office of Communications took on tasks it had not handled under Nixon. The "News Summary" was prepared by a series of communications aides, engaging in "much less editorializing" than under Patrick Buchanan's tutelage, and it was circulated more widely.[210] Communications also established contacts with the press secretaries of Republican governors throughout the United States.

As the 1976 election approached, Ronald Reagan's nomination threat deepened, and the PFC campaign manager resigned in the midst of allegations of scandal. White House officials thus redoubled their efforts to gain tighter control over both the campaign and White House political staffs. As part of an attempt to "centralize control over the messages that were going out from the administration,"[211] Staff Coordinator Dick Cheney took advantage of Margita White's departure for the Federal Communications Commission and took the Office of Communications out of the press secretary's orbit. It became an independent unit reporting directly to Cheney. By July 1976, Cheney aide David Gergen was named its director.

The reorganized communications unit was "the formal apparatus for controlling the public image of the Administration."[212] From the outset, it was closely involved in the 1976 election campaign. Gergen became a primary influence in interjecting partisan learning into the operation. He had worked with Charles Colson during Nixon's reelection campaign in "planning the administration's line-of-the-day and . . . coordinating the flow of news" from the White House, and he had participated in "scripting the 1972 Republican convention."[213] One of Gergen's first projects as director was to work on the Republican National Convention, a task he shared with another former Nixon staffer, William Rhatican, who had been named deputy director of communications.[214]

Internally, the office remained structured as a relatively shallow hierarchy, and it retained virtually all the responsibilities it had undertaken under White. According to Maltese, Gergen concentrated on "strategic planning," while his deputy director emphasized "implementing the plan."[215] In addition, Gergen and Rhatican oversaw five subunits: Research, Editorial Services, Presidential Spokesmen, Television, and Special Services. The Research subunit handled the "News Summary," performed the research needed by other parts of the communications office, and prepared briefing books for the president (including those for the televised presidential debates). Meanwhile, aides in Editorial Services ghostwrote magazine articles and opinion columns for administration officials, as well as more "substantive" speech excerpts for the presidential surrogates. Although the Presidential Spokesmen subunit arranged appearances for members of the Ford family and cabinet members, it worked with the PFC in scheduling other campaign speakers in an effort to avoid running afoul of both federal law and public expectations about the distinction between campaigning and governing. Gergen introduced the Television Office into the communications operation; previously, it had been lodged under the press secretary. The director of communications also enlisted a former Nixon colleague—William Carruthers—to serve as a consultant. Finally, the Special Services unit housed staffers such as Richard Brannon, who wrote speeches, and Don Penny, the president's joke writer.[216]

Meanwhile, Gergen continued to participate in the publicity activities he had become involved with while working in Cheney's office. He and two other Cheney aides, Michael Raoul-Duval and James Cavanaugh, had suggested the formation of a "Communications Group" to formulate and implement "news plans." In effect, showing a form of partisan learning from the Nixon years, they proposed a collegial-consensual structure that would have brought together staffers from communications, writing, scheduling, the press office, each of the policy units, congressional relations, and the PFC.[217] Although such a group began meeting in the late spring of 1976, it became more active when Gergen moved into the communications post and took over as chair. The group's original composition had proved unwieldy, and Gergen proposed to Cheney that "the new communications group should be set up so that (1) we have a mechanism that both determines and executes daily communications plans; (2) we have a smooth flow of meetings each day that keep people plugged in but do not consume enormous portions of our time; and (3) we maintain a high degree of confidentiality prior to execution."[218] Ultimately, the Communications Group was pared down to include only Gergen, Rhatican, Press Secretary Nessen, and PFC Communications Director William Greener Jr. These four met daily at 7:15 A.M.; after an hour session, the members dispersed to touch base with policy aides and others before reconvening around

9 A.M. The group then made recommendations to Cheney (linking it back to the WHO hierarchy) and implemented those he approved.[219]

By mid-fall 1976, Dom Bonafede wrote in the *National Journal:* "David Gergen and the White House Office of Communication . . . generally act as a public relations service. . . . White House press policy has mostly been taken over by William I. Greener . . . , and by Gergen."[220] Despite ongoing pressures from an environment still reacting against the publicity abuses associated with Watergate, the Ford White House had reinvented a communications operation that was quite similar to Nixon's.

The Carter Years. Like Ford, Carter sought at the outset to fashion an open and decentralized administration, hoping to highlight the contrast between Nixon's approach to governing and his own. Even though the term began without an Office of Communications, by its midpoint, one had reemerged. Furthermore, few of the tasks undertaken by past communications staffers went unperformed.

Initially, communications tasks were lodged in the White House press office under Press Secretary Jody Powell. For example, maintaining relations with the non-Washington media became the primary responsibility of the Office of Media Liaison, directed by Patricia Bario. This function had grown into a clear expectation following Klein's efforts in the Nixon White House. Nurturing these links included responding to phone inquiries from media without regular Washington correspondents, inviting out-of-town editors to White House briefings with administration officials, and sending out "background reports" to editorial writers.[221] By the end of the term, staffer Ray Jenkins reported that the media liaison operation handled 300 to 400 calls each day and had organized 58 groups of 20 to 200 non-Washington media representatives who attended day-long briefings and spent "a half hour with the President." Underscoring the general lack of institutional memory in the White House, he also claimed that the unit "was the first to maintain an extensive mailing program with out-of-town media," developing a list that ultimately included more than 10,000 names; at least forty-five separate background reports went out each year.[222] Moreover, much like the Ford communications office, media liaison established ties with the press secretaries of Democratic governors.[223]

The signal innovation of the Carter Office of Media Liaison was installing an "audio actualities" service in the White House, which Deputy Press Secretary Walter Wurfel touted as the "best available audio equivalent of the printed news releases issued here daily."[224] This permitted twice-daily "feeds" from administration officials to radio stations through a WATS telephone line. Jenkins noted that the calls per feed ranged from 200 to 600, which was the system's capacity.[225]

Wurfel, one of two deputy press secretaries, supervised both the media liaison office and one charged with producing the "News Summary." He also was involved in other communications jobs. Wurfel met monthly with department and agency PIOs, and he created "Public Affairs Advisory Groups." The deputy press secretary turned to these groups of "corporate PIOs and public relations people" for "advice on how to promote administration programs and improve the president's image."[226] Elsewhere in the press office was a presidential television coordinator, who reported directly to the special assistant for media and public affairs, Barry Jagoda. Even though there was no separate editorial unit, Powell also formally supervised the speechwriting office.[227]

By most accounts, this early press operation was typically a loosely coupled system. Powell was frequently occupied by presidential advising, and his main internal focus was on daily dealings with the White House press. The hierarchical structuring that did exist appeared within units such as the Office of Media Liaison and speechwriting, and among media liaison, the "News Summary" office, and Wurfel. At the same time, Powell claimed that both press and communications operations were helped by having a "friend in court" in charge, someone with direct access to Carter. Patricia Bario, who later assumed Wurfel's role as liaison to department PIOs, agreed: "Having Powell's weight to throw around did help."[228] Nonetheless, Wurfel contended that Powell was spread too thin, which undermined the deputy's ability to coordinate administration messages.[229]

More important, during the first year of the administration, no single person or unit in the press office or elsewhere was responsible for longer-term communications planning. By the spring of 1978, Carter and his advisers were convinced of the need for a major effort to boost the president's image and support among the public. Difficult problems in the broader political environment no doubt helped focus their attention. Inflation continued, seemingly unabated by high unemployment. At the end of April 1978, Carter's public approval rating stood at 41 percent, evidently influenced by both the economy and his vacillation during a 109-day strike by the United Mine Workers, but unaffected by legislative victories on the Panama Canal treaties and the sale of F-15s to Saudi Arabia.[230] Finally, the president took unofficial media consultant Gerald Rafshoon's advice to name a director of communications, and Carter pushed Rafshoon to accept the position in May.[231]

The new communications unit was transferred out of the press office. With it came the press advance and speechwriting units, as well as Jagoda's television operation. (The Office of Media Liaison and the "News Summary" unit continued to report to Powell.) Directly under Rafshoon was Deputy Director of Communications Gregory Schneiders, a former campaigner who had been director of White House projects and a Watson assistant. The communications unit (with approximately twenty staffers) was structured hierarchically, with Schneiders "running the day-to-day operations" of the office.[232] He oversaw and passed on Rafshoon's directives to several other aides. Anne Edwards, for example, "handle[d] the technical aspects of press conferences and television . . . appearances."[233] Meanwhile, Communications Coordinator (and later Special Projects Director) Alan Raymond (a television newsman from Boston and former press secretary for Governor Michael Dukakis) was responsible for booking administration officials on television news shows; he also served as the unit's liaison with the various policy task forces (see below).[234] A second communications coordinator, copywriter Carol Coleman, wrote and produced brochures, public service announcements, films, radio scripts, and audiovisuals to be used in presenting presidential programs.[235]

Rafshoon himself undertook a variety of tasks, striving to bring a greater "discipline of themes" to the statements and activities of administration officials.[236] Within the Office of Communications, he worked perhaps most closely with the speechwriters. Rafshoon was the "go-between for them and the President," telling them "what the President wants to say or what we need to have in a speech." The communications director often assigned the writer for specific speeches, and he edited the resulting drafts.[237] In addition, communications staffers pulled together the briefing books before every presidential press conference, and Rafshoon "prepared Carter for town meetings [and] press conferences."[238] He also persuaded the president to permit his rehearsals of important speeches to be videotaped.[239]

Rafshoon tried to increase the effectiveness of Wurfel's efforts to coordinate the statements and activities of executive branch departments and officials. Toward the beginning of his White House tenure, Rafshoon talked with the PIOs about the need for the administration to speak with one voice and asked them to contact his office before their bosses made appearances so that they could receive timely "theme papers." He recalled some of these early meetings: "I have never been in a more hostile atmosphere. . . . They felt like they were going to be controlled. I heard Califano's PIO saying, 'This sounds like Nixon.' "[240] Nonetheless, in an effort to increase the extent of hierarchical guidance to departments and agencies, the office sent a weekly newsletter to White House staffers and senior executive branch officials on the "accomplishments and priorities of the White House." It also started clearing television appearances by administration officials and providing relevant "talking points."[241]

Despite the potential for triggering turf battles, Rafshoon's arrival and the splitting of the press office generated relatively few problems. In large part, this probably reflected Powell's long-term relationship with the new communications director. In his exit interview, Rafshoon recalled that he and Powell had worked with each other since 1969. "The day-to-day reaction stuff, the things that are in the headlines—Jody deals with. The things that might happen a few weeks down the road, getting ready for something, setting events, speeches—that's my area. But we work together, you know; he has input on my stuff; I have input on his."[242]

Even so, some problems of coordination arose, which was scarcely surprising, given the difficulty of sharply distinguishing between short- and long-term activities. For example, Wurfel, who remained in the press office and continued as the unit's link with agency PIOs, asked to be copied on the materials they received from the communications office. "I don't want to mix into long-range planning, but that long-range planning does have a way of affecting the day-to-day operations of the PIOs. If I am to be an effective liaison with them for the Press Office . . . I need to know what they're doing for [Rafshoon] and you."[243] Wurfel promised in return to invite Schneiders and Rafshoon to all his sessions with PIOs. The simple relationship between the two deputies evidently resolved any problems.

In addition, the Office of Communications responded to proposed additions to the president's schedule. Rafshoon claimed that he tried to limit Carter's activity to avoid "overexposure."[244]

The communications staff also worked frequently with Anne Wexler and the Office of Public Liaison in a largely collegial-consensual structure, coordinating information packets and other written materials for dissemination outside the White House. Members of the two staffs were among the multiple participants in several task forces designed to build support for specific administration policy goals. These goals included defending Carter's veto of a 1979 defense authorization bill, pushing for passage of energy and civil service reform legislation, and mobilizing support for Senate ratification of the SALT II treaty.[245] A Rafshoon aide (typically Raymond) participated in all the task force meetings. The communications unit served as the "booking agency" for these efforts, assembling useful information, drafting talking points, and mobilizing administration spokespeople. When presidential statements were necessary, either the speechwriters or Deputy Director Schneiders produced the drafts.[246] Although Rafshoon and Wexler saw the potential for turf battles between their operations, for the most part, few developed.[247]

As 1980 approached, Rafshoon, Schneiders, and ultimately Hamilton Jordan left the White House to work on Carter's reelection campaign. The departure of such a senior and influential aide as Rafshoon evidently persuaded Jordan and others that it would be difficult to find an adequate replacement. In August 1979, the decision was made to abolish the Office of Communications and distribute its various parts. Writing was placed under Alonzo McDonald's supervision, and press advance returned to the press office. Within the larger press operation, the Office of Media Liaison was "enlarged and given more authority."[248] For example, Special Projects Director Alan Raymond and his responsibilities with the policy task forces were placed in media liaison. The liaison unit also worked with Wexler's staff to schedule surrogate speakers, a task that became especially important after the taking of U.S. hostages in Iran in November 1979.

Indeed, given the expanded role of the Office of Media Liaison late in the Carter presidency, it is not surprising that some who joined the press staff in the final eighteen months considered the unit "the renamed Office of Communications."[249] It did not, however, take on all the tasks of its predecessor. Much communication strategy emanated from outside the WHO. Meanwhile, at least for a time, inside the White House, Alonzo McDonald "convened a small task force to deal with presidential communications and presidential communications postures."[250]

As under Ford, the presidential electoral cycle seemed to be the key influence in producing these changes. At the same time, the negative reactions of the media to Rafshoon's presence in the WHO may have made his departure for an explicit campaign role and the virtual transfer of the communications operation to the DNC and the Carter campaign committee especially appealing. Rafshoon's White House presence produced initial media "fascination," generating a "series of new adjectives, new verbs, and new nouns—Rafshooning, Rafshoonery."[251] The same media, though, soon began charging that the Office of Communications sought to manipulate them: the unit and its director became "a handicap."[252]

CONCLUSION: THE FUTILITY OF CHANGE?

Clearly, the post-Watergate political environment continued to influence the public-relations activities of the Carter White House. Press Secretary Powell observed at the end of the administration that the press had been more traumatized by Watergate than any other segment of U.S. society. Bario elaborated: "[Reporters] always went away giving you the impression of believing 'I just know the s.o.b. dodged or lied to me and later I'm going to be able to say that if they'd just answered my tough questions I would have caught it.' There's always the sense that they're out to catch you."[253] Such suspicions also constrained the adoption of developing media technologies. The technology for making "audio actualities" available, for example, had existed for over a decade before Carter assumed the presidency, and it was widely used in campaigns and by some federal departments (including the so-called Spotmasters that Herbert Klein urged on cabinet officers). Yet both the Nixon and Ford White Houses decided not to institute audio feeds from the White House. Indeed, during the 1973 Watergate investigations, some members of Congress criticized such services as "propaganda mechanisms,"[254] and the initial media reaction to the Carter innovation and to the entire media liaison operation was that they were "Nixonian."[255] Ultimately, however, other journalists' demands for and expectations of information, coupled with the White House desire to cast the administration in the most favorable possible light, triumphed.

Since the 1970s, structuring for public outreach has become, if anything, more elaborate and more important than it was in the Nixon administration. White House (or essentially indistinguishable National Committee) polling is routine and incessant.[256] The press and communications offices not only have become institutions but also have expanded and refined their operations in response to the phenomenon of the "24-hour news cycle."[257] This has led to a legitimate concern that public relations and related "political" purposes might tend to dominate "good policy" advocacy within the contemporary White House.[258] Nevertheless, as the institutional presidency responds to its environment, this growth is seemingly inevitable.

4
Interest Group Outreach:
The Office of Public Liaison

At least since FDR, presidents have sought to forge ties and maintain contact with external constituencies and to mobilize support among them. Yet not until the Nixon years did systematic efforts emerge to use specialized White House aides to perform these tasks. Previous administrations rarely devoted full-time staff effort to cultivating relations with external groups, and often erratic market structuring prevailed as environmental demand for and presidential interest in such activities fluctuated.[1]

As in first-era presidencies, structuring for group outreach under Richard Nixon reflected the influences of both environmental and presidential choice factors. The 1960s and 1970s, for example, saw an explosion of constituency groups and a marked diversification of interests. Meanwhile, demands for greater governmental accountability to citizens and heightened attention to public input mounted—and focused increasingly on presidents and the White House. Taking office in 1969, Nixon faced even stronger environmental pressures than his Democratic predecessors had, pushing him to pay attention to external groups. Nixon was elected in a close race, with only a plurality of the popular vote, and he confronted a Congress (and, in his view, an executive branch bureaucracy) controlled by the opposition party. For his part, the new president did not shy away from appearing visibly "political," a sharp contrast to the most recent Republican chief executive, Dwight Eisenhower.

Under Nixon, Charles Colson became the first "to concentrate full time on the core [group] liaison activities."[2] Indeed, except for its title, Colson's unit functioned as the "Office of Public Liaison" (OPL), as it came to be called under Gerald Ford.[3] Although OPL's location in the White House has varied somewhat over time, it persists as a distinct unit. Since Colson—and, by implication, the public liaison unit—became closely identified with Watergate-related activities, both Ford and Carter tried to restrict the office's range of activities and its prominence within the White House. In fact, midway through Carter's term, OPL as such was essentially abandoned. At the same time, however, interest group outreach actually intensified as the 1980 presidential election neared.

As the preceding suggests, in the White Houses examined here, OPL neither monopolized group liaison nor confined itself to such relationship-sustaining activities. Other members of the White House staff also maintained ties with particular constituencies. And, as chapter 3 suggested, staffers such as Colson spent considerable time on more generalized public- and congressional-relations activities. Underscored, in turn, are both the difficulties of distinguishing *empirically* among staffers' tasks and the numerous governance issues raised by such overlapping activities.

NIXON: THE EMERGENCE OF GROUP LIAISON

As in earlier White Houses, some Nixon staffers were responsible for communicating the views of and maintaining ties with identifiable external groups and interests. Jay Wilkinson, for instance, handled organized religion and youth concerns during his short time in the White House.[4] As he would throughout the administration, writer Patrick Buchanan served as a link to Roman Catholics and to the Catholic hierarchy. Meanwhile, Peter Flanigan—who handled economic, commercial, and financial policy issues—had numerous contacts in the business world[5]; on occasion, he also worked with the Catholic community.[6] Nixon's former law partner, Leonard Garment, was among those who focused on civil rights issues and sought to develop relations with minority groups[7]; his assistant, Bradley H. Patterson Jr., became the White House's "resident overseer" of issues involving Indians.[8] Garment also worked at times with the "arts and humanities,"[9] the elderly,[10] and the U.S. Jewish communities.

As in the past, the constituencies that received attention in large part reflected the salient issues and demands of the time (in the late 1960s and early 1970s, these included the Vietnam conflict, race relations, sex discrimination, inflation), the president's party, and the political and policy objectives of the president. By the fall of his first year in office, Nixon increasingly felt under siege, battling a worsening economy, antiwar demonstrations in Washington, and an uncooperative Congress. The president responded in part by stepping up White House efforts to mobilize external supporters.

The First Director

Among the changes in the White House was the addition of Charles Colson, a lawyer who had served on the staff of Senator Leverett Saltonstall, a Republican from Massachusetts. H. R. Haldeman recalled that Colson, named special counsel on November 6, 1969, "was originally brought into the White House to work in the congressional liaison area, but his assignments were expanded to include outside interest groups."[11] Even though the new aide soon became a "special assignment man" for the president[12] and became enmeshed in broader public-relations and communications initiatives (as chapter 3 detailed), much of his own work revolved around mobilizing particular constituencies. Moreover, he directed an expanding staff of group liaisons.

Colson himself spent considerable time cultivating relations with organized labor.[13] For instance, he accompanied Nixon when the president met with union leaders, and Colson wrote the accompanying briefing papers.[14] Colson passed on intelligence about labor leaders' views and reactions to Haldeman and other administration officials; he also transmitted names of possible union nominees for positions in the Department of Labor.[15] Nixon, of course, sought to attract support from the largely Democratic union members, especially "those leaders in the labor movement who basically are conservative in their views"; he directed Colson to be sure that his "labor friends know that the President is with them all the way."[16] AFL-CIO President George Meany, whom Nixon called "an all out Democrat, but a great patriot,"[17] received particular attention. Through ongoing communications with Jay Lovestone, a member of the AFL-CIO's board, Colson reported the labor leader's policy views and his reactions to the administration's efforts to battle inflation.[18] Somewhat less clear, however, is whether these efforts had much impact. Despite Meany's concerns about presidential initiatives to slow the growth in wages and his opposition to both the Philadelphia Plan and the Family Assistance Plan, Nixon pursued each, albeit with varying intensity and often few results.[19] The president secured only Meany's neutrality in the 1972 election.[20]

Much of Colson's stress was on what he saw as a crucial voting bloc: "an emerging conservative, middle class/labor vote."[21] In the special counsel's view, these "white ethnic, middle class working" people were key "swing voters" who wanted "stability and order" in the economy and in society more generally.[22] Besides labor, he focused on Catholics, and he pushed successfully to add an ethnic group liaison to his staff. Meanwhile, Colson, himself a conservative, joined in efforts to link Nixon with the provision of aid to parochial schools and with opposition to busing.

Yet, one must be careful not to paint with too broad a brush. Colson apparently tried as well to suggest both blacks and women for various presidential appointments.[23] His primary objective—which, by most accounts, he pursued relentlessly—was to find additional support for the president.[24]

Structuring for Public Outreach: The Colson Unit

In his group outreach efforts, Colson oversaw several others, working at the top of a loose hierarchical structure. He, of course, was part of the overall White House hierarchy, reporting to and receiving orders from the president through the chief of staff's office.[25]

At least two of Colson's assistants—George Bell and Henry Cashen—already worked in the White House Office (WHO) when he arrived. Bell was a staff assistant to personnel director Harry Flemming until early 1970, when he joined Colson. Until Bell resigned for health reasons in late 1972, he served primarily as a liaison with labor, taking directions from and reporting to Colson on meetings with local labor leaders and on labor issues in particular states.[26] Yet Bell also performed a range of other activities. He met with representatives of business groups, frequently to gather their views of the economic outlook in their industries.[27] On occasion, Bell focused on senior citizens and religious groups.[28] Like others in the Colson unit, he was deployed to seek statements of support for the administration's economic initiatives, emphasizing, for example, "Small Business Groups" and local labor organizations.[29] More generally, Bell often acted as Colson's deputy, supervising other aides' contacting efforts,[30] organizing the office's "system" for recommending direct presidential contacts,[31] and serving as Colson's channel to the personnel office for suggestions on appointments.[32]

Cashen (a Nixon advance man in the 1966 and 1968 campaigns) initially worked under John Ehrlichman, first as deputy counsel and then as deputy assistant to the president for domestic affairs; he served as liaison to the Post Office and the Departments of Housing and Urban Development (HUD) and Transportation.[33] This experience in dealing with executive branch officials evidently helped Cashen in his activities as a virtual caseworker for various groups.[34] Still, under Colson, he primarily "dealt with most of the business and trade association guys."[35] Despite this specialty, Cashen also handled other areas, for example, serving as a contact with Catholic groups on issues such as parochial school aid,[36] developing a "good Irish mailing list,"[37] and trying to organize "celebrity" supporters of Richard Nixon.[38]

Colson's office soon expanded. W. Richard (Dick) Howard was detailed to the White House from the Department of Commerce in July 1970, becoming a full-time aide the following year. Most of his work focused on liaison with business groups, as did that of staffer Roger Johnson. Donald Rodgers served as a consultant to the president, working under Colson doing labor liaison.

The unit continued to grow as the 1972 election approached, reaching at least twenty-three.[39] Its internal structure remained a loose hierarchy, and Howard gradually took on some of Bell's responsibilities for supervising other Colson aides.[40] The new staffers sought to develop relations with and mobilize support from a variety of groups considered key to Nixon's reelection. For instance, as noted earlier, Colson and others believed that the blue-collar, white ethnic vote was critical. At least at first, Haldeman hoped to keep the task of mobilizing such voters at the Republican National Committee (RNC), but gradually he was persuaded to add liaison with ethnic groups to both the Committee to Reelect the President and the White House.[41] In February 1972, Michael Balzano, a thirty-six-year-old former garbage collector who, after hurting his back, had received a doctorate in political theory from Georgetown University, joined Colson's staff to serve as "liaison man with blue-collar and ethnic groups."[42] Colson directed Balzano to, for example, help ensure that "our busing road shows [are] geared right into ethnic forums in key Northern cities,"[43] including using a "special political advance fund" to oversee the production and placement of anti-busing TV ads in ethnic areas around major cities.[44]

Also receiving attention were Hispanics, dubbed the "Spanish-surnamed." William H. Marumoto divided his time between the personnel office and Colson's unit. Among his tasks were finding appropriate forums for "top Spanish speaking appointees" and visitors such as the president of Mexico,[45] as well as mobilizing those opposed to U.S. recognition of Cuba.[46] Colson also expected Marumoto to participate in discussions of "substantive" policy issues, such as housing, bilingual education, and efforts to encourage Department of Commerce and Small Business Administration programs to "increase Spanish enterprise."[47]

Meanwhile, Melville L. Stephens and William F. Rhatican focused on veterans,[48] and Jamie McLane handled both youth and senior citizens. Specialization was scarcely complete, and assignments frequently overlapped. McLane, Howard Cohen, and Douglas Hallett all took on youth liaison tasks, and Llewellyn (Bud) Evans Jr. joined McLane as a link with senior citizens.[49] Colson asked Hallett, who had been assigned to work with Hispanic groups before Marumoto joined the public liaison staff, to "ride herd" on the Spanish-surname operation.[50]

In addition to trying to strengthen relations with existing groups and voting blocs, Colson helped organize "independent" citizen groups. Entities such as Tell It to Hanoi and Citizens to Safeguard America were meant to heighten support for the president through letter-writing campaigns and newspaper ads.[51] Moreover, Colson relied on such groups to assist in efforts to push administration initiatives in Congress.

Other Group Liaisons

Even so, the nascent office of public liaison scarcely monopolized group outreach in the White House. To an extent, the market structuring of past administrations persisted, as numerous aides had ties with external constituencies throughout the Nixon years. In some cases, these relationships reflected particular staffers' jobs before joining the WHO; in other cases, aides volunteered or were pressed into service based on their descriptive characteristics (such as religious membership or race). On still other occasions, external demand and others' lack of interest led to staffers assuming tasks.

As already mentioned, senior aides such as Buchanan, Flanigan, and Garment maintained ties with external constituencies throughout their time in the White House. Others assumed such responsibilities more sporadically. Even before leaving his cabinet post to become counselor to the president in mid-1970, for example, Robert Finch functioned at times as a youth liaison, although aides on Colson's staff gradually took over the task. As counselor, Finch also became involved from time to time in issues related to Hispanics, blacks, and women.[52]

Minority Groups. Other aides pursued group outreach tasks on a more regular basis. Robert J. Brown, for instance, was a special assistant to the president whose main responsibility was minority affairs, focusing mostly on African Americans. Kotlowski credits him with "forc[ing] the issue of minority procurement" and, along with Garment, generating results from administration efforts to boost minority businesses. In late 1969, Nixon signed a Brown-drafted presidential memorandum that "invit[ed] federal agencies to help 'set goals' to expand purchases from minority firms"; thus, the "first minority contract set-asides" were born.[53] In addition, Brown served as liaison to many black businesses ("Brown's negro businessmen-bankers-Elks")[54] and religious groups, and he pushed for stronger efforts to hire minorities in the executive branch.[55] Although formally lodged in the Domestic Council (DC) staff for much of his time in the White House, as the election approached, Brown moved back to the WHO, where he and others sought to influence the contract-awarding process of the Office of Minority Business Enterprise, hoping to boost Nixon's reelection support.[56]

Other African American aides also took on group outreach tasks. A former reporter and assistant director of public relations for the NAACP, Stanley S. Scott originally joined the Office of Communications to develop ties with minority media,[57] but he soon became involved in group outreach. By the end of 1972, he described his job as including the following tasks: being a "central White House contact point for blacks," helping convey information about blacks within the administration, and working with the Department of Defense on "racial conflict."[58] Although Scott and Brown appear to have worked together only rarely, there is no indication that their relationship was competitive.[59]

Brown left to start his own company in North Carolina in early 1973, and Scott was elevated to special assistant to the president with responsibility for "minority affairs." In that position, he continued his previous activities and also began to make recommendations for White House briefings, presidential press coverage, and political appointments. In addition, Scott sought to heighten the visibility of Africa within the administration.[60] Much of the actual impact of such efforts, however, was limited to public-relations activities. Scott accompanied Pat Nixon on a trip to visit drought-stricken areas of Africa and was responsible for "coordinating the impact of Mrs. Nixon's trip with the black community."[61] As the president's Watergate-related difficulties mounted, Scott joined the "surrogates program" to defend Nixon.

The position of liaison for minority affairs was lodged in numerous units as the second-term administration struggled to cope with growing criticism and increased fiscal restraints. First listed as a member of the group liaison unit headed by William J. Baroody Jr. (who joined the staff in December 1972 as Colson's replacement), Scott was later placed (along with Baroody) under Counselor Melvin Laird.[62] By early 1974, Staff Secretary Bruce Kehrli recommended to Chief of Staff Al Haig that Scott (and his assistant, John C. Calhoun) be transferred back to the Office of Communications, working this time under director Kenneth Clawson.[63]

Although several White House staffers spent at least some of their time on "civil rights" and on issues of interest to racial minorities,[64] such concerns were never high on the Nixon administration's list of priorities. Colson sometimes expressed borderline indifference to efforts directed at "minority groups," although he had long suggested the names of blacks and Hispanics for political appointments.[65] In part, this may have reflected Nixon's mounting resistance to reaching out to many blacks, among them civil rights leaders and those he deprecatingly termed "integrationists."[66] Plausibly, too, before 1972, both men's views "stemmed from electoral considerations, the need to woo [white] blue-collar voters."[67]

Women. Meanwhile, an even larger constituency began to demand serious attention: women. The president understood the political need to place women in more senior and more visible posts in the federal government and to have policy development pay greater attention to women's views and problems.[68] Yet, when the President's Task Force on Women's Rights and Responsibilities issued its report in late 1969, it received virtually no attention and was not even published until June 1970. Among other recommendations, the task force "urged Nixon to name an assistant for women's rights and send Congress a message on discrimination against women. It endorsed ERA [the equal rights amendment] as well as legislation to empower EEOC [the Equal Employment Opportunity Commission], provide child care and access to education, expand the Civil Rights Commission's charge, and end [sex] distinctions in Social Security benefits."[69] Of most relevance here, the idea of an assistant for women's rights went nowhere, vetoed by the senior staff as "not an effective addition."[70] More generally, "unlike minority rights, gender issues were not on Nixon's agenda."[71]

Nonetheless, pressure from both inside and outside the administration continued for more jobs and enhanced opportunities for women. Within, it was often conservatives such as personnel chief Fred Malek and Colson who pushed for these initiatives, looking always to sway women's votes. Malek sought to increase the number of female political appointees and assigned his assistant Barbara Franklin to identify possible candidates and pass their names on to departmental officials; Malek and Franklin then tried to encourage the departments to hire women from the list. As the 1972 campaign approached, Franklin also became "project supervisor" for outreach efforts directed at women.[72] Externally, criticism from many feminists may have helped encourage the adoption of "Revised Order number 4," under which the "Labor Department used goals and timetables to open high-paying jobs to women."[73]

After the election, Anne L. Armstrong joined the staff as counselor to the president; until George W. Bush took office, this was the most senior WHO position formally held by a woman. Armstrong, the outgoing cochair of the RNC, had no explicit assignment. Although one of her primary jobs was liaison with grassroots party members, she also became, in effect, an assistant for women's affairs, maintaining ties with myriad women's groups.[74] Rather quickly, however, Armstrong accumulated a spectrum of not fully related tasks, as had her predecessor, Robert Finch. She defined her "areas of responsibility" as encompassing "women, youth, Spanish-speaking Americans, the Bicentennial, the Cost of Living Council, the National Commission on Critical Choices for Americans, the Federal Property Council, and the Commission on the Organization of Government for the Conduct of Foreign Policy."[75] Moreover, as Watergate grew more serious, one journalist observed that Armstrong—a key Nixon loyalist who spent considerable time speaking in the president's defense—became overloaded.[76]

Armstrong had a small staff—never totaling more than ten—to help with her varied tasks. For the most part, her office operated as a hierarchy, with Armstrong at the top. She transmitted their questions and requests to others in the executive branch,[77] and her aides both reported to her and briefed her on meetings with groups and individuals from around the world.[78] Even though Armstrong reportedly spent only 25 percent of her time on "civil rights,"[79] she was often an advocate for women. In fall 1973, for example, she tried to intercede with Chief of Staff Haig on behalf of Nola Smith, who had been hired as a women's recruiter to replace Barbara Franklin in the personnel office but had received none of the resources of her predecessor.[80]

The Armstrong staff was organized around her responsibilities. Most important here was her establishment of an "Office of Women's Programs," a step her boss had refused to take. A draft speech written for Armstrong notes that the unit was designed to "act as an advocate for progress and change, both in the Government and in the private sector." It served as a "liaison with national women's organizations, . . . disseminate[d] information about statutes and regulations that deal with issues of sex discrimination, [and] channel[ed] complaints . . . to the proper officials in Government."[81] Aides also tracked female appointees throughout the executive branch and on the federal bench, commented on legislation, and gave speeches.[82]

The new unit had a skeletal staff of two professionals. At the outset, Jill Ruckelshaus, serving formally as a consultant, oversaw the full-time director of the office, Vera Hirschberg, who previously had worked as a presidential speechwriter. Ruckelshaus ultimately was forced to leave in March 1974 due to mounting distrust after her husband, William Ruckelshaus, resigned as deputy attorney general during the "Saturday Night Massacre" in fall 1973. Hirschberg followed in May 1974. Patricia Lindh replaced Jill Ruckelshaus in June 1974, and Karen Keesling joined the staff as her assistant in early July.[83]

Other Armstrong aides assisted with different aspects of her group outreach responsibilities. In addition to working on the bicentennial, for example, Pamela Powell spent part of her time on liaison with youth groups, as well as overseeing White House internships.[84] Fred Slight, who, as a former RNC colleague, worked mainly as Armstrong's "political liaison," transferred to her staff from the Cabinet Committee on Opportunities for Spanish Speaking People and often served as a liaison with the Spanish-speaking.[85] Just as the Nixon administration was limping to a close, Armstrong finally received news that the aide hired to help with Hispanic liaison, Fernando DeBaca, was scheduled to begin working.[86] Despite Armstrong's concerns that Hispanic liaison was not receiving sufficient attention, others in the White House praised her commitment. Bradley Patterson commented, for instance, that until Armstrong took it over, "we really handled [the Spanish-speaking in a] very poor way here in the White House. It was passed around back and forth to one set of hands and another, and it was really very unhappily . . . sort of bucked about."[87]

Armstrong's activities also got her involved in the internal politics of the White House. As mentioned earlier, she took a stand on behalf of women in the White House by objecting to the shabby treatment accorded to Nola Smith. Among other indignities Smith, unlike her peers and her predecessor, was excluded from the White House Mess.[88] And, as noted in chapter 2, Armstrong took on Kehrli and Haig in demanding that women get access to the male-only White House health unit. The initial resistance was firm, with Haig observing that this was "not a good idea . . . [the] place just isn't suited for ladies."[89] In the end, however, Armstrong prevailed, and women got access to the unit.

Group Liaison and Governance Issues

As one would expect, participation in group liaison by numerous individuals lodged in multiple offices frequently raised issues of governance. As Colson cautioned Bell, "What we don't need are a lot of independent agents handling different groups. When we use someone . . . from someone else's staff it is fine so long as we have the right working relationship."[90] Called for were structures to coordinate activities or, sometimes, to resolve disputes.

Efforts to mobilize group support in developing and supporting particular pieces of legislation frequently involved several parts of the staff, working mostly in collegial-consensual structures. For instance, Colson's office and DC staffers joined to explore possible approaches to legislation that would outlaw a few specific handguns, which, along with a rising crime rate, were generating increasing controversy. Early in 1971, Cashen briefed representatives of gun manufacturers, hunters' associations, and firearms periodicals on possible gun legislation.[91] Later in the year, DC staffer Egil (Bud) Krogh held similar discussions and commissioned a report by an "independent ballistics organization [that] will indicate that objective standards are feasible for eliminating poorly constructed junk handguns." He suggested to Colson that they jointly hold additional meetings with gun supporters to "place the report in context" and to reach "consensus on acceptable legislation to outlaw 'Saturday Night Specials.'" Although Colson expressed some concern that the "gun lobby's" close involvement in writing legislation "leaves us open to a very political attack," he agreed to allow Cashen to continue to work with the DC staff on the project.[92]

By the early 1970s, DC aides typically worked in particular policy areas (rather than with specific departments or agencies), and Colson frequently sought to link such staffers with his own group specialists.[93] On occasion, too, John Ehrlichman directed DC staff to work with Colson's office in galvanizing group support for specific bills.[94]

Not all attempts at joint activity unfolded smoothly. In early 1970, in an effort to maximize the "follow-up benefit" of presidential meetings with "outside groups,"

DC Deputy Director Kenneth Cole and Colson laid out in a formal memo a "modus operandi" for cooperation among the group outreach, domestic policy, and scheduling units. Colson agreed to consult with all "substantive people" before seeking to schedule a presidential meeting with a group. "Once the meeting is approved, the domestic affairs staff will ensure that policy decisions made are consonant with the aims of the meeting, i.e., don't announce population control on the day the President is to meet with the Catholics." The relevant DC deputy would review and approve the presidential briefing memo that went to Nixon before the meeting, and the appropriate cabinet member, DC chief Ehrlichman, or the deputy would sit in on the meeting. Afterward, the deputy also "would have the prime responsibility for [following up on] any substantive issues. . . . Colson should assume responsibility if there is a political matter or if it is merely seeing to it that a policy is carried out." Although noting that the DC deputy and Colson would "need to work in close cooperation," the memo concluded that "problems of coordination would be Cole's to solve."[95]

In effect, this arrangement can be viewed as an effort to impose a hybrid hierarchical/collegial-competitive structure. All three potentially conflicting units (group outreach, DC staff, and scheduling) were involved, and the DC deputy and Colson were charged with "ensur[ing] that whatever follow-up required is consistent with the President's commitments, the policy established in the domestic affairs staff and the political goal to be reached."[96] Yet, at least formally, "substantive domestic policy" goals appear to have been given priority in terms of initial approval of group meetings, approval of the president's briefing memo, and resolution of coordination problems.

This scheduling agreement did not put an end to coordination difficulties, which worsened as the 1972 election drew nearer. Not only did "domestic policy" include a wide range of substantive areas, but it also raised myriad questions of public relations, legislative strategy, media coverage, and group liaison. At least from Cole's perspective, the collegial-competitive features of White House activities suffered from a lack of clear decision rules. There was a "sort of group responsibility for things. The responsibility [is] divided amongst the departments and agencies, Herb Klein's office, Chuck Colson's office, Bill Timmons's office, and Ron Ziegler's office. No man has been in charge."[97] Soon, Cole recommended the imposition of hierarchical structuring: "*one* man ought to be in charge of any given issue. . . . He makes the decision as to what does or doesn't happen in the areas of policy development/tradeoffs, legislative strategy, special interest groups, and PR/media and background."[98]

Perhaps not surprisingly, relations between the DC staff and Colson were not always cooperative. Sometimes, senior aides disagreed over administration goals and strategies. Colson, for example, recalled "head-on . . . deadly conflict with Ehrlichman" over busing. In the former's telling, while the latter "was worrying about the substance of the issue," the group liaison head focused on the impact of the busing issue on the president's support among blue-collar whites.[99] As often happened during the Nixon years, the electoral argument persuaded the ultimate arbiters, Haldeman and the president. Other times, Colson evidently took matters into his own hands, bypassing DC staffers altogether. Serving on occasion as an advocate for some of the groups with which his office dealt, he sought to persuade administration officials of particular policy positions. In mid-1972, for instance, Colson enlisted Office of Management and Budget (OMB) Deputy Director Caspar Weinberger's "assistance in changing the Administration's position" on pending House legislation that increased funding for the GI Bill and for military widows' compensation.[100]

Meanwhile, Cashen routinely reported to Colson on pending legislation he was tracking,[101] and Colson pressed aides such as Cohen and Rhatican for information on "what has been accomplished in terms of bringing organized groups in to lobby the Congress."[102] Somewhat curiously, even though Colson and his aides focused a good deal of their attention on Congress, there were relatively few ties between the group outreach office and the congressional liaison operation.[103] In part, this may reflect the comparative status of the two units in the WHO. As chapter 6 details, the Office of Congressional Relations (OCR) in the Nixon White House ranked relatively low in the staff hierarchy. Its director for much of the administration, William Timmons, did not have regularly scheduled meetings with the president, and he and his staff "became second-class citizens as far as the rest of the White House staff was concerned."[104] Moreover, the evident resistance to cooperation came from both sides. OCR Director Timmons tried to hire an additional aide to maintain ties with organized groups, triggering a swift response from Colson that this would be "very ill-advised."[105]

At the same time, the absence of structural mechanisms for linking congressional and group liaison and for resolving conflicts over strategy was important. The sort of collegial structuring that emerged between group liaison and other staff units did not appear. Within the White House more generally, technical controversy over how best to deal with a Congress controlled by Democrats existed: "Haldeman, Ehrlichman, Pat Buchanan, and Chuck Colson . . . had very little experience in Washington and a much more combative approach to Congress than [Bryce] Harlow or Timmons."[106] Rather than hearing arguments over strategy in an adversarial structure, the president listened mostly to the views of his most senior aides.

To be sure, the problems of coordination surfaced in part because of the nature of group liaison. At least from Colson's perspective, the job had "an inherent conflict[:] The people in the White House who were dealing with substance . . . exclusively want to do just that, they want to carry things out . . . the way they see the particular problem. When you inject how the world outside sees it, there is an understandable conflict, and my job had to be at times to be an advocate for a point of view."[107] Moreover, many of these external constituencies had competing priorities and interests; it is scarcely surprising that some of the resulting conflicts suffused White House political and policy discussions. Nonetheless, Colson's competitiveness and relentless pursuit of what he believed were the president's goals doubtless added to the complexity of addressing problems.

Stabilization

Although Charles Colson finally left the White House, the tasks associated with group outreach did not. They became the responsibility of William Baroody in December 1972. Several of Colson's aides stayed on, including his chief deputy, Dick Howard; Mike Balzano, the ethnics liaison; Don Rodgers, whose specialty was labor groups; and Kathleen Balsdon, who kept track of the unit's numerous lists of "contacts."[108] As noted earlier, minority affairs liaison Stan Scott also was lodged in Baroody's office. Nonetheless, the group outreach operation was placed further down in the overall White House hierarchy. For a time, both the Baroody operation and the Office of Communications were placed under Press Secretary Ron Ziegler.[109]

As the second-term Nixon White House continued to adjust to the departure of some aides, the arrival of others, and the distraction of the increasing menace of Watergate, structuring grew more fluid. By October 1973, the group outreach unit operated under Counselor for Domestic Affairs Melvin Laird, for whom Baroody was a deputy.[110] Laird's departure in early 1974 generated a new round of restructuring. On January 28, the White House announced that Kenneth Clawson had been named director of communications, formally replacing Herbert Klein; Baroody was promoted to special consultant to the president (the title just below assistant to the president), and his position as Colson's replacement as head of group outreach was officially acknowledged. It was in this context that Baroody encouraged Deputy Press Secretary Gerald Warren to describe him as "not a new Colson, . . . but a new Baroody."[111]

For the most part, Baroody and his aides concentrated on maintaining ties with external groups and constituencies, especially those that had "come to be known as the 'New Majority' "; they continued Colson's "direct mail operation" and "group cultivation" (developing "contact" lists).[112] Even so, when describing his office's tasks to the new chief of staff, Al Haig, Baroody added that the unit continued to be involved in public relations and political activities: it served as a "switchboard for our friends on the outside such as the Lou Harris's and Sindlinger's, key Democrats for Nixon, . . . and others; [as well as being a] liaison with the RNC, congressional campaign and policy committees."[113] In Baroody's view, three basic elements of support for the president were available: the media, Congress, and outside groups. Although his operation focused on the third, it played a "major role" in the other two.[114]

Underscoring the increasing importance of Congress, by mid-1973, the outreach unit had acquired two additional aides whose focus was legislative. Powell Moore replaced Patrick O'Donnell (who had handled the Speakers' Bureau under

Colson), but the new staffer's job was to serve as liaison to OCR and to work directly with members of Congress. Meanwhile, Wayne Valis's charge was to track legislative issues. In May 1974, Moore formally moved to OCR, and Theodore Marrs and Jeffrey Eves joined group liaison, the latter specializing in veterans' issues.[115]

Formal boundaries among these specialized White House subunits likely mattered less and less as the pressures of external scrutiny and criticism mounted. Galvanized by the "Saturday Night Massacre," the *Washington Star-News* reported, "old and new pressure groups are gearing up to mobilize public opinion and constituent pressure on the House committee [on impeachment] and other members of Congress."[116] As might be anticipated in response to such a massive perceived threat, White House staffers from numerous units joined in an informal collegial-consensual structure to respond. For example, the follow-up for the 1974 State of the Union Address involved OCR staff making "congressional calls," Peter Flanigan joining Baroody "with selected constituencies," Anne Armstrong and her aides fielding "political calls," Director of Communications Ken Clawson calling editors and publishers, and still others taking calls from the general public or checking with state and local elected officials.[117] Such "impeachment support" activities continued. In May 1974, Flanigan and Baroody sent President Nixon one of numerous "progress reports" in which they summarized efforts of staffers and supporters around the country to try to persuade members of Congress to "expedite the constitutional process of impeachment . . . and put Watergate behind us immediately."[118]

Of course, they failed. Yet the Nixon administration's experiment with more systematic outreach to organized groups and identifiable constituencies both survived and generated expectations that future presidencies would sometimes struggle to meet.

FORD: EVOLUTION OF THE OFFICE OF PUBLIC LIAISON

When Gerald Ford became president, he was initially greeted with considerable relief and overwhelming public support. After less than a month, however, his pardon of Richard Nixon unleashed a firestorm of criticism, a reaction amplified by a Congress controlled by the opposing party and facing midterm elections in three months. That the president's "approval rating plummeted from 71% to 50% in less than a week" only reinforced congressional anxiety. Meanwhile, Press Secretary Jerald terHorst's resignation triggered "the first salvo in a war [with the press] that would rage" for the remainder of the administration.[119]

In such an environment, the new president sought to develop relations not only with legislators and the press but also with groups throughout the United States. Baroody, who had "previously pitched the idea" of a separate Office of Public Liaison to Nixon, found Ford "almost immediately . . . 100 percent behind the idea."[120]

The president saw OPL as one vehicle in his effort to "generate a new climate of confidence and understanding of national issues."[121]

Formally established in September 1974, the new unit included not only Baroody's aides but also a variety of other staff liaisons, including Virginia Knauer, who maintained ties with consumer groups. OPL merged with Anne Armstrong's office when she resigned in December. By mid-1975, the group outreach unit had grown to thirty.[122] Much as it had been under Nixon, OPL was structured as a loose hierarchy, with Baroody and a deputy director at the top. Reporting to Baroody or his deputy were several specialized subunits for particular constituencies such as consumers, women, and blacks. Other staffers focused on relations with, for example, business and trade associations, youth, "ethnics," and Hispanics.[123] One professional, Wayne Valis, was primarily responsible for research and for drafting speeches to be delivered by administration officials to particular groups.[124]

Formally, OPL was located in the office of Counselor John Marsh. Marsh, a former Democratic member of Congress from Virginia, also oversaw OCR and, in the view of many, paid more attention to the administration's dealings with Congress.[125] Indeed, Reichley contends that OPL "operated somewhat outside the direct chain of command."[126]

From the start, OPL sought to convey the image of a presidency that was far more open than Nixon's had been. It began by organizing conferences, both around the country and in Washington, which brought together diverse groups and administration officials. In Baroody's view, the "roadshows"—for instance, the twenty-four OPL-sponsored regional conferences on subjects such as "consumer representation"—were particularly successful. The president spoke at several of these meetings, and senior administration officials attended all of them.[127] At the same time, OPL oversaw a series of meetings in Washington, D.C., where cabinet secretaries and others met with representatives of a variety of interests. Tuesday mornings and afternoons were reserved for sessions with "human services groups," whereas on alternate Wednesdays, twenty or more trade association representatives or corporate chief executive officers met with government officials.[128] Although journalists sometimes poked fun at such "Baroody briefings," they noted that "Baroody's men go to great length to emphasize that the businessmen should feel free to follow-up on the briefing by telephoning the government official personally for more individual give and take."[129]

Although arranging and following up on such sessions took a considerable amount of the OPL staff's time, the unit also continued the Nixon-era group liaison activities. Donald Webster, for instance, was in charge of coordinating the Wednesday meetings; an economist, he also maintained contacts with "other economists, business groups, agricultural organizations, and people in the investment field."[130] Theodore Marrs, a former military physician and deputy assistant secretary of defense, oversaw the Tuesday briefings; served as a link to veterans, military groups, and medical associations; and supervised outreach on several other "human resources" issues.[131] In addition, once Donald Rodgers left the White House,

Baroody, Marrs, and Webster maintained contact with labor unions, and Valis passed on intelligence from his contacts with the United Auto Workers and public employees' unions.[132]

Nor was there much change in efforts to maintain links with women, blacks, and Hispanics. Patricia Lindh, named special assistant to the president for women after Armstrong's departure, continued her work with a variety of national women's organizations, focusing on the enforcement of Title IX and activities associated with the observance of International Women's Year.[133] Similarly, Stanley Scott sought to provide information to black newspapers about "Administration activities relevant to the concerns of blacks," as well as to sustain ties with "black leaders and organizations."[134] The aide with responsibility for liaison with Hispanics, Fernando DeBaca, started in September1974 and began to develop relationships between the new presidency and Hispanic organizations.[135]

Despite its broader reach, OPL did not monopolize outreach to external groups and constituencies. Several other aides, for example, had ties with religious groups. White House Counsel Philip Buchen frequently tracked the political and policy reactions of various segments of the Jewish community.[136] David Lissy moved from the DC staff's payroll to the White House in 1976 so that he could have "political" as well as "substantive" discussions with the Jewish officials he dealt with as the "President's liaison to the American Jewish community."[137] As the 1976 election approached, Richard S. Brannon joined the communications office as a liaison to Christian religious organizations.[138]

Other interests also received attention from staffers not formally lodged in OPL. Gwen Anderson from Counselor Robert Hartmann's office served as the White House contact for the National Republican Heritage Groups Council (an RNC "auxiliary") on "Republican partisan matters and related Ethnic affairs."[139] Meanwhile, Robert Goldwin, who had worked as a staff assistant for NATO Ambassador Donald Rumsfeld, followed Rumsfeld to the White House, where Goldwin "had responsibility for seeking ideas from scholars outside the administration."[140]

At the same time, in the more permeable Ford White House, senior staffers were approached by a variety of interest groups. Jerry Jones, for instance, was lobbied by representatives of oil companies on energy legislation. He reported on their arguments to Staff Coordinator Dick Cheney, although apparently not to either OPL or OCR.[141]

Governance Structuring: Links beyond OPL

Despite the persistent overlap of responsibilities, for the most part, informal collegial-consensual structuring linked OPL staffers with other units, with few problems. Relatively early in the administration, for example, Press Secretary Ron Nessen assigned Larry Speakes to act as liaison with Baroody for arranging coverage of White House press conferences. Congressional-relations aides were invited to OPL-sponsored White House receptions for trade associations and labor unions,[142] and Baroody sent draft correspondence to members of Congress to OCR Director Max Friedersdorf for his approval.[143] Because of Baroody's and OPL's ongoing contact with the business community, he routinely offered policy suggestions to the president's economic adviser William Seidman, as well as other administration officials.[144] OPL and DC staff also worked together on briefing sessions for regulated industries and following up on complaints and suggestions made at the White House Conferences on Domestic and Economic Affairs.[145] Similarly, the National Security Council (NSC) staff and OPL cooperated and coordinated with each other on the scheduling of proposals for presidential meetings with foreign policy–related interest groups and individuals and on the preparation of speeches delivered by administration officials to such groups.[146] National Security Assistant Brent Scowcroft occasionally alerted Baroody to the possible foreign policy implications of outreach efforts to particular nationality groups.[147]

Considerably more complex were the arrangements that followed the inclusion of consumer liaison in OPL. This involved the public liaison unit in activities that included the congressional-relations unit, domestic and economic policy staffers, and the Office of Consumer Affairs in the Department of Health, Education, and Welfare. With mounting demands from consumer advocates, the administration found itself under increasing pressure to take action. As the newly elected Congress convened in early 1975, the prospects looked promising for passage of legislation to establish an independent consumer agency, an action that the president and many Republican business interests strongly opposed.

Within the administration, differences emerged over the appropriate response (which, for the most part, reflected technical rather than goal conflict). Baroody, noting that "consumer issues . . . will continue to have broad political appeal," urged Ford to adopt a "comprehensive and credible alternative proposal" that would be announced in a special presidential message.[148] The public liaison director outlined several substantive proposals for inclusion in such a message, which Knauer and her staff had evidently produced. Before a decision could be made, however, Senator Abraham Ribicoff introduced a bill to create a consumer protection agency, and the White House moved quickly to mobilize opposition. John Byington, deputy special assistant for consumer affairs, sent materials for "needed decisions and action" to economic policy aide Seidman.[149] The public liaison staff also drafted a presidential letter to "certain Members of Congress" that outlined the administration's opposition to the Ribicoff legislation. Yet DC staff director James Cannon did not approve the draft and substantially revised it to include alternative plans for enhancing consumer protection. Working within an ad hoc adversarial structure, John Marsh then asked congressional-relations, policy, and senior White House staff, as well as top OMB officials, for comments and suggestions on the Cannon version.[150] Ford refused to take a public position until the DC staff outlined specific consumer protection alternatives for him to choose among. Ultimately, the president rejected recommendations to expand the Office of Consumer Affairs, to establish consumer representation units in each cabinet department, and to send a special message to Congress; he agreed only to take less radical steps.[151]

Baroody predicted a "number of adverse political consequences" of this decision. Chief among them, he feared, was "serious criticism from the conservative segment" of the business community, which had helped formulate the compromise proposal Ford had rejected. Meanwhile, Knauer had persuaded "liberal [business] elements" to switch to the administration alternative; she also "had done quiet spadework within the consumer movement and expected to be able to neutralize a substantial segment of the consumer movement [with] our package."[152]

Instead, part of the administration's response was a presidential directive to executive branch departments and agencies to "better represent consumer interests," which staffer Knauer was charged with overseeing.[153] The final versions of the agency "Consumer Representation Plans" that were generated as part of this effort were approved by Knauer, OMB officials, and the DC staff, under Baroody's supervision.[154] In addition, consumer affairs and other OPL staffers joined with OMB officials to hold "consumer representation hearings" in several U.S. cities.[155]

Much as Baroody had predicted, "consumer advocates and groups . . . lashed out at the plans and hearings as a politically inspired, worthless 'hoax' designed as a 'smokescreen' to make more acceptable Ford's announced intention to veto the proposed consumer protection agency," which had passed both houses of Congress.[156] Presented with several alternative paths and with information about the advantages and disadvantages of those choices, the president evidently followed his party's traditions and his own policy preferences.

Conclusion

By the end of the Ford administration, group outreach had gained a "respectable face."[157] No longer were the activities of the newly labeled OPL associated with the excesses of Charles Colson. Although the incoming Democratic administration would seek to reorient OPL, the demands and expectations of the multiplying groups and interests outside the White House would severely constrain any lasting change.

CARTER: CHANGE, THEN CONTINUITY

Jimmy Carter took office with a deep distrust of "special" interests and a populist desire for a more open presidency.[158] The initial Office of Public Liaison strove to extend White House outreach to a range of "alienated groups."[159] Yet many other elements of the fragmenting Democratic coalition clamored for attention from the first Democratic president in almost a decade, while organized interests generally had come to expect ready access to the president and senior staff. Although OPL had ceased to exist as a distinct unit by mid-1978, the tasks it and other White House staffers had performed in previous administrations continued, and novel governance structuring emerged. By the end of the Carter years, group outreach had become institutionalized.

OPL under Costanza

The new president named Margaret (Midge) Costanza as director of OPL. The former vice mayor of Rochester, New York, and cochair of candidate Carter's New York campaign, Costanza was charged with using OPL to "concentrate on those special interest groups that would not ordinarily have the resources or financing to have their voices heard in an effective and meaningful way."[160]

Costanza headed a staff that numbered as many as ten permanent professionals, supplemented by a handful of detailees.[161] Especially at the outset, Costanza herself traveled around the United States making speeches to a variety of groups. While in Washington, she reportedly saw "everybody who has a gripe or question for Carter," reporting by memo to the president about what was discussed and the agencies to which she referred problems or questions.[162] She acted as well as OPL's "principal press spokesperson."[163] Costanza was near the top of the overall White House hierarchy, attending senior staff meetings and submitting scheduling and speech proposals.[164] Yet she met individually with Carter only rarely.[165]

Meanwhile, OPL was structured internally in a hybrid hierarchical-collegial fashion. A deputy assistant for public liaison typically served as a direct link to Costanza and also oversaw and coordinated the activities of the rest of the staff.[166] Moreover, Costanza's peripatetic activity often led individual public liaison aides to be assigned to help her prepare for senior staff meetings, for example.[167] Among other tasks, Ed Smith wrote speeches for Costanza and handled her routine correspondence.[168] Additional communication about objectives, problems, and tasks took place at weekly staff meetings. On occasion, OPL staff evidently needed to be reminded of Costanza's position within the unit. In April 1977, she sent an emphatic memo written in all capital letters: "No one is to independently offer or hold a meeting related to issues in the press without explicit authorization and instruction."[169]

OPL aides were assigned broad policy areas and interests to follow and with which to establish and maintain contact. For example, throughout her time in the White House (which ended in late 1979), Jane Wales spent much of her time on issues and groups involving women, consumers, and energy. On various occasions, she also handled outreach to "Asian-American groups, post-secondary education, . . . government reform, minorities, [and] wildlife."[170] Among Marilyn Haft's responsibilities were the "arts, civil and human rights, food and nutrition groups, humanities, Indians, medicine, [over]population, [and] professional groups."[171] After OPL Administrative Assistant (AA) Janice Peterson moved out of the White House, Haft took on some of her work as liaison to "ethnics"[172] while also serving as OPL's "legislative liaison" (see later). Similarly, Smith expanded his portfolio to include Peterson's responsibilities for neighborhoods, blacks, and urban affairs.[173] By early 1978, his assignments also included religion and Asian Americans.[174]

Despite the president's concerns about group access to the White House, many of the more traditional interests with which previous administrations had cultivated relations also received attention from the Carter OPL. For instance, AA Richard (Richie) Reiman focused on veterans and assisted S. Stephen Selig III (a special assistant and later deputy assistant) with outreach to business and industry and to trade associations.[175] After Peterson left, the two took on additional responsibilities, including energy, the environment, wildlife, higher education, and liaison with agricultural and rural groups.[176] Selig also served for a time as OPL's "agency liaison."[177]

In addition, relations with the U.S. Jewish community remained a matter of serious concern. In OPL, the primary aide involved in outreach to Jewish groups was Joyce Starr, a sociology Ph.D. who had worked as the "press coordinator [for] Jewish community affairs" during the 1976 campaign. Although her other responsibilities at various times included the "handicapped," Hispanics, and health,[178] her clear emphasis was on issues of concern to Jewish groups, such as the treatment of Jews by the Soviet Union. Indeed, one enthusiastic journalist called Starr "the first to be designated official spokesperson on behalf of Soviet Jews on the White House staff."[179]

Nonetheless, OPL scarcely monopolized White House relations with Jewish groups. Robert Lipshutz, counsel to the president, and Domestic Policy Staff (DPS) Director Stuart Eizenstat served as the main channels for input from the Jewish community, and both had considerable contact with the National Security Council (NSC) staff on issues involving the Middle East and Soviet Jews.[180] Available evidence suggests that Starr worked easily with the two, as well with Joseph Aragon and, on occasion, Hamilton Jordan and his aide Mark Siegel. Throughout her time in the White House, she sent Eizenstat, Lipshutz, and Aragon a steady stream of memos reporting on the views expressed at briefings she had arranged with Jewish groups and on her efforts at "human rights outreach."[181]

Not surprisingly, outreach to Jewish communities was not the only activity in which OPL aides worked with others in the WHO. Especially early on, for example, OPL "cleared and checked" nominees for presidential boards and commissions.[182] Selig and Reiman worked with Deputy Press Secretary Walter Wurfel in preparing for Press Secretary Jody Powell's "advisory group" meetings with business and labor public-affairs executives to counsel President Carter on his "image."[183] Meanwhile, Peterson and Patricia Bario, associate press secretary for media liaison, explored ways of more "effectively us[ing] the Ethnic press."[184]

OPL aides' broad assignments frequently involved them in substantive policy issues, which in turn brought them in contact with counterparts in the policy units and elsewhere in the White House. For the most part, these interactions relied on collegial-consensual structuring. For instance, Selig joined James Bishop of the energy staff and Amelia Parker and Mark Siegel from Jordan's office to explore how the Carter energy program might best be sold to the business community as well as to the general public.[185] Selig and Reiman worked with Siegel, Bishop, and energy aide Kevin Gorman to form a "Business People's Committee to support the seven goals of the energy policy."[186] By comparison, OPL contacts with NSC staffers more typically involved the exchange of information on issues of particular interest to constituency groups.[187]

Meanwhile, OPL relations with the Domestic Policy Staff were more regular, although they apparently grew more difficult. Public liaison staffers initially attended the weekly DPS meetings, and DPS aides sometimes participated in sessions with interest groups that OPL organized.[188] Costanza, Wales, Haft, and Reiman joined Eizenstat and Mary Schuman from DPS in a meeting to discuss lobbying efforts for airline regulation reform, a session joined by representatives of Common Cause and the National Association of Manufacturers.[189] By late 1977, however, Costanza reported to the OPL staff that DPS "meetings are expected to take on a new concept, going into more depth and our staff may be disinvited." If that happened, she or Deputy Director Seymour Wishman would attend and report back to the full staff.[190]

Like much of the rest of the WHO, some OPL aides spent considerable time on legislative activities. In March 1977, Les Francis joined the Office of Congressional Relations as the "legislative programs coordinator." Charged with coordinating "all White House efforts to shepherd legislation and policy through Congress,"[191] Francis oversaw a collegial-consensual structure that included representatives from DPS, OPL, intergovernmental relations, scheduling, political affairs, and the vice president's office. The group met twice weekly to discuss presidential legislation and what needed to be done to support it on Capitol Hill.[192] OPL's representative was Marilyn Haft, its "legislative issue coordinator." The Francis group developed "legislative push" strategies for particular initiatives. For example, Joyce Starr participated on the legislative team working on the administration's hospital cost-containment bill, and Jane Wales joined in efforts to influence legislation designed to create a separate consumer protection agency.[193] As part of a considerably more massive undertaking, OPL aides Selig and Reiman joined in the legislative push for ratification of the Panama Canal treaties, working to generate support from business groups, veterans, and a range of other organizations.[194] In addition, the two were often joined by Wales in organizing briefings on the Panama Canal treaties for a variety of groups.[195]

Despite the bustling activity and evident commitment of OPL staffers, problems soon emerged, both within the unit and in its dealings with those outside. First, as already mentioned, the unit struggled with internal administration, especially with maintaining the hierarchical flow of authority. Ten months into the administration, Costanza stressed at a staff meeting that she had to approve all major memos, and she emphasized "the need for follow-up of every meeting and every issue in which OPL is involved."[196] Yet, to a significant extent, the difficulties may have been woven into the initial structuring of the White House staff. According to an observer of the early Carter administration, for instance, " 'flack-catching' offices" like OPL did not have clear "role definition[s]," a situation exacerbated by the "lack of knowledge of presidential priorities."[197] In other words, OPL was not well integrated into an overall White House hierarchy.

Second, OPL's tasks overlapped with those of other White House units. Despite Wales's involvement in consumer issues, Esther Peterson was named special assistant for consumer affairs. And Peterson was not placed in OPL (as the consumer liaison had been in the previous two administrations); instead, she "work[ed] out of Stu Eizenstat's [domestic policy] shop."[198] Meanwhile, DPS Director Eizenstat and staffer Simon Lazarus participated actively in policy making related to consumers.[199]

Nor were consumers the only interests handled by those outside OPL. As noted earlier, outreach to U.S. Jewish groups involved several in the WHO. The DPS housed Nelson Cruikshank, the counselor to the president on aging, and Elizabeth Abramowitz, the assistant director for education and women's issues. Similarly, Landon Butler (and later Bernard Aronson) in Hamilton Jordan's office developed ties with organized labor, and Martha (Bunny) Mitchell's "primary assignment" was to "serve as a link between Carter" and African Americans.[200]

Hispanics, too, received attention from White House aides located outside of OPL. Although Joyce Starr was formally designated OPL's Hispanic liaison, at the outset, she could not even speak Spanish.[201] She worked with others, primarily Joseph Aragon, in trying to provide outreach until the Office of Hispanic Liaison opened in 1979 (see later). Aragon started as the "White House ombudsman," but he also oversaw the Community Services Administration until a director could be confirmed by the Senate and worked on special projects such as government reorganization, civil service reform, and the Panama Canal treaties. Even so, many in the Hispanic community believed that his main responsibility was to serve as their channel into the White House. Despite Aragon's estimate that he spent only about 10 percent of his time "advis[ing the] president on matters regarding the Hispanic community,"[202] he undertook many tasks associated with outreach to minority groups. Among other activities, he compiled and updated lists of Hispanic appointees, authored preparatory memos for presidential and vice-presidential meetings with representatives of Hispanic organizations (including the congressional Hispanic Caucus), and advised the Office of Media Relations on working with Spanish-language media.[203] On occasion, Aragon was assisted by other Hispanic staffers such as Associate Counsel Patrick Apodaca and OPL detailee Ruth Sanchez-Dirks.[204]

Third, by most accounts, Costanza's tenure in OPL generated controversy. She became a lightning rod in part because of her charge to provide outreach to previously excluded groups, a task she undertook with considerable energy and enthusiasm. "She loves it, wisecracking her way through the day, meeting and talking with groups as various as gays and Indians."[205] Such sessions and others—for example, with supporters of amnesty for Vietnam draft evaders[206]—frequently generated criticism both inside and outside the White House; even a vegetarian group's "Food

Day buffet at 1600 Pennsylvania Avenue had the cattlemen up in arms."[207] Meanwhile, Costanza herself took controversial stands. Among the actions that her White House colleagues found hard to tolerate were her calls for OMB Director Bert Lance's resignation following charges of illegal banking practices and her calling of a meeting of senior female appointees who disagreed with the president's public opposition to Medicaid-financed abortions.[208]

At the same time, Costanza's overall lack of appropriate skills hurt her. Reportedly, she was "perceived by a number of insiders as 'a lightweight' . . . it [was] a specific reference to her 'lack of administrative ability, the fact that from the beginning she was not allowed to pick and choose most of her own staff, and that the amount of responsibility overcame her,' according to a woman inside the administration who asked to remain anonymous."[209] Costanza also "rapidly developed the reputation among women's groups of being ill-prepared for meetings, not being savvy on issues, of compounding these shortcomings by blaming her staff and an abrasiveness that offended people inside the White House and out. She was a token."[210] Even so, at least some of the difficulties attributed to Costanza's weaknesses could also be explained by the problems her male colleagues had working with a strong, assertive woman.[211]

Whatever the reason, in April 1978, in yet another round of general staff reorganization, Anne Wexler was named an assistant to the president, with responsibilities for liaison with organized interests. Costanza shifted to handling only women's and "domestic human rights issues," her staff was reduced to a single person, and she was moved from near the Oval Office to the White House basement.[212] By the time Costanza formally resigned in August 1978, OPL had "effectively ceased to operate."[213]

Reorienting Interest Group Outreach

Despite the contemporary press's description of Wexler's position as the "assistant for public liaison,"[214] her approach and activities differed dramatically from Midge Costanza's. As chapter 6 describes, Wexler concentrated on formulating legislative strategies and garnering longer-term public support, not working with individual interests. Indeed, she recalled turning down an initial White House job offer specifying that "besides developing the Public Liaison's contribution to the development and [attainment] of presidential priorities," the liaison would "also be responsible for the special assistants to deal with . . . particular interest groups." Instead, Wexler saw her role as "essentially being the president's advocate, and I had to protect that role to be able to work substantively with the interest groups."[215]

In addition to Wexler (and her small professional staff), the Carter White House added personnel charged with outreach to specific groups, returning to the approach of earlier administrations that it had rejected at the outset and then haltingly began to adopt. Besides Esther Peterson, the consumer liaison; Landon Butler and Bernard Aronson, liaisons to labor[216]; and Nelson Cruikshank, the staff link to the elderly,[217] the White House soon added aides to nurture relations with women, blacks, Hispanics, "ethnics," and Jews. Structurally, such staffers were not lodged in a distinct unit, as many of them had been early in the administration; nor did they report to Wexler. Their interactions were characterized mostly by market structuring, although their formal title of special assistant placed them at a particular level of the emerging overall White House hierarchy. From Wexler's perspective, such structuring was useful: "There was always a filter between me and those special assistants who essentially were advocates. . . . We tried to insulate my special role by having special assistants. I was often able to use the advocates for lobbying purposes and for helping us on policy coalitions, but they took [on] their own day-to-day problems and the interest groups usually directed their individual concerns to the person who was perceived as being their advocate."[218]

By many accounts, several of the aides who pursued what Wexler termed group advocacy roles were more successful than their predecessors had been. Sarah Weddington, for instance, replaced Costanza as the liaison for women's issues. Almost immediately, she directed the administration's successful effort to persuade the Senate to extend the deadline for ratification of the equal rights amendment. Weddington and her staff also worked with OCR on other legislative issues, pushed for ratification of the ERA in states that had not yet done so, sought to increase the number of women named as federal judges, coordinated the efforts of an Interdepartmental Task Force on Women, and spoke throughout the United States.[219] Although she too generated occasional controversy,[220] Weddington evidently won White House respect for her skill. This was signaled by her August 1979 elevation to assistant to the president and member of the senior staff, as well as by her assignment to numerous political liaison tasks when Timothy Kraft was formally named Carter's 1980 campaign manager.[221]

Although Starr, Eizenstat, and others continued to serve as White House channels for the concerns of Jewish groups, in mid-1978, Edward Sanders joined the administration as a senior adviser to both the president and the secretary of state. His primary emphasis was liaison with the Jewish community, seeking to "rebuild" support.[222] Sanders and an assistant, Marvin Feuerwerger, organized numerous White House briefings for representatives of Jewish organizations and met with religious leaders. As the focus of U.S. foreign policy shifted from relations between Israel and Egypt to the crises in Afghanistan and Iran, Sanders's involvement in foreign policy issues waned.[223] When he left the White House payroll in early 1980, Sanders was replaced by Alfred H. Moses (a Washington, D.C., lawyer), whose attention increasingly centered on the approaching election.[224]

About the same time that Sanders joined the WHO, Louis Martin, the "godfather of black politics,"[225] was brought in (moving from the staff of Senator Adlai Stevenson). Amid ongoing criticism of Bunny Mitchell's "political inexperience and inability to deliver"[226] and White House officials' private concessions that they had "done a poor job dealing with the black community,"[227] Martin was expected to perform tasks similar to those he had undertaken in the Kennedy and Johnson administrations. He headed a shallow hierarchy of two or three deputies, an administrative assistant, and two secretaries.[228] Like Weddington, Martin's office published and distributed a newsletter aimed at elected officials and community-based organizations.[229] The unit also arranged White House briefings for black leaders and groups, held state and regional "Federal Economic Assistance Conferences" to introduce community leaders to African American federal administrators, recommended individuals for and "sign[ed] off on many senior level appointments," and handled casework.[230] A Martin deputy, Karen Zuniga, served as the unit's link to the White House personnel office,[231] and she maintained contact with black political appointees throughout the executive branch, organizing "team meetings" at which Martin encouraged them to help "build a stronger [presidential] team."[232] Zuniga also monitored the administration's Black College Initiative, which was designed to increase federal support of historically black institutions.[233] In addition, the office had a legal deputy, Julia Dobbs, who tracked legislative and policy initiatives that affected blacks; worked with the Small Business Administration, the Commerce Department, and other agencies involved in procurement; and focused more generally on "all aspects of minority business development."[234] A third deputy, I. Ray Miller Jr., arrived in early 1980; among his responsibilities were office administration and "coordination of the legislative and political activities" of the unit.[235]

Within the overall White House hierarchy, Martin reported on his unit's activities to a staffer in Hamilton Jordan's, and later Jack Watson's, office. Martin and his aides also worked routinely (and, by all appearances, collegially) with colleagues in the personnel and counsel's units on executive and judicial appointments, as well as with those in the Office of Media Affairs and on the Domestic Policy Staff. Other links were more ad hoc. In response to a Civil Rights Commission report showing that women and minorities were underrepresented and stereotyped on television shows, for example, Martin organized a "White House Media Task Force," which included representatives from DPS as well as agencies with jurisdiction over these issues, such as the Federal Communications Commission, the Equal Employment Opportunity Commission, and the Office of Federal Contract Compliance.[236]

Meanwhile, White House handling of outreach to Hispanics did not become the responsibility of a formal staff unit until the summer of 1979, when the White House Office of Hispanic Affairs (OHA) was created. Joseph Aragon had resigned and returned to California in January 1979, amid criticism of the White House from Hispanic groups and his own rumored dissatisfaction with the administration.[237] Designed "to be a link between the White House and the Hispanic community," OHA performed tasks similar to those of the other "group advocacy" units. It provided information on federal housing, education, and economic development programs, and it sought to increase the number of Hispanic political appointees.[238] Like the liaisons with blacks and with women, OHA published a newsletter,[239] and much like those handling Jewish outreach activities, it focused on specific foreign policy issues, such as the mounting number of Cuban refugees.[240] Moreover, working with others in the executive branch, OHA pushed legislative initiatives (e.g., on bilingual education), undertook what it called "the first major farmworker consultation in the White House," and implemented the "first National Bilingual Hispanic Consumer Education/Outreach Project."[241]

The special assistant named to head OHA was Esteban Torres, "the highest ranking Mexican-American in the administration."[242] He, too, headed a small, shallow hierarchy, including as many as three relatively specialized deputies, an AA, and an intern.[243] One of the deputies, Gilbert Colon, oversaw the unit's daily activities[244]; another, Miriam Cruz, focused on outreach to Hispanic communities across the United States and sought to raise awareness of the special problems faced by Hispanic women.[245] Deputy Paul Tapia spent much of his time staying in touch with Hispanic leaders, arranging sensitive meetings for Torres (e.g., on the treatment of striking migrant workers by local law-enforcement officials),[246] following pending legislation, and briefing Torres in preparation for his travels around the country.[247]

"Ethnic Americans" were the final people the Carter administration formally acknowledged, in a new White House Office of Ethnic Affairs created in early 1980. Prior to that, ethnic liaison was handled by Wexler's office.[248] According to the new unit's director, Stephen Aiello, "ethnic-Americans have been defined as persons of Eastern European, Southern European, Middle Eastern, and Asian backgrounds."[249] Despite the inclusion of Asian Americans, most observers read the action as a "belated" recognition of the heightened consciousness of white ethnics.[250] Working with Vicky Mongiardo (who had been a deputy special assistant for ethnic affairs on Wexler's staff) and an assistant, Aiello maintained contacts with ethnic groups around the country, screened candidates to act as U.S. delegates to international conferences, and assembled and distributed a White House newsletter. On occasion, he was dispatched to explain administration foreign policy that particular groups had criticized.[251] Even more than the other group outreach units, the Office of Ethnic Affairs appeared to focus almost entirely on shoring up the president's electoral support.

Despite the emphasis of the group outreach units on particular constituencies, efforts to coordinate some of their activities arose sporadically. Some of the special assistants, for example, worked to keep one another informed of their units' activities.[252] In addition, more senior staffers saw the group outreach aides as potentially helpful extensions of their own political, public-relations, and policy responsibilities. In late 1978 and early 1979, under the direction of Timothy Kraft, Bertram Carp, and Anne Wexler, Jane Wales (a Wexler aide and former OPL staffer) assembled a "public liaison committee" composed of constituency outreach staffers whose ostensible purpose was to discuss "the goals of a program of public outreach and procedures which would be most helpful to you."[253] Wexler and Kraft apparently used the temporary collegial-consensual structure mostly for their own intelligence-gathering and political coalition-building activities. Constituency outreach aides, for instance, were asked to discuss ideas for working with interest groups on particular presidential initiatives and to find out more about groups' "legislative priorities" or "new directions."[254] After committee members met with the leaders of their constituency groups, they shared and discussed notes of the sessions. Wexler and Kraft then communicated substantive policy ideas to DPS, which also drafted reports on the administration's achievements "from the point of view of constituency groups." The public liaison committee also provided Wexler with contacts for budget briefings, State of the Union mailings, and possible presidential phone calls.[255]

Meanwhile, Wexler sought to use the special assistants' (and other senior aides') specialized knowledge when developing lists of the "most important" meetings of interest groups "for possible Presidential, Vice Presidential, or First Lady involvement as well as potential messages, Senior Staff attention, or forwarding of special materials."[256] Finally, beginning in April 1980, Weddington's office introduced a limited information hierarchy, attempting to monitor the speaking schedules of senior aides in the group liaison units (as well as those in executive branch departments and agencies) and entering the scheduled engagements into a computerized "Speakertrack."[257]

By the end of the Carter administration, then, public liaison had become an expected responsibility of the presidential staff. Indeed, Pika concludes that Jimmy Carter "open[ed] still more avenues of access and [mounted] a more systematic effort to enlist support than any of his predecessors."[258]

CONCLUSION

With structuring for public liaison emerging and stabilizing across three presidencies and in both Republican and Democratic administrations, it meets our requirements for evidence of institutionalization. Although the precise nature of the structuring for public liaison continued to vary within and between administrations, the notion that diverse constituencies should have channels into the White House had come to be accepted.

After Jimmy Carter, all subsequent presidents have included an OPL in the White House. The unit's location in the overall staff hierarchy, however, has been somewhat less stable.

During the first term of Ronald Reagan's presidency, OPL was headed by an assistant to the president, Elizabeth Hanford Dole, who reported directly to James Baker. In the second term, under Chief of Staff Donald Regan, the unit was moved down in the White House hierarchy, shifted to the Office of Communications, and headed by a deputy assistant to the president who reported to the director of communications. At the time, many viewed this shift (along with the appointment of only women to direct public liaison throughout the Reagan presidency)[259] as a clear sign that OPL was not "a major policy-making force; charged with improving White House relations with women, minorities and religious groups, it is often dismissed as something of a hand-holding operation."[260] When George H. W. Bush continued the arrangement, Pika concluded that public liaison had "gradually declined in significance."[261] He noted as well that placement in the communications office appeared appropriate, since OPL was "increasingly involved in the distribution of fact sheets and newsletters to specialized audiences,"[262] emphasizing only some of the tasks undertaken by Carter's "group advocates" (and virtually none of those Wexler pursued).

Under Bill Clinton, OPL was structured much as it had been in the Ford, early Carter, and first-term Reagan administrations. Headed again by an assistant to the president, the "well-regarded" Alexis Herman, the unit once more reported to the chief of staff.[263] Much like Wexler in the Carter White House, Herman "hosted low-profile sessions with lobbyists each Wednesday."[264] Moreover, through the Clinton years, OPL continued to specialize. In mid-1995, for example, a distinct Office for Women's Initiatives and Outreach, with its own director and small staff, was created within OPL.[265] Although the Office on the President's Initiative for One America, created in early 1999 to "follow up on the work of [Clinton's] initiative on race," reported to the president, its director, Ben Johnson, had worked in OPL since 1993.[266] Nonetheless, changes in the political environment, particularly the 1994 Republican takeover of Congress, may well have reduced the policy significance of White House interest group liaison activities, having much the same impact as the exhausted Reagan domestic policy agenda did by 1985.[267]

Although the Office of Public Liaison continues in the George W. Bush White House, the specialized subunits for outreach to women and to African Americans do not. Nor has OPL remained an independent office; it is one of several overseen by senior political adviser Karl Rove.[268] At the outset, OPL notably did not report to communications czar Karen Hughes; Rove's move into that area after Hughes's June 2002 departure may suggest an increased resemblance to the structural arrangements of Republican predecessors Reagan and Bush.[269] As in previous presidencies, however, constituency groups have made it clear that they expect and value channels to the White House, and they loudly protested the elimination of formal subunits for women and blacks. Angry objections to the reported abolition of the Clinton administration's White House office that coordinated AIDS policy led Bush officials to quickly restore it.[270]

The emergence and stabilization of White House structuring for public outreach suggest that partisan learning in this area had waned. Partisan variation continued, however, in the nature of the groups and constituencies to which administrations paid the most attention. The Nixon innovation persisted, reinforced by the environmental expectations and demands it helped generate.

5
White House Counsel

Another innovation that Richard Nixon brought to the White House Office (WHO) was a unit that specialized in legal work. Although presidents since Franklin Roosevelt had had aides with the titles of "special counsel" or "counsel," such staffers typically undertook more wide-ranging policy responsibilities. The origin of the title "special counsel" can be traced to Samuel Rosenman, the FDR speechwriter who oversaw much of domestic policy during World War II. Rosenman served on New York State's court of last resort until Roosevelt finally persuaded him to move to Washington to work full-time for the president in the early 1940s. "Special counsel" was viewed as an appropriate title for the lawyer and former judge. Later aides with the title (for example, Clark Clifford and Charles Murphy in the Truman administration, Theodore Sorensen under Kennedy, Harry McPherson in the Johnson White House, and John Ehrlichman in the first year of the Nixon administration) also were lawyers and typically participated in policy development and speechwriting.[1]

The Eisenhower White House was an exception to some extent. Gerald Morgan, named special counsel in 1955, and Edward McCabe, an associate special counsel, worked on tasks similar to some of those in the contemporary counsel's office. Even so, both men also assisted with congressional liaison responsibilities, probably in large part because the counsel's office was first created to deal with congressional investigations of the executive branch in the mid-1950s, and the two had transferred from the congressional liaison unit.[2] Moreover, much like their counterparts in other pre-Nixon White Houses, Morgan and McCabe paid considerable attention to "coordinating the development of the proposed legislative program for the President."[3]

Even if Nixon's reintroduction of the White House counsel's office was merely another illustration of partisan learning, the unit took root. Both Gerald Ford and Jimmy Carter established counsel's offices consistent with the Nixon model. When Carter's second counsel, Lloyd Cutler, tried to broaden his mandate in the direction of policy development, it had little impact on the office itself, which had become firmly institutionalized. However, his status as a key presidential adviser on matters that went beyond the purely legal has been emulated by his successors. The counsel's office that emerged in the 1970s has appeared in White Houses ever since, its importance sustained and often enhanced by the continuing environmental demands on presidents.

NIXON: EMERGENCE OF A SPECIALIZED UNIT

At the outset, Richard Nixon, following the precedent of his Democratic predecessors, gave one of his most senior aides, John Ehrlichman, the title "counsel to
the president." Ehrlichman and his staff, virtually all of whom were lawyers, did
perform routine legal tasks, such as examining proposed legislative language and
handling presidential pardons. Yet much of their work began to focus on domestic
policy issues, and Ehrlichman found himself frequently serving as mediator
between warring domestic policy advisers Arthur Burns and Daniel Patrick Moynihan. By November 1969, Burns and Moynihan were shifted to other positions on
the staff, and Ehrlichman was named "assistant to the president for domestic
affairs."[4]

Nixon then "retired the title" of counsel to the president for a while and
bestowed the label "special counsel" simultaneously on three political affairs
staffers—Murray Chotiner, Charles Colson, and Harry Dent.[5] By the time John
Dean joined the WHO as counsel in July 1970, Ehrlichman had shifted "most of
the people who had been involved . . . in substantive matters" to the Domestic
Council (DC) staff. Dean "was left with the rudimentary issues of the counsel's
office such as clearance of personnel, presidential pardons, [and] legal questions
involving presidential gifts."[6]

Like Ehrlichman, Dean was formally a subordinate to Chief of Staff H. R.
Haldeman. Yet, unlike his predecessor, Dean was not a member of the "senior
staff," and for at least the first two years, he had little contact with the president.[7]
Besides being "just an appendage to Bob Haldeman's staff," Dean recalled receiving "periodic" assignments from Ehrlichman.[8]

Remembered by colleagues as driven by ambition,[9] Dean set about expanding
the reach of the counsel's operation. When he hired Fred Fielding to serve as an
assistant, Dean told him that the counsel's office should be considered "a small
law firm at the White House. . . . We have to build our practice like any other law
firm."[10] Dean's idea was to involve the office in identifying and handling potential
conflict-of-interest problems, first of presidential nominees and later of White
House staffers and others in the Executive Office. Dean predicted that if the unit
were "alert in conflict-of-interest reviews and investigations, [it] would have a small
say in presidential appointments" and ultimately become an indispensable part of
the larger staff.[11] Indeed, Fielding began by "drafting a system for pre-screening
political appointees for conflict of interest problems."[12]

Such an initial emphasis likely was not accidental. In part, it may have reflected
the Nixon White House's early cautiousness "about appearances of impropriety relative to personal finances and conflicts of interests,"[13] possibly based on the Eisenhower administration's experiences. Probably more significant were the changing
political and legal environments: "The first full-length treatises on federal conflict-
of-interest requirements had appeared only in the early 1960s, and President John-

son opened a still undeveloped field by issuing his 1965 executive order [EO 11222] on standards for executive personnel to avoid conflicts of interest."[14]

Yet the new counsel did not stop there. After a few months in the White House, for example, Dean began tracking "potential or planned activities by terrorist groups in the U.S." as well as other protests and demonstrations, reporting to Haldeman and Ehrlichman.[15] He also occasionally updated Nixon, who actively encouraged such intelligence gathering.[16] In August 1971, Haldeman circulated a memo (which Dean drafted) that directed White House staffers to channel "not only information regarding civil disorders, activities of domestic insurgents [but] also . . . reports of civil rights problems of note, political information, and material related to potential 1972 opposition candidates or the campaign itself" to the counsel's office, where it would be "gathered and included in a summary . . . for presentation to the President."[17]

Meanwhile, Dean sought to develop relations with those White House colleagues who appeared to be growing in stature and influence. Among them was Charles Colson, to whom Dean directed a steady stream of memos on issues ranging from civil disturbances to campaign finance to American Civil Liberties Union activities to internal AFL-CIO politics.[18] Early on, too, Dean sent memos to Jeb Magruder and Lyn Nofziger, commenting on possible public-relations strategies.[19]

The counsel's office was also involved in commenting on, providing legal analyses of, and approving a range of other activities in which White House staffers were involved. Dean, for instance, sought to join ongoing discussions in the DC staff about the use of illegal drugs by U.S. service personnel in Vietnam and on publicizing the administration's "crime fight."[20] He chaired an ad hoc collegial-consensual group with representatives from the communications, press, and DC staffs to discuss appropriate presidential responses to the report of the presidential obscenity commission, from which the administration sought to distance itself.[21] The counsel's office was represented on other similar structures, such as that to discuss presidential positions on legalizing abortion (joined by aides from communications, group liaison, and DC). Counsel aides on occasion also provided interpretations of statutes and legislative debates to economic policy and national security staffers.[22]

Dean's efforts at expansion were mostly successful. In late October 1971, he reported to Haldeman on the range of activities in which the counsel's office had become involved. The unit had grown to include several professional staffers besides Dean and Fielding. Attorneys David Wilson and M. Darlene Moulds handled a variety of tasks, such as writing memos on the applicability of the Hatch Act to White House aides, tracking specific antitrust actions, monitoring military justice issues, and examining requests for presidential memberships and use of the presidential seal.[23] In addition, Jack Caulfield and Tom Huston worked in the office for a time, handling mostly "domestic intelligence" and investigations, often at Haldeman's direction.[24] Also in the unit was a staff assistant for security who handled

FBI files (and reported to Alexander Butterfield as well). Besides routine legal tasks such as clearing executive orders and handling requests for presidential pardons, the unit's diverse activities included monitoring demonstrations and coordinating law-enforcement control efforts, clearing all proposed presidential appointees, providing conflict-of-interest "clearance and counseling" for Executive Office staff, and disseminating "domestic intelligence."[25] Commenting on Dean's report, the chief of staff noted his concern that the office was "functioning too much as a service facility to the Domestic Council and OMB . . . and not enough as the President's counsel." Nonetheless, Haldeman agreed that the unit needed to "improve its capacity and emphasis in the collection and dissemination of domestic intelligence and [of] information and tactics regarding political enemies," even as he indicated disapproval of Dean's request to "increase our capacity to provide more assistance to the campaign."[26]

At the same time, as part of the White House management review, Fred Malek focused on the internal operations of the counsel's office. His assessment called for more internal hierarchy, with Dean spending more time on supervision and Fielding helping to direct the work of the associate counsels and other staff.[27]

Although Dean appeared to follow Malek's general recommendations, he continued to seek to expand the unit's reach. After Nixon announced that he would seek reelection, the counsel's office provided legal assistance on campaign-related issues and worked to ensure compliance with federal and state election laws. As the party conventions neared in summer 1972, the unit also collected information on possible "disruptions."[28]

Following the president's landslide victory, Dean attempted to couple his bid to stay in the White House with a plea for further enlarging the scope of the counsel's job. Arguing that the "assignments and the objectives" of the office had not been "clearly defined," he recommended that the unit "be given the mandate to be responsible for the handling and resolution of all questions of law, and the formulation of all related policy, which affect the President or arise incident to the presidency," and that it have "overview responsibility of insuring that all legal issues in the executive branch are handled in a manner consistent with the President's policy and objectives and with the activities of other departments and agencies." Besides including the counsel's office in policy development, Dean envisioned naming associate counsels for domestic, economic, and foreign affairs, as well as using staff assistants in numerous liaison capacities.[29]

Little came of this effort, of course, as both Dean and Haldeman succumbed to the Watergate scandal and soon departed. The counsel's suggestions, however, highlighted the recurrent competition over organizational turf in the Nixon White House. They returned as well to previous administrations' more encompassing notions about the responsibilities of the counsel's office, which in Dean's plans ranged far beyond domestic policy. That his concerns included economic and foreign policy arguably reflected more than Dean's own ambitions; they likely underscored the impact of the political and policy problems of the time—among them, the court-martial of Lieutenant William Calley, consideration of war powers leg-islation, antitrust actions, hijackings of American planes, opening relations with the People's Republic of China, and trade negotiations.

Leonard Garment, Nixon's former law partner and an assistant to the presi-dent with responsibilities for minority and youth liaison, stepped in as acting White House counsel after Dean was fired in late April 1973. Garment has written that as early as March 1973, Ehrlichman asked him to "help negotiate ground rules for White House witnesses in the coming Senate hearings" on Watergate. In agreeing, Garment found that he had become a member of a clandestine group that included Press Secretary Ron Ziegler and Special Counsel Richard Moore. They met to "mull over Watergate 'facts' and strategy," with Ziegler serving as both the White House spokesperson and the link between the three of them and higher-level ses-sions involving Nixon, Haldeman, Ehrlichman, and Dean. Ultimately, with Ehrlich-man again acting on the president's behalf, Garment was asked to become "an acting defense counsel."[30]

Given the increasingly threatening Washington environment and the departure of Nixon's most senior aides, Garment moved to near the top of the White House hierarchy, at first speaking to and hearing from the president frequently.[31] As the problems of Watergate deepened and Nixon "dug deeper into his private shell," Chief of Staff Al Haig became the "principal communications link between Nixon and his lawyers."[32] With the assistance of the new chief of staff, Garment assem-bled a small legal team to focus on Watergate. It included Fred Buzhardt (the Defense Department's general counsel), Douglas Parker, and University of Texas law professor and constitutional scholar Charles Alan Wright.[33] Over the course of several months, the four developed certain specialties, with Buzhardt responsible for listening to the presidential tapes and Wright advising on constitutional issues and arguing in various federal courts.[34]

Especially after the Saturday Night Massacre of October 1973 and the furor it provoked, the president's legal team slowly concluded that he would need to resign. When Nixon refused, the senior staff agreed that Garment "had outlived his effectiveness as the president's lawyer" and that he would be "gradually phase[d] out of Watergate."[35] Garment returned to his previous duties, and Buzhardt took over as counsel. A mostly new group of special counsels, headed by trial lawyer James St. Clair, was assembled to defend the president.[36]

Fielding remained as deputy counsel, overseeing the non-Watergate-related work of the office, until he left the White House in January 1974.[37] He was not formally replaced, although in early 1974, three new associate counsels—Richard Hauser, Kenneth Lazarus, and George Williams—joined the counsel staff (which included Associate Counsel Dudley Chapman and Security Chief Jane Dannenhauer).

Given both the mounting external pressures and the internal staff efforts to save the Nixon presidency,[38] it is not surprising that there is little evidence of other significant nonroutine work in the counsel's office. Nonetheless, the counsel's office survived and would continue through the Ford presidency.

FORD: CONTINUITY IN THE COUNSEL'S OFFICE

The new president's longtime friend and former law partner, Philip Buchen, took over as White House counsel. A key member of an informal transition team that formed in May 1974, Buchen continued to assist in efforts to reorient the White House staff.[39]

Not surprisingly, the counsel's office—a key element in the Watergate cover-up—was an important focus of attention. Among those who offered recommendations on the appropriate tasks and organization of the unit were former Eisenhower aides Gerald Morgan and Edward McCabe. In perhaps a classic illustration of the attempt to inject partisan learning into a new White House, the two suggested a return to the kind of unit that had served Eisenhower. The counsel's office would be responsible for "White House legal affairs," but included in its responsibilities would be a host of matters involving legislative affairs.[40]

Buchen recalled that McCabe and Morgan did a "first class job of getting [him] oriented," and former Eisenhower domestic policy adviser Philip Areeda "really gave [the] job some of the content it seemed to be lacking."[41] Yet both organizational inertia and environmental influences evidently worked against a return to the Eisenhower arrangements. Areeda served only briefly in the counsel's office, leaving the administration in early 1975.[42] Meanwhile, outgoing Nixon Counsel Fred Buzhardt and Associate Counsel Dudley Chapman (who stayed through the Ford administration) wrote memos that emphasized the range of routine legal activities performed by the unit under Nixon, most of which remained in place.[43] Buzhardt noted as well the likely increased involvement of the office in matters related to changes in the Washington legal and political environments, most of which pointed to heightened involvement with the executive and judicial, rather than the legislative, branches. "Discovery-related procedures . . . and contests of Administrative actions" triggered by Watergate could be expected to continue, and they would probably be reinforced by the federal courts' easing of standing-to-sue requirements and the rise of public-interest legal activities. At the same time, issues of executive privilege and the impact of procedures under the new Freedom of Information Act would create additional work. By December 1974, neither the description nor the titles of those working in the Office of White House Counsel included any mention of involvement in the president's legislative program.[44]

Much like John Dean and Leonard Garment, Buchen operated in a shallow hierarchical structure, with a deputy counsel who oversaw the work of the office and substituted when the counsel was not available. All three deputy counsels who worked for Buchen—Areeda, followed by Roderick Hills and then Edward Schmults—also were involved in issues of regulatory reform.[45] Similar to earlier counsel's offices, the unit's work was divided among several staff assistants and associate and assistant counsels, with a total number of eight to ten professionals.[46] Jane Dannenhauer, for instance, continued to head the Security Office and to handle FBI investigations, reporting to Associate Counsel Kenneth Lazarus and Assistant Counsel Jay T.

French.[47] Lazarus, who served throughout the administration, also dealt with conflict-of-interest clearances and issues involving the Hatch Act.[48] Initially, he shared responsibility for reviewing presidential appointments with Associate Counsel Chapman and Counsel William E. Casselman II; when the latter left to return to private law practice in October 1975, Lazarus took over the entire personnel operation.[49] Chapman, who spent an estimated 60 percent of his time providing "routine services," assumed Casselman's tasks of conducting "heavy-duty briefings" of new White House aides and presidential appointees and "periodic upbraidings of the senior staff" on standards of appropriate conduct; Assistant Counsel Barry Roth frequently assisted.[50] Associate Counsel Barbara (Bobbie) Greene Kilberg formally replaced Casselman, but she spent most of her time on routine issues (e.g., use of the presidential seal, presidential memberships in organizations) and working with the Domestic Council staff, especially on Indian concerns.[51]

Much of the work of the counsel's office was in response to a still-hostile post-Watergate environment. In addition to paying careful attention to potential conflict-of-interest issues, for example, Casselman handled "the many problems which arose with the Nixon tapes and documents, the litigation brought by the former President, and the need to respond to requests and subpoenas from the Special Prosecutor and others for access to the Nixon materials."[52] At the same time, congressional resurgence and suspicion placed increased demands on the White House. Associate Counsel James A. Wilderotter (who served from April 1975 through April 1976) spent most of his time tracking and responding to requests from the Church and other congressional committees investigating the CIA and other executive branch national security operations.[53] Lazarus estimated that such matters also occupied approximately 25 percent of Buchen's and Hill's time and took up almost half of French's time.[54]

Other members of the counsel staff responded to demands related to policy problems that President Ford had inherited. French, for example, handled files on the president's clemency board and the amnesty program for draft evaders and military absence offenders.

Participation of the counsel's office in myriad White House tasks likely reflected not only Buchen's status as a friend and colleague of the president but also the new administration's concern that its activities be above legal or ethical reproach—yet another reaction to a skeptical Washington environment. The counsel's unit was among the offices represented at the frequent senior staff meetings held throughout the term.[55] Members of the counsel's office also participated in DC staff meetings,[56] and Hills chaired the DC's Task Force on Regulatory Reform.[57] On occasion, a counsel aide acted as the mediator among economic and domestic policy staffers, the Department of Justice, and industry representatives.[58] The White House counsel's office ultimately became involved in legislative issues as well; chief among them, according to Buchen, was Frank Zarb's proposed comprehensive energy reform initiative.[59] Meanwhile, the counsel himself sometimes served as a liaison with parts of the U.S. Jewish community.

Nonetheless, much as in the initial years under Dean, the Office of White House Counsel focused primarily on legal issues. By the end of the Ford administration, the counsel's operation had become a mostly stable unit that performed both routine tasks and those driven by politically charged environmental demands.

CARTER: EVIDENCE OF INSTITUTIONALIZATION?

As we have noted, the most persuasive evidence that structuring has become institutionalized is persistence across two or more presidencies of *differing* political parties. Considerable support for that conclusion appears in the activities and structuring of the counsel's office during the Carter administration. At the same time, Jimmy Carter's second White House counsel, Lloyd Cutler, indicates the persistence of residual partisan learning.

Continuity: Counsel Robert Lipshutz

The emphasis on legal issues involving the presidency continued into the Carter White House and largely defined the activities of the counsel's office. The first White House counsel was Robert J. Lipshutz, an Atlanta lawyer who, although he had never worked in government at any level, was a longtime political associate of the president and the national campaign treasurer.[60] Indeed, Lipshutz insisted that any work he did in the new administration had to allow his "not los[ing his] identity as a lawyer either in perception [or] in reality."[61]

Under Lipshutz, the counsel's office was structured much as it had been under Ford. Formally, the counsel was at the top of a shallow hierarchy, with a deputy (Margaret McKenna) as second in command and three associate counsels.[62] As counsel, Lipshutz provided direct advice to the president and served on the collegial structures of the senior staff, such as the "management committee" that examined the White House budget.[63] Lipshutz and McKenna evidently divided some tasks between them, with the former handling intelligence liaison and the latter focusing on executive privilege claims and responding to document requests from Congress and concerning litigation.

Again, the other attorneys in the unit undertook relatively specialized activities. Associate Counsel Patrick Apodaca, for instance, oversaw the Security Office and was responsible for FBI clearances for presidential appointees. Senior Associate Counsel Michael Cardozo worked on conflict-of-interest issues, provided legal advice to both East and West Wing aides, and handled presidential papers. Meanwhile, senior Associate Counsel Douglas Huron worked on executive orders, issues of equal employment opportunity, and matters involving the Federal Election Commission.[64]

Once more, such specialization was scarcely complete. For example, Lloyd Cutler, Lipshutz's successor as counsel, asserted that the interests of Israel and problems in the Middle East had "almost totally absorbed" Lipshutz's time.[65] Although this is no doubt an exaggeration, Lipshutz himself recalled that he "spent a lot of time" on such issues, particularly leading up to the Camp David agreement.[66] In addition, Apodaca acted on occasion as a Hispanic liaison.

At the same time, the president's political and policy goals influenced the activities of the counsel's office. For example, the unit became more involved in the selection of lower court judges than had many of its predecessors, pursuing Carter's voiced objective of diversifying the federal judiciary. Lipshutz, McKenna, and Huron paid special attention to the administration's efforts to ensure that those considered for nomination to the federal circuit courts included women and racial minorities.[67] Before potential nominees were recommended to Carter, they were reviewed by a collegial-competitive group that included not only Attorney General Griffin Bell but also Lipshutz, congressional relations head Frank Moore, political adviser Tim Kraft, and, occasionally, Hamilton Jordan. The counsel contended that in such sessions he "took the lead role on the affirmative action aspect of things."[68] Throughout, Lipshutz recalled, the White House struggled with an attorney general and a Justice Department that believed that judicial selection "should be strictly their prerogative."[69]

President Carter's own beliefs about "good government," which both reflected and reinforced the influence of the prevailing political environment, also affected the counsel staff. For instance, the president's efforts to "depoliticize the Justice Department" led to the practice that "all White House staff contacts with lawyers in the department were filtered through the White House counsel's office."[70] Furthermore, even before the president was inaugurated, Lipshutz and John Moore (who would become chair of the Export-Import Bank) drafted rules on conflicts of interest for those considering joining the new administration. With Associate Counsel Cardozo, Lipshutz continued to modify these guidelines, and counsel aides typically represented the administration in working with Congress on what would become the Ethics in Government Act of 1978.[71]

Indeed, this act—along with other products of the post-Watergate "climate of suspicion" (such as the 1976 Federal Records Management Act)—doubtless increased the pressure on the White House counsel's office "to provide close scrutiny of potential nominees for high positions." Moreover, the "tightening of disclosure and conflict-of-interest requirements for those already in office created new demands for legal clarification, putting further burdens on the counsel's office."[72]

Return to Partisan Learning? Counsel Lloyd Cutler

As the Carter administration's problems mounted and it entered its "so-called 'malaise' period,"[73] changes in the staff were among the responses. Lipshutz left as counsel in August 1979 and was replaced by Washington lawyer Lloyd Cutler. In June, Cutler had agreed to become a "President's Special Representative," working with Secretary of State Cyrus Vance in negotiating two maritime and fisheries treaties with Canada.[74] This involvement soon led to Cutler's becoming the "single point of contact to deal with the Senators" in discussions of the SALT II treaty, presenting the administration's "position on proposed amendments, the reasons why the treaty should be approved, etc."[75] Not until he was named as Lipshutz's replacement in October 1979 did Cutler sever ties with his law firm and formally work for the White House.[76]

Many contemporary observers noted that Cutler's assumption of the counsel's job produced major changes. The office "suddenly was transferred from a quiet, lawyerly operation that tended to legal business to a highly visible force in shaping and executing presidential policies."[77] Comparisons to past White House staffers who had had the title of counsel multiplied, and names such as Theodore Sorensen and Harry McPherson soon reappeared in press reports.[78] Cutler did little to quell such comparisons. Indeed, he recalled that President Carter asked him " 'to play sort of a Clark Clifford role.' I got that in writing and, of course, Clifford was so venerable and such a great storyteller, everybody thought that Harry Truman never made a move without consulting Clark Clifford. And every time I got left out of a meeting I would go to [Chief of Staff Hamilton] Jordan or I would go to the President and I would say, 'I think that Harry Truman would have wanted Clark Clifford in this meeting.' I was older than all the rest of them so nobody could gainsay me."[79]

Little suggests, however, that Cutler's appointment was an explicit administration effort to return to the wide-ranging involvement of previous Democratic counsels, a type of partisan learning. Since Lyndon Johnson left office, the scope of WHO activities had broadened, and senior policy and political advisers had multiplied. Cutler himself was not the president's personal confidant, nor was he involved in most activities of the Carter presidency (such as speechwriting or designing communication strategies), as earlier Democratic counsels had been. Moreover, Cutler inherited an office that had assumed numerous responsibilities in areas such as federal judicial selection, compliance with ethics and conflict-of-interest laws, and investigations of presidential nominees.

Nonetheless, Cutler participated in a broader range of more visible activities than had Lipshutz or any of their Republican predecessors. Cutler, for example, "kept the job of being in effect the counsel to present the SALT Treaty to the Senate," a task that he maintained "we were doing very, very well . . . until the invasion of Afghanistan and the seizures of hostages in Iran came along."[80] Later, he helped design and carry out the administration's responses to these crises, working on the grain embargo and the boycott of the 1980 Olympics, as well as on negotiating with the shah of Iran to leave the United States.[81] At least in Cutler's telling, much of this work was linked to his job as the president's lawyer. For instance, he was asked to handle "a continuous set of Iranian problems," including whether the War Powers Resolution required the administration to consult with Congress in advance of the mission to rescue the U.S. hostages in Iran, and how to respond to demonstrations by Iranian students and by anti-Iranian groups in the United States that might be televised in Tehran and exacerbate matters there.[82] At the same time, the counsel became involved in two more "personal" administration crises: Billy Carter's alleged representation of the Libyan government, and Hamilton Jordan's alleged drug use.[83]

Although Cutler estimated that he spent "not more than ten or fifteen percent" of his time on the more routine activities of the counsel's office, he oversaw those tasks, which continued to be performed by a staff of five to six additional lawyers.[84] The office remained structured as a relatively shallow hierarchy, although it had two deputy counsels (Michael Cardozo and Joseph Onek), a senior associate counsel (Douglas Huron), and as many as three associate counsels. Internal specialization persisted, as counsel staff handled executive branch appointments, conflict-of-interest issues, and allegations of official misconduct. Cardozo joined Huron in pushing to increase the White House's role in the selection of federal judges, albeit still in competition with Attorney General Bell.[85]

Environmental dynamics also shaped the activities of the counsel staff. For example, an additional lawyer, Philip Bobbitt, was hired to help handle the increasing national security–related work generated by world events.[86] Somewhat similarly, ongoing congressional use of the legislative veto and the pending *Chadha* appeal against the Immigration and Naturalization Service focused the attention of counsel staffers Cutler, Onek, and Bobbitt, as well as many agency officials, on both the constitutionality of the veto and politically appropriate responses.[87] At the same time, external pressures may have constrained the performance of some tasks by the White House counsel's office. Rozell has contended, for example, that the "taint of Watergate" led the administration to avoid "the phrase 'executive privilege' " and "to accommodate requests for information without resorting to executive privilege, even when there appeared to be a compelling reason for withholding information."[88]

By the end of the Carter presidency, then, the tasks of the White House counsel and the structuring of the counsel's office appear to have stabilized. Introduced by Richard Nixon, the unit persisted, even as both of his successors sought to distance themselves from his administration's legacy of secrecy and duplicity. Indeed, the myriad efforts by those in Congress, the federal courts, and the executive branch to avoid repetition of the "excesses" associated with Watergate generated even more work for the White House counsel's office, as conflict-of-interest, financial disclosure, and general "ethics" laws multiplied. Although Lloyd Cutler's actions as counsel may remind some of his revered (and criticized) Democratic predecessors, signaling the persistence of partisan learning, the structuring and tasks of the counsel's office changed little from its genesis under a Republican president.

CONCLUSION

Nixon's introduction of a WHO unit charged mostly with "lawyering" at once reflected partisan learning and a more lasting innovation. Once put in place by John

Dean, the counsel's office has appeared in subsequent White Houses under both Republican and Democratic presidents.

Examination of the emergence of structuring for the White House counsel's operation and its institutionalization provides support for several of our initial propositions. As Propositions 3 and 4 predicted, few changes in staff structuring took place between either the Nixon and Ford years or the Ford and Carter presidencies. Consistent with the first part of the fifth proposition, the activities and at least some of the informal structuring of the Nixon counsel staff differed in purpose from those in the Eisenhower White House. Moreover, as the second part of Proposition 5 leads us to expect, the structuring and activities of the Carter White House counsel differed from those of LBJ's special counsel.

Nonetheless, Lloyd Cutler's presence in the latter part of the Carter administration and his perceived attempts to define problems more as "policy" or "political" questions rather than "legal" ones[89] may indicate the presence of some residual partisan learning. That he returned in the next Democratic administration after the evident failure of a similarly "political" counsel (if one less well schooled in Washington and presidential politics) may reinforce such a conclusion. Even so, the structuring and activities of the members of the counsel's *staff* remained notably stable. Meanwhile, a recent report on the White House counsel suggests that individual counsels may generally be more like Cutler, regardless of party. The White House counsel, as a senior presidential adviser, participates in myriad activities and issues, many of which cannot be predicted or planned for. Indeed, the counsel's time is often almost completely consumed by the handling of crises or unexpected demands.[90]

In part, this may be because the political environment has grown even more threatening to presidents than it was in the 1970s. Cutler, counsel for Presidents Carter and Clinton, observed that the job has become more driven by scandal and congressional efforts to probe more deeply into administrations.

> We were doing executive privilege in the Carter days; we were doing it in the Clinton days. We had demands from congressional committees for White House documents and agency documents; drafts of legal opinions, for example, were so much more pervasive. Mostly it's the difference that when I worked for Carter while we did have the Billy Carter problem and a few others, Hamilton Jordan's alleged drug violations which turned out to be entirely untrue, while we had a couple of those, most of what I did was substantive. . . . In Clinton's time I had the same understanding that I could be in on all these things but I had to put in so much of my own daily effort and my staff did on the investigations of the President, Whitewater, et cetera that I had no time. . . . I would say working for Carter which was a year and a half, not more than 20 per cent [of the counsel's work] was what I call playing defense. Under Clinton it was closer to 80 per cent.[91]

The same hostile setting may help explain the increased size of the counsel's office, which expanded from two to three attorneys in the early 1970s to more than forty lawyers at times during the Clinton administration.

The counsel's office, a Nixon-era innovation, first began to institutionalize in response to an environment that was actively wary of the reemergence of presidential abuses of power. Then, the roots of such structuring continued to deepen as distrust and suspicion of presidents and presidential power reappeared. Now, even absent the immediate need to "play defense," the counsel's office remains a stable and valuable aspect of the institutional presidency.

6
Congressional Relations

Unlike most other White House outreach efforts, structuring for congressional relations was already relatively stable by the time Richard Nixon was elected president. The Eisenhower administration created the model: a legislative liaison office headed by a highly placed presidential aide, employing a handful of people whose full-time job was lobbying and keeping track of Congress.[1] The Kennedy and Johnson units largely emulated Eisenhower's.[2] Generally successful, this arrangement for representing the president on Capitol Hill had come to be expected by members of Congress. Nixon not only continued the pattern but also brought back Ike's last head of congressional relations, Bryce Harlow, to head the office.

Despite the nearly impossible task of attempting to lead the legislative branch, Gerald Ford retained a fully staffed congressional-relations office under the overall guidance of Counselor to the President John Marsh, a former Democratic representative from Virginia. As an erstwhile legislative leader, Ford supplemented the staff by approaching Congress personally in a manner that recalled Lyndon Johnson more than it did Nixon.

By the time Jimmy Carter entered the Oval Office, the question of structuring for congressional liaison had passed beyond partisan learning and into the realm of institutionalization. Despite Carter's initial aloofness from Congress, he largely replicated the existing model for handling legislative affairs. As the administration's legislative efforts faltered (due in part, many charged, to the relative inexperience of liaison chief Frank Moore), the president and his top advisers responded with an innovation, creating a series of collegial-consensual task forces that used personnel from throughout the executive branch in a coordinated effort to back major legislation.

NIXON

The first head of Nixon's Office of Congressional Relations (OCR), Bryce Harlow, was virtually the only senior White House staffer with whom members of Congress were familiar. A War Department legislative liaison and House committee staffer before serving in the Eisenhower White House, Harlow was highly respected on the Hill, and his appointment seemed to signal a high priority for legislative initiatives.

The staff assembled under Harlow was much smaller than LBJ's had been at the end of his administration. Nixon and Harlow believed that Johnson's aides had grown too involved in providing services to members and were determined to "wean Congress off the White House teat."[3] As in earlier administrations, the unit was structured as a shallow hierarchy, initially with four professional staff reporting to Harlow through a deputy. Kenneth BeLieu had responsibility for Senate liaison, and William Timmons had the House (and was Harlow's top deputy), with Dale Grubb assisting each. Lamar Alexander handled research and administrative matters. Soon, however, the staff grew, responding in part to requests from attention-starved Republican members of Congress. By mid-1969, Eugene Cowen, Tom Korologos, and John Nidecker were added to the Senate group, and William Casselman (from Harry Flemming's personnel staff) and Richard Cook joined to work with the House. Lyn Nofziger, a Nixon veteran from California, was brought in to assist members on publicity, including writing speeches and press releases for them. In keeping with Nixon's preference for liaison people with Hill experience, the staff consisted mainly of people who had worked in Congress and could reflect a congressional viewpoint.[4]

Even with this expansion, the congressional liaison staff was relatively lean. Part of the reason for this was Nixon's desire to make as much use as possible of departmental legislative liaison personnel.[5] In general, this proved to be a dubious strategy. White House congressional liaison staffers openly complained about their departmental counterparts. House aide Max Friedersdorf, for instance, lamented the tendency of departmental people to push their own viewpoints instead of the president's.[6] Senate assistant Wallace Johnson noted that sometimes bills were too far gone to salvage by the time White House operatives became aware of problems.[7]

As the Nixon legislative program advanced, the need for the White House to take the lead grew evident, and the liaison staff expanded to as many as twelve professionals in the spring of 1971. Yet second-term efforts to shrink the White House staff, plus Nixon's loss of faith in a legislation-based approach to governance, ultimately led the unit to shrink to as few as six.[8]

Harlow left after two years, replaced by Timmons. Soon, however, in the face of complaints from Congress, former Congressman Clark MacGregor was hired to reprise Harlow's role at the top of the congressional liaison hierarchy. When MacGregor left for the campaign committee in mid-1972, Timmons resumed his position as head, where he remained into the early months of the Ford administration.

Specialization among the liaison specialists resembled that of the Kennedy and Johnson congressional-relations offices. On the House side, staffers divided the membership among them, while the smaller Senate staff operated more flexibly. Whereas the JFK and LBJ House staffs specialized mainly according to geographic area, Nixon's aides tended to concentrate on the committees assigned to them according to subject matter.[9] William Casselman, for instance, dealt primarily with the Judiciary and Public Works Committees and their members. Nonetheless, the staff also took advantage of their particular backgrounds and connections. For example, BeLieu, who had worked under both Kennedy and Johnson, paid special attention to Senate Democrats and to organized labor.[10] Because the attention that needed to be paid to specific subgroups could vary greatly, some market structuring emerged, and assignments sometimes followed no identifiable pattern as the office "sort of took things as they came."[11]

Harlow worked with both houses of Congress, specializing mainly in dealing with senior Republicans.[12] His successor, MacGregor, made at best a modest impact; the former Minnesota representative "had little meaningful interaction with Congress or the congressional relations staff."[13]

The Organizational Scheme

Overall, the Nixon White House steadily evolved into a tighter hierarchy throughout the first term, although that hierarchy was always supplemented by an array of more informal governance structures. At the outset, the preeminent position of the chief of staff and his control structures was not fully clear. Bryce Harlow, the only senior aide with extensive Washington experience, was generally thought to be one of the most powerful people in the White House. Indeed, Harlow's prominence led to a problem for the president. So venerated was Harlow that the administration's initial difficulties with Congress were widely blamed on Nixon rather than on his adviser. Thus, "Nixon was left without the traditional protection that advisors' service as a lightning rod can provide."[14]

As the Nixon approach to organizing for domestic policy evolved, so did informal structuring, including outreach to Congress through the liaison operation. Each morning, collegial-consensual meetings with representatives of the Domestic Council (DC) staff and the Office of Management and Budget (OMB) kept congressional-relations aides abreast of substantive policy issues and kept the policy people aware of the situation in Congress.[15]

In 1969, the presidential isolation that would later be observed was not a problem. Not only Harlow but also his subordinates had regular access to Nixon.[16] Struggles in Congress took a toll, however, as did Nixon's preference for focusing on foreign rather than domestic policy. As a result, Harlow never became a presidential intimate, and the congressional liaison staff lacked the strong link to the president that they had anticipated. Over time, as Harlow's influence waned and he finally left, access to Nixon became more difficult; congressional-relations aides were confronted with other staffers above them in the White House hierarchy who were more "formal and rigid" toward them.[17] Collier suggests that part of the problem was that the "downtown" staff, such as H. R. Haldeman, John Ehrlichman, and Peter Flanigan, failed to fully understand the realities of Congress.[18]

Nonetheless, after Harlow left, Timmons maintained a good personal relationship with the president. Eugene Cowen, who dealt with the Senate during most of Nixon's first term, recalled that Nixon would even unburden himself to Timmons at the end of the day.[19] Timmons, in turn, respected Nixon's "feel" for Congress, even while lamenting that the president would never directly ask a member for a vote, even when urged to do so.[20]

Yet liaison staffers below Timmons seldom saw the president and had a minimal relationship with him. Patrick O'Donnell, a Senate liaison under both Nixon (second term) and Ford, recalled, "Nixon only knew Timmons and there was no sense of personal warmth between the President and his legislative people. He was not comfortable dealing with Congress on a daily basis and that showed in his attitude towards us. We were the bearers of bad news because we were the congressional aides."[21]

White House Contacts with Congress

A recurring problem in modern presidencies has been the coordination of the legislative efforts of the larger White House staff.[22] Such congressional contacts are inevitable, as the expertise of particular aides becomes relevant to Congress's purposes and staffers work on behalf of their issues or constituencies. Congressional liaison units typically hope to exert some control over these activities, encouraging staffers with useful expertise and thwarting those they deem unhelpful or unwise. More often, liaison specialists struggle just to keep track of White House contacts with Congress.

The problem of orchestrating and monitoring the legislative activity of the White House staff appeared midway in Nixon's first year in office, when Haldeman had to urge staff members to notify Harlow of all congressional contacts and to clear in advance those that were "substantive."[23] The need for constant staff monitoring remained, however. In January 1970, for instance, Lamar Alexander of congressional relations had to admonish Nixon assistant Clay (Tom) Whitehead about sending a letter on communications satellites to members of Congress (MCs) when it should have gone out from BeLieu or Timmons: "It confuses the Members AND the congressional relations staff when various persons on the White House staff write to members."[24] Nor did such difficulties easily disappear. In 1971, for example, MacGregor chastised the White House staff for accompanying MCs to the Kennedy Center without notifying the congressional-relations office.[25] Later, after Haldeman had left the White House and staff discipline became more problematic, the issue of presidential aides cutting deals with Congress unbeknownst to liaison staff surfaced yet again.[26]

Of course, one reason for White House staffers to go directly to Congress was suspicion that the congressional-relations staff was not doing the job as well as it could be. This attitude was reflected in a 1972 memo to Charles Colson that criticized the liaison staff, arguing that "they do not nurture relations based on frequent personal contact" and the development of strong, reciprocal relations.[27] John Ehrlichman's domestic policy staff likewise complained. A late 1970 internal memo contended that congressional relations was overburdened and that there was no "clear, consistent 'signal caller' " in the White House.[28] The conclusion was that the DC staff should no longer "stay in the back room—green eye shades and all," but rather should interact more with Congress.[29]

It seems obvious that although the White House staff was formally organized as a hierarchy, it was not a tightly controlled one, because it could not be. Different units and officials had their own priorities, such as Colson's emphasis on group relations and the DC staff's concern for the fate of policy proposals. The modest-sized congressional-relations office could not adequately represent all these interests; nor is it clear that a larger staff could have done much better. Thus, direct approaches to Congress by non-OCR staff likely were inevitable. Merely keeping track of these contacts was all that the congressional liaison specialists could realistically aspire to, and even that was not always accomplished.

Congressional Access to the President

One of the most frequent observations about Richard Nixon, both during and after his presidency, concerns his "isolation" in the Oval Office. Key sources of such complaints while he was in office were members of Congress, who frequently expressed resentment at being neglected or disregarded. At the beginning of the first term, however, Nixon and Harlow tried hard to develop strong relationships with Congress, focusing not only on the GOP but also on whatever elements of the majority Democrats they could attract, issue by issue. The president met regularly with Republican leaders and with bipartisan leadership groups[30] and made time for "short visits that would permit members of Congress to see the President in the Oval Office . . . so that they could claim they had seen the President."[31] Although the scheduling was a subject of constant tweaking, these meetings continued throughout the administration, even after Nixon had concluded that working with Congress bore little fruit.

Despite these efforts, Nixon's congressional relations were never warm. He "could be persuaded to meet with members, but he did so as a duty."[32] He did not enjoy the meetings, would not press hard or effectively for votes, and made an overall impression that contrasted sharply and negatively with that of his predecessor, Lyndon Johnson. Nixon's suspicion that such sessions were not productive was compounded by occasional leaks to the press by members of Congress. One such episode led Timmons to write to Haldeman: "Obviously there is a dirty traitor in our midst who is purposely trying to harm the President and other leaders."[33] Nonetheless, the congressional-relations office persisted in urging Nixon to work with Congress. Ultimately, though, congressional-relations efforts suffered from another kind of access problem. Despite such high-profile leadership as Harlow and MacGregor, the liaison staff was never at the center of the Nixon White House, and legislative aides never had the president's ear in the way that a Haldeman, Ehrlichman, or Kissinger did.

Nixon, Haldeman, and the Problem of Staff Access

Any White House is hierarchical in ways that go beyond the organizational chart. Most important, there is a hierarchy of access and influence. Those who command the president's time and attention tend to shape policy decisions far more than those who do not. Congressional relations, despite having sporadic leadership from staffers near the top of the organizational chart (Harlow, MacGregor), never approached the peak of the access hierarchy. In light of Harlow's stature in particular, this may seem curious. A variety of explanations involving both presidential choice and environmental factors can be suggested. Among the possible reasons for the limited influence of congressional concerns in the White House were Nixon's distaste for lobbying, his focus on foreign policy, and a Congress dominated by Democrats but lacking the traditional strong leaders.[34] And virtually any congressional-relations office, as a "boundary" unit that interacts intensely with the external environment, faces problems of credibility within the White House.[35]

In addition, some of the problem was tied directly to organizational governance issues. One can begin with the seemingly apt strategy of placing the head of OCR high in the White House hierarchy. The purpose was to ensure that members of Congress had access to President Nixon to voice their concerns. Yet unintended consequences surfaced. First, the stature of the head of congressional relations diminished that of the rest of the OCR staff, at least in the eyes of the MCs.[36] Second, after Harlow's promotion in 1969 took him away from most day-to-day congressional contact, his access (and later MacGregor's) tended to reduce that of aides who spent most of their time on the Hill. Even Timmons lacked the kind of access to Nixon that Larry O'Brien had enjoyed to JFK or Barefoot Sanders to LBJ. This problem was compounded when Harlow's star waned. Nixon's frustration with Congress, along with Harlow's lack of inner-circle credentials, resulted in a relationship to Nixon that never rivaled that of Haldeman. By the time Harlow left at the end of 1970, the OCR staff was without a strong tie to Nixon. As noted earlier, replacing Harlow with MacGregor did little to alleviate the problem. Congressional relations had become established as no better than a second-level unit in the White House.[37]

Meanwhile, as the influence of Haldeman, Ehrlichman, and later Colson grew, key decisions came under the sway of those neither directly connected to legislative liaison nor necessarily sympathetic to the perspectives of Congress. As Collier notes, "with the liaison staff continually passed over and counselors continually passing through, the only authoritative channels to the president for members of Congress were the relatively unfriendly Haldeman and Ehrlichman," whom MCs tended not to trust.[38] OCR staffer Eugene Cowen recalled a "paranoid" sense of us-versus-them among the top White House aides. He recalled asking in a staff meeting, "Why are you treating the Republic of China better than you are treating the Congress?"[39] In effect, advisers lacking experience with Congress had short-circuited the access and influence that congressional liaison required in the White House hierarchy.

Of course, the revelations of Watergate and the implosion of the Haldeman White House changed matters in the second term. By mid-1974, Carl Bernstein and Bob Woodward reported that Timmons's staff had almost ceased its efforts on the Hill, in the face of a lack of support from the White House. Timmons "has no ammunition and no guidance," a source reported.[40]

Ad Hoc Structuring

Nixon's predecessors had, on occasion, augmented the usual congressional ties with special staff structures to pursue especially important legislation. John Kennedy, for instance, had created a virtual mini-staff to pursue the Trade Expansion Act of 1962.[41] Although Nixon never went that far, he did experiment with White House direction and coordination of a legislative effort when he put Alexander Butterfield in charge of the Senate campaign for the "Safeguard" antiballistic missile system (see chapter 2). Not only was Butterfield the "action coordinator" for this effort, but he and four other White House aides composed a steering committee for the effort. Only one, Kenneth BeLieu, was from congressional relations, and he had earlier opposed the entire plan.[42]

The project did not go well. BeLieu evidently was recalcitrant throughout,[43] and the campaign was ultimately unsuccessful. Upon reflection, Haldeman later advised that efforts on behalf of the president's program should be headed by representatives of relevant agencies, who could then call on such units as OCR for expertise as needed.[44] OCR representatives also served on the policy "working groups" set up by the Domestic Council, but they acted as resources, never as leaders.[45]

Evaluation

In congressional liaison, much as in speechwriting (see chapter 8), a key to success is to connect the staff activity to the president. Without presidential attention, the work of the congressional-relations staff will carry far less weight, and members of Congress will seek other avenues of access to the highest reaches of the White House. Although Nixon's first-term strategy of placing responsibility for congressional relations in the hands of a respected senior adviser seemingly had the potential to forge the necessary connection, in fact it did not. A large part of the explanation for this lies less in structuring than in the inability of Harlow, and later MacGregor, to compete for influence with Nixon's White House intimates, especially Haldeman and Ehrlichman.

The difficult political environment the Nixon administration confronted in Congress, along with the president's primary interest in foreign policy, added to the problems of OCR. Similarly, Nixon's reluctance to undertake the task of influencing Congress, and his lack of enthusiasm when forced to do so, made the successful pursuit of the administration's legislative efforts especially problematic. As the priority placed on legislative strategy waned in the second half of Nixon's first term, the chance of repairing the hierarchical connection to the president was lost. By the second term, the administration's organizational approach had changed.

Nixon's second-term counselors did not supervise OCR. Timmons and his staff became formally, and in fact, a second-tier White House unit.

The structuring and senior leadership of Nixon's OCR followed the patterns established by Eisenhower, Kennedy, and Johnson. Staff members specialized in either the House or the Senate. In the latter, assignments were highly flexible. In the former, some specialization by committee or issue area supplemented ideological affinity and geography as the basis for assignments, but flexibility was considerable there as well. As in previous administrations, too, organizational turf became an issue as aides from elsewhere in the White House sought to cultivate relations with Congress. Despite the inevitable complaints, especially from long-neglected Republican legislators, the Nixon staff did as well as could be expected. When they failed to do the near impossible, they began to suffer relative neglect. At the end, in mid-1974, doing what they could meant doing very little, as Nixon's position in Congress became impossible to sustain.[46]

FORD

The legislative affairs office passed intact from Richard Nixon to Gerald Ford, with William Timmons at the head. Ford, however, restored the unit to its former stature when he placed it under his new counselor, John O. (Jack) Marsh. A former U.S. House member from Virginia, Marsh oversaw the Office of Public Liaison and preparations for the bicentennial celebration as well, but his primary focus was the Office of Congressional Relations. The result, this time, was better, although Ford's primary claim to congressional success lay in having his vetoes sustained.

Below Marsh, a housecleaning process replaced most Nixon aides with Ford recruits. Liaison head Timmons was gone by the end of 1974, although his replacement was holdover Max Friedersdorf, who served until Ford left office. Ford and Marsh chose an experienced if small staff—two people to handle the Senate, and three or four for the House. The smallness of this staff, though perhaps appropriate for an administration with limited legislative aspirations, was nonetheless a problem. Blaming White House budget limitations—severe in the aftermath of Watergate—in part for the difficulty, staffer Vernon Loen noted, "Congress is very liberal in voting itself staffs. . . . But, they are very niggardly with the White House."[47]

The Organizational Scheme

Reacting to the perception that hierarchy had isolated Nixon, Ford attempted to institute a formal spokes-of-the-wheel arrangement. Although he was mostly unsuccessful, with staff directors Donald Rumsfeld and Richard Cheney becoming de facto chiefs of staff (see chapter 2), more people had guaranteed personal access to Ford than to Nixon. One of these was Jack Marsh, the president's former

House colleague who had assisted Ford during his vice presidency. Raising Marsh's profile in the White House was the fact that the president placed a high value on his congressional contacts. Marsh was thus more favorably positioned than either Harlow or MacGregor had been in the Nixon White House.

Marsh's status was enhanced by his ability to maintain good relationships with Rumsfeld and Cheney. The legislative-relations office had a "red tag" system to alert the staff secretariat to memos that had to go to Ford. Although paper still flowed through Rumsfeld or Cheney, it moved faster than it had under Haldeman, and Marsh or Friedersdorf could, if necessary, "make sure the information gets through."[48] The disconnect in the hierarchy from OCR to the president that had developed under Nixon was not evident in the Ford White House.

The informal collegial-consensual structuring that had linked OCR with the DC staff and OMB survived under Ford. The meetings dropped from daily to three times a week and involved fewer participants, but the informational function was preserved. OMB and DC officials also attended Ford's 8:30 staff meetings, along with Friedersdorf.[49] The liaison staff itself had little role in policy making, but it had input. Staff member Joe Jenckes recalled: "We were allowed to play the role that liaison people should play in the White House policy making process. The system was structured so that we would have access to provide all our intelligence to the key policy participants. We were salesmen for the President's programs. We applied his legislative strategies. We were allowed to review the options papers as they flowed through the White House policy channels. We were encouraged to advise on which options would stand a chance in the Senate."[50]

White House Contacts with Congress

The Ford congressional-relations team employed departmental liaison specialists in much the same way Nixon's aides had, but with better results. Departmental representatives were "charged with the responsibility for carrying the work of their own department from the subcommittees up to the committee, even on to the Floor."[51] The White House liaison people were mobilized "only when a controversy arose."[52] As with Nixon, the size of the Ford staff made this sort of division of labor mandatory.

At the same time, Ford's liaison aides had occasional problems with DC staff who tried to involve themselves in congressional relations. Those efforts, said Loen, "were usually bad experiences," because the policy staffers simply lacked sufficient understanding of Congress.[53]

At the top of the White House, only Marsh was aggressive in pursuing congressional contacts. Such efforts were hardly needed when the president was a former legislative leader and his own top lobbyist. At ground level, liaison staffers operated much as their predecessors had. If there was a major difference, it probably reflected the fact that, realistically, the Ford team had little chance of advancing a significant legislative agenda. Rather, their primary accomplishments lay in persuading a congressional minority to sustain the president's vetoes.[54]

In terms of technique, the Ford staff dealt more than Nixon's had with ordinary MCs, but their tactics were much the same. They handled case work, Kennedy Center tickets, White House tours for constituents, and invitations to the White House to woo the membership.[55] And, as usual, congressional liaison served as a link to the White House personnel office in matters pertaining to patronage.

Congressional Access to the President

Whereas Nixon had resisted his aides' efforts to push him to have more personal dealings with members of Congress, Ford approached this task eagerly. He held both partisan and bipartisan leadership meetings, usually weekly or biweekly, but sometimes as many as two of each in a week.[56] When liaison aides suggested that he make phone calls to MCs, Ford was reliably happy to oblige.[57] Unlike Nixon, who had a hard time asking for votes, Ford was so comfortable doing so that he served as a role model of sorts for his staff. Liaison head William Kendall explained: "He doesn't threaten or cajole or use any other form of selling except friendly persuasion and education. How he does it is how we try to do it. That's just get yourself involved in what you're trying to sell to the point that you understand it, you can argue it, you know what the objections are and you can answer those."[58] Liaison aide Charles Leppert put it succinctly: "Jerry Ford was our best lobbyist."[59]

The key to Ford's approach, of course, was his experience as Republican House leader and the fact that he genuinely liked and respected his former colleagues. As Bryce Harlow recalled, "Nixon respected the Congress as an institution but he was not often impressed by its individual members."[60] Nonetheless, despite the credit he had built with Congress, Ford's initiatives were "overwhelmed" by events, including his own decision to pardon Nixon.[61]

Evaluation

Assuming the presidency under the most trying conditions, Gerald Ford left intact most of Richard Nixon's staff governance structures, including those for congressional relations. Although most of the people were finally replaced, the structuring remained the same until Ford left office. Nonetheless, comparing Nixon's OCR with Ford's underscores the limitations of structuring alone. Even though the formal structures were almost identical on paper, clearly Ford's version was more effective. Moreover, despite his strong liaison operation and his own personal skills, Ford could do little more than get Congress to sustain his vetoes. People and circumstances clearly condition what structuring can accomplish.

In the process of disavowing Nixon's hierarchical and closed White House, Ford made some important organizational changes, such as refusing to name a chief of staff and de-emphasizing the office of communications. However, the only thought given to OCR concerned bringing in new personnel to make it more effective. Ford depended on his experience to recruit people who knew Congress well. This emphasized the thoroughgoing institutionalization of the congressional-relations office, which would be reaffirmed under his successor. Regarding personnel, though, Jimmy Carter's approach would be different.

CARTER

As already noted, much of Jimmy Carter's approach to the organization and activities of the White House was a reaction to the excesses of the Nixon years. Believing that the size and strength of Nixon's staff had contributed to his downfall, Carter was determined that his staff would be smaller and that the cabinet would be closer to the president and more influential. Accordingly, Carter kept his liaison staff (formally dubbed the congressional-relations office) small at the outset of the administration, expecting (as had Nixon initially) that much of its work would involve coordination of department and agency liaison staff.[62] Assisting congressional liaison head Frank Moore were just three House staffers (Rick Merrill, Valerie Pinson, and James Free) and one Senate aide (Danny Tate), plus a small support staff. Deference to the agencies was reflected in the fact that at the outset, congressional relations did not have responsibility for announcing federal grants made to particular congressional districts.[63] Over time, although the core liaison staff would expand only modestly, administration efforts in Congress would intensify, White House coordination would come to be seen as essential, and the congressional liaison unit would serve as a key element in the "task forces" created to push major initiatives.

Moore had experience as Carter's legislative liaison in Georgia but little experience with Congress. Not surprisingly, as relations with Congress soured early in the administration, Moore's (and Carter's) unfamiliarity with Washington in general and Congress in particular became the focus of criticism. Even so, Moore survived the full term.

During the transition period, Moore sought advice on the structuring and operation of congressional liaison from experienced sources, most of them partisan. Moore and his transition aide Joe Mitchell talked with Claude Desautels and Jean Lewis from John Kennedy's staff and with Henry Hall Wilson from Lyndon Johnson's. Moreover, they met twice with Larry O'Brien, who had headed both those staffs. Moving beyond pure partisan learning, Moore also talked with Bryce Harlow, "who was very helpful in giving me some good advice on the sequence and pace of things, and generally what to expect."[64] Such influences could be seen in the formal structuring of the liaison office and its position in the overall White House organizational scheme.

Policy Substance versus Shoe Leather

The small Senate operation worked much like those before it, but an early experiment with assigning House liaison staff on the basis of departmental or substantive specialties played to poor reviews. This approach differed from that under JFK and LBJ, whereby congressional liaison staffers had been assigned mainly—though not exclusively—on the basis of geography. Thus, some have characterized the early Carter approach as reflecting "Jimmy Carter's belief in depoliticizing government and advancing legislation based on logical argument rather than back-slapping and trading favors."[65] In fact, however, it probably owed as much to the small size of the liaison staff, which almost precluded a geographic or ideological approach to assignments. Moreover, the Carter approach did not differ a great deal from that in the Nixon White House, where staffers specializing in the House had substantive (by House committee) portfolios while also exploiting geographic and ideological affinities.

Nonetheless, in its primary attention to policy "substance" over "shoe leather" as an organizing principle, the early Carter approach went somewhat further.[66] Despite the potential advantage of having liaison staff with a better command of particular issues, however, the approach came to be seen as a failure, largely because it tended to inhibit the formation of the kind of personal relationships essential to lobbying.

Although sometimes cited as a source of Carter's troubles with Congress, the "substance" strategy for House liaison lasted only a short time. When veteran Hill aide William Cable became chief House liaison staffer in the spring of 1977, he instituted a geography-based system, albeit one in which each staffer took responsibility for states from various regions.[67] At the same time, as in prior administrations, assignment by issue also persisted. Cable recalled: "Oh, those were simultaneous. That explains why when we'd ask various people, some of them said, 'Yes. We were organized by region,' and some said, 'No. We were organized by issue.' "[68] In sum, although the House liaison staff needed to learn the importance of the personal touch in lobbying, the differences between Carter and Moore's approach and that of their predecessors were, over the course of the administration, minimal.

The Organizational Scheme

Formally, the Carter liaison office was situated similarly to congressional-relations units in prior administrations. The division between House and Senate responsibilities also was conventional, although Robert Beckel's 1978 arrival as a foreign policy specialist who spanned both chambers was an innovation. Moore, as head, enjoyed the rank of assistant to the president rather than the more exalted title of counselor, and his formal responsibilities were limited to working with Congress. Yet, as a key member of Carter's Georgia gubernatorial staff, Moore was a member of the president's inner circle, with daily access to the Oval Office. In this respect, his status within the administration was roughly comparable to that of Marsh in the Ford White House and higher than that of any of Nixon's congressional aides, even Harlow. "Moore's access to the president was never in question and the White House often went out of its way to demonstrate this. Moore had a standing 8:15 appointment with the President every morning, and it was not unusual for him to see Carter four or five times a day. Moore was a personal friend of Carter and the two families were very close."[69] Moore's access provided an entrée for some of his staff as well. Beckel observed that he and other congressional liaison staffers had, by virtue of their daily meetings with Carter, far greater access than other White House aides, including those on the National Security Council staff and the Domestic Policy Staff.[70] Such access was especially important in the first year of the administration because, as Hamilton Jordan's top aide Landon Butler has noted, the White House had no mechanism below the presidential office for bringing together political and policy considerations.[71] It took Jordan and others more than a year to routinize the morning staff meetings; this hurt congressional relations, which sorely needed regular interaction with other parts of the White House.[72]

At the outset, this organizational uncertainly, combined with Moore's unfamiliarity with Congress (and vice versa), created problems for the administration. Indeed, Moore's difficulties began during the transition, when, lacking virtually any staff support, he developed a reputation for failing to return calls to important members of the Washington community. His subsequent problems included failing to connect Carter to key legislators such as Speaker Tip O'Neill, neglecting to respond promptly to members' requests, and slighting certain members when inviting guests to state dinners. These seemingly small matters loomed large in the minds of some in Washington as indicators of incompetence. In this case, as in other areas of the Carter presidency, these early missteps created an aura of ineffectuality that persisted long after the problems had largely been solved. As Carter aide Les Francis noted, "once you get a reputation, especially in this town, it just sticks with you like glue."[73] Cable was even more emphatic: "Frank [Moore] was very responsive to members of Congress. I found him to be after I got there. . . . But the question was did we ever recover from [the bad reputation]? And, I guess the popular perception is that we didn't ever recover from it. . . . It's hard in this town. Once something gets in your clip file it's hard to ever get it out . . . it is part of the literature at that point and it's hard to ever get it out even if it is inaccurate."[74] The experience of Moore and the congressional-relations office was something of a microcosm of the entire Carter administration.

Managing Congressional Relations

The congressional-relations office's early problems with responsiveness brought immediate attention from the more organizationally minded elements of the Carter White House. Beginning in early 1977, Richard Harden and his staff suggested and, with Moore's support, implemented procedural changes. A legislative projects coordinator, Robert Russell, held weekly liaison staff meetings at which aides worked to develop priorities and coordinate "work plans" for important bills. The staff developed and maintained timetables and collected systematic information on pending legislation.[75] Harden's office also set up a computerized system for tracking legislation, marking one of the earliest applications of this technology in the White House.[76] The system held files on each member of Congress that contained demographic and political data, including voting records, seniority, and ratings by interest groups such as Americans for Democratic Action.[77]

All these innovations improved the capability of the congressional liaison office, even though they did little to address the problem of linking the staff more closely to the White House policy process. That would be addressed by Harden's successor as Carter's management expert, Alonzo McDonald.

McDonald was singularly unimpressed by the state in which he found the congressional liaison office, which he called "a random organization."[78] He initially responded by physically consolidating the unit's personnel in the Old Executive Office Building, broadening the use of the computer system, and installing (following his usual strategy) a deputy, Bob Thomson, to oversee operations. Yet these changes did not address the main problems he detected: the lack of involvement of congressional liaison staff in the policy decision process and a continuing inability to effectively prioritize and plan. The former tended to leave the legislative perspective out of policy decisions, leading to difficulties. The latter produced a "crisis orientation toward almost every little tactical move."[79] Beyond that, McDonald was convinced that executive branch departments and agencies needed to assume more of a leadership role (and accept both credit and blame) in pushing legislation.

McDonald's most important response to these problems was to emphasize and (along with Anne Wexler) refine the "task force" approach to major legislation that Hamilton Jordan had pioneered in the successful effort to gain ratification of the Panama Canal treaty, and then extend it to other issues, including the budget, inflation, and civil service reform.[80] The task forces were formal but temporary collegial-consensual structures geared toward developing and gaining acceptance for policies in particular issue areas, such as defense or energy.

The task forces represented a mobilization of congressional liaison experts, public-information officers, and substantive specialists from relevant departments and agencies, along with their White House counterparts. They developed agendas, crafted policy positions, mobilized public support, and lobbied Congress on the issues (see chapter 4 for additional details). Although congressional liaison contributed to several task forces, it was not necessarily the lead unit. In a case such as energy policy, however, where winning congressional approval was the major obstacle, the White House congressional-relations office provided the organizational focal point, with several representatives from other agencies detailed to the White House for the duration of the task force.[81]

The task force approach was a well-conceived strategy for mobilizing administration resources. It registered signal successes, although not in every case; SALT, for example, was not ratified. Overall, however, the task forces were congruent with the multifaceted political environment the administration faced on important issues.

Congressional Access to the President

Jimmy Carter's relations with Congress, rocky at first, improved markedly over the course of the administration. Initially perceived as aloof, Carter ultimately, according to Beckel, "spent more time with members of Congress than any other president in history."[82] Beckel speculated that Carter's willingness to meet with legislators may have undercut Moore: "Whenever the President would see a member of Congress, he'd say, 'If you ever have a problem, call me up personally.' "[83] Many of them did so. Thus, Carter inadvertently reinforced the impression that Moore was not the key to gaining the president's ear, in spite of his well-known access. In fact, this view may have had some substance. Moore, although often in the Oval Office, was not close to Carter in the way that Hamilton Jordan was, and he was not necessarily present when the most important conversations took place.

More generally, according to White House Counsel Lloyd Cutler, members "didn't feel comfortable dealing with the White House staff and did not feel they were getting heard."[84] At least in his view, only the arrival of Anne Wexler in the spring of 1978 alleviated the situation, and only when Wexler became involved with particular items of legislation.[85]

Despite Carter's determination to see members of Congress, success in congressional relations continued to elude him. Members' trust in the president, once damaged by the administration's early failures, proved difficult to restore. Carter's approach to the task did not help. Although more comfortable than Nixon had been with asking for members' votes, he disliked "the give-and-take of political bargaining."[86] Often, by the time Carter met with lawmakers, he "had already made his judgment and was moving ahead."[87] Convinced of his rectitude and mastery of the substance of issues, the president routinely impressed but could not always persuade.

Evaluation

Overall, the Carter congressional-relations operation followed the basic patterns of its predecessors, including the hierarchical connection to the president through the head of the office and specialization by chamber below. At the outset, it was handicapped by Moore's inexperience and Carter's failure to fully recognize the difference between Congress and the Georgia legislature. Yet, by the end of the administration, the office had become successful on its own terms, and it served as the focal point of several innovations.

The computerization of routine record keeping that Harden introduced and McDonald expanded significantly improved the internal working of the unit.

Carter's interest in placing staffers with backgrounds in business consulting in key positions in his administration bore fruit in this area, as well as helping to bring order to the overall administration of the office.

More important, the Carter White House's extensive use of task forces as a way of focusing attention on an issue across the administration and integrating policy formulation with lobbying of both Congress and the public provided a model for future presidencies. Although not a completely novel approach, task force structuring had never been employed as widely as it was under Carter, with generally positive results. This success, along with the relatively impressive ability of the Carter staff to learn, justifies the positive assessments that the operation received in retrospect and even toward the end of the Carter years.[88]

CONCLUSION

The period encompassing the Nixon, Ford, and Carter administrations was a time of further institutionalization of the structuring for congressional relations that Eisenhower had first fashioned and Democrats Kennedy and Johnson then employed. This occurred despite the fact that success in Congress generally eluded all three of the later presidents. Nixon, of course, faced a Democratic Congress, and Ford's situation was virtually impossible. Even Carter, although a member of the majority party, was a party outsider at a time when Congress was becoming increasingly difficult to lead, both internally and from the White House.[89] Thus, disappointing legislative results did not cause these presidents to reconsider their organizational arrangements for dealing with Congress. For similar reasons, only modest results did not necessarily lead to the dismissal of liaison heads Timmons and Moore, even though both received much critical comment.

Key features of the hierarchical structuring that linked the congressional liaison office to the president and to the processes of integrating policy and politics proved problematic in all three second-era administrations. No matter how it was attempted—whether through a virtual White House legend (Harlow), a former member of Congress (MacGregor, Marsh), or a longtime friend of the president (Moore)—tying the congressional liaison operation to the rest of the administration generated ongoing difficulties. Such problems were probably exacerbated by the fact that the White House chiefs of staff of the time—who might have acted, for example, to coordinate broader legislative outreach activities or to adjudicate conflicts over appropriate strategies—either had little to do with Congress (Haldeman) or were notably unsuccessful when they tried (Jordan).

The main structural innovation of the period, the Carter administration's simultaneous use of multiple task forces, spoke directly to these difficulties. Task forces permitted the integration of legislative considerations with both substantive policy and public-relations concerns by bringing together executive branch representatives of all these perspectives in collegial and mostly consensual governance structures. Although scarcely a panacea, this approach worked well and has since been imitated, most notably by the Clinton administration in its use of "war rooms." Perhaps the central lesson to be learned from this particular structural "fix" is that, in times of kaleidoscopic politics and growing White House permeability, White House governance must extend beyond 1600 Pennsylvania Avenue and undergo frequent changes in the makeup of specific structural arrangements.

7
Structuring for Policy Processes

The White House has become the focal point for the integration of politics and policy. Previous chapters have suggested the growth of White House structuring for political outreach and for the promotion of administration policy. What remains is to examine the sources of substantive policy, with the purpose of analyzing how structuring for policy development and decision making not only shapes policy content but also affects its political impact. This chapter looks at the evolution of White House structures in the three major policy arenas: national security, domestic, and economic. None of these is *terra nova,* as all have been amply explored in the secondary literature, on which we often rely. Our purpose here is to summarize the main structural developments and relate them to the overall analysis of evolution and institutionalization in the presidency generally and in the White House particularly. In these policy areas, one can see evidence of the trend toward centralization of authority and discretion over public policy processes in the White House that Moe has highlighted.[1] At the same time, we note that such developments did not always work as intended, nor has the trend toward centralization been entirely linear.

The organizational structuring most commonly used to coordinate and plan policy has been some variant of the "cabinet council." This entails a group of cabinet members (or subcabinet officials and agency heads) as the formal governing body, assisted by a staff (formally lodged in the Executive Office of the President [EOP]) whose top official is typically a White House aide, usually with the title of assistant to the president. This kind of arrangement, designed to link collegial structures of departmental and agency representatives to the president via a specialized staff, was pioneered when the National Security Council (NSC) was thrust by Congress on a reluctant President Truman. In the Nixon administration, variants of this basic mechanism were developed for domestic and economic policy as well. Such structuring was seen not only as a coordination and planning tool but also as a way of bringing policy control into the White House and closer to the president. Nixon made no major changes in the structures he inherited in the foreign policy arena. However, he did significantly enhance White House control of foreign policy when his national security assistant, Henry Kissinger, became the most powerful individual ever to hold the office. Nixon's successors modified his innovations, but the basic structural approach to policy decision making remained relatively stable throughout the 1970s.

Nixon's successors, however, did not always share the priority he placed on moving policy control closer to the White House. Thus, although subsequent presidents maintained the structures, these did not always have the same centralizing effect. Moreover, especially in the diffuse realm of domestic policy, no single structural device proved capable of covering the full range of issues and policy areas. Still, Nixon's Domestic Council (DC) and its successors served, in one way or another, to bring more coherence to the policy process. The most notable change occurred when Jimmy Carter dropped the cabinet council format but kept the staff intact. Meanwhile, the relationship between the domestic policy staffs and the Office of Management and Budget (OMB) proved, over all three administrations, to be problematic.

In the economic area, Nixon developed the Council on Economic Policy to supplement existing advisory arrangements, formalizing a kind of comprehensive advising that his predecessors had frequently sought. His successors elaborated, with different degrees of success, on this model. Integrating domestic and foreign economic policy proved to be a persistent problem.

NATIONAL SECURITY POLICY

White House structuring for national security has long revolved around the National Security Council and its staff, directed by the assistant to the president for national security affairs (formally called the national security assistant, or NSA). Established under Harry Truman and shaped variously by Dwight Eisenhower and his successors, the NSC staff operation has been a notably stable element of the modern White House. The congruence of this basic arrangement and its decision setting has been noted before.[2] Whether structurally and procedurally complex, as under Eisenhower, or more nimble and flexible, as under Kennedy, the NSC staff's mostly collegial structuring has adapted to handle competitive policy advocacy as well as mediation and coordination.

Beginning with the strong policy role played by McGeorge Bundy under Kennedy, the NSC has often featured dominant personalities in the NSA position. The period covered here has been the high-water mark in that respect, as the two most influential and controversial NSAs, Henry Kissinger and Zbigniew Brzezinski, served Nixon, Ford, and Carter. At the same time, however, this was a period when NSC staff operations achieved greater stability and permanent stature. After rising to prominence under Kennedy but then suffering neglect under Johnson, this was a marked change.

Nixon and Ford

The story of the Nixon White House serving as the incubator for so many of the structures of the modern White House extends to the national security area as well. NSC chronicler Shoemaker has observed, "For a variety of reasons, the National Security Council and its supporting staff reached functional maturity during the

Nixon administration. . . . Nixon, an ardent centralizer and highly suspicious of the State Department, sought to formalize a system under which the White House was clearly in charge."[3] For this task, Nixon appointed Harvard professor and Rockefeller adviser Henry Kissinger as his NSA. Kissinger asserted White House priority within the NSC's interdepartmental committee system, denying the State Department its former "first among equals" status and chairing six of the seven committees himself.[4] Nixon and Kissinger dramatically expanded the size of the professional staff from around a dozen to more than fifty, giving it the capacity to perform the kind of policy formulation work first undertaken by Bundy's staff, while also serving as the main point of coordination for the diverse elements of the national security apparatus. Nixon's respect for Kissinger's expertise was matched by his lack of regard for that of his old friend William Rogers, the secretary of state. That, plus Nixon's desire for personal control of major foreign policy decisions, led to the virtual exclusion of the State Department from major administration initiatives, while Kissinger played a key role in such affairs as the opening of China and the negotiations that ended U.S. participation in the Vietnam conflict.

Nixon also essayed one innovation that would not last when, in his second term, he combined in Kissinger the jobs of NSA and secretary of state. When Gerald Ford inherited the presidency, he kept Kissinger as secretary but appointed General Brent Scowcroft to be his NSA. Otherwise, Ford made no significant changes, and Kissinger remained the dominant force in foreign policy decision making. A gradual reduction in the size of the NSC staff, begun in Nixon's second term, continued. Yet the basic model, vesting primary foreign policy responsibility in the White House office of the NSA, was maintained.

Carter

In the national security area, Ford continued the general pattern of incorporating most of Nixon's White House structuring, and Carter repeated his questioning of the Nixon-Ford arrangements. Consistent with his general view of cabinet government, Carter initially sought to decentralize national security decision making, along with restoring the State Department's leading role. The NSC staff, shrunk to about thirty professionals, would coordinate but would not lead.[5] This was the understanding when Cyrus Vance signed on as secretary of state.

At the same time, the president turned to an academic to serve as NSA. A Kissinger-like figure, Zbigniew Brzezinski attempted to recentralize initiative and control within the NSC staff, which led to early struggles with Vance. For most of the first half of the Carter administration, Vance prevailed. When the Iranian crisis came to the fore, however, beginning with the fall of the shah in 1978, Brzezinski "was able to assume the dominant position in the national security structure, a position he did not surrender until the administration ended."[6] Vance ultimately resigned after losing his argument against the attempt to rescue the American hostages in Tehran.

Initially, Carter made important modifications in NSC staff structuring, eliminating committees and seeking to simplify the system—much as Kennedy had done to Eisenhower's NSC structures. Ironically, perhaps, he replaced them with two committees designed to focus on, respectively, planning and coordination. The latter, the Special Coordination Committee (SCC), bore a strong resemblance to Eisenhower's Operations Coordinating Board, which Kennedy had eliminated.[7] The former, the Policy Review Committee (PRC), was dominated by cabinet officers, but the SCC, with the same membership, was chaired by Brzezinski. Not surprisingly, the two became competitors, and one of the signs of Brzezinski's success was the greater frequency and wider agenda scope of SCC meetings.[8] Among the reasons for the SCC's rise to preeminence was that the NSC staff provided support to both bodies, including preparation of formal summaries of PRC meetings. As a result, the report would go to the president from Brzezinski. Under the circumstances, the perception that the NSA was in charge was inevitable.[9]

Structuring for national security policy under Carter recapitulated in miniature the overall Carter experience. Determined at the outset to do things differently from Nixon and Ford, Carter tried to push some responsibility out of the White House, while experimenting with new structures inside it. But over time, the new structures performed in unanticipated ways, and the decentralization in the structuring that reached from the White House into the executive branch generated conflict and uncertainty. The upshot was that, in terms of structuring and location of responsibility, the Carter White House increasingly resembled the Nixon model. If Brzezinski was never quite Kissinger, he certainly was a more formidable actor than Scowcroft or most of his predecessors and successors. Nevertheless, Carter's efforts to rein in the power of the NSA may have served as a precedent, since his own successor, Ronald Reagan, largely accomplished that goal.

Analysis

Nixon's design for the NSC, like so many of his structural creations, clearly was congruent with the expanding needs of national security policy in the Cold War era. At the same time, in its actual operation, it became problematic. Collegial structures within the overall NSC framework were a useful innovation, but their domination by Kissinger and his staff imposed a kind of informal hierarchy that compromised the collegial design. Kissinger and his successors were, in effect, placed in the same kind of position vis-à-vis national security that the chief of staff occupied within the White House generally. Yet Kissinger and Brzezinski had little intention of playing the "honest broker"; rather, they sought to prevail in the bureaucratic struggles for policy primacy. In those battles, control of the NSC staff and the staffing process proved decisive. Ford's effort to rebalance the system by bringing in Scowcroft and restricting Kissinger to a cabinet role was at least a step in the right direction if collegial-competitive structures were to function as intended.

Ford's and Carter's efforts to downsize the NSC staff made sense as efforts to restrain the power of the NSA within the national security community, but they were not clearly desirable otherwise, in light of the demands of coordination and planning. It is perhaps noteworthy that when Reagan became president, despite the absence of a dominant NSA, the size of the NSC staff immediately headed back toward Nixon-era levels.

Carter's restructuring of the NSC staff failed, not because simplification was a bad idea, but because he inadvertently created competing collegial bodies with potentially overlapping responsibilities. In addition, each body was controlled by one of the rivals for influence in national security policy, and there was no accepted means of adjudicating conflicts. If Brzezinski and Vance had been more inclined toward cooperation, the arrangement would have worked better, but the design itself was still problematic.

DOMESTIC POLICY

The term *domestic policy* covers a tremendous range of policies—essentially everything that is not clearly "foreign" or "economic." Although White House structuring for the latter arenas was well established before Nixon's presidency, that for domestic policy had proved difficult, and solutions were ephemeral.[10] Primary responsibility for domestic policy was, for the most part, spread among several departments and dozens of agencies in the executive branch. Nevertheless, significant change had been made under Lyndon Johnson. For the first time, a specialized staff, under Joseph Califano, had placed the Johnson White House at the center of significant aspects of much, though not all, domestic policy development.[11] Richard Nixon would take this initiative much further. Under Nixon, the trend toward the housing of policy specialists in the White House culminated in the creation of the Domestic Council and its staff. This set up an enduring dynamic not only of potential centralization but also of competition for policy influence among the White House domestic policy staff, the well-established staff of the Office of Management and Budget (formerly the Bureau of the Budget), and, of course, executive branch departments and agencies.

Nixon

Richard Nixon's interests and priorities lay in the realm of foreign policy, but he entered the White House with a robust domestic agenda as well. Determined to roll back some of his predecessor's Great Society programs, he was at the same time willing to innovate in such areas as environmental and health policy. During his first term, he invested White House resources heavily in domestic policy. Despite some success, his story was, overall, one of frustration.

Moynihan and Burns. Initially, Nixon had two, roughly coequal, domestic policy staffs, each headed by a member of his senior staff. Counselor to the President Daniel Patrick Moynihan, a Democrat and veteran of the Kennedy administration, was Nixon's somewhat surprising choice to head a new White House unit, the Urban Affairs Council. In an era marked by recognition of the problems of urban poverty and crime, as well as the outbreak of urban rioting, urban affairs had an unusually high priority. To address it, Nixon created the Urban Affairs Council, a collegial-competitive structure deliberately modeled on the National Security Council, whose formal membership consisted of the president, vice president, and seven cabinet members. Moynihan and his assistant Stephen Hess headed a small staff of about a half dozen mostly moderate to liberal professionals.[12]

Although much attention focused on Moynihan and his staff from the start, they were originally conceived as distinctly subordinate to the council members. Nixon had declared in 1968 that he did not want White House staff running domestic policy in the way that Joseph Califano's staff had during Johnson's presidency. "Nixon lieutenants and Nixon himself had heard stories of Joe Califano, the tough young lawyer from Brooklyn by way of Harvard, harassing and riding herd on distinguished Cabinet members many years his senior. There would be no repetition of this in the Nixon administration where power would flow back to the Cabinet-level departments."[13] Thus, the early months of the Nixon administration featured lengthy, sometimes frustrating meetings at which cabinet members advocated for the perspectives and clientele of their respective agencies.

At the same time, Nixon needed to find a place for his "favorite economist,"[14] Arthur Burns, who had organized domestic policy task forces during the presidential transition. At least until a position on the Federal Reserve Board opened, Burns needed a White House slot. So, considerably after the Moynihan appointment, Nixon named Burns counselor to the president and White House economic and domestic policy adviser. Burns was assisted by a small staff of conservatives that included domestic affairs specialist Martin Anderson.

The presence of two counselors with relatively loosely defined responsibility for domestic policy clearly presented a potential problem. Worse, those counselors were an orthodox, conservative, Republican economist (Burns) and an idiosyncratically liberal, Democratic political sociologist (Moynihan). And although Burns was a Nixon favorite of some standing, the charismatic Moynihan quickly intrigued his boss and gained the kind of access that anyone in the White House would envy.[15] The clashes that ensued were virtually inevitable. As Warshaw has observed, "the original concept of a domestic policy operation focused on the Urban Affairs Council, which would parallel the responsibilities of the National Security Council, fell apart once Burns was added to the White House staff."[16]

Burns and Moynihan competed with each other, with each man reaching into territory that arguably belonged to the other. Burns, for instance, strongly opposed Moynihan's pet welfare reform project, the Family Assistance Plan (FAP). Moynihan and his talented staff, for their part, had interests that went well beyond the bounds of "urban" policy. Meanwhile, as if to confuse matters more, Nixon added additional units, including a Council on Rural Affairs and a Cabinet Committee on the Environment, the forerunner of the Council on Environmental Quality. These units reported not through Moynihan or Burns but through Counsel to the President John Ehrlichman.[17]

Ehrlichman's rise to prominence in the domestic policy area was clearly a response to the need for some sort of structuring to coordinate, or at least mediate between, the Moynihan and Burns operations. As early as the spring of 1969, Nixon called on Ehrlichman to resolve disputes between them. Undoctrinaire and open to ideas, Ehrlichman managed to gain the respect of most of the domestic policy actors[18] and showed adeptness at weaving diverse ideas together. Ironically, in moving in this direction, Ehrlichman for a time expanded the counsel's responsibilities along the lines pioneered by his Democratic predecessors, from Samuel Rosenman through Harry McPherson.

Even so, Ehrlichman's best efforts did not solve the inherent structural problem of competing domestic policy staffs. At the same time as Burns was preparing to leave, Moynihan, his FAP proposal frustrated by the Senate, was falling from favor.[19] As a result, the issue of White House and EOP structuring for domestic policy became a central item on the agenda of the Commission on Government Reorganization, headed by Roy Ash. In August 1969, possessed of recommendations dating from the Eisenhower administration as well as a transition report, the commission recommended the creation of both the Office of Management and Budget (expanding on the existing Budget Bureau) and a Domestic Policy Council.[20] The latter, structured along the lines of the Urban Affairs Council, encompassed the full range of domestic policy responsibilities. It would be headed by Ehrlichman, who had consulted with Ash during the course of the commission's work. Analogous to structuring for national security, Ehrlichman became the assistant to the president for domestic affairs, with a staff located formally in the EOP and comprised of parts of both the Moynihan and the Burns units. The council itself consisted of the president, the vice president, nine cabinet members, the postmaster, and the head of the Office of Economic Opportunity.[21] The Domestic Council began operations in November 1969, although formal authorization from Congress did not come until the following June.

Domestic Council. Like both the Urban Affairs Council and the NSC, the DC was a "cabinet council," with cabinet members (plus, in this case, the president and vice president) constituting the policy-making body at the top, supported by a professional staff. Like the NSC, the DC was designed to integrate and coordinate the processes of making and implementing policy in an area where these had been notably lacking. The council itself represented a blend of hierarchy (inevitable with the president as a member) and collegial governance among the secretaries— ideally, mostly consensual, but bound to be competitive at times. In the NSC case, as noted earlier, staff members were initially understood to be functionaries, with little expectation of policy initiative, because President Truman wanted it that way. The urban affairs staff was similarly conceived as being subordinate to the cabinet secretaries on the council. In contrast, the DC staff was aggressive from the start, largely because President Nixon saw it as a device for drawing domestic policy processes away from the departments and into the White House.

The creation of the Domestic Council was evidently the result of not only Nixon's dissatisfaction with the Moynihan-Burns rivalry but also his growing frustration with both policy making in the domestic departments and his inability to lead Congress in this area. The decision to try to centralize domestic decision making in the White House was Nixon's response and represented the first phase of what Nathan has called the "administrative presidency."[22] The new structuring had the immediate effect of creating a buffer between the White House and most cabinet members and increasing the presence of the White House (DC) staff.[23] Ehrlichman created a series of "working groups" for policy development; these groups included departmental representatives (not the secretaries) but were chaired by one of Ehrlichman's six assistant directors.[24]

These groups linked the White House, elements of the EOP (such as OMB), and the departments in collegial structures, with the degree of competition varying by issue. Clearly, they were congruent with the policy environments surrounding domestic issues. Those environments, shifting with technology and public attention and suffused with the claims and efforts of diverse and overlapping interest groups and agencies, needed to be addressed by collegial structures that could represent varying views of policy goals and the means of achieving them. Yet, for all their apparent virtue, the working groups had a downside, if an intended one as far as the administration was concerned. Although they succeeded in forging useful links between White House staff and agency officials, the groups also had the effect of reducing the participation, knowledge, and relevance of the cabinet secretaries. This was exacerbated by the fact that the DC as such seldom met. As Nathan has noted: "If a member of a working group could not win his point by effective argument, he could go back and persuade his secretary to become personally involved. But by then, the cabinet officer had the difficult task of arguing an intricate policy position when most of the other participants were already knowledgeable about and committed to another policy. It was no wonder that cabinet members intervened less and less frequently during this period."[25]

In effect, then, working-group structures occupied the nexus of several hierarchies—that of the White House (and EOP) and those of the relevant departments. They facilitated the operation of the former but tended to truncate the latter. Indeed, the working groups even met at times with President Nixon. This contrasted with the well-publicized complaints by some cabinet members, such as Walter Hickel and George Romney, that they were unable to get in to see the president.

The cultivation of contacts between DC staffers and midlevel agency personnel gave White House aides access to policy implementation in its most detailed aspects. This increased both White House supervision of the details of agency processes and the power of Ehrlichman and his staff. As Nathan observed, "White House clearance was required on more and more issues and became harder to obtain. On occasion, cabinet members were completely left out of White House deliberations."[26] Thus, structures that initially seemed to be designed for the collegial integration of agency and White House perspectives became hierarchical devices for exercising White House control. Adding to the trend was the increased effort by the administration, beginning in the fall of 1970, to ensure that new subcabinet appointees passed rigorous White House scrutiny for loyalty to the president's programs.[27]

The relationship between the DC staff and the OMB was another problematic element of Nixon's design. During the Ehrlichman years at the DC, the two units had a generally cooperative relationship. Roy Ash, architect of much of Nixon's organizational reform and budget director during the second term, observed that the DC focused on "what to do," while the OMB looked more closely at "how" and "how well." The division of labor, though, was never that neat, in part because OMB heads insisted on a traditional budgeting focus and were not aggressive on the "management" side.[28] In any case, Nixon's first-term budget directors, Robert Mayo, George Shultz, and Caspar Weinberger, reported to Ehrlichman, which put the DC in the driver's seat.[29]

The DC staff clearly became the preeminent force in Nixon's domestic policy making. By the end of 1971, as Warshaw states, "Ehrlichman's Domestic Council staff was firmly in control of the domestic agenda."[30] Ehrlichman, the key player in the DC's successes, began to focus more on special projects, such as government reorganization, and turned day-to-day operations over to his deputy, Kenneth Cole. But the arrangement was not entirely stable. White House management of the details of departmental administration came at a cost. This was first identified by Wood, with reference to President Johnson's much more modest domestic staff: "Confusion is created when men try to do too much at the top. . . . The separate responsibilities of the White House, the Executive Office, and the agencies are fudged, and the demarcation of who does what becomes uncertain. . . . As this confusion continues, a curious inversion occurs. Operational matters flow to the top . . . policymaking emerges at the bottom. At the top, minor problems squeeze out major ones and individuals lower down the echelons who have the time for reflection and mischief-making take up issues of fundamental philosophical and political significance."[31] Despite the formal division of labor with OMB, Nixon's DC staff, reacting to the president's suspicions about disloyalty in the bureaucracy, experienced the same "curious inversion." With OMB focused on budgeting, DC staff moved toward micromanagement, with dubious success.

Still dissatisfied with his control of domestic policy, in his second term, Nixon proposed a final innovation in domestic policy—a reorganization of the executive branch that would have shrunk the number of cabinet departments. Although this scheme never passed Congress, a version of it was tried without legislative approval when Nixon designated certain members of his cabinet "supersecretaries." This approach coincided with efforts to shrink the White House staff and reintegrate cabinet members into domestic policy processes through committees chaired by cabinet members and composed of other cabinet members along with White House and EOP staff.[32] In 1973, there were fourteen such committees.

The Watergate investigations, of course, soon relegated domestic policy efforts to the administration's back burners. Ehrlichman resigned in disgrace and was replaced by Cole. Although the structures of the DC remained intact, they were of little use. As Ash observed, Cole did not have the president's confidence the way Ehrlichman had.[33] Nor did Ash, now budget director, report to Nixon through Cole. In any event, as Watergate preoccupied Nixon, the window for new domestic initiatives closed. The introduction of former Wisconsin representative and Defense Secretary Melvin Laird as assistant to the president for domestic affairs had minimal impact. The DC staff and most of its personnel became part of the legacy the Nixon administration left to Gerald Ford.

Other Policy Structures. Even though the OMB and the DC and its staff played central roles in bringing the threads of domestic policy together, it was not possible for them to handle the entire range of issues falling under that rubric. Moreover, others in the White House with policy expertise and interests played important roles. As chapter 4 noted, for instance, Anne Armstrong, as an advocate for women, had an impact on administration policy on such issues as the equal rights amendment and Title IX. Likewise, Leonard Garment and his assistant Bradley Patterson were given the lead in dealing with American Indian issues. They were the ones who successfully navigated such controversies as Wounded Knee and the occupation of the former Alcatraz penitentiary by Indian militants.[34] Garment was also heavily involved in civil rights policy.[35] Charles Colson, though principally a "political" aide, was omnipresent as well in policy discussions—an expected consequence of the interdependence of politics and policy. In the view of DC staffer Lewis Engman, however, Colson "would not sustain interest in much of anything."[36] Others also became involved, as would nonpolicy staff or specialized policy staff in all subsequent White Houses.

Ford

Gerald Ford's transition team (Donald Rumsfeld, John Marsh, William Scranton, and Rogers Morton) initially endorsed an effort to remove the DC staff from the White House to facilitate a return to cabinet government.[37] However, nothing came of this, and the Domestic Council and its staff remained intact, with Ken Cole staying on as head. Once again, this supports our Proposition 3—that, despite disclaimers, the Ford White House would strongly resemble Nixon's.

In one area, however, there was a significant change. The Economic Policy Board (discussed later) was created to coordinate economic policy, which had the effect of formally removing the DC from the coordinating role it had sometimes played under Nixon. The board was viewed as one of Ford's major successes.[38] Yet it, like so many other structural initiatives that sought greater coordination, simultaneously created new problems. In this case, moving the DC away from economic policy created a problem in integrating the two areas. The difficulty was compounded by the growing influence of OMB under the leadership of Roy Ash, his successor James Lynn, and their deputy Paul O'Neill. During the Ford years, OMB continued to overshadow the DC, as it had ever since Ehrlichman resigned.[39] Although a testimonial to the competence and influence of top OMB leaders, the situation also narrowed the policy perspective of the administration, as OMB continued to approach issues primarily from a budgetary perspective.[40]

Ford, initially interested in returning policy influence to the departments, reversed course dramatically in February 1975 when he appointed his newly confirmed vice president, Nelson Rockefeller, to head the DC as its vice chair. Rockefeller's vision was similar to Nixon's early intentions for the DC staff as a body "in which broad policy decisions could be formulated with implementation handled by the departments."[41] In other words, the DC staff was to be gotten out of the business of micromanaging the executive branch, but it was to seize the high ground of policy formulation and planning. Unfortunately, as Warshaw has pointed out, this vision was basically inconsistent with that of Ford and his advisers. They "saw the Domestic Council as a vehicle for controlling the proliferation of federal programs and supporting a stronger role for state and local governments in policy making."[42] Thus were sown the seeds of failure.

Rockefeller took control of the DC, naming his aide James Cannon to replace the departed Cole as assistant to the president for domestic affairs and head of the DC staff. Yet he encountered resistance, especially from Rumsfeld, when he sought to give the DC staff full control of domestic policy staffing and to place its operation (e.g., hiring personnel) outside the staff director's purview.[43] Ultimately, Rumsfeld failed, but tension between the conservative staff coordinator and the more liberal vice president plagued the White House domestic policy process for the duration of Rockefeller's ten-month run as vice chair of the DC.

Rockefeller added aides of his own choosing and tried to reorient the DC staff toward long-range planning. Still, he was never able to get the DC staff out of the routine business of "preparing decision papers; reviewing proposed testimony when policy issues were involved; providing information to the departments on congressionally originated bills on the president's position; providing answers to the congressional relations staff, to agencies or other White House staff on possible compromise positions involving changes from stated positions."[44] Between staffing domestic policy issues and coping with political and policy developments as they arose, the unit had too little time and too few staff to accomplish the planning Rockefeller wanted. Moreover, resistance from the Rumsfeld side of the White House continued. When Rockefeller sought proposals for domestic initiatives from the departments, Dick Cheney countered with a memo urging DC task forces to "consider doing nothing as an option, and also the possibility of doing less as an option."[45] Ford backed Cheney.

The final blow to Rockefeller's hopes for the Domestic Council came when Ford decided that his 1977 budget would require some serious cuts. That decision, made without participation by Rockefeller or Cannon, rendered the DC's ongoing review of priorities "a moot operation."[46] Rockefeller announced in November 1975 that he would not run in 1976, and a month later he resigned as vice chair of the DC. The DC staff returned to its most basic role, the one it had played under Cole, that of "firefighter."[47] Consigned to the fringes and poorly integrated into the rest of the White House operation, the DC staff realized little of its potential and found itself in the shadow of the OMB as far as domestic policy making was concerned.[48]

Carter

Jimmy Carter entered office with a strong commitment to cabinet government, a conviction that was at least reinforced by the suspicion that a strong White House had been part of Nixon's undoing. Shortly after his inauguration, Carter obtained authority from Congress to reorganize the White House and Executive Office of the President. Carter appointed a task force, led by Harrison Wellford, to examine, among other things, the workings of the Domestic Council and its staff. What ensued, however, was actually a testimonial to the congruence between the basic DC staff structuring and its decision setting: a collegial structure, capable of including internal competition but operating mainly consensually, coping with policy areas characterized by both persistent uncertainty and sporadic conflict.

The task force, working in concert with domestic policy adviser Stuart Eizenstat, came up with a model that, though abolishing the Domestic Council per se (i.e., the statutory council made up of cabinet members), preserved the staff of the DC, along with most of its functions. As Warshaw summarized, "The Domestic Council had survived reorganization and emerged with a new name but essentially the same functions. The institutionalized presidency continued to include domestic policy management with Stu Eizenstat firmly at the helm."[49] Institutionalization, however, did not mean stasis. As it had under Ford and Nixon, the domestic policy operation, now dubbed the Domestic Policy Staff (DPS), would undergo a change of philosophy.

Carter's commitment to cabinet government meant that he was not looking to the White House as a source of policy development. As domestic policy aide Bertram Carp put it, the domestic staff was "put together in order to function within the parameters of Carter's very strong commitment to the departments. That meant we were process managers, not program designers."[50] Thus, the Rockefeller model of farsighted domestic planning was out of the question. Instead, cabinet departments were to be the source of policy initiatives, with Eizenstat's staff responsible mainly for reviewing, staffing, and preparing decision papers for the president. In Carter's view, the conduit to the departments provided by the DC was, if meaningful at all, an indicator of White House control; thus it had to be abandoned. Nonetheless, the president did attempt to impose some central direction on domestic policy. He "met ten to twelve times per year with the domestic policy office staff to reinforce the direction he wanted the administration to take, direction that the domestic policy office staff could build into departmental policy initiatives."[51] Since Carter's emphasis was on implementation more than new programs, Eizenstat's staff also became involved in a version of the kind of oversight seen in Nixon's first-term DC staff. The difference, of course, was that the relationship between the White House and the domestic departments under Carter was far less fraught with tension and suspicion than it had been under Nixon.[52]

In the initial burst of enthusiasm for cabinet government, Cabinet Secretary Jack Watson loomed as a potential rival to Eizenstat's influence. The former was initially responsible for assembling ad hoc "cabinet clusters," groups of cabinet members brought together to deal with particular issues.[53] Watson's performance was not strong, however, and he provided the clusters "little direction on administration priorities nor did he reinforce campaign themes."[54] Equally problematic was the presence of two distinct policy processes in the White House—not fiercely competing, but not integrated, either. In response, the August 1977 reorganization of the White House Office and EOP moved responsibility for the clusters to Eizenstat and basically took Watson and his staff out of the domestic policy arena. At the same time, Eizenstat received a mandate to utilize interagency processes and to have his aides function as process managers, not advocates.[55]

Responsibility for creating and using the cabinet clusters brought new clout to the Domestic Policy Staff. Eizenstat operated the clusters on a continuing basis and assigned his assistants to staff them, which entailed a significant amount of policy "guidance" as well. Likewise, DPS aides participated on the task forces that were assembled to push major administration policy initiatives. As a result, the idea of independent cabinet departments as primary sources of policy initiatives began to erode early in the administration, as policy control gravitated once again toward the White House. Yet the shift did not take place without a struggle, as several cabinet secretaries—notably Bob Bergland of Agriculture, Brock Adams of Transportation, and Joseph Califano of Health, Education, and Welfare—firmly asserted their independence in policy matters. This led to Carter's reinforcing the role of the DPS both by lecturing the cabinet and by expanding Eizenstat's professional staff to more than twenty-five. As Warshaw has concluded, this meant that cabinet government "was being dismantled and the White House was asserting its role as policy manager."[56]

White House assertiveness notwithstanding, the president remained unable to control his most independent cabinet secretaries. As a result, in July 1979, Carter fired four of them: Califano, Adams, Michael Blumenthal of Treasury, and James Schlesinger of Energy. The president was admitting that cabinet government had been a failure. At the same time, Hamilton Jordan was made chief of staff, which meant that Eizenstat, among others, would report to the president through him. At this point, Eizenstat actually assumed more control, not because of organizational arrangements but because Carter's last year in office was largely devoted to coping with the Iranian hostage crisis and running for reelection. By the time Eizenstat asserted his control over the domestic agenda and was finally able to give the administration the "clear direction and coordination"[57] it needed, the issues had come to matter less. Further limiting the influence of the DPS was the continuing complexity of domestic policy and the consequent difficulty of containing it in a single unit. At the outset of the Carter administration, for instance, Peter Bourne's Drug Policy Office operated semi-independently of the DPS, and Midge Costanza's public liaison staff was involved in policy issues relevant to women and minorities. Although Bourne left early and his staff was absorbed into the DPS, other aides, primarily those involved in group liaison (see chapter 4) but with strong policy interests, emerged throughout the administration: Sarah Weddington on women's issues, Nelson Cruikshank on aging, Edward Sanders on issues affecting the Jewish community, and Louis Martin on policy matters of concern to African Americans. Whatever the pros and cons of any particular structural arrangement, the diversity of the policy environment was bound to be reflected in the White House itself and thus to defy being fully subsumed under the aegis of a single "domestic policy" unit.

By the third year of the Carter presidency, a consensus emerged both inside and outside the White House that the DPS was doing its job well, with Eizenstat especially drawing praise as an honest broker of diverse interests. Nonetheless, the limitations of DPS's mandate precluded it from being a source of comprehensive planning or bold initiatives. Indeed, the main criticism of Eizenstat as a policy manager was that although he was politically oriented and astute, he "was basically unwilling to deal with Jordan. If he couldn't deal with Ham, there could be no fusion of policy and politics."[58] Recognizing this, top advisers such as (by then) Chief of Staff Jordan and pollster Pat Caddell began in mid-1979 to mull the need for additional structuring, including an "Executive Committee of the Senior Staff" to develop "unconventional" approaches and a separate planning unit.[59] Little was done to pursue such ideas, however, as the need to gear up for the upcoming presidential election, plus the Iranian hostage seizures, took domestic policy innovation off the table.

Analysis

Domestic policy is less a coherent policy area than a collection of odds and ends whose importance varies with the circumstances and the priorities of each administration. As such, it has been difficult to capture structurally.[60] Prior to Nixon, nobody had fully tried, although Johnson's staff, driven by the need to formulate and implement Great Society legislation, provided a preliminary model. Likewise, the staffs of Burns and especially Moynihan in Nixon's first year provided points of reference. Nixon's design went beyond Johnson's both in connecting the policy staff to the cabinet through a cabinet-council structure and in dealing comprehensively with the full range of domestic policy issues. In either case, structuring was, for the most part, congruent with the prevailing policy environments. Although the

staff was formally structured as a rather shallow hierarchy, it operated more collegially. In a turbulent and often conflictual policy area, the staff sought consensus
or to mediate among competing views. In the face of greatest controversy, however, rather than having the capacity to impose a decision itself, the policy staff
relied on its links to the overall White House hierarchy, running through John
Ehrlichman (or Ken Cole) to the president himself.

Yet the structuring of the Domestic Council was problematic in at least two
ways. First, the cabinet was not adequately connected to the work of the staff. For
this feature to work, the cabinet members would have had to actively negotiate
with one another, making up a good part of the collegial-competitive (or consensual) interaction. In fact, though, cabinet participation was far below this expectation, partly because the officials had other priorities, but also because the policy
area was so fragmented that few issues could engage all or even most of the council. Thus, initiative gravitated to the staff.

Second, when the mission of the DC staff was redefined to emphasize the
monitoring of implementation, the collegial structuring of the formal council
became largely irrelevant, and the hierarchical aspect of the staff structure assumed
greater importance. However, even when hierarchical structuring had clearly
become most congruent with the decision setting, the DC staff remained a rather
flat hierarchy, originally designed more to mediate and negotiate than to supervise.
That it was virtually overwhelmed by the administrative demands of its new task
was thus unsurprising.

Still, the structuring of the DC staff was about as close to congruent with its
complex policy environment as one could reasonably expect. A version of it persisted through the Carter administration and, indeed, up to the present time. As a
result of this evident congruence, our expectations about continuity fare quite well.
The DC staff could be considered a rather large, if incremental, step beyond Johnson's policy staff, and it amounted to a similar, though more ambitious, response
to features of the policy environment that could not be ignored. It persisted intact
through the Ford administration, as expected. Also as anticipated, it resurfaced
under Carter, surviving initial competition for policy influence with the cabinet
secretariat. As predicted, too, Carter and his advisers contemplated alternatives but
ultimately settled on the inherited model, minus the less-than-useful connection to
the cabinet via the council. Finally, these transfers of experience—first from Johnson to Nixon, then from Ford to Carter—illustrate that learning had become more
bipartisan than in earlier times. The White House apparatus for domestic policy
was becoming institutionalized.

ECONOMIC POLICY

White House structuring for economic policy goes back as far as John Steelman's
staff, transferred to the White House from the Office of War Mobilization and

Reconversion, early in the Truman administration.[61] Steelman was formally the White House liaison to the Council of Economic Advisers (CEA), and he, as well as other White House aides, took an active advocacy role. White House economic advisers were present in subsequent administrations as well, but the CEA moved to a position of primacy during the Kennedy and Johnson administrations. During the 1960s, the "troika" of the CEA chair, the director of the Budget Bureau, and the secretary of the treasury met regularly on economic matters, "with the CEA clearly the dominant participant."[62]

Nixon

Initially, Richard Nixon relied heavily on Secretaries of the Treasury John Connally and George Shultz, with the active participation of the Domestic Council staff on domestic economic issues. Connally "worked primarily through the troika," while Shultz created interagency committees for specific purposes.[63] Nixon's innovation during his first term was the creation of the Council on International Economic Policy (CIEP) to fill an increasingly important policy niche. CIEP, a cabinet-level body, was tied to the overall White House hierarchy through its staff, which was led by senior Nixon White House aides: Peter Peterson, then Peter Flanigan. Henry Kissinger's NSC staff eschewed involvement in economic issues, removing one source of potential competition. Nevertheless, "CIEP's relationship to both the Treasury Department and the Special Trade Representative was somewhat problematic," as each resisted CIEP's asserting a role in its particular bailiwick.[64]

In his second term, Nixon moved toward greater coordination of domestic and international economic policy with the creation of the Council on Economic Policy (CEP), which was modeled roughly on the existing cabinet-council bodies for foreign and domestic policy. Shultz, the treasury secretary, was the council chair, assisted by a staff headed by Kenneth Dam. The new body did not mean the demise of CIEP, however; it lasted through the Ford administration before finally being terminated by President Carter in 1977. The scope of CIEP's activities, however, contracted; it became limited to "selected trade issues" and generally lost out in competition with the special trade representative.[65]

Ford

The Ford administration not only emulated the Nixon experiment in economic policy coordination but, in most observers' eyes, also improved on the model. Ford's Economic Policy Board (EPB) included as formal participants nine cabinet members, the director of OMB, the chair of CEA, and the executive director of CIEP, bringing together virtually all the major players in economic policy. Executive Director William Seidman supervised the staff.[66] EPB not only engaged in policy planning but also met daily to monitor developments. It was an excellent example of collegial-competitive decision making (or "multiple advocacy"), in large part because it was able to accept and consider a full range of competing points of view from the various actors in its policy area.[67]

EPB also helped realize Ford's ambition of restoring power to the cabinet departments, as well as tapping their expertise on economic issues. This outreach to multiple sources of advice was facilitated by Seidman's ability to play the role of honest broker, which in turn was related to his long-standing relationship with the president. Nevertheless, Roger Porter, an EPB staff member, faulted the body for being somewhat impervious to political considerations, making it less effective than it might have been at integrating these factors into policy deliberations.[68]

Carter

Perhaps not surprisingly, the Carter administration tried to reinvent the EPB (and CEP). Carter's Economic Policy Group (EPG) was cochaired by Secretary of the Treasury Michael Blumenthal and CEA chair Charles Schultze, and its responsibilities encompassed both domestic and international economic policy. However, it was less successful than its predecessors. Carter's NSC staff, unlike Nixon's and Ford's, was actively engaged in the international economic policy arena and ultimately became the primary venue for handling such issues.[69] Even in the domestic policy sphere, the EPG found itself in competition with the Domestic Policy Staff, and as a result, the EPG generally failed to realize its potential as a collegial-competitive structure. The Carter White House's difficulty in coordinating across units became part of the story in the economic area as well.

Analysis

Once again, the Nixon administration, building on the experience of its predecessors, created structuring that was congruent with the policy environment: a collegial-competitive (or multiple-advocacy) structure that drew on the major actors and perspectives in the administration. As expected, Ford continued the structure, although he renamed and refined it. The congruence of such a structure with the policy environment is best illustrated by Ford's EPB. However, as if to underscore the obvious point that structure alone is not everything, a version of the same approach worked far less well for Carter, mainly due to the unregulated competition it experienced from other White House advisory bodies.

CONCLUSION

The necessity of creating structures to integrate diverse sources of policy advice and oversight first became evident in the early years of the New Deal, when Franklin Roosevelt's proliferating structural innovations compelled a search for coordinating mechanisms.[70] The matter became more urgent during World War II, leading to the early development of the Joint Chiefs of Staff and ultimately to the integration of the armed services and the creation of the National Security Council. The NSC then became the model for structuring in other policy areas when the complexity of the policy environment—a consequence of the increasingly ambitious policy aims of presidents and members of Congress and the rising demands of constituency interests—threatened to overwhelm any administration's capacity to plan and to supervise implementation. Thus, one can attribute the emergence of the NSC largely to environmental causes (World War II), but in the case of structuring for domestic policy, environmental demands clearly interacted with presidential priorities. In the domestic sphere, Nixon's relatively ambitious agenda[71] led to structural experimentation that resembled but went beyond that of his immediate predecessor. The difficult economic circumstances of the 1970s were a primary stimulus to structural innovation in that area, but presidential priorities—especially Ford's—put a focus on the need for innovative policy structuring. Finally, the selection of the basic cabinet-council arrangement seems to have been partly an organizational phenomenon, as the NSC continued to serve as a handy model for structuring in other areas.

As in other structural aspects of the White House, we find that in these three policy areas, partisan learning began breaking down in the 1970s as short-term experience—including reactions to Nixon's downfall—and environmental pressures intervened. Hence, in national security, Nixon relied on a strong NSA, like Kennedy and Johnson but unlike Eisenhower. Ford improvised around this approach, keeping Kissinger in a position of power, but not as NSA. Carter initially tried to reject it, along with almost anything else that smacked of a powerful, Nixonian White House. He failed, however, as Brzezinski ultimately attained a stature nearly equal to Kissinger's, and the White House reasserted its primacy in the national security policy process. This evidently happened less because Carter wanted it that way and more because Brzezinski was the superior bureaucratic politician. Yet it also reflected a logic by which senior White House aides, presumably reflecting the interests of the president alone, would prevail in competition for the president's ear over agencies encumbered by both clients and diverse organizational cultures and outlooks.

The story of domestic policy structuring is consistent with that of national security. In the domestic area, Nixon emulated Johnson more than Eisenhower in building a strong staff structure for domestic policy, beginning with the Burns and Moynihan staffs. He then mimicked the NSC model in the design of the Domestic Council. In this case, Ford did not modify Nixon's creation significantly (even though the DC staff lost power), but Carter made the predictable effort to return power to the cabinet and downplay the influence of his Domestic Policy Staff. In the end, that staff asserted itself, becoming more crucial to policy processes under Carter than it had been under Ford or during the last years of the Nixon administration.

In economic policy, the pattern is somewhat different. Nixon was relatively slow to move toward fuller coordination of economic policy under the CEP; it was Ford who pushed the model closer to its potential with the creation of the EPB. Carter seemingly embraced the idea in the form of his EPG. Here, there is evidence of nonpartisan learning where it might not have been expected. In actual practice, however, the EPG fell far short of Ford's EPB in power and effectiveness.

Overall, Propositions 3 and 4—that there would be little change from Nixon to Ford and (though not without a struggle) from Ford to Carter—are supported. The dynamic in the latter dyad, at least in national security and domestic policy, seems to be similar structural reactions to common environmental imperatives rather than conscious nonpartisan learning. However, one key expectation was not met. Nixon's formal policy structures bear little similarity to Eisenhower's. In national security, Nixon seems to have learned more from Kennedy, and in domestic policy, more from Johnson. In economic policy, Nixon was an innovator; he evidently sensed, after experimentation with CIEP, that the location of the United States in the world economy would demand fuller integration of domestic and foreign economic policy.

The structural decisions of the 1970s reverberated in later decades. NSC structuring has continued as a predictable part of any new administration. Likewise, domestic policy staffs have become standard parts of new White Houses, although experimentation and some degree of uncertainty persist. The first-term Reagan experiment with multiple cabinet councils did not endure, and the first Bush administration saw Roger Porter's domestic staff somewhat outgunned by Richard Darman's OMB. Still, specialized domestic policy staffing has clearly become institutionalized, as evidenced by both Bush administrations as well as that of Bill Clinton. Similarly, Ford's EPB model has been closely followed, most notably in the structuring of Clinton's National Economic Council, a design that his successor left mostly intact. The innovation and experimentation of Nixon, Ford, and Carter in the White House management of public policy produced a basis for both learning and the long-term enlargement of the institutional presidency.

8
Speechwriting

Writing the president's speeches, major and minor, from the State of the Union Address to Rose Garden remarks, has long been an important part of the work of the White House staff. Besides being opportunities for outreach to the public, presidential speeches can be catalysts for the formulation of public policy and political strategy, compelling presidents and their advisers to make policy decisions in order to be able to articulate them.[1] Speechwriting, then, is a technique for informing and persuading various publics, as well as an element of the policy process. The integration of these two purposes has posed a persistent challenge to those who design White House governance structures.

From George Washington through Harry Truman, and again under John Kennedy, most presidential speeches were written either by the president himself or by highly placed advisers.[2] Franklin Roosevelt pioneered the use of collegial speechwriting teams and also began the practice of having top White House aides as speechwriters, luring one of his writers, New York State Judge Samuel Rosenman, to the White House as special counsel to the president. Truman continued FDR's practices, but Dwight Eisenhower rejected that approach in favor of delegating his writing to aides who were speechwriting specialists but were not otherwise heavily involved in advising. Kennedy revived the FDR-HST pattern, another reflection of partisan learning, and Lyndon Johnson attempted to continue it.

Johnson's arrangements were more internally competitive, in part because a wide range of aides was necessary to produce the many speeches now expected of a president. The importance of the speechwriting process for policy decisions also encouraged competition among advisers for access to it. By 1965, in the face of perceived disorganization and an ever-increasing demand for the president's words, LBJ supplemented top aides with specialized writers, hired mainly to help with minor speeches and messages.[3] Almost immediately, this created a governance problem: how to integrate the writing specialists into the flow of information and decisions surrounding policy issues.

As the Johnson administration progressed, various structural "fixes" did not fully solve the problems of coordinating the overall writing process, and at the same time, the stable of writing specialists grew. The result was the emergence of two pathologies that would plague Johnson's successors. The first was conflict over access to the writing process and control of the content of speeches. Aides with policy or political portfolios recognized the importance of that kind of influence. Second was the relative isolation of some speechwriters—the specialists—from direct knowledge of the policy or political decisions that should have shaped the speeches they wrote. These writers were left to "write blind," in relative ignorance of the administration's position. This generated a long series of complaints and efforts at amelioration, but the problems continued to the end of LBJ's presidency.[4]

In his first term, Richard Nixon seemingly overcame the difficulties that had plagued Johnson. He relied on writing specialists but was careful to link them to the policy decision process and, in the case of important speeches, to participate heavily in the writing himself. In the second term, however, under the pressures of Watergate and staff turnover, this approach faltered. Both Gerald Ford and Jimmy Carter copied the basics of Nixon's structural design. Ford in particular was attentive to the need to link the writers to the president and to the work of the rest of the White House. Still, neither was able to emulate Nixon's first-term success. In the Ford White House, the problems included a lack of adequate collegial structuring, exacerbated by tensions among the staff. In Carter's case, the intended linkages between the speechwriters and the policy process were inadequate, and the writing staff was never permitted to become as large as it probably should have been.

THE NIXON SYSTEM

Richard Nixon's approach to the structuring of speechwriting clearly drew on the experiences of the Eisenhower White House. It also bore some similarity to LBJ's, but Nixon's people may have viewed the Johnson operation largely in terms of problems to be avoided.[5] From the beginning of his administration, all of Nixon's writers were writing specialists, not generalist policy or political advisers. In that regard, his arrangements most clearly harked back to Eisenhower. But Nixon's plans were more elaborate, as was necessary in light of the increased demand for presidential words. He lodged the writers in an Office of Speechwriting and Research, set within the newly created Office of Communications. This arrangement thus had a clear element of partisan learning, albeit adapted to fit Nixon's organizational and political needs and preferences.

Nixon's staff was substantially larger than Eisenhower's, consisting of as many as ten writers, supported by a similar-sized staff of researchers. The first director of the office, James Keogh, was not a writer; he focused on editing and making writing assignments. His successors, Raymond Price and David Gergen, however, were writers. Below Keogh in the initial setup were two tiers of hierarchy. Senior writers such as Price and William Safire worked on more substantive speeches, statements, and messages, with Price usually being primarily responsible for drafting the annual State of the Union Address. In the next tier were writers more analogous to LBJ's specialists, who drafted speeches to interest groups, ceremonial remarks, formal toasts, and the like. The staff also wrote remarks for members of the president's family and speeches for Vice President Spiro Agnew and various cabinet members.[6]

The writing staff did not entirely monopolize speechwriting in the Nixon White House, though they came close. Patrick Buchanan, who began on Keogh's staff but soon became independent of it, continued to write speeches for Nixon, and especially for Agnew.[7] Likewise, aides such as Ken Khachigian and John McLaughlin, who did stints on the writing staff and elsewhere in communications, contributed some writing, as did National Security Council staffers and others. The break from the pattern set by the Democrats, however, was clear. Senior staffers, such as heads of major White House units, were not expected to be speechwriters. Thus, rivalry among top advisers did not express itself in the writing process in the disruptive way it had under LBJ. Moreover, writers were buffered from influences outside the White House. Cabinet officials, for instance, were to meet only with Chief of Staff H. R. Haldeman or three other top White House officials—not with the writers.[8]

The second problem that had bedeviled Johnson—the distancing of the full-time writers from decision processes—also was addressed in Nixon's scheme. Two different kinds of structures emerged. The first involved hierarchy. In an overall White House staff system characterized by clear lines of communication and authority running to the chief of staff, writers could be included in regular communications channels and could rely on guidance from Haldeman or his staff. Although Nixon himself rarely interacted personally with his writers, the hierarchy permitted two-way communication between the president and his writers over speech content. Nixon or his most senior aides typically laid down the key elements of a speech in the initial instructions to the writer, then followed up with aggressive editing. For Nixon's 1971 speech that introduced wage and price controls and closed the "gold window," the president arranged for writer William Safire to meet with top economic and foreign policy advisers.[9]

As a further check on policy content and appropriateness, speech drafts were routinely "staffed" in a manner similar to that in which decision memoranda were handled. Top White House and cabinet officials with relevant expertise were asked to review and comment on speech drafts, a process that lengthened preparation time but promoted orderly multiple advocacy.

To supplement the communication of policy directions and political strategies from the chief of staff, the Nixon White House made a practice of including writers in sessions at which policy issues were discussed, such as senior staff meetings. Johnson's full-time writers had demanded exactly this kind of access but had been refused. In the Nixon scheme, the inclusion of writers in such meetings did not necessarily elevate them to the status of policy makers. Rather, it simply "help[ed] them to understand what the President's current thinking may be on several subjects."[10]

Hierarchical structuring for informing writers presupposes that a degree of consensus has been reached prior to the writers' involvement. This was the case in the Nixon White House—the writers generally were not participants at those meetings where consensus was developed but became involved later on. Nevertheless, Nixon supplemented hierarchical structuring by a practice of assigning writers to speeches on the basis of their policy views. For example, he would turn to Price for idealistic prose, to Safire for a philosophical or humorous touch, and to Buchanan for combative, conservative rhetoric.[11]

Moreover, at times, Nixon modified his reliance on hierarchy and used speechwriting to explore policy and strategic options. In such cases, he would assign multiple writers with divergent views to either submit multiple drafts of a speech or sequentially revise it. In effect, this replaced the usual hierarchy with an adversarial structure in which the writers aired their views and rationales before a final decision maker, the president. For example, in April 1970, Henry Kissinger, Buchanan, and Price each prepared drafts for a televised "Progress Report on Vietnam."[12] In such situations, according to John Ehrlichman, "all the ideological factions of the White House staff—came creeping out of the bushes. . . . [There was] healthy, vigorous, good-spirited argument which persisted until Nixon signaled that he'd made his final decision."[13] In other words, the writing process was effectively used to produce multiple advocacy in political and policy advice. In addition, in such contexts, the senior writers were, and understood themselves to be, acting as genuine advisers.

Thus, Nixon's design of the speechwriting process by and large overcame the "writing blind" problems that had emerged during the Johnson administration. However, this emphasis on policy content and advice is not the entire story. As chapter 3 detailed, virtually all the work of the Nixon White House was pervaded by a concern for public relations in a broad sense. Not surprisingly, speechwriting was included; not only were some of the writers drawn from the larger communications office, but some of those on the writing staff also performed PR functions. Safire, for example, was occasionally used as a channel to the media,[14] and he attended, with Buchanan, the News Calendar meetings, during which it was decided which presidential events and activities would be emphasized to the media.[15] Along with Price and Keogh, Safire also participated in Herb Klein's Saturday Morning Planning Committee meetings.[16] Such public-relations efforts were often aimed at publicizing and shaping public reaction to presidential speeches.

Nixon's design and use of the speechwriting process during his first term were generally successful in terms of connecting writing to both policy and public relations. In particular, he overcame the problems Johnson had experienced in terms of conveying policy content. However, Nixon himself was far from completely satisfied with the product he received. Perhaps ironically, his main complaint was that his speeches focused too much on the details of policy, as well as being both too long and deficient in terms of "color" and "flair."[17] Despite persistent efforts to dig up colorful anecdotes and edit aggressively for style, the writing process never fulfilled the president's aspirations.

In Nixon's second term, although the basic structuring for speechwriting remained the same, problems developed that recalled Johnson's experience. In particular, the "writing blind" complaint surfaced once again. The explanation lay in a combination of staff turnover and the monumental distraction of the president's efforts to deal with Watergate.

In January 1973, Price stepped down as head of the writing office and was replaced by his deputy Gergen, who was neither as senior nor as personally close to Nixon as Price was. Price remained in the White House and ultimately took charge of writing most of Nixon's Watergate-related speeches.[18] Meanwhile, Safire left the White House, and there were more important Watergate-induced changes elsewhere on the president's staff, particularly the forced resignation of Haldeman in late April 1973. His successor, Alexander Haig, was less meticulous an overseer than Haldeman and was compelled to deal with unprecedented turmoil both inside and outside the White House. As the environment grew increasingly hostile, Nixon became more isolated within the White House, and his attention to such things as drafting and editing speeches and mediating policy disputes waned.[19]

Organizationally, policy direction was weakened when senior staff meetings ceased to include any representatives of the writing staff. In February 1974, Gergen complained to Haig: "From the writer's point of view, it is particularly difficult to be out of touch with the daily currents. Our writing should reflect the nuances as well as the broad outlines of policy. We should have a sense of the President's moods as well as his long-range goals. And with the cumbersome bureaucracy we now face in order to clear Presidential messages and statements, we should have close relationships with all of the President's major advisors . . . all of the writers need much better access than we now have."[20] The first-term White House hierarchy for providing policy guidance to writers had weakened, and no substitute mechanism surfaced to take its place. This was mitigated somewhat by the fact that the speeches most critical to Nixon, those relating to his efforts to survive the Watergate investigations, were written by Price, who had unlimited access to the president.

Analysis

The Nixon administration marked the demise of speechwriting by senior policy advisers. Despite the troubles of the second term, Nixon provided an organizational model that his successors would seek to emulate. This would prove difficult, however, because Nixon's system relied on more than hierarchical structuring to be effective. In the first term, Nixon's senior writers carried a certain weight, as policy advocates, that their successors did not. Likewise, Gergen did not have the stature in the White House enjoyed by his predecessors. One consequence was his inability to get the writing staff access to top-level policy discussions. Haldeman, likewise a key link to the writers, was similarly missed, as Haig's attention was understandably focused elsewhere. In addition, Nixon himself, a key element in the system, grew increasingly distant. Although structure mattered, the approach clearly required more than structure.

When Gerald Ford succeeded Nixon, he inherited Nixon's basic formal gov-

ernance structures, including the full-time writers and researchers. His experience
with speechwriting, though, would be different from Nixon's.

FORD: COPING WITH CONFLICT

The editorial office under Gerald Ford was structured like Nixon's, but Ford
quickly replaced almost all its members, including bringing Paul Theis into Gergen's position.[21] He also produced one organizational innovation, assigning Counselor to the President Robert Hartmann overall responsibility for speechwriting.
Given Hartmann's rank and long association with the new president, this arrangement seemed to promise greater access for writers and their concerns than they had
enjoyed under Nixon. Moreover, Hartmann, a former journalist and chief of Ford's
presidential and vice presidential staffs, was an accomplished speechwriter whose
most memorable contribution to the Ford presidency may have been the phrase,
"Our long, national nightmare is over." He would personally draft major speeches.
    Hartmann described his own scope of influence aptly: "to approve every sin-
gle word that went out of the White House in the President's name—with the
exception of statements [Ford] authorized the Press Secretary to make."[22] This reinforced the idea that Hartmann's relationship to Ford would be the key to bridging
the gap between writers and policy makers that had appeared late in Nixon's presidency. Hartmann responded by instituting the kind of communication channels
that had been lacking. Hartmann or Theis attended daily senior staff meetings,
occasionally bringing a writer along.[23] Better yet, Hartmann saw to it that writers
were routinely involved in meetings with the president prior to their work on particular speeches.[24]
    Despite the apparent congruence between Ford's writing structures and the
task at hand, the president's speeches were criticized for both blandness of style
and vagueness of policy direction.[25] Part of the problem was Ford, who was not a
gifted public speaker. But another significant element traced back to the effort at
spokes-of-the-wheel staff organization (see chapter 2) and the competition that
emerged.
    The primary internal problem the Ford White House faced was organizational
politics, especially a fierce rivalry between Hartmann and Staff Coordinator Donald Rumsfeld. Rumsfeld's efforts to control paper flow and harmonize the activities of the staff units led to friction with Hartmann, who resisted any attempt to
interfere with his access to or influence with Ford. Moreover, Hartmann's contempt
for the Nixon holdovers on the staff (the "praetorians") included Rumsfeld. The
tension between them led Rumsfeld to try to compete with Hartmann's staff in
drafting and influencing major speeches; he even called on Gergen, then at the
Treasury Department, for assistance with alternative drafts.[26]
    Hartmann fought back, taking his case both to Ford and to his old friends in the
press. But the acrimony distracted Hartmann from the task of linking his writers to

the policy process. When he began missing senior staff meetings in protest against Rumsfeld, who chaired them, his ability to guide the writers suffered. Rumsfeld, for his part, made no effort to work with the writers. Ford, perhaps accustomed to such conflict in the congressional setting, where its consequences were more benign, failed to deal with the problem. As a consequence, the gap between writing and policy, the "writing blind" problem, was allowed to reemerge in spite of structuring that should have minimized it.

Staff tensions were not the only flaw in the Ford speechwriting operation. A related problem—one that would appear in succeeding White Houses—was "staffing" speeches, or circulating them to appropriate officials for comment. Early on, Rumsfeld had complained of inadequate staffing (see chapter 2). Poor staffing led to such outcomes as Hartmann's insertion of the WIN (Whip Inflation Now) slogan, which many would come to view as an embarrassment, into a Ford speech that no one else saw before it was delivered.[27] In response, Rumsfeld instituted a more formal staffing system, with clearance forms routinely attached to drafts—a reasonable response, under the circumstances. Once initiated, however, staffing seemed to grow out of control. A minor speech such as Ford's remarks at a Christmas party for the press corps needed clearance by eight different offices.[28] Excessive staffing led to more than red tape. Speechwriter Pat Butler recalled the result: "Ford and his staff assistants were being so careful that they just took everything controversial and politically upbeat out of his speeches. A bureaucracy had been established that did not serve the President's best interests."[29] From the standpoint of style, Hartmann summed up the problem: "This is not only a time-consuming process, but a speech thus produced ends up about as exciting and artistic as an Act of Congress."[30]

Here, Ford's staff performed poorly compared with Nixon's. Although speeches were staffed for Nixon, his ex-aides have tended to praise the process, and none has blamed it for flaws in the final product.[31] The problem for Ford was the underlying dissensus. Sometime before a speech is given, a consensus on policy must be reached—in the writing process itself, if need be. In the Ford White House, this frequently failed to happen. Speech staffing sometimes became an invitation to renewed argument and strategic maneuvering, even over relatively minor speeches. For instance, speechwriter Kaye Pullen, exhausted from battling over a 1975 Ford speech to the NAACP, lamented to a colleague, "I am rewriting this thing because no one can make up his mind what we're supposed to say."[32] In the face of that kind of uncertainty, one frustrated writer even turned for inspiration and information about administration policy to the *Wall Street Journal* and *Congressional Quarterly.*[33]

Structural "fixes" were tried. Meetings between the writers and Hartmann or department head Theis were deemed unsatisfactory.[34] Even regular sessions between Ford and the writers, presided over by Hartmann, were unhelpful because, according to Gergen, all concerned came in unprepared.[35] As Hartmann was increasingly distracted by staff infighting, and as policy decisions proved harder to make, the link to the writers became attenuated. Finally, Dick Cheney, now the staff coordinator, opted to formally go around the writing staff. He brought Gergen back into the White House, as a writer, on Cheney's staff.[36] In response, Hartmann reorganized the writing staff, placing the researchers in a separate unit, replacing Theis with former joke writer Robert Orben, and bringing in new writers.[37]

The result was at least a certain redundancy. Speeches were reviewed by a group representing both the Cheney and the Hartmann writing efforts, with Ford at the center of this adjudicative structure. Butler, who became Orben's deputy, recalled that Ford began to take a stronger role, spending "an unusually large amount of time reviewing the details of these speeches. Usually there would be a draft from Gergen and another from our shop. The President would review the drafts and take what he wanted. He seemed to find some way to take something from both drafts. He always found a compromise that made all of the principals feel that their work was being appreciated."[38] Tension remained, but the enlarged role of the president and the solidarity and pressure of the campaign reduced both the excessive editing and the backbiting. The nature of campaign speaking also tended to minimize any problems in policy formation and to place a greater premium on style, which had been Orben's forte all along. Thus, environmental change surely worked in favor of Ford's beleaguered speechwriters.

Analysis

Despite a promising approach to hierarchical structuring, the Ford White House experienced problems at least as daunting as those plaguing Johnson or Nixon. Part of the difficulty lay in the larger, more or less hierarchical structuring of the White House, in which writing was only a subordinate part. However congruent Ford's writing structure may have been with the demands of the political environment beyond the White House, it fell victim to the more proximate milieu of the staff itself. Leadership, by Hartmann and Ford especially, was another key variable. Attempts at adjudicative structuring (e.g., the writers' meetings with Theis, Hartmann, and Ford) were inadequate to solve the problems. A notable lack of collegial structuring—indeed, of collegiality across White House offices—inhibited the flow of ideas. Until the exigencies of campaigning caused Ford to take an enhanced role, the arrangements did not function well.

CARTER: RESPONDING TO THE WRONG DIAGNOSIS

Jimmy Carter's transition team knew that the Ford speechwriting process had been problematic. They recommended not only eliminating the Hartmann position, which was done, but also downsizing the writing office to as few as three.[39] This, of course, reflected the general predisposition of Carter and his advisers to address organizational problems by downsizing—in part, a product of the lingering suspicion that Nixon's difficulties had been tied to the excessive size of the White House staff. The size of the writing unit finally was set at a normal complement of five or six writers and no researchers at all, reporting to Press Secretary Jody Powell. This was in spite of a political environment that was demanding more rhetoric from Carter than from his predecessors.[40] Carter, in effect, addressed these demands by reducing his capacity to respond.

Shrinking the writing staff also reflected what some saw as Carter's relative indifference to (perhaps even "suspicion" of) the process of speechwriting.[41] As a candidate, Carter had written his own speeches. In any event, his placement of writing under a trusted aide (Powell) was superficially reminiscent of Ford's use of Hartmann. But Hartmann was a writer. Powell's main obligation was to the press office, with the result that writing was often neglected. Powell, in retrospect, conceded that putting writing under his office was "not the correct decision," blaming it on his campaign experience and his desire to maintain control of too many things.[42]

The downsizing of the writing staff further hampered the writing effort. As early as the second month of Carter's term, head writer James Fallows complained that his staff was overburdened and asked for research help.[43] It did no good, then or later. Throughout the course of the administration, the writing staff was kept at the same level of personnel, without researchers.[44]

The placement of writing under the somewhat indifferent press secretary also had a predictable consequence. The writers had no reliable conduit to the policy process or to the president himself. When Fallows asked to be included in senior staff meetings, Carter's grudging reply was, "OK—don't overdo it."[45] That was optimistic. In fact, Fallows seldom saw the president and was isolated from policy decision settings. Congressional-relations head and Carter intimate Frank Moore once guessed that "Fallows spent maybe an hour with the President all told."[46] Fallows complained that even when he did see Carter, the advice he got was usually "vague."[47]

Out of such circumstances, the emergence of the sort of gap between writing and policy seen in prior administrations was virtually inevitable. As writer Caryl Conner put it in a memo to Fallows in August 1978, "it is difficult to write in a vacuum. Speechwriters should sit in on policy discussions related to the substance of their assignments. This eliminates the problem of 'writing blind,' and of loaded or incomplete reporting by one party to the meeting. More important, the exposure makes the writer familiar with the thinking behind the decisions."[48] As a remedy, Conner echoed Fallows's earlier proposals for writers to be present at policy meetings and to have access to President Carter. Despite formal endorsement of these ideas by Powell, domestic policy chief Stuart Eizenstat, and national security adviser Zbigniew Brzezinski, little came of it.

For the rest of the administration, according to writer Chris Matthews, writers coped with this lack of guidance by poring over Carter's *Why Not the Best?* and his old speeches "like . . . biblical scholars."[49] Perversely, this sometimes led writers to take an off-the-cuff Carter statement, such as his promise to cut the number of government agencies, as virtual prophecy, regardless of the seriousness or the quality of the idea.

Another problem, particularly early in the Carter administration, was that speech staffing was erratic. In the relatively collegial Carter White House, the clearance process did not reflect political rivalry as it had under Ford. Rather, the problem was getting speech drafts to the right people at the right time. Mistakes, including errors of fact, sometimes crept into the speeches.[50] Later, the "Too Many Cooks Syndrome" of overstaffing, which had been a considerable problem for Ford, emerged under Carter.[51] Meanwhile, in areas such as foreign policy, where rivalry reminiscent of the Ford White House could surface, the result was similar. In at least one instance, contending speech drafts were simply combined into one speech whose internal tensions remained unresolved.[52]

In mid-1978, Carter, like Ford before him, attempted to address what he finally saw as a problem by undertaking a modest reorganization, placing the writers in the communications office under Gerald Rafshoon. By the writers' account, this changed little procedurally, although Rafshoon did take a stronger interest in speech content than Powell had, running through new themes every few days.[53]

More change followed the reorganization that made Hamilton Jordan chief of staff and brought Alonzo McDonald to the White House. Chief writer Hendrik Hertzberg greeted McDonald by identifying for him the central problems the writers had: limited access to Carter and lack of "clout" to prevent speeches from being watered down through overstaffing.[54] McDonald responded by addressing a different aspect of the staffing problem, creating standardized forms and an orderly speech clearance process—a system Hertzberg called "a roaring success," as far as it went.[55] But although they brought order, McDonald's reforms did not address the overstaffing problem, which, if anything, got worse as even more people became involved.[56] In terms of access to the president, nothing changed.

Analysis

The Carter writing system was structured much like Ford's. Again, in terms of formal structuring, one might have predicted success, since initially a Carter intimate connected the writers to the president. But Powell was even less effective than Hartmann had been. At the same time, staff shrinkage took a toll on the writers, and "writing blind" became a familiar challenge. Thus, the formal hierarchy's inherent potential was lost. And, like the Ford case, informal structuring that might have compensated failed to appear.

In the generally collegial Carter White House, speech staffing did not provoke the conflict it sometimes did under Ford. Nonetheless, over time, overstaffing became the same problem for Carter that it had been for his predecessor. When an organizational expert was brought in to fix matters, he wound up addressing neither problem, seeking instead a more efficient version of what was already there. Striving for efficiency is normally praiseworthy, but it missed the mark in this case.

McDonald, whose commitment to informal governance structures was useful in other areas, failed to introduce the kind of communication opportunities for the writers that might have strengthened the speechwriting operation.

CONCLUSION

The pathologies that had begun to surface under Johnson finally reemerged under Nixon and plagued both Ford and Carter. The cures, access and clout, seem obvious. But access to the president is precious, and there are many claimants. Access to policy processes on the part of non–policy makers is apt to be resisted. And widespread staffing is rational in terms of minimizing errors and respecting legitimate claims to involvement, even if it is not the way to write the best speeches. As in many other areas of organizational design, the issue is one of priorities. The experience of subsequent administrations would demonstrate the elusiveness of the "right" organizational structures and routines for integrating policy and outreach through presidential rhetoric.

The problems that bedeviled Nixon, Ford, and Carter—especially too much staffing and "writing blind"—persisted beyond the Carter administration. Former writers as well as journalists have identified and lamented such problems in the Reagan,[57] George H. W. Bush,[58] and Clinton[59] administrations. In an era when a daily supply of presidential rhetoric is routinely anticipated by the media and the public, generating appropriate blends of policy content and rhetorical quality remains a challenge for the White House.

9
Analysis and Conclusions

We began this investigation with a relatively simple narrative about the organization of the White House over the course of the Nixon, Ford, and Carter administrations. Consistent with much existing scholarship, we looked at the decade of the 1970s as the period during which, in terms of organizational structuring and institutionalization, the presidency became more clearly and distinctively "modern." During the first era of the modern presidency (the early modern period), the beginnings of most structural aspects of the contemporary White House could be identified, but their presence in any given administration was frequently hit-or-miss, and they sometimes amounted to little more than a single individual assigned temporarily to a particular policy or liaison responsibility. Beginning with the presidency of Richard Nixon, however, those tasks that would survive as elements of the White House Office began to be the responsibility of relatively well-staffed units linked to a more fully realized hierarchical governance system emanating from the office of the chief of staff.

In developing this more modern version of White House organization, Nixon and H. R. Haldeman built on those features that had already become expected elements of any White House, such as congressional liaison and the press office. In addition, they created staff structuring for a number of tasks that had been pursued only sporadically, such as interest group liaison and economic policy making. And they took what had been nascent structures under Lyndon Johnson, such as arrangements for specialized speechwriting and domestic policy decision making, and elevated them to full-blown organizational units. Thus, the Nixon White House became the largest White House Office in the history of the presidency, as well as the most structurally diverse.[1] Of course, it also became the most controversial. In the immediate aftermath of Watergate, commentators blamed Nixon's closed, hierarchical White House, as well as the sheer size of its staff, for some or all of the pathologies that led to the president's forced resignation. Under those circumstances, Nixon's successors, Gerald Ford and Jimmy Carter, had little choice but to take a stance, rhetorically at least, in opposition to Nixon's practices.

PROPOSITIONS AND EXPECTATIONS

This study sought to document and to add texture and detail to the story of Nixon's building of the White House Office, as well as to systematically investigate, in structural terms, the nature of the Ford and Carter responses. Our relatively conventional understanding of the Nixon administration, along with the organizational-theoretical ideas outlined earlier, helped us craft the questions and propositions found in chapter 1. In what follows, we return to those propositions and summarize how they fared in the face of the evidence presented in chapters 2 through 8. Moreover, we speculate about some of the findings for which the theoretical framework failed to fully account.

Nixon Administration as a Tipping Point

Although the number of staffers in the White House grew under Nixon, and structures multiplied, one can reasonably inquire whether these shifts represented a break point so sharp as to suggest a transition in the institutional presidency from an early modern (or first) era to a distinguishable second era that was more fully modern. To assess such a claim, at least four factors can be examined. One is the size of the White House Office and ancillary staffs, such as those for domestic policy and national security affairs. Second is the range of tasks incorporated into the White House. A third, related factor is the purposes to which these White House staff elements were put. Finally, one can examine the relative stability, or the extent of institutionalization, of Nixon's innovations in particular and of his overall organizational strategy more generally.

Size. On the matter of staff size, the evidence is relatively clear. Counting detailees and "special projects" aides, the White House staff, by the best available count, numbered 456 in 1968, Lyndon Johnson's final year. In 1969, the number jumped to 632, before declining to 553 by 1974. Yet this growth proved temporary. By 1978, Carter had cut the staff to 362.[2] Other data, reflecting different methods of counting, show roughly the same pattern and suggest that although the White House has grown back some since then, it has neither frequently hit nor long sustained the levels reached under Nixon. In any event, as John Hart has commented, "the data on White House staff growth need to be treated cautiously, qualitatively as well as quantitatively. In general, the post-Watergate critics handled [those] data rather casually, using crude statistics as the basis for their diagnosis of what was wrong with the presidency."[3] In other words, the numerical data are neither entirely clear nor definitive, and their interpretation is contestable. The growth in White House staff size under Nixon may direct attention to that administration as breaking the patterns of its predecessors, but considered in isolation, it establishes little.

Range of Tasks. A more convincing case that the Nixon presidency marks a discontinuity in the evolution of the White House can be made by examining the range of tasks that became fully identifiable features of the White House for the first time under Nixon. The list is impressive. It includes public (i.e., interest group) liaison, communications (including outreach to non-Washington media), the counsel's office (as a unit focused more on law than on policy), and speechwriting, along with coordination of domestic and economic policy. In narrower areas as well, the Nixon White House incorporated and nurtured activities rarely seen there before, including the collection and analysis of public-opinion polling data and, of course, the identification and investigation of presidential "enemies." For better or worse, the White House under Nixon became home to an unprecedented array of activities and clearly represented a major leap forward in the centralization of the power of the presidency in the White House Office itself.

Use of Staff. At least as clear as the diversity of the tasks performed by aides in the Nixon White House is the overall move toward a "public-relations" presidency. With an advertising executive as his chief operating officer and a staff heavy with public-relations and journalistic talent, Nixon oriented the White House more toward public outreach than had any of his predecessors. At the same time, it is notable that Nixon also continued in a direction that Johnson had explored when he made the White House the focal point for the coordination and oversight of domestic and, eventually, economic policy. This enhancement of the president's reach into the workings of the larger executive branch, the pursuit of an "administrative presidency," arguably was as portentous as the public-relations efforts. All in all, when one probes beyond how the White House looked and focuses on what its occupants were actually doing, the case for discontinuity is strengthened.

Institutionalization. As we conceive this discontinuity, it is not merely an aberration but a more lasting alteration of the political and organizational landscape. One can look at institutionalization in the relatively short run by asking whether Nixon's innovations survived through the Ford and Carter administrations. In many ways, this was a hard test, for Ford and Carter were virtually compelled to seek alternatives to Nixon's organizational innovations. Yet, as the preceding chapters have shown and as we review below, for the most part, this did not happen. Instead, sometimes after a period of resistance and experimentation, the main elements of the Nixon system kept returning.

One can look at institutionalization over the longer run by asking whether the organizational elements that Nixon put in place remain today. Without a notable exception, the answer is yes. Indeed, the Nixon White House still supplies the basic model for White House structuring and overall organization, and its key features have been reproduced in virtually every administration through that of George W. Bush.[4] In the era of the "permanent campaign," Nixon's focus on outreach to various publics appears, in retrospect, to have been farsighted.

In sum, we contend that the evidence for discontinuity is persuasive. Richard Nixon's White House Office contained many features that were missing or only sporadically present in its predecessors; it channeled staff structuring toward a broader and more ambitious range of goals than had been attempted before; and it established precedents that survived short-term rhetorical rejection, changes in party control, and the longer-term test of time. In light of the evident importance of this change in the nature of the White House and the expectations of it, it seems appropriate to return to the questions of how and why Nixon created the organization that he did.

Explaining Discontinuity

Chapter 1 outlined three clusters of variables that we employed to help explain why changes in White House structuring take place. Presidents may emulate their predecessors, especially fellow partisans, or they may feel compelled to respond to the demands of their environments. Typical organizational processes, such as the tendency toward increasing differentiation over time and the dynamics of "office politics," also may come into play. Finally, we considered the impact of presidential preferences and strategies.

Rather clearly, no single cluster of factors can explain all structural changes and continuities. Nor is any one change likely to be fully accounted for by a single influence. Nonetheless, we can identify patterns and tendencies that add some depth to our understanding of the structural evolution of the White House. Accordingly, we look closely at the major changes that Nixon brought to the White House in an effort both to explain them and to explore more broadly how the sources of change have themselves shifted (and persisted) over the course of the modern presidency.

Structuring for Coordination and Supervision. Nixon's basic White House design is easy to attribute largely to partisan learning, the tendency of presidents to emulate their partisan predecessors. We identified this as a recurrent pattern in first-era White Houses.[5] Nixon had served eight years as Dwight Eisenhower's vice president and had come, like many, to greatly admire Ike's organizational skills, so it is not surprising that key elements of Nixon's White House—especially the office of the chief of staff and the staff secretariat—mirrored the Eisenhower design. This is even less surprising in light of the fact that Democrats had been unstinting in their criticism of Ike's White House arrangements, charging that they were too bureaucratized, slow, and dependent on a military staff model. Nixon's decision to emulate Eisenhower can be seen as not just an adaptation of what he had learned but also a defense of his mentor and his party.

At the same time, however, other factors impelled Nixon and Haldeman toward the model they chose. Conspicuous among them was the recent experience of Lyndon Johnson, who seemingly understood that the volume of problems facing the White House was overwhelming his spokes-of-the-wheel system of more or less generalist advisers. Despite pleading with staffers such as Robert Kintner to provide management fixes, Johnson never solved the problem.[6] LBJ's difficulties were well known to Nixon, and they certainly would have suggested to any incoming president that higher degrees of formalization and more hierarchical structuring were indicated. In effect, the political environment—growing harsher and more contentious in an era of unpopular war, economic downturns, urban unrest, and rising numbers of clamorous interest groups—virtually compelled some sort of change from LBJ's approach.

Finally, the broader historical circumstances of Nixon's presidency may have played a role. As noted in the introduction, Nixon has been described as a "preemptive" president, challenging an existing regime and hoping to remake the politics of his time. Faced with hostile majorities in Congress and an executive branch that he suspected was committed to a Democratic agenda, Nixon quite reasonably sought to empower the one part of the government he more clearly controlled. This objective would account for many things over the course of the administration, but initially, it seems at least consistent with the creation of a strong, hierarchical staff system premised on command and control from the Oval Office.

Structuring for Outreach. Much of Nixon's imprint on the White House as an organization lies in the realm of outreach. Our Proposition 1 predicted, in part, that structuring in this area would reflect presidential choice variables more than it had in previous presidencies. In effect, we expected to find a reversal of the pattern we had identified in studying the Hoover through Johnson presidencies, when structuring for outreach seemed to be driven mostly by environmental factors.[7] Given Nixon's avowed ambition of building a new Republican majority, we anticipated that White House outreach structures would show the imprint of presidential objectives and strategies.

When one looks closely at Nixon's structural innovations in the outreach area, one finds clear support for this expectation. In the area of public outreach especially, Nixon and Haldeman's interest in public-relations strategies and polling pushed the White House far beyond anything seen before, even in the absence of contemporaneous changes in PR techniques or polling strategies. The cluster of informal governance structures devoted to outreach strategies was likewise unprecedented. At the level of more formal structuring, the emergence of the Office of Communications reflected Nixon's strategy of trying to go around and over the Washington press corps, which he profoundly distrusted.

Similarly, Nixon's stress on attracting support from elements of the fragmenting New Deal coalition provides a persuasive explanation for the emergence of Charles Colson's unit, later dubbed the Office of Public Liaison. Rather clearly, too, the president was encouraged by the arguments, analyses, and activities of senior aides such as Colson. Environmental changes figured here as well, with the presidency enmeshed in the political maelstrom of the civil rights and Vietnam eras. Interest group organization had grown increasingly salient, most obviously among African Americans but also among Hispanics, whom Nixon saw as potential allies. Antiwar protest had strengthened the group identities and visibility of other groups, notably "hard-hat" blue-collar workers and "white ethnics." This "Silent Majority" formed an inviting target for a preemptive president seeking to construct a majority coalition. Still, the identification and exploitation of such opportunities arguably was one of Nixon's (and his staff's) major strategic accomplishments. It is not at all clear that, confronting similar opportunities, a Barry Goldwater or a Nelson Rockefeller, for instance, would have seized them in the same way.

Structuring for speechwriting also changed in important ways under Nixon. In part, this was due to the continuing increase, observable since at least the time of Herbert Hoover, in the demand for the president's words. Partisan learning may well have played a role here as well. Nixon's segregation of his writing team in a unit of its own had its clearest parallel, albeit on a much smaller scale, under Eisenhower. Yet Nixon's attention to speech style and content and his carefully targeted use of various writers also suggest presidential strategic influence. Notably, as Nixon became distracted by the Watergate investigation, and as Ray Price came to specialize in Watergate speeches, the balance of the writing staff grew isolated from the president and the policy decision process. The informal governance structures that had effectively linked the writers to both during the first term atrophied without active presidential participation.

Although the counsel's office can be seen as having features of both policy and coordination, we have grouped it with outreach in light of the way Nixon used it. Nixon's counsels were not the policy advisers they had been under Democratic presidents. Beginning with John Dean, they were more concerned with such activities as vetting executive branch and judicial appointments, maintaining liaison with the Justice Department, and representing the administration in the courts. Despite being something of a throwback to Eisenhower's counsel, Nixon's office represented a sharp break with the precedents set by Democratic presidents, as well as a significant enlargement of the unit and its duties beyond the Eisenhower model.

At the same time, as Proposition 2 predicted, one outreach structure, congressional liaison, was far less influenced by presidential choice variables. In this instance, a well-established model existed—a legacy of Eisenhower, but one that both Kennedy and Johnson had embraced. Nixon innovated only at the margins, awarding the effective head of the office, Bryce Harlow (and later Clark MacGregor), the rank of counselor. This initiative—aimed at strengthening the hierarchical relationship between White House legislative activities and presidential priorities—was effective only sporadically. Overall, as expected, the structuring of the legislative liaison unit remained mostly stable and seemed to be a thoroughly institutionalized operation. To be sure, Nixon's preferences and strategies affected congressional relations, mostly negatively, but they exercised little influence over White House structuring.

Structuring for Policy Processing. In the early modern presidency, with the exception of national security, structuring for policy processing was largely hit-or-miss. Not until the Johnson administration did a specialized policy staff emerge in the area of domestic policy, and even that did not have full control over domestic initiatives within the White House. Structuring for economic policy in the Executive

Office became institutionalized, but its appearance in the White House itself was rare. When we did find such structuring, we attributed it mostly to presidential goals and strategies, as well as to the relative priority a president put on a given policy arena.[8] Clearly, Nixon was an innovator here, creating the Domestic Council (DC) and, in the area of economics, both the Council on International Economic Policy and the Council on Economic Policy. Were these reflections of Nixon's specific policy objectives or perhaps of an overall structural strategy? The answer is complex.

The cabinet-council plus staff format in national security policy was distinctly *not* a product of Harry Truman's preferences; he opposed the idea and used the National Security Council (NSC) apparatus far less than he might have. Nevertheless, with the Cold War impending, the kind of policy planning and coordination that such structuring could provide seemed essential. After Congress basically forced the NSC on Truman, all his successors used it actively and tended to expand its influence, including that of the NSC staff. Something similar might be said about Nixon and domestic policy. After experimenting with the odd couple of Arthur Burns and Daniel Patrick Moynihan as domestic advisers, Nixon concluded that more orderly structuring was necessary, both to bring decision closure and to reduce the amount of time he and senior staffers spent refereeing disputes. At the same time, although he was beginning to withdraw from domestic policy innovation as an administration priority, the president evidently understood that integration and control of the work of the executive branch departments and the Office of Management and Budget (OMB) was essential—hence the creation of the Domestic Council and its staff. To this extent, one can attribute the establishment of the DC to Nixon's objectives.

Nonetheless, the demand for solutions to the domestic crises of the day— whether urban rioting, campus disorder, or longer-term issues such as health care and education—had escalated under Nixon's predecessors. Johnson's prototype domestic policy staff was a response, and it laid down something of a precedent. The NSC provided yet another model. In the face of environmental demand for at least the articulation of policy positions, Nixon relied on nonpartisan learning in the form of recent White House experience. Thus, there was more to Nixon's innovation than his particular preferences, an interpretation consistent with the observation that he did not adopt the idea of the DC until the feuding between Burns and Moynihan (and the mediating efforts of John Ehrlichman) convinced him that he needed something better.

In economic policy, Nixon followed in Eisenhower's footsteps when he brought the issue area into the White House Office proper. Once more, there was clear environmental pressure on the administration: a weak domestic economy. At the same time, Nixon's evident affection for the cabinet-council form and his desire to centralize policy matters in the White House were important influences. Indeed, Nixon's failed effort to reorganize the domestic and economic cabinet departments, followed by his quixotic designation of "supersecretaries" in lieu of congressional cooperation on reorganization, underscored his interest in integrating the domestic and economic policy streams.

Only in national security policy was the story a relatively simple one. Nixon and Henry Kissinger inherited an NSC system that had proved itself under Eisenhower and (in a different form) Kennedy, although it had fallen into some disarray under LBJ. Nixon also accepted the precedent, from Kennedy, of a strong assistant for national security affairs, something of a counterpart to the chief of staff. On the whole, it is safe to conclude that structuring in this area was, much like congressional relations, already institutionalized and was likely to be modified only at the margins. Here, although there was some change, nothing approached clear discontinuity.

From Nixon to Ford

On its face, Proposition 3 may seem obvious: organization of the White House would change little under Gerald Ford. Ford assumed the presidency under the worst possible circumstances and had little time and no mandate to make major changes in organization. Yet in the post-Watergate atmosphere, any new president needed to assure the public that he was as unlike Nixon as possible. Ford did this, promising an "open" administration with, in particular, no dominant chief of staff interposed between the president and the cabinet or his other advisers. In addition, some of Ford's closest advisers, such as Robert Hartmann, adamantly urged him to dismantle the Nixon staff system and dismiss virtually all of Nixon's aides. Much about his situation might have impelled Ford to attempt a major housecleaning and restructuring.

Nevertheless, our examination of the Ford White House revealed little in the way of serious restructuring. Although he formally kept his vow not to have a chief of staff, Ford invested his "staff coordinators" with nearly all the powers common to a chief of staff other than control of access to the president—and even there, the coordinators ultimately exercised some leverage. This change was more terminological than substantive. The structures for coordination and supervision, along with the relevant processes (e.g., decision memoranda coordinated by the staff secretary), remained in place. The only notable alteration was Ford's restoration of the job of cabinet secretary.

Elsewhere, in almost every case, Ford continued in Nixon's footsteps. His policy staffs mirrored Nixon's, although the Economic Policy Board had more clout and more success than Nixon's Council on Economic Policy. The basic workings of the NSC staff did not change. In domestic policy, Ford seemed to signal an aggressive new approach when he turned Domestic Council operations over to Vice President Nelson Rockefeller. Yet that approach was short-lived, principally because Ford did not share his vice president's desire for a proactive administration role in the area. Structurally, the DC staff simply persisted, although its actual influence continued the decline that had begun in the later months of the Nixon administration.

Since much of the blame for White House excesses under Nixon had focused on Charles Colson and his public liaison operation, one might have expected change there. Yet once more, none occurred. William Baroody, Colson's successor in Nixon's second term, continued to head the unit, albeit formally reporting to Counselor John Marsh. Obviously, the tactics of the office had to change, in accord with Ford's theme of openness, but it seems that abandoning the idea of linking interest groups directly to the White House was never even contemplated. Similar stories can be told about the counsel's office and the writing staff, where minor changes did not amount to anything like a rejection of Nixon's basic approach.

The Office of Communications was the main exception to Proposition 3, at least for a time. By the end of Nixon's first term, the unit had fallen under the influence of Colson, and much of his souring reputation had rubbed off on it, even after he left the White House. Ford did act to de-emphasize the office, relying more on the Republican National Committee. Even so, in 1976, in the face of the pressures of a presidential campaign, Ford and Dick Cheney brought back Nixon veteran David Gergen to head a revitalized communications operation, staffed mainly with Nixon veterans. In a similar vein, the Ford White House was less obsessed with polling and less aggressive about seeking public-opinion data than the Nixon people had been. Nevertheless, Ford aides did not pull back entirely, and an active polling and poll analysis capability remained, located in the staff coordinator's hierarchy, essentially where it had been under Nixon.

From Ford to Carter

The prediction in Proposition 4, that little would change in the transition from Gerald Ford to Jimmy Carter, certainly flies in the face of the conventional wisdom and presidential pronouncements of the time. Carter ran for president as the "anti-Nixon," promising, among other things, to run his White House in a way that was altogether different not only from Nixon but also from Ford. That meant having no chief of staff (or anything resembling one), implementing a spokes-of-the-wheel staffing system, and having a smaller, leaner White House. Not only Carter's rhetoric but also much of his early planning reflected predictable partisan learning, harking back to the golden ages of Truman and Kennedy.

Newly elected President Carter carried through with his plan to forgo a chief of staff. Although top aide Hamilton Jordan was clearly "first among equals," he eschewed management responsibility and functioned more as a political adviser. A management committee of senior aides handled routine matters, while Carter himself became at least sporadically involved in the details of White House management. Indeed, the president's staffing arrangements, along with his proclivity for detail, were widely blamed for his evident overload and difficulties focusing on the larger issues of public policy. Finally, in the face of public and inside-the-beltway criticism, Carter relented and named Jordan chief of staff.

In the areas of outreach and policy, however, the changes wrought by the Carter

White House were far less extensive than might have been anticipated. Nixon's most controversial innovation, the Office of Public Liaison, was retained, although at the outset, it focused rather narrowly on disadvantaged groups. When Midge Costanza's star faded, she was partially replaced by Anne Wexler, whose mandate extended beyond public liaison. With the 1980 political season looming, however, a cluster of aides with specific interest group responsibilities came on board. In effect, then, although structuring for public liaison fragmented under Carter (less a consequence of planning than of White House turf politics), the overall effort to keep interest groups connected to the White House was probably greater than it had been under either Nixon or Ford. Here, the political environment probably was key. The expectations of constituency groups, especially those directed toward a Democratic president, virtually compelled a White House response.

The Office of Communications was not a part of the Carter design, although some of its activities were retained in the Office of Media Liaison, attached to the press office. Yet when Gerald Rafshoon came into the White House, communications activities became at least as central to Carter as they had been to Ford. Even when Rafshoon left for the reelection campaign, media liaison's role expanded to the point where it could fairly be viewed as a continuation of the Nixon-Ford design. Again, although structuring under Carter was more fluid, the underlying task never went away. Neither did attention to polling, which was probably at least as strong under Carter as under his predecessors, enhanced by the presence of pollster Pat Caddell on the staff. Once more, an increasingly complex political environment required continuation of the main structures and strategies of Carter's predecessors.

Carter's counsel's office initially followed the Nixon-Ford script closely, focusing on, for example, relations with the Justice Department and clearing presidential appointees. When Lloyd Cutler arrived, however, the veteran Democrat saw himself returning to the tradition of a Clark Clifford; he sought to play more of a policy role in the administration and to focus less on narrow legal issues. Below Cutler, the unit itself retained the same structuring and performed basically the same tasks it had under Robert Lipshutz. The result was a kind of triumph of structure over ambition: Cutler partially succeeded in defining his own activities as White House counsel, but he left the office he headed much as it had been.

Meanwhile, in speechwriting, the organizational turmoil that helped define the Carter White House was most evident, with the writers failing to flourish under the wing of Press Secretary Jody Powell, then faring only marginally better under Gerald Rafshoon and Alonzo McDonald. Most important for our analysis, however, is that Carter apparently never considered doing without a specialized writing staff; nor were any of his top aides major speechwriters. Even though neither Ford nor Carter discovered a way to duplicate Nixon's first-term success in managing his writers, the writing staff had become a stable part of the White House. Given the ever-increasing demand for presidential words, one might argue that it could hardly have been otherwise.

Carter's most notable contribution to the annals of White House structuring came in an unexpected area: congressional relations. In this most clearly institutionalized realm, Carter initially set up a staff under Frank Moore that soon resembled its predecessors in structuring and operation. Yet, goaded by legislative frustrations (and criticism of Moore), Jordan, Wexler, and McDonald developed the "task force" approach to focus assets from throughout the administration on high-priority legislative items, using the congressional liaison office as a point of coordination. This did not alter the basic structuring or operations of the unit itself, but it was an innovative strategy for using it. Here, presidential (and senior aides') priorities and strategy were important in pushing congressional relations toward a new structural pattern.

The least changed aspects of the Carter White House were the policy structures. The Domestic Policy Staff lost the cabinet-council format but otherwise continued to do much the same work as its predecessors. In the economic policy arena, Carter, like Nixon and Ford, established a White House coordinating unit, the Economic Policy Group. Although less successful than Ford's Economic Policy Board, it gave bipartisan validation to the idea that White House coordination was central to economic policy planning. Finally, the NSC staff operated much as it had under the Republicans, with Zbigniew Brzezinski treating Henry Kissinger as something of a role model for a strong national security assistant. Roughly congruent structuring was thus rewarded by longevity and, in our use of the term, institutionalization.

On the whole, then, Jimmy Carter began with a good deal of the Nixon-Ford White House apparatus and finished with more of it. With this kind of adoption by a Democrat, the basic Nixon model of White House organization had passed the initial test of institutionalization. Moreover, it became, for all of Carter's successors to date, something of a standard model of White House organization and governance.

PARTISAN LEARNING AND THE STANDARD MODEL

During the first era of the modern presidency, two general approaches to governing the White House clearly emerged. The Democrats' model, descended from Franklin Roosevelt and, especially, Harry Truman, stressed relatively small staffs, generalist advisers at the top, and an overall spokes-of-the-wheel structuring, with the president as the hub and a half dozen or more advisers with direct access to him. The Republicans' model, established by Dwight Eisenhower, stressed a clearer division of labor and an overall formal hierarchical structure, managed by a strong chief of staff and supplemented by an array of formal and informal governance structures linking the various elements of the system. Richard Nixon brought the Eisenhower model back, emphatically, with additions to try to respond to the more complex and more demanding political and policy environments of the late 1960s and early 1970s. Mostly against his will, but driven by perceived environmental expectations and imperatives, Jimmy Carter acquiesced in keeping or reinventing virtually the entire Nixon model. For the most part, consistent with Proposition 5, the era of sharp partisan difference over the structuring of the White House was over.

Although Carter's successors would modify this standard model in a variety of ways (such as Ronald Reagan's first-term "troika"), none would abandon it. Still, partisan differences lingered. Carter's only Democratic successor, Bill Clinton, initially established what could be called at best a "weak" chief of staff system, headed by Mack McLarty. The results, widely criticized as chaotic, may have spelled doom for even that modification of the Nixon model. When Leon Panetta replaced McLarty and brought discipline to the White House, he essentially reimposed the kind of "strong" chief of staff system favored by Republicans since Eisenhower.

Below the level of the chief of staff, the key elements of Nixon's model clearly have become institutionalized parts of the White House. One could hardly conceive of a contemporary presidency without communications, public liaison, press, and congressional-relations offices. Polling and public-opinion analyses are pursued avidly in the modern White House, even to the extent of using focus groups.[9] Likewise, speechwriting staffs, legal counsel's offices, and White House–Executive Office policy staffs have become routine elements of the presidency. The nonpartisan learning that reinforces the standard model has come to be embodied in networks of individuals who held similar jobs in different White Houses, such as the "Judson Welliver Society" of former speechwriters.[10] Major Washington think tanks and associated scholars now produce volumes of advice on staffing the White House, virtually all of it embodying the "conventional wisdom" of the standard model.[11] Indeed, scholarly debate over White House structuring has largely died down, and what Nixon wrought is widely accepted as the template for all.[12]

GOVERNANCE STRUCTURING: VARIATION AND IMPLICATIONS

Even though the model may be standardized, the actual operation of any White House is distinctive. In part, this reflects the strong individuals who populate administrations, beginning with the president. In part, it is due to considerable variation in the nature of structuring in different White Houses. One can see such a contrast in the administrations of the 1970s. The Nixon White House, much like Eisenhower's,[13] supplemented the hierarchical staff system with a wide array of governance structures, many of them collegial-consensual, for planning such things as public-relations activities, media strategies, and presidential travel. Virtually all our accounts of Nixon's staff describe participation in such structures, which formed a kind of communications web that helped the diverse elements of the staff work mostly in concert. In its routine activities, at least, Nixon's White House showed important—and arguably necessary—adaptations to the limitations of sheer hierarchy and the dangers of specialization. Chief of Staff Bob Haldeman, a veteran of the advertising business and someone familiar with the sharing of plans and ideas, played a key role in establishing such informal responses.

At the same time, the Nixon experience highlights the dangers of informal or ad hoc structuring that is not directly linked to more formal procedures of approval and oversight. The activities that got Nixon in trouble—such as those involving the "plumbers" and the Watergate cover-up—took place *outside* of the White House staffing system and were unconnected to other governance structures.

The Ford administration, although emulating Nixon's in most ways, was less successful in creating structures that brought relevant players and necessary expertise from various parts of the White House to bear on common problems. A differentiation dynamic that might have been expected to generate such structuring rarely operated. In part, this was because certain key actors, notably Counselor Robert Hartmann, were suspicious of almost any routinely used structures and preferred to hold themselves aloof from active participation in them. The results, perhaps shown most clearly in the working of Hartmann's speechwriting shop, were jealousy, lack of necessary communication, and occasional outright rivalry and conflict.

Similar difficulties plagued the Carter White House. There, the problem was not the kind of classic "office politics" that Ford confronted but rather an excessive "turfiness," which stemmed at least in part from the lack of a unifying, hierarchical backbone. Carter staffers commonly referred to their operations as overly "compartmentalized," with too little communication across unit boundaries. Again, the differentiation dynamic was blocked, and the governance structuring needed to facilitate coordination simply did not emerge.

Thus, the appearance of congruent governance structuring is, as the Ford and Carter examples suggest, not an inevitable phenomenon. It must be established, and that creation is an act of organizational leadership.

Informal governance structures are often temporary. Yet the White House in the 1970s and beyond has featured highly formal structures as well, mainly in the policy areas.[14] These structures, meant to link the diverse inputs of departments and agencies and to both integrate information and mediate among different perspectives, are among the most difficult to operate. Moreover, they cannot be seen as any single type of structure. Sometimes, they abet consensual sharing; on other occasions, they must resolve conflict through mediation, argumentation, or the intervention of an adjudicator, such as the president or chief of staff. The analysis of these structures presented here shows that although all were similarly designed, not all were similarly successful.

If one looks at those structures that cannot be counted as great successes, one sees that key players either opposed them (e.g., OMB and sometimes the president in the case of Ford's DC staff; Brzezinski and the NSC staff in the case of the Economic Policy Group under Carter) or were reluctant to cede authority to them (as cabinet secretaries were in dealing with Carter's Domestic Policy Staff). In some instances, strong staff leadership was lacking (for example, Nixon's DC after

Ehrlichman left). No simple prescriptions can prevent such problems, but it is important to note both their existence and possible sources of the difficulties.

CONCLUSION

A consideration of the relationship between structuring and success leads to—indeed, in a sense, presupposes—one final consideration. From the standpoint of a president, what exactly does a well-governed White House provide? Why, for instance, have many scholars and White House veterans alike insisted that the "standard model" be adopted? What would happen if it weren't? What is lost if informal structuring does not effectively supplement the formal structures of the model?

The negative examples in our account of White House governance may be instructive in addressing these questions. For instance, Jimmy Carter's determination to work without a chief of staff cost him dearly, in the estimation of participants and observers alike. More dramatically, Richard Nixon's placement of his most nefarious operations outside the formal and informal governance structures of his White House led directly to his downfall. One could argue that insulating such activities from the scrutiny provided by orderly decision processes led to the dysfunctional perceptions and choices that Janis has labeled "groupthink."[15] More recently, Bill Clinton's first eighteen months in office, with a weak chief of staff and a general lack of formal structuring, were widely criticized, and poor staff governance was blamed in part for his series of public-relations gaffes.[16]

One can also learn from an inspection of what has worked well. After all, the standard model emerged mainly out of experience with what worked or, as we would put it, with structures that were congruent with their decision settings. The policy structures of the Nixon White House, for instance, probably provided as close an approximation to "multiple advocacy" as one could find in a large organization that operates in a complex and turbulent environment. At the same time, the hierarchical structuring evident in Nixon's overall staff system allowed a quick response to the kind of crises that leave no time for careful scrutiny or diverse inputs. Similarly, the Nixon White House created structures that reached out to the public and to interest groups; this permitted the administration to gauge with some accuracy which environmental demands were particularly salient (as well as zones of indifference), and it evoked positive reactions from at least some constituency groups. Perhaps most important, the Nixon White House was thick with collegial structuring that brought together political and public-relations experts and policy specialists and generally achieved the difficult task of blending their ideas. For presidents needing to "test reality" in order to respond wisely to it, nothing—except perhaps the wisdom of the president—is as important.[17]

Rather clearly, the value of governance structuring interacts with presidential objectives and strategies. The fate of the various domestic policy staffs offers an apt illustration. Nixon's DC staff showed promise as a link between the White

House and the departments, but it failed when it turned to the task of micro-managing administrators. For Ford, who had little in the way of a domestic policy agenda, the Domestic Council under the aggressive leadership of Vice President Rockefeller became a nuisance. Later, with Rockefeller gone, the DC staff was almost superfluous. Under Carter, however, the domestic staff took on the task of mediating between the departments and the president and became, in the end, a generally effective part of the White House.

A study like this presents complex stories and evidence, not simple lessons. Yet there appears to be some wisdom that can be gleaned. The presidency is necessarily a hierarchical organization, since nobody is the president's peer. Experience, especially since the 1970s, shows that it is probably best to accept this and to make hierarchy the baseline principle for structuring a president's staff. It appears equally important, however, to understand that hierarchical structuring in isolation cannot bring about the kind of cooperative planning, multiple-advocacy decision making, and coordinated reactions to complex circumstances that White Houses frequently require. Collegial governance structuring, both formal and informal, is also essential to a successful White House. In a time when the once unfamiliar term *homeland security* suggests an urgent need for organizational planning and cooperation and conjures up dire consequences should they be lacking, this lesson is only more powerful and compelling.

Notes

INTRODUCTION

1. See, e.g., John P. Burke, *The Institutional Presidency: Organizing and Managing the White House from FDR to Clinton,* 2d ed. (Baltimore: Johns Hopkins University Press, 2000); George A. Krause and Jeffrey E. Cohen, "Opportunity, Constraints, and the Development of the Institutional Presidency: The Issuance of Executive Orders," *Journal of Politics* 62 (February 2000): 88–114.

2. Burke, *Institutional Presidency,* 24. Giving advice during transitions has become virtually a cottage industry. Burke, e.g., footnotes Stephen Hess, "Advice for a President-elect, 1976–77," in *Organizing the Presidency,* 2d ed. (Washington, D.C.: Brookings Institution, 1988); Benjamin W. Heineman and Curtis Hessler, *Memorandum for the President: A Strategic Approach to Domestic Affairs in the 1980s* (New York: Random House, 1980); NAPA, *A Presidency for the 1980s* (Washington, D.C.: National Academy of Public Administration, 1980); and Richard Neustadt's memoranda to Kennedy before he took office (233). One could add the efforts in 2000 by the Center for the Study of the Presidency, the American Enterprise Institute, the Brookings Institution, the Heritage Foundation, and the White House Interview Program.

3. Burke, *Institutional Presidency,* xiii.

4. Charles E. Walcott and Karen M. Hult, *Governing the White House: From Hoover through LBJ* (Lawrence: University Press of Kansas, 1995).

5. Krause and Cohen, "Opportunity, Constraints, and Development."

6. Lyn Ragsdale and John J. Theis III, "The Institutionalization of the American Presidency, 1924–92," *American Journal of Political Science* 41 (October 1997): 1314–15.

7. Our emphasis continues to be the White House Office, along with the National Security Council staff and, for second-era presidents, the domestic and economic policy staffs (most of whom were lodged in separate units in the larger Executive Office of the President).

8. We see such dynamics as being mediated by presidents' or advisers' perceptions (or "constructions") of the relevant environment.

9. More typically, attention (including our own) has focused on the size of the White House staff. Richard Neustadt, for example, noted the "quantum jump" in the number of senior staffers in the Nixon White House (Neustadt to Kenneth Hechler, October 15, 1981, Neustadt Papers, Box 6, Truman Presidential Library); see also Krause and Cohen, "Opportunity, Constraints, and Development"; Walcott and Hult, *Governing the White House,* 8. Yet size can be a misleading indicator, varying in part by how *staff* is defined (e.g., whether total numbers include detailees). More important, in Nixon's case, the key changes were in how the White House staff was used, its increasing complexity, and the associated evolutionary dynamics. In addition, the changes in staff numbers since the late 1960s have not

always involved increases, and much of the change has been discontinuous, with sharp increases or steep declines in particular years. There is often considerable variation across White House subunits, which has led to calls for additional efforts to disaggregate information at least by subunit. See, e.g., John Hart, *The Presidential Branch: From Washington to Clinton* (Chatham, N.J.: Chatham House, 1995), chap.6; Charles E. Walcott and Karen M. Hult, "White House Staff Size: Explanations and Implications," *Presidential Studies Quarterly* 29 (September 1999): 638–56.

10. Cf. Sidney Tarrow, "Bridging the Quantitative-Qualitative Divide in Political Science," *American Political Science Review* 89 (June 1995): 471–74.

11. See also Ragsdale and Theis, "Institutionalization of the American Presidency," 1303, 1315ff.

12. This appears to be consistent with Skowronek, who dates the waning of "pluralist politics" and the emergence of "plebiscitary politics" to 1972. See Stephen Skowronek, *The Politics Presidents Make: Leadership from John Adams to Bill Clinton* (Cambridge: Harvard University Press, 1997), 54–55.

13. Ibid., 44.

14. Such a view is generally consistent with Crockett's definition of an opposition leader: "A president is an opposition leader if he is elected from a political party that does not command the power to define terms of political debate" (David A. Crockett, *The Opposition Presidency: Leadership and the Constraints of History* [College Station: Texas A&M University Press, 2002], 22). Crockett sees Nixon as having entered the presidency at a time that "coincided with a change in electoral arrangements, but not in governing philosophies" (152).

15. Crockett undertakes such an analysis, focusing on "opposition presidents," only some of whom pursued preemptive strategies, as Richard Nixon did (see ibid.).

16. Skowronek, *Politics Presidents Make,* 43.

17. "Third way alternatives of preemptive leaders have not proven very durable" (ibid., 451).

1. SETTING THE STAGE

1. Charles E. Walcott and Karen M. Hult, *Governing the White House: From Hoover through LBJ* (Lawrence: University Press of Kansas, 1995), 11.

2. See, e.g., Karen M. Hult and Charles E. Walcott, *Governing Public Organizations: Politics, Structures, and Institutional Design* (Pacific Grove, Calif.: Brooks/Cole, 1990); Walcott and Hult, *Governing the White House.*

3. Sewell notes that " 'structure' is one of the most important, elusive, and undertheorized concepts in the social sciences" (William H. Sewell, "A Theory of Structure: Duality, Agency, and Transformation," *American Journal of Sociology* 98 [July 1992]: 1). In the literature on the U.S. presidency, discussing the "structure" of the entire White House does not strike us as being very helpful; at least since the presidency of Herbert Hoover, the White House staff has contained multiple structures. An influential example of work that focuses on a single White House structure is Richard Tanner Johnson, *Managing the White House* (New York: Harper and Row, 1974). Although his emphases differ from ours, Kessel similarly highlights multiple staff structures. See, e.g., John Kessel, "The Structure of the Carter White House," *American Journal of Political Science* 27 (1983): 231–63; "The Structure of the Reagan White House," *American Journal of Political Science* 28 (1984): 231–58.

4. For an elaboration of these ideas, see Hult and Walcott, *Governing Public Organizations;* Walcott and Hult, *Governing the White House.*

5. We identified structures empirically by noting the recurrence of interactions (typically, at least three) among individual actors about a limited range of problems or decisions. The greater the number of interactions that involved the same people (or representatives of the same units) and subjects, the greater our confidence that structuring was present. A structure was considered formal if it was mandated or approved by hierarchical authorities. As we reported elsewhere (Karen M. Hult, Charles E. Walcott, and Thomas Weko, "Qualitative Research and the Study of the U.S. Presidency," *Congress and the Presidency* 26 [fall 1999]: 133–52), "formal structures were relatively easy to identify, with indicators of their existence including written procedures, statutory requirements, and agendas and minutes of meetings" (139). Indicators of more informal structures (where there was evidence of repeated exchanges in a task area) included reports on or notes about telephone calls or in-person meetings, exchanges of memos, and copying patterns on memos.

6. Concerns with stability weave throughout the definitive Ragsdale and Theis examination of the institutionalization of the U.S. presidency. See Lyn Ragsdale and John J. Theis III, "The Institutionalization of the American Presidency, 1924–92," *American Journal of Political Science* 41 (October 1997): especially 1282–84.

7. Walcott and Hult, *Governing the White House,* 18.

8. Ibid.

9. The emergence of new governance structures typically increases an organization's internal complexity. This may heighten the extent of uncertainty or conflict, which may in turn generate demand for additional governance mechanisms; these demands, if met, can further heighten complexity, causing the cycle to continue. For further discussion, see, e.g., Hult and Walcott, *Governing Public Organizations,* 38–39; Walcott and Hult, *Governing the White House,* 16ff.

10. For example, Karen M. Hult, "Strengthening Presidential Decision-Making Capacity," *Presidential Studies Quarterly* 30 (March 2000): 27–46; B. Guy Peters, *The Future of Governing: Four Models,* 2d rev. ed. (Lawrence: University Press of Kansas, 2001), 192ff.; Andrew Rudalevige, *Managing the President's Program: Presidential Leadership and Legislative Policy Formulation* (Princeton, N.J.: Princeton University Press, 2002); Walcott and Hult, *Governing the White House.*

11. For example, Terry M. Moe, "The Politicized Presidency," in *The New Direction in American Politics,* ed. John E. Chubb and Paul E. Peterson (Washington, D.C.: Brookings Institution, 1985); Thomas J. Weko, *The Politicizing Presidency: The White House Personnel Office, 1948–1994* (Lawrence: University Press of Kansas, 1995); Rudalevige, *Managing the President's Program;* David E. Lewis, *Presidents and the Politics of Agency Design: Political Insulation in the United States Government Bureaucracy, 1946–1997* (Stanford, Calif.: Stanford University Press, 2003). Cf. Kathleen Thelen, "Historical Institutionalism in Comparative Politics," *Annual Review of Political Science* 2 (1999): 369–404.

12. For findings that support such a focus on strategic presidents, see Rudalevige, *Managing the President's Program,* 98–99, 112. In King, Keohane, and Verba's terms, then, our interest here is on the *systematic* variance in presidential behavior; see Gary King, Robert O. Keohane, and Sidney Verba, *Designing Social Inquiry: Scientific Inference in Qualitative Research* (Princeton, N.J.: Princeton University Press, 1994).

13. See also Hult, "Strengthening Presidential Decision-Making Capacity," 29; Walcott and Hult, *Governing the White House,* 21–22.

14. Walcott and Hult, *Governing the White House,* 259–63.

15. Ibid., 254–55.

16. Cf. Hult, "Strengthening Presidential Decision-Making Capacity," 43.

17. Stephen Skowronek, *The Politics Presidents Make: Leadership from John Adams to Bill Clinton* (Cambridge: Harvard University Press, 1997), 49, 46.

18. To enhance comparability, we coded the data obtained from these multiple sources using the same categories we employed in studying the Hoover through Johnson presidencies, supplemented by new categories to capture the additional tasks and units that appeared in the Nixon, Ford, and Carter administrations. Since we collected and coded most of the data electronically, we were able to use a computerized database management program (SuperFile) to search for key words within and across administrations. Data and additional information are available from the authors.

19. Tim Buthe, "Taking Temporality Seriously: Modeling History and the Use of Narratives as Evidence," *American Political Science Review* 96 (September 2002): 482.

20. Gary King, "The Methodology of Presidential Research," in *Researching the Presidency: Vital Questions, New Approaches,* ed. George C. Edwards III, John Kessel, and Bert Rockman (Pittsburgh: University of Pittsburgh Press, 1993), 404. For more general reflections on the challenges of this sort of empirical work (as well as possible ways of addressing them), see Hult, Walcott, and Weko, "Qualitative Research."

2. STAFF ORGANIZATION AND GOVERNANCE

1. As Dickinson has noted, FDR got advice to the contrary from the scholars of the Brownlow Committee, who called for a staff head, perhaps modeled on the British cabinet secretary. FDR, of course, rejected this advice. See Matthew Dickinson, *Bitter Harvest: FDR, Presidential Power, and the Growth of the Presidential Branch* (New York: Cambridge University Press, 1997), chap. 3.

2. Johnson has made the strongest case for collegiality, citing the Truman and Kennedy White Houses in particular. See Richard Tanner Johnson, *Managing the White House* (New York: Harper and Row, 1974).

3. Richard E. Neustadt, *Presidential Power* (New York: Wiley, 1960). What we call the Democratic model encompasses what Richard Tanner Johnson called "collegial" and "competitive" styles. Johnson's "formalistic" style corresponds to what we call the Republican model.

4. Descriptions of the Eisenhower model can be found in Andrew J. Goodpaster, "Organizing the White House," in *The Eisenhower Presidency: Eleven Intimate Perspectives of Dwight D. Eisenhower,* ed. Kenneth W. Thompson (Lanham, Md.: University Press of America, 1982), and Stephen Hess with James P. Pfiffner, *Organizing the Presidency,* 3d ed. (Washington, D.C.: Brookings Institution, 2002). For an argument that this system was less rigid and formal than often thought, see Charles Walcott and Karen M. Hult, "White House Organization as a Problem of Governance: The Eisenhower System," *Presidential Studies Quarterly* 24 (1994): 334–35.

5. See Walcott and Hult, "White House Organization as a Problem of Governance." For further elaboration and general praise of Eisenhower's decision-making arrangements, see Phillip G. Henderson, *Managing the Presidency: The Eisenhower Legacy—From Kennedy to Reagan* (Boulder, Colo.: Westview, 1988), and John P. Burke and Fred I. Greenstein, in

collaboration with Larry Berman and Richard Immerman, *How Presidents Test Reality: Decisions on Vietnam, 1954 and 1965* (New York: Basic Books, 1988).

6. Charles E. Walcott and Karen M. Hult, *Governing the White House: From Hoover through LBJ* (Lawrence: University Press of Kansas, 1995), 248–50. As early as December 1964, Johnson was asking for an inventory of staff titles, duties, and salaries, hoping (vainly) to cut his staff. See Jack Valenti to Bill Moyers, 12/11/64, Subject File Ex FG 11-8, Box 70, Johnson Presidential Library. As late as March 1968, essentially the same request was being made, this time of Chief Executive Clerk William Hopkins. Tom Johnson to Hopkin (*sic*), 3/13/68, Subject File, Ex FG 11-8, Box 68. Johnson also demanded organizational charts. Staffers, knowing that LBJ's interest would wane, simply recycled charts that had been made previously. See Robert Kintner to Bill Moyers, et al., 5/16/66, and Kintner to staff, 8/15/66, Subject File Gen FG 11-8, Box 70, Johnson Presidential Library.

7. H. R. Haldeman with Joseph DiMona, *The Ends of Power* (New York: Times Books, 1978), 50.

8. The "Prussian efficiency" of Haldeman's White House was conceded even by its critics, and it had many admirers. For instance, Jerry Jones, who served under both Nixon and Ford, said that he considered Haldeman the best manager he had ever seen. Jones, interview with Stephen Wayne, Hyde/Wayne Interviews, 3, Ford Presidential Library.

9. The best known of these arguments is Thomas Cronin, "The Swelling of the Presidency," *Saturday Review* 1 (February 1973): 30–36; reprinted in Harry A. Bailey Jr., ed., *Classics of the American Presidency* (Oak Park, Ill.: Moore, 1980).

10. Haldeman, *Ends of Power,* 51–52.

11. Dan Rather and Gary Paul Gates, *The Palace Guard* (New York: Warner, 1975), 37.

12. Haldeman, *Ends of Power,* 52.

13. Rather and Gates, *Palace Guard,* 183–84.

14. The atmosphere around Haldeman and Nixon could only be described as "macho," right down to the deprecation of women as administrators. For instance, political adviser Harry Dent tried to convince Haldeman to give Dent's assistant, Rose Smith, the title of staff assistant (an administrator's title). At one point, Haldeman relented and gave it to her, but then he took it back and would not budge further. Later, in a letter to Anne Armstrong in the White House, Dent noted, "I wrestled with Haldeman and his office on this matter before leaving the White House, but I still could not do any good in correcting this injustice." He blamed the problem on a "hang-up he [Haldeman] had on rewarding women with key positions and titles." Dent to Armstrong, 10/4/73, White House Special Files, Staff Member and Office Files, David C. Hoopes, Box 10, "White House Certificates—1973," Nixon Papers.

15. Haldeman, *Ends of Power,* 53.

16. Rather and Gates, *Palace Guard,* 66.

17. He did, however, participate in "political" group meetings along with Harry Dent, Bryce Harlow, Robert Finch, Donald Rumsfeld, and Dwight Chapin, beginning in mid-1970.

18. Haig to Senior Staff, 5/23/73, White House Special Files, Staff Member and Office Files, Alexander M. Haig, Box 40, "Haig Memoranda—1973," Nixon Papers.

19. Transcript of Dom Bonafede interview with Haig, August 16, 1973, White House Special Files, Staff Member and Office Files, Alexander M. Haig 1970–1974, Box 4, "Haig Chron—August," 1.

20. Timmons to Haig, May 11, 1973, White House Special Files, Staff Member and Office Files, Alexander M. Haig, Box 40, "Haig Memoranda—1973," Nixon Papers. Haig sent the memo promptly.

21. Jerry Jones, staff secretary under both Nixon and Ford, noted that there were really two Nixon White Houses, Haldeman's and Haig's. Haldeman's, he argued, was "outstanding" in terms of management. Haig's, like Ford's, was more loosely and less proactively run. Jones, Wayne interview, 3–4.

22. Alexander M. Haig Jr. with Charles McCarry, *Inner Circles: How America Changed the World: A Memoir* (New York: Warner, 1992), 345.

23. Roy L. Ash, oral history interview with Raymond H. Geselbracht and Frederick J. Graboske, 1/13/88, Middleburg, Va., Oral Histories, Nixon Presidential Materials, 53.

24. Ibid., 12.

25. Butterfield to Haldeman, January 2, 1973, White House Special Files, Staff Member and Office Files, Alexander P. Butterfield, Box 5, "Alex Butterfield (January, 1973)," Nixon Papers. In summarizing his job, which by then also included cabinet secretary, Butterfield listed twenty-six separate responsibilities, some broken down into as many as nine distinct tasks or areas.

26. These included the Security Office, the Office of Presidential Papers (run in conjunction with the National Archives), the Office of Special Files, and the president's receptionists.

27. One of Butterfield's recurrent headaches was getting staff members to write and submit such memos. See, e.g., Butterfield to Haldeman, April 7, 1969, Butterfield to Peter Flanigan, March 3, 1970, Butterfield to Ray Price, March 31, 1970, all in Butterfield Files, Box 1, Nixon Papers.

28. See Charles E. Walcott, Shirley Anne Warshaw, and Stephen J. Wayne, "The Chief of Staff," *Presidential Studies Quarterly* 31 (2001): 478–79, 482.

29. For instance, during a February 5, 1969, meeting between Nixon and science adviser Lee DuBridge, Butterfield noted that " 'Tim' [King Timahoe, the president's Irish setter] pulled down one of the large flags which stand to the right of the President's desk." White House Special Files, Staff Member and Office Files, Alexander P. Butterfield, Box 1, "Alex Butterfield (Feb 1969)," Nixon Papers.

30. Congressional-relations staffer Ken BeLieu initially resisted Butterfield's intrusion into the effort, though he relented when Butterfield, as "action coordinator," was put under BeLieu's overall supervision. BeLieu to Nixon, May 1, 1969, White House Special Files, Staff Member and Office Files, Alexander P. Butterfield, Box 1, "Alex Butterfield (May 1969)," Nixon Papers. After the ABM campaign ended, Butterfield was not given similar tasks again.

31. This group eventually expanded to include Staff Secretary Ken Cole, political adviser Lyn Nofziger, Klein aide Jeb Magruder, and William Safire, with Haldeman sometimes sitting in instead of Butterfield. Butterfield to Nixon, October 12, 1969, White House Special Files, Staff Member and Office Files, Alexander P. Butterfield, Box 1, "Alex Butterfield (Oct 1969)," Nixon Papers.

32. Haldeman to Safire, Nofziger, Magruder, Chapin, Ziegler, Klein, Harry Dent, Cole, Butterfield, October 10, 1969, White House Special Files, Staff Member and Office Files, Alexander P. Butterfield, Box 8, "Memoranda Received Oct thru Dec '69," Nixon Papers. The recipients of this memo constituted the group. After a few months, they abandoned regular meetings for ad hoc meetings of only "needed" participants. See the memo from Magruder to the (now expanded) group, April 15, 1970, Staff Member and Office Files, Harry S. Dent, Box 12, "Presidential Objective[s] Planning Group (2)," Nixon Papers.

33. See Cole to Harlow, et al., n.d., 1969, Staff Member and Office Files, Harry S. Dent,

Box 2, "1969 Staff Memos #4," and Dent to Butterfield, January 21, 1970, Staff Member and Office Files, Alexander P. Butterfield, "Memoranda Received Jan–June 1970," Nixon Papers.

34. Butterfield to Chapin, Brown and Bull, 7/9/70, White House Special Files, Staff Member and Office Files, Alexander P. Butterfield, Box 2, "Alex Butterfield (Jul 1970)," Nixon Papers.

35. Butterfield to Nixon, December 5, 1969, Staff Member and Office Files, Alexander P. Butterfield, Box 1, "Alex Butterfield (Dec 1969)," Nixon Papers. In a December 1, 1969, memo to Haldeman (same folder), Butterfield explained why Ross Perot had backed out of funding the production of "Silent Majority" pins: the only slogan Perot liked was "United We Stand."

36. For instance, Butterfield to Daniel Patrick Moynihan, July 8, 1970: "The President appreciated your memorandum concerning the NAACP denunciation. He wants you to know that he does understand." White House Special Files, Staff Member and Office Files, Alexander P. Butterfield, "Alex Butterfield (Jul 1970)," Nixon Papers.

37. Geoffrey Shepard to Jim Fazio, November 22, 1972. White House Special Files, Staff Member and Office Files, Box 10, "General Memoranda Rec'd Oct–Dec 1972," Nixon Papers.

38. Agenda for Five O'clock meeting, March 20, 1969, White House Central Files, Subject Files, White House Administration, Box 21, "Ex WH 7 Staff Meetings, Beginning 7/31/69," Nixon Papers.

39. Unsurprisingly, this led to occasional embarrassments. For instance, the son of a wealthy GOP donor was part of a student group that went to the White House to meet Donald Rumsfeld. However, he was held at the gate because he was on a "do not admit" list— he had been arrested once after a peace demonstration. Rumsfeld finally got him in, then complained to Butterfield on April 8, 1971. White House Special Files, Staff Member and Office Files, Alexander P. Butterfield, Box 9, "General Memoranda Rec'd Jan–Mar 1971," Nixon Papers.

40. Butterfield to Tom Maxwell, April 23, 1970, White House Special Files, Staff Member and Office Files, Alexander P. Butterfield, Box 1, "Alex Butterfield (Apr 1970)," Nixon Papers.

41. Butterfield to Jean Robb, February 26, 1971. White House Special Files, Staff Member and Office Files, Alexander P. Butterfield, Box 2, "Alex Butterfield (Feb 1971)," Nixon Papers.

42. Butterfield to Haldeman, July 9, 1970, White House Special Files, Staff Member and Office Files, Alexander P. Butterfield, Box 2, "Alex Butterfield (Jul 1970)," Nixon Papers.

43. See Butterfield to Haldeman, October 5, 1970, White House Special Files, Staff Member and Office Files, Box 2, "Alex Butterfield (Oct 1970)," Nixon Papers. Problems in this area persisted, however, especially with policy staffers such as Ken Cole and Henry Kissinger.

44. Butterfield to Haldeman, September 15, 1971, White House Special Files, Staff Member and Office Files, Alexander P. Butterfield, "Alex Butterfield (Sep 1970)," Nixon Papers.

45. See Walcott and Hult, *Governing the White House,* 100, 246ff.; also Walcott and Hult, "White House Organization as a Problem of Governance."

46. John Whitaker, interview with A. James Reichley, February 15, 1978, Reichley Interviews, 1, Ford Presidential Library.

47. John Whitaker, interview with Susan Yowell, May 4, 1973, Exit Interviews, 28–29, Nixon Papers.

48. Whitaker to Cabinet members, May 27, 1969, White House Special Files, Staff Member and Office Files, Peter Millspaugh, Box 1, "Coordinators Meeting," Nixon Papers.

49. See Walcott and Hult, *Governing the White House,* 110–11, for a brief description of "staff notes" under Eisenhower.

50. On the later efforts, see Richard Nathan, *The Administrative Presidency* (New York: Wiley, 1983).

51. Cole to Whitaker, January 11, 1969, White House Central Files, Subject Files, WH (White House Adm), Box 17, "Ex WH 5 Personnel Mgt, Begin 5/12/69," Nixon Papers.

52. Ibid.

53. Haldeman to Dwight Chapin, April 21, 1969, White House Special Files, Staff Member and Office Files, Dwight L. Chapin, Box 18, "Memoranda From H. R. Haldeman— 1969," Nixon Papers.

54. Butterfield to Haldeman, January 2, 1973 (same memo referred to earlier), White House Special Files, Staff Member and Office Files, Alexander P. Butterfield, Box 5, "Alex Butterfield (January, 1973)," Nixon Papers.

55. Ibid.

56. Dom Bonafede, *National Journal,* May 3, 1975. See also White House Special Files, Staff Member and Office Files, Alexander M. Haig, 1970–1974, Box 12, "Interstaff Communication, 1973—Dave Parker," Nixon Papers.

57. The appointments secretary was not listed under Haldeman's office in the initial White House organizational charts, but Dwight Chapin reported directly to Haldeman and was clearly as much a Haldeman aide as anyone in the White House.

58. As early as June 18, 1969, Chapin was making it clear in a memo to Haldeman that he wanted to concentrate on "planning and over-all guidance" of the appointments operation. White House Special Files, White House Central Files, Subject Files: Confidential Files, 1969–74, Box 51, "PR 7-1 [Granted] 1/20/69 to 5/31/70 [1969–70] [2 of 2]," Nixon Papers.

59. He would be replaced at the outset of Nixon's second term by his assistant, William Henkel.

60. Nixon to Haldeman, October 1, 1969, White House Special Files, White House Central Files, Subject Files: Confidential Files, 1969–74, Box 51, "PR 7-1 [Granted] 1/20/69 to 5/31/70 [1969–70] [2 of 2],"Nixon Papers.

61. Ibid.

62. This was one of four staff groups set up in 1969; the others were domestic policy (chaired by John Ehrlichman), foreign policy (Henry Kissinger), and urban policy (Daniel Patrick Moynihan). Chapin to Haldeman, 9/24/69, White House Central Files, Subject Files, WH (White House Administration), Box 22, "Ex WH 7 Staff Meetings, 8/1/69–12/31/69," Nixon Papers.

63. Safire to Chapin, September 11, 1969, White House Central Files, Subject Files, WH (White House Administration), Box 22, "Ex WH 7 Staff Meetings, 8/1/69–12/31/69," Nixon Papers.

64. Chapin, memo to file, June 15, 1970, White House Central Files, Subject File, WH (White House Administration), Box 22, "Ex WH 7 (Staff Meetings) 1/1/70–8/31/70 (cont.)," Nixon Papers.

65. He would eventually serve time in prison in connection with campaign "dirty tricks" performed at his behest by old college friend Donald Segretti.

66. Noble Melencamp to Bruce Kehrli, n.d. (probably early 1972), White House Staff

Files, Staff Member and Office Files: Office of the Staff Secretary, Box 191, "Staff Secretary Setup [#2]," Nixon Papers.

67. Basic arrangements for control of communications to the president were outlined in a memo from Chief Executive Clerk William Hopkins to Cole, January 24, 1969, White House Central Files, Subject Files, WH (WH Administration), Box 9, "Ex WH 4-1 (Mail), Begin–1/28/69," Nixon Papers. The same file series contains details of relatively minor adjustments made in this process in the early months of the administration.

68. Cole to Haldeman, March 18, 1969, White House Central Files, Subject Files, WH (White House Administration), Box 9, "Ex WH 4-1 (Mail) 3/1/69–4/30/69," Nixon Papers.

69. Ibid.

70. The staff secretary's responsibilities were outlined in a memo from Chief Executive Clerk Noble Melencamp to Bruce Kehrli, evidently upon Kehrli's acceptance of the job. White House Staff Files, Staff Member and Office Files: Office of the Staff Secretary, "Staff Secretary Setup [#2]," Nixon Papers. A list of the responsibilities of the deputy staff secretary was provided by Hoopes toward the end of Nixon's first term. Hoopes to Butterfield, August 4, 1972, White House Special Files, Staff Member and Office Files, Alexander P. Butterfield, Box 10, "General Memoranda Rec'd Jul–Sep 1972," Nixon Papers.

71. Kehrli was perhaps the ideal person for the job: a UCLA graduate who had worked at Haldeman's agency, J. Walter Thompson, before leaving for service in the marines.

72. Wardell was added in part because Kehrli had indicated a desire to leave, with Hoopes being his designated successor. Kehrli to Haig, August 3, 1973, White House Staff Files, Staff Member and Office Files: Office of the Staff Secretary, Box 191, "Staff Secretary Setup [#1]," Nixon Papers.

73. Here and elsewhere, for clarity's sake, we use the spelling "Counselor," which has been employed in recent presidencies. Nixon and Ford, however, actually used the somewhat grander "Counsellor."

74. Kehrli to Haig, February 19, 1974, White House Special Files, Staff Member and Office Files, Hoopes, Box 10, "White House Health Unit—Women," Nixon Papers. Eighty-seven women joined for the same $20 membership fee paid by men. There is no evidence that interest faded.

75. Butterfield to David Parker, July 25, 1972, White House Special Files, Staff Member and Office Files, Alexander P. Butterfield, Box 5, "Alex Butterfield (July 1972)," Nixon Papers.

76. Kehrli to Bennett, June 30, 1973, White House Staff Files, Staff Member and Office Files: Office of the Staff Secretary, Box 191, "Staff Secretary Setup [#1]," Nixon Papers.

77. Ibid.

78. This was the lowest "professional" rank in the White House.

79. For instance, on October 19, 1971, Higby sent to Counsel John Dean a list of action items "outstanding." The list included preparation of an antitrust suit against the *Los Angeles Times,* at which Dean balked. Higby to Dean, White House Special Files, Staff Member and Office Files: John W. Dean III, Box 53, "Office [of Counsel to the President] Activities," Nixon Papers.

80. For example, Higby to Ziegler, White House Special Files, Staff Member and Office Files, Ronald Ziegler, Box 1, "Basic Reorganization of Press Office [1 of 3]," Nixon Papers.

81. Colson to W. Richard Howard, July 7, 1971, White House Special Files, White House Central Files, Subject Files: Confidential Files, 1969–74, Box 12, "[CF] FG-1 [The P], 5/1/70–12/30/70 [1969–70]," Nixon Papers.

82. For instance, Colson to Cole, January 31, 1972, and Colson to Higby, 2/4/72, White House Special Files, Staff Member and Office Files, Charles W. Colson, "Ken Cole [1972]," Nixon Papers.

83. See, e.g., Chapin to Haldeman, October 13, 1969, Higby to Chapin, 10/13/69, White House Special Files, Staff Member and Office Files, Stephen B. Bull, Box 1, "Stephen Bull: Phone Calls Submitted to President [1969]," Nixon Papers.

84. See, e.g., Strachan to Higby, 3/8/71, and Higby to Magruder, January 21, 1971, White House Special Files, Staff Member and Office Files, Gordon Strachan, Box 12, "Republican National Committee Letters to Editor Project," Nixon Papers.

85. Strachan memo, recipient not specified (though clearly to Haldeman), November 27, 1972, White House Special Files, Staff Member and Office Files: Office of the Staff Secretary, Box 162, "White House Office Members; Functions and Current Assignments, 1972, #3," Nixon Papers. Haldeman required all staff members to provide such job descriptions, along with their resignations, after the 1972 election.

86. Ibid.

87. For example, Bull to Chapin, October 3, 1969, White House Special Files, Staff Member and Office Files, Stephen B. Bull, Box 1, "Memoranda for D.L.C. [Dwight L. Chapin] Sept. 1969–May 1970," Nixon Papers.

88. Cole to Chapin, Bull, August 13, 1969, White House Central Files, WH (White House Administration), Box 8, "Ex WH 4 Office Management, Beginning 12/31/69," Nixon Papers.

89. Chapin to Haldeman, November 12, 1969, White House Special Files, Staff Member and Office Files, Dwight L. Chapin, Box 8, "Chronological—Chapin—November 1969," Nixon Papers.

90. Karen M. Hult and Charles E. Walcott, *Governing Public Organizations: Politics, Structures, and Institutional Design* (Pacific Grove, Calif.: Brooks/Cole, 1990), 44, 75, 94.

91. Haldeman, *Ends of Power,* 58–59.

92. The latter criticism was voiced in the Ford White House as the rationale for involving more people in face-to-face decision making with the president. See Robert T. Hartmann, interview with William A. Syers, William A. Syers Papers, Box 1, "Files, 1985—Interviews," Ford Presidential Library. Nonetheless, the decision memo continued to be used in the Ford White House.

93. Haldeman, *Ends of Power,* 57.

94. See, e.g., ibid., 108–9. J. Edgar Hoover, though involved in the plan's preparation, was ultimately the one who scuttled it.

95. Ibid., 319.

96. One could, of course, question the absence of "checks and balances" in the White House decision system. Ultimately, though, because the White House is a hierarchy, efforts to check and balance the president will seldom succeed.

97. Quoted in Robert T. Hartmann, *Palace Politics: An Inside Account of the Ford Years* (New York: McGraw-Hill, 1980), 166.

98. Ibid.

99. Ibid. Ford was urged to pick a chief of staff "who will not be perceived to be eager to be chief of staff."

100. Ibid., 167–68.

101. John Robert Greene, *The Limits of Power: The Nixon and Ford Administrations* (Bloomington: Indiana University Press, 1992), 194.

102. Even the most routine procedures had to be reinvented. For example, the process whereby a member of the counsel's office would meet with demonstrators to receive their petitions had to be explained, cleared, and accepted by the new top aides. See Brent Scowcroft to Haig, 9/2/74, Jerry Jones to Buchen, 9/10/74, Philip Buchen Files, General Subject File, Box 9, "Desegregation—Boston School Busing," Ford Presidential Library.

103. Hartmann, *Palace Politics,* 205–6.

104. Greene, *Limits of Power,* 195.

105. John T. Garrity (of McKinsey) to Thadeus Beal (WH Personnel Office), September 19, 1974, Philip Buchen Files, General Subject File, Box 63, "Transition—Personnel Issues," Ford Presidential Library.

106. Beal to Buchen, September 20, 1974, Philip Buchen Files, General Subject File, Box 63, "Transition—Personnel Issues," Ford Presidential Library.

107. Hartmann, *Palace Politics,* 276–77.

108. Cheney noted that although staffing proceeded as before, Ford, who was more likely to supplement paper with direct conversation, did not always limit himself to the options presented to him. Richard B. Cheney, interview with Stephen Wayne, June 27, 1975, James F. C. Hyde Jr. and Stephen J. Wayne Oral History Collection, Ford Presidential Library.

109. Hartmann, *Palace Politics,* 275.

110. Ibid., 276. Hartmann exempts himself, but not everyone would. See, e.g., Greene, *Limits of Power,* 195.

111. Cf. Cheney, Wayne interview, 12–15; Donald Rumsfeld, interview with A. James Reichley, January 25, 1978, Reichley Interviews, Box 1, "Ford White House Interviews," 5, Ford Presidential Library.

112. Rumsfeld to Ford, October 15, 1974, Jerry H. Jones Files, Box 15, "W.H. Memos— Rumsfeld, Don—for discussion," Ford Presidential Library. This, of course, pointed the finger directly at Hartmann, who was an irregular attendee at senior staff meetings.

113. Ron Nessen to Rumsfeld, October 7, 1974, Ronald H. Nessen Files, Box 44, "WH Staff memoranda, 1974—Rumsfeld," Ford Presidential Library.

114. White House Press Release, December 18, 1974, William J. Baroody, 1974–77 Subject Files, Box 20, "WH Staff Reorg 12/18/74," Ford Presidential Library.

115. Jones, Wayne interview, 3–4.

116. Ibid., 4. Hartmann concurred that Ford was the key but argued (approvingly) that the White House really did not have a definite overall organizational structure because "Ford had never come down hard on the way he wanted the White House to operate." Hartmann, interview with A. James Reichley, December 8, 1977, Reichley Interview Transcripts, Box 1, "Ford White House Interviews," 7, Ford Presidential Library. Rumsfeld tended to agree, noting that Ford did not believe in "the concept of an all-powerful White House" or that "it was necessary to draw all the threads through a single needle head." Rumsfeld, interview with A. James Reichley, January 25, 1978, Reichley Interview Transcripts, Box 1, "Ford White House Interviews," 6, Ford Presidential Library.

117. Rumsfeld to staff, June 13, 1975, James E. Connor Files, Box 15, "Presidential meetings—Follow-up on Presidential Directives (1)," Ford Presidential Library. The memo directed staff to report back through Staff Secretary Connor. Replies were still filtering in as late as December.

118. Max Friedersdorf (congressional-relations office) to Rumsfeld, October 7, 1975, John O. Marsh, General Subject File, Box 10, "Congressional Relations Office (3)," Ford Presidential Library.

119. Rumsfeld to Senior Staff, October 28, 1975, James E. Connor Files, Box 8, "Cheney, Richard (3)," Ford Presidential Library.

120. Philip Buchen, interview with William A. Syers, March 13, 1985, William A. Syers Papers, Box 1, "Files, 1985—Interviews," 2, Ford Presidential Library.

121. James Connor, interview with A. James Reichley, October 19, 1977, Reichley Interviews, Box 1, Ford White House Interviews, 3, Ford Presidential Library.

122. For instance, William Seidman labeled Rumsfeld "a chief of staff," adding that one was necessary in the White House. Interview with William A. Syers, June 12, 1985, William A. Syers Papers, Box 1, "Files, 1985—Interviews," 4, Ford Presidential Library. White House public liaison chief William Baroody agreed that although Rumsfeld was no Haldeman, he was "a lot more than a staff coordinator." Interview with Syers, February 6, 1985, William A. Syers Papers, Box 1, "Files, 1985—Interviews," 2, Ford Presidential Library.

123. Bobby Greene Kilberg (counsel's office), interview with A. James Reichley, December 28, 1977, Reichley Interview Transcripts, Box 1, Ford White House Interviews, 4, Ford Presidential Library; Nelson Rockefeller, interview with A. James Reichley, March 24, 1978, Reichley Interview Transcripts, Box 1, Ford White House Interviews, Ford Presidential Library.

124. Foster O. Chanock, interview with Stephen J. Wayne, December 2, 1976, James F. C. Hyde and Stephen J. Wayne Oral History Collection, 14, Ford Presidential Library. Chanock noted that once the 1976 campaign began in earnest, all the backbiting "just sort of disappeared."

125. White House Study Project, Report No. 1—December 7, 1976, "Analysis of Present White House Office," Ford Presidential Library. This study was prepared by the Carter transition team.

126. See Kathryn D. Tenpas, *Presidents as Candidates: Inside the White House for the Presidential Campaign* (New York: Garland, 1997), especially chaps. 2–3.

127. For instance, Chanock was liaison to the campaign committee for polling information and advertising (obtaining ads so they could be screened by Cheney or Ford), and he worked in scheduling. See Chanock, Wayne interview, 14–15.

128. Wayne suggested this (he had previously written it) during his interview with Cheney, 16, Hyde and Wayne Collection, Ford Presidential Library. Cheney's response (16–18) was that the campaign required new functions, and Cheney was trying to allocate them to the people who could perform them best.

129. Dom Bonafede, *National Journal,* October 9, 1976, 1439. Bonafede also claimed that Gergen and his allies had largely taken over public relations and press policy.

130. For instance, Joe Jenckes (congressional relations, interviewed August 8, 1985) told Syers, "I was never convinced that Cheney was really the chief of staff." Robert Hartmann (interviewed May 3, 1985, by Syers) concurred and suggested that this frustrated Cheney. William A. Syers Papers, Box 1, "Files, 1985—Interviews," Ford Presidential Library.

131. Jones to Rumsfeld, March 11, 1975, Jerry H. Jones Files, Box 20, "Domestic Council," Ford Presidential Library.

132. James E. Connor, interview with Stephen J. Wayne, November 2, 1976, James F. C. Hyde and Stephen J. Wayne Oral History Collection, 12–13, Ford Presidential Library.

133. One result, according to Jerry Jones, was that people in the Ford White House could do mediocre work without anyone saying anything. Still, he thought, "in the end what tended to happen is that all of the good guys tended to come to the top and push aside all the people that couldn't cut it." But it was a long, frustrating process. Jones, Wayne interview, 6–7.

134. Rumsfeld to Connor, September 2, 1975, James E. Connor Files, Box 17, Ford Presidential Library. Rumsfeld was concerned that when Ford wanted a quick response, he was "going out of the system."

135. See Robert T. Hartmann Files, Box 13, "Office—Organization," "Office—Personnel (1)," and "Office—Personnel (2)," Ford Presidential Library. At one point, Hartmann even asked Ford to intervene, at Cheney's suggestion.

136. Connor, Reichley interview, 2–3.

137. Prior to this, cabinet relations had been handled by David Parker, whose principal duties lay in scheduling and advance. See Dom Bonafede, *National Journal,* May 3, 1975.

138. Rustand to Connor, December 31, 1974, James E. Connor Files, Box 1, "Cabinet Secretary—Responsibilities," Ford Presidential Library.

139. Rustand to Rumsfeld, December 13, 1974, James E. Connor Files, Box 15, "Presidential Schedule—Long-Range Planning Meeting with the President," Ford Presidential Library. Rustand's planning documents formed the basis for a meeting among Ford, Rumsfeld, Cheney, Connor, and Rustand.

140. Gerald Ford, interview with Martha Joynt Kumar, October 10, 2000, quoted in Walcott, Warshaw, and Wayne, "Chief of Staff," 466.

141. Hartmann's critique can be found in *Palace Politics,* especially chapters 12 and 15. For examples of the consequences of staff conflict in one area, speechwriting, see Karen M. Hult and Charles E. Walcott, "Separating Rhetoric from Policy: Speechwriting under Gerald Ford and Jimmy Carter," *White House Studies* 1, no. 4 (2001): 463–78.

142. For a thorough discussion of this operation and the rivalry between it and such campaign leaders as Hamilton Jordan and Stuart Eizenstat, see John P. Burke, *Presidential Transitions: From Politics to Practice* (Boulder, Colo.: Lynne Rienner, 2000).

143. Quoted in Peter G. Bourne, *Jimmy Carter: A Comprehensive Biography from Plains to Post Presidency* (New York: Scribner, 1997), 359.

144. Quoted in ibid., 360. The quote is from an interview done shortly after Carter left the White House.

145. See ibid., 360–61.

146. Ibid., 361. Jack Watson's aide Bruce Kirschenbaum made the same point, attributing Carter's organizational choices to an overreaction to "the excesses of Watergate"; Watson concurred. Jack Watson (including Berry Crawford, Jane Hansen, Bruce Kirschenbaum), Miller Center interview, April 17–18, 1981, Carter Presidency Project, Vol. III, Carter Presidential Library.

147. White House Study Project, Report No. 1, December 7, 1976, "Analysis of President White House Office," Ford Presidential Library. In fact, the public liaison office was not eliminated.

148. Bourne, *Jimmy Carter,* 360.

149. Harden had also been part of the transition team that studied the Ford operation and prepared organizational blueprints for the new administration.

150. This was soon supplemented by a subcommittee called the Personnel Committee, consisting of Lipshutz, Jordan, Harden, and Hugh Carter. It reviewed and approved all White House decisions on personnel matters, including the use of detailees and consultants. It took the lead in Carter's efforts to shrink the size of the White House staff. The Personnel Committee's mandate was outlined in a memo from Lipshutz to Responsibility Center Directors, April 18, 1977, Joseph W. Aragon Staff Offices Papers, Box 9, "Newsclippings 1/77–10/77," Carter Presidential Library.

151. Watson, Miller Center interview, 61–62; Watson's deputies, such as Jane Frank, often played the go-between role. See Rex Granum to Jody Powell, n.d. (probably October 1977), Jody Powell Files, Box 42, "Memoranda: Granum, Rex 2/2/77–11/29/77 [CF, O/A 55]," Carter Presidential Library.

152. Watson, Miller Center interview, 64.

153. Ibid., 15–16.

154. For example, Watson and Frank to Carter, November 17, 1977, Staff Offices—Counsel, Lipshutz, Box 5, "Business Leaders 11/10/77 Meeting, 11/10/77 [O/A 7751D]," Carter Presidential Library. This meeting with business leaders included secretaries Blumenthal, Kreps, and Strauss, plus budget director McIntyre, CEA chair Schultze, Eizenstat, and Jordan.

155. Kirschenbaum (Watson), Miller Center interview, 23; Watson, Miller Center interview, 48.

156. Watson, Miller Center interview, 3.

157. Ibid., 54–58.

158. Dennis Farney, *Wall Street Journal* article (n.d.), Richard Harden Papers, Box 12, "Executive Office of the President [Reorganization] Study 1/27/77 [CF/OA 61]," Carter Presidential Library.

159. Harden to Management Committee, January 26, 1977, Richard Harden Papers, Box 18, "Management Committee [White House Staff and Budget] 1/77 [CF/OA 63]," Carter Presidential Library. "Responsibility centers" were in fact simply the staff offices.

160. Farney, *Wall Street Journal* article.

161. Harden and Frank Press to EOP Unit Heads, Senior White House staff, September 14, 1977, Richard Harden Papers, Box 3, "Advisory Group on White House Information Systems 8/22/77–12/26/77 [CF/OA 59]," Carter Presidential Library.

162. Frank Moore to Members of the Management Team, 3/1/77; Harden to Robert Russell and Leslie Francis, 5/2/77; Harden to Lipshutz, 10/4/77, Richard Harden Papers, Box 18, "Legislative Projects Coordinator 2/3/77–3/24/78 [CF/OA 62]," Carter Presidential Library.

163. It was announced at a press conference, which immediately touched off speculation about which top staff members' offices were winners (Jordan, Watson) and losers (Eizenstat, Midge Costanza). Fred Barnes, "The Winners and Losers in WH Shakeup," *Washington Star,* July 17, 1977, Joseph W. Aragon Staff Offices Papers, Box 9, "Newsclippings 1/77–10/77," Carter Presidential Library.

164. EOP Reorganization Plan, transmitted to Congress on July 15, 1977, Richard Harden Papers, Box 12, "Executive Office of the President [Reorganization] Study 6/17/77–9/12/77 [CF/OA 61]," Carter Presidential Library.

165. Carter had asked Congress to await his reorganization study before acting on its own plan to cut the White House staff by 30 percent. Edward Walsh, "White House Asks Staff Cut Delay," *Washington Post,* April 27, 1977, Richard Harden Papers, Box 19, "Newspaper and Magazine Clippings 12/76–1/78 [CF/OA 63]," Carter Presidential Library.

166. Skeptical accounts of the reality and impact of the cuts appeared immediately. See, e.g., "White House Watch," *New Republic,* July 30, 1977, Richard Harden Papers, Box 12, "Executive Office of the President [Reorganization] Study 6/17/77–9/12/77 [CF/OA 61]," Carter Presidential Library. The argument that certain offices, such as speechwriting, were seriously hurt by the cuts is made by Hult and Walcott, "Separating Rhetoric from Policy."

167. Bourne, *Jimmy Carter,* 366.

168. Doug Colton to A. D. Frazier, March 26, 1977, Richard Harden Papers, Box 12,

"Executive Office of the President [Reorganization] Study 1/27/77 [CF/OA 61]," Carter Presidential Library.

169. Jack Watson and Jane Frank (deputy cabinet secretary) to executive departments and agencies, October 7, 1977, Domestic Policy Staff: Eizenstat, Box 187, "Dom Policy Review—NSC (PRM) and General Organization [1]," Carter Presidential Library.

170. Dom Bonafede, "Carter White House Slowly Taking Shape," *National Journal,* February 12, 1977, Richard Harden Papers, Box 19, "Newspaper and Magazine Clippings 12/76–1/78 [CF/OA 63]," Carter Presidential Library.

171. Hutcheson to Senior Staff, January 24, 1977, Jody Powell Files, Box 43, "Hutcheson, Rick 1/24/77–2/1/77 [CF/OA 2]," Carter Presidential Library.

172. Memo on appointments, December 14, 1977, Staff Offices—Counsel, Lipshutz, Box 51, "White House Executive Committee, 9–12/77 [CF/OA 714]," Carter Presidential Library.

173. Kraft to White House staff, November 7, 1977, Hugh Carter Files, Box 38, "Kraft, Tim—1977 [CF/OA 375]," Carter Presidential Library.

174. Frank Moore, Miller Center interview (including William Cable, Dan Tate, Robert Thomson), September 18–19, 1981, Carter Presidency Project, Vol. IV, 94, Carter Presidential Library.

175. Bourne, *Jimmy Carter,* 372.

176. Ibid.

177. Carter's return was marked by an initially well-received speech sometimes misleadingly referred to as the "malaise" speech (Carter did not use the term). Any resulting momentum was crushed, however, when Carter followed it with a cabinet shake-up that resulted in the five resignations. The administration did indeed project an image of despair.

178. Zbigniew Brzezinski paraphrased from an interview with Peter Bourne, in Bourne, *Jimmy Carter,* 447.

179. Ibid.

180. Jack Watson advanced this view in his Miller Center interview, 20.

181. Burton I. Kaufman, *The Presidency of James Earl Carter* (Lawrence: University Press of Kansas, 1993), 147.

182. Watson, Miller Center interview, 41.

183. When McDonald arrived, Harden was moved out of the White House and into the Executive Office Building. Walter Mondale noted the importance of the move: "If you are there [the Executive Office Building], you might as well be in Baltimore." Quoted in Herman Nickel, "Can a Managerial Maestro End the White House Cacophony?" *Fortune,* October 22, 1979, 58, Hugh Carter Files, Box 43, "McDonald [Alonzo] Office—1980," Carter Presidential Library.

184. Al McDonald, Miller Center interview (including Michael Rowny), March 13–14, 1981, Carter Presidency Project, Vol. II, 95, Carter Presidential Library. McDonald's claims to be nonpolitical can also be found on pp. 19, 35, and 36.

185. Ibid., 105.

186. See Nickel, "Can a Managerial Maestro," 60; McDonald, Miller Center interview, 96. Jordan had introduced regular staff meetings of any kind only in early 1979.

187. Hendrik Hertzberg, Miller Center interview (including Christopher Matthews, Achsah Nesmith, Gordon Stewart), December 3–4, 1981, Carter Presidency Project, Vol. VIII, 43, Carter Presidential Library.

188. Ibid., 44.

189. See, e.g., McDonald to Issues Planning Group, June 12, 1980, Office of the Assistant

to the President for Women's Affairs [Weddington], Box 60, "Policy Coordination [3]," Carter Presidential Library.

190. Rowny (McDonald), Miller Center interview, 20–21.

191. Ibid. McDonald and Rowny (ibid., 108) were actually unaware that the Ford White House had a deputy system (albeit for somewhat different purposes).

192. McDonald, Miller Center interview, 30–31. DPS leaders agreed. David Rubenstein of the DPS suggested that McDonald's efforts "didn't quite work out because Al didn't have the political backing nor did he have the support in the White House staff to be able to carry that function off." Miller Center interview with Bertram Carp and Rubenstein, March 6, 1982, Carter Presidency Project, Vol. XIV, 63, Carter Presidential Library.

193. McDonald, Miller Center interview, 41.

194. Organization chart, November 26, 1979, Staff Offices, Domestic Policy Staff, Again (Sheppard), Box 5, "White House Bulletins, Directives, Etc., 11/8/79–3/31/80 [2]," Carter Presidential Library.

195. Watson's deputy, Eugene Eidenberg, replaced him as cabinet secretary.

196. Watson, Miller Center interview, 30.

197. Anne Wexler, Miller Center interview (including Michael Chanin, Richard Neustadt, John Ryor), February 12–13, 1981, Carter Presidency Project, Vol. I, 91–95, Carter Presidential Library.

198. Moore, Miller Center interview, 128.

199. Rubenstein, Miller Center interview, 63.

200. See, e.g., Walcott, Warshaw, and Wayne, "Chief of Staff." See also Karen M. Hult and Kathryn Dunn Tenpas, "The Office of the Staff Secretary," *Presidential Studies Quarterly* 31 (June 2001): 262–80. Revised versions of both articles appear in Martha Joynt Kumar and Terry Sullivan, eds., *The White House World: Transitions, Organization, and Office Operations* (College Station: Texas A&M University Press, 2003). This volume is the closest thing there is to a compendium of the conventional wisdom on White House operations now shared by scholars and practitioners alike.

3. PUBLIC OUTREACH

1. Phillips captured Nixon's reaction well: "This 'New York–Washington axis,' with its 'Ivy League elitist adversary culture,' . . . triggered conservative animosity." See Kevin P. Phillips, *Mediacracy: American Parties and Politics in the Communications Age* (Garden City, N.Y.: Doubleday, 1975), 26. See also Stephen E. Ambrose, *Nixon,* vol. 2, *The Triumph of a Politician, 1969–1972* (New York: Simon and Schuster, 1989), 251, 409–12, and passim.

2. The *Haldeman Diaries* provides one indicator. A search for "public relations" (in the notes, typically "PR") yielded 330 mentions in 221 entries (*Haldeman Diaries* CD-ROM). See also Ambrose, *Nixon,* 6; Jeb Stuart Magruder, *An American Life: One Man's Road to Watergate* (New York: Scribner, 1974), 85.

3. Marshall Edward Dimock and Gladys Ogden Dimock, *Public Administration* (New York: Rinehart, 1953): 403, quoted in Mordecai Lee, "Public Relations in Contemporary Public Administration Curricula: A Disappearing Act," *SPAE's Forum* 9 (June 1999): 9. Similarly, those in the Nixon White House (and in most other second-era administrations) often appeared to operate in ways that were roughly consistent with Edward Bernays's 1955

definition of public relations: " 'the attempt, by information, persuasion, and adjustment, to engineer public support for an activity, cause, movement or institution.' " Quoted in James G. Hutton, "The Definition, Dimensions, and Domain of Public Relations," *Public Relations Review* 25 (summer 1999): 200.

4. See, e.g., Hutton, "Definition, Dimensions, and Domain."

5. The dimensions are interest served, source of initiative, and focus on image or substance.

6. Hutton, "Definition, Dimensions, and Domain," 208. The example that Hutton used for the "image" extreme of the image–substance continuum was "Richard Nixon's admonition, during the Watergate scandal, 'let's PR it' " (205).

7. John Ehrlichman, *Witness to Power: The Nixon Years* (New York: Simon and Schuster, 1982), 266.

8. Magruder, *An American Life,* 89.

9. Thomas W. Benham [Vice President, Opinion Research Corporation] to Gordon Strachan, "Polls Chron July–Aug 1971," H. R. Haldeman Files, Box 335, Nixon Papers. See also, e.g., Diane J. Heith, "Presidential Polling and the Potential for Leadership," in *Presidential Power: Forging the Presidency for the 21st Century,* ed. Robert Y. Shapiro, Martha Joynt Kumar, and Lawrence R. Jacobs (New York: Columbia University Press, 2000); Lawrence R. Jacobs and Robert Y. Shapiro, "The Rise of Presidential Polling: The Nixon White House in Historical Perspective," *Public Opinion Quarterly* 59 (summer 1995): 163–95.

10. Charles E. Walcott and Karen M. Hult, *Governing the White House: From Hoover through LBJ* (Lawrence: University Press of Kansas, 1995), 69–70.

11. Cf. Heith, "Presidential Polling," 384.

12. Jacobs and Shapiro, "Rise of Presidential Polling," 180.

13. See, e.g., Robert Martin Eisinger, "The Illusion of Certainty: Explaining the Evolution of Presidential Polling" (doctoral dissertation, University of Chicago, 1996). Much of this material appears in Eisinger, *The Evolution of Presidential Polling* (New York: Cambridge University Press, 2003).

14. For example, John G. Geer, *From Tea Leaves to Opinion Polls: A Theory of Democratic Leadership* (New York: Columbia University Press, 1996), 84.

15. Bert A. Rockman, *The Leadership Question: The Presidency and the American System* (New York: Praeger, 1984).

16. Lawrence R. Jacobs and Melinda Jackson, "Reconciling the Influence of Policy Issues and Candidate Image on Election Campaigns: The Private Polling and Campaign Strategy of the Nixon White House" (paper presented at the annual meeting of the American Political Science Association, 2000), 19.

17. See, e.g., Jacobs and Shapiro, "Rise of Presidential Polling."

18. Nixon to Haldeman, January 15, 1969 [passed on to Haldeman by Rose Mary Wood on January 23, 1969], White House Special Files, President's Personal File, Memoranda from the President, 1969–74, Box 1, "Memos—Jan 1969," Folder 2, Nixon Papers.

19. *Haldeman Diaries* CD-ROM, April 14, 1969.

20. Included were sixty-three matches in fifty-two entries for Gallup, thirty matches in twenty-five entries for Harris, and ten mentions in eight entries for polling consultant David Derge.

21. For example, on January 12, 1970, Haldeman reported (*Haldeman Diaries* CD-ROM) that the president "spent most of the afternoon sessions reviewing and reverting to the Derge poll. Was fascinated with the findings and had made a lot of notes on analysis." See also July 10, 1970.

22. Ibid., July 13, 1970, January 19, 1971, February 7, 1973.

23. For example, Nixon to Haldeman, March 2, 1970, and Nixon to Haldeman, May 25, 1970, White House Special Files, President's Personal File, Memoranda from the President 1969–74, Box 2; Nixon to Ehrlichman, December 28, 1972, White House Special Files, President's Personal File, Memoranda from the President 1969–74, Box 4. Cf. Diane Joy Heith, "Polling for Policy: Public Opinion and Presidential Leadership" (doctoral dissertation, Brown University, 1997), 67; Jacobs and Shapiro, "Rise of Presidential Polling," 173; Richard Sobel, *Public Opinion in American Foreign Policy* (New York: Oxford University Press, 2001), 81.

24. See White House Special Files, White House Central Files, Subject Files: Confidential Files, 1969–74, "[CF] PR 15 Public Opinion Polls," Nixon Papers.

25. Howard to Haig, September 5, 1973, White House Special Files, Staff Member and Office Files, Alexander M. Haig 1970–74, "Interstaff Communications, 1973," Box 5—Sept, "Dick Howard." On Howard's poll-related activities more generally, see Howard to Haig, May 7, 1973, White House Special Files, Staff Member and Office Files, Ronald Ziegler, Box 1, "Basic Reorganization of the Press Office [3 of 3]," Nixon Papers.

26. For example, Chapin to Haldeman, September 26, 1969, "Chronological: Chapin—September 1969," October 10, 1969, "Chronological: Chapin—October 1969," November 14, 1969, "Chronological: Chapin—November 1969," Box 8; Chapin to Haldeman, May 4, 1970, "Chronological: Chapin—May 1970," Box 10; Chapin to Haldeman, November 19, 1970, "Chronological: Chapin—November 1970," Box 12; all in White House Special Files, Staff Member and Office Files, Dwight L. Chapin, Nixon Papers.

27. Haldeman to Chapin, March 17, 1970, White House Special Files, Staff Member and Office Files, Dwight L. Chapin, Box 18, "Memoranda from Mr. Haldeman January 1970–August 1970 [2 of 2]," Nixon Papers.

28. Chapin to Haldeman, October 8, 1969, White House Special Files, Staff Member and Office Files, Dwight L. Chapin, Box 8, "Chronological: Chapin—October 1969," Nixon Papers.

29. Chapin to Haldeman, March 11, 1970, White House Special Files, Staff Member and Office Files, Dwight L. Chapin, Box 9, "Chronological: Chapin—March 1970," Nixon Papers.

30. Chapin to Haldeman, November 19, 1970, White House Special Files, Staff Member and Office Files, Dwight L. Chapin, Box 12, "Chronological: Chapin—November 1970 [2 of 2]," Nixon Papers.

31. Haldeman to Rumsfeld, September 17, 1971, White House Special Files, White House Central Files, Box 53, "[CF] PR 15 Public Opinion Polls [1971–74] [1 of 2]," Nixon Papers.

32. For example, Colson to Haldeman, December 23, 1970, "HRH Memos 1969–70 (complete) [1 of 3]," Box 1; August 1, 1971, "H. R. Haldeman June–Dec 1971 [2 of 3]," Box 3; September 25, 1972, "H. R. Haldeman September 1972," Box 3; White House Special Files, Staff Member and Office Files, Charles W. Colson, Nixon Papers.

33. On Harris polls, see, e.g., Howard to President via Haig, July 25, 1973, September 5, 1973, October 25, 1973, November 14, 1973, White House Special Files, White House Central Files, Subject Files: Confidential Files, 1969–74, Box 53, "[CF] PR 15 Public Opinion Polls [1971–74] [1 of 2]," Nixon Papers. Howard transmitted information from Sindlinger polls and from discussions with the pollster in, e.g., Howard to President via Haig, July 26, 1973, August 2, 1973, September 11, 1973, September 27, 1973, November 9, 1973, November 21, 1973, February 27, 1974, May 14, 1974, White House Special Files,

White House Central Files, Subject Files: Confidential Files, 1969–74, Box 53, "[CF] PR 15 Public Opinion Polls [1971–74] [1 of 2]"; Howard to Haig, August 20, 1973, White House Special Files, Staff Member and Office Files, Alexander M. Haig 1970–74, "Interstaff Communications, 1973," Box 2, "Dick Howard," Nixon Papers.

34. Jacobs and Shapiro, "Rise of Presidential Polling," 178, n. 57.

35. Ibid. Jacobs and Shapiro note that through 1971, the Opinion Research Center (ORC) and Chilton conducted most of Nixon's private polls.

36. Magruder, *An American Life,* 182.

37. Heith, "Polling for Policy," 40, table 3.1.

38. Ibid., 39.

39. See Jacobs and Shapiro, "Rise of Presidential Polling," 177.

40. For example, Higby to Haig, September 25, 1973, September 28, 1973, White House Special Files, Staff Member and Office Files, Alexander M. Haig 1970–74, "Interstaff Communications, 1973," Box 6—September, "Misc.," Nixon Papers.

41. Buchanan to President per Haig, October 21, 1973, White House Special Files, White House Central Files, Subject Files: Confidential Files, 1969–74, Box 53, "[CF] PR 15 Public Opinion Polls [1971–74] [1 of 2]." Buchanan also conveyed Sindlinger's results in the summer of 1973. See, e.g., Buchanan to President per Al Haig, June 22, 1973, White House Special Files, Staff Member and Office Files, Office of the Staff Secretary, Administrative Files [Courier Files], Box 39, "June 27, 1973 Courier to San Clemente, CA," Nixon Papers.

42. For example, Harlow to Haig, October 2, 1973, White House Special Files, Staff Member and Office Files, Alexander M. Haig 1970–74, "Interstaff Communications, 1973," Box 7—October, "Bryce Harlow," Nixon Papers.

43. For example, George Bush to President via Haig, March 20, 1974, White House Special Files, Staff Member and Office Files, Office of Staff Secretary, Administrative Files [Courier Files], Box 40, "March 23, 1974 Sat 1:30 SS Courier Run to Camp David," Nixon Papers.

44. Jacobs and Shapiro, "Rise of Presidential Polling," n. 54.

45. Similarly, Jacobs and Jackson argue that Richard Nixon and his staff were "confident" about their capacities for "identifying voters' attitudes and . . . attempting to manipulate the public's issue preferences, candidate perceptions, and vote choice" ("Reconciling the Influence," 17).

46. *Haldeman Diaries* CD-ROM, January 19, 1971.

47. Eisinger, "Illusion of Certainty," 319.

48. Chapin to Haldeman, May 4, 1970, White House Special Files, Staff Member and Office Files, Dwight L. Chapin, Box 10, "Chapin Chronological, May 1970," Nixon Papers. More generally, see Lawrence R. Jacobs and Robert Y. Shapiro, "Presidential Manipulation of Polls and Public Opinion: The Nixon Administration and the Pollsters," *Political Science Quarterly* 110, no. 4 (1995–1996): 529–30.

49. Jacobs and Shapiro, "Presidential Manipulation of Polls," 525. See, e.g., *Haldeman Diaries* CD-ROM.

50. November 24, 1970, "Tentative Plan: November 29 Gallup Poll," White House Special Files, Staff Member and Office Files, Charles W. Colson, Box 1, "HRH memos 1969–70 (complete) [1 of 3]," Nixon Papers.

51. Ibid. Virtually all the actions included in the November 24 memo were listed in Odle's report on actions taken in response to the Gallup poll (Odle to Haldeman, cc: Chapin, Klein, December 2, 1970, in the same file).

52. Strachan to Nofziger, October 2, 1970, White House Special Files, Staff Member and Office Files, Box 10, "Polls—Gallup," Nixon Papers.

53. Colson to President, April 14, 1972, White House Special Files, Staff Member and Office Files, Charles W. Colson, Box 1, "Memorandums for the President [1 of 2]," Nixon Papers.

54. Thus, Heith writes, "The White House would routinely disseminate selected questions and the responses which were supportive of White House actions to various influential political figures" ("Polling for Policy," 40). See also Eisinger, "Illusion of Certainty."

55. Shumway to Thomas W. Benham [Executive Vice President, ORC], July 12, 1971, cc: Klein, Colson, Strachan, White House Special Files, Staff Member and Office Files, Charles W. Colson, Box 12, "Van Shumway [1 of 3] [1971]," 1, Nixon Papers.

56. Ibid., 2.

57. Eisinger, "Illusion of Certainty," 244.

58. Sobel, *Public Opinion*, 58.

59. Colson to Haldeman, May 20, 1971, White House Special Files, Staff Member and Office Files, Charles W. Colson, Box 4, "H R H Memos [3 of 3] [12/19/70–6/30/71]," Nixon Papers. Examples of similar mailings appear throughout Colson's files. Indeed, on the same day, Republican Senator Hugh Scott added the cover letter to an ORC poll on Vietnamization sent to more than 17,000 state and local veterans and military organizations.

60. Buchanan to Gordon Strachan, September 15, 1971, White House Special Files, Staff Member Office Files, Box 1, Buchanan Chronological Files, "September 1971," Nixon Papers.

61. Buchanan to John Lofton and Lyn Nofziger, September 20, 1970, White House Special Files, Staff Member Office Files, Box 1, Buchanan Chronological Files, "September 1971," Nixon Papers.

62. Charles Colson quoted in John Anthony Maltese, *Spin Control: The White House Office of Communications and the Management of Presidential News*, 2d rev. ed. (Chapel Hill: University of North Carolina Press, 1994), 94.

63. See, e.g., *Haldeman Diaries* CD-ROM, January 12, 1970, 119; August 6, 1970, 146; July 23, 1970, 184. The *Haldeman Diaries* also mentions poll results in discussions with Nixon on October 31 and November 22, 1969; April 6 and July 23, 1970; and January 17 and April 23, 1971. Cf. Heith, "Polling for Policy," 53 and passim; Eisinger, "Illusion of Certainty," chap. 7.

64. Jacobs and Shapiro, "Rise of Presidential Polling," 176ff.

65. Heith, "Polling for Policy," 153.

66. The "diagnostic" and "therapeutic" labels are from Jacobs and Jackson, "Reconciling the Influence." Their focus is on private polling for the 1972 election.

67. *Haldeman Diaries* CD-ROM, January 29, 1969.

68. Haldeman to John Brown, cc: Ehrlichman, January 27, 1969, White House Central Files, Subject Files, WH (White House Administration), Box 15, "Ex WH 4-1-1 (Mail Reports), Begin 6/30/69, 1 of 2," Nixon Papers.

69. See, e.g., reports from Melencamp to President, with "JK" [James Keogh] approval, White House Central Files, Subject Files, WH (White House Administration), Box 15, "Ex WH 4-1-1 (Mail Reports), Begin 6/30/69, 1 of 2," "Ex WH 4-1-1 (Mail Reports), 2/1/70–3/31/70," Nixon Papers.

70. See, e.g., responses to the November 3, 1969, presidential speech on Vietnam (*Haldeman Diaries*, 105); summary of mail detailing reactions to the president's televised inter-

actions with the press between January 1969 and 1971 (Price to Higby, January 26, 1971, White House Central Files, Subject Files, WH, Box 16, "Ex WH 4-1-1 [Mail reports], 1/1/71–12/30/72"); summary and analysis of mail on the Pentagon Papers (Price to President, July 2, 1971, White House Central Files, Subject Files, WH, Box 11, "Ex WH 4-1 [Mail] 7/1/71–7/15/71"); reactions to a possible 1973 Vietnam peace agreement (Roland Elliot to President, January 24 and 25, 1973, White House Central Files, Subject Files, WH, "Ex WH 4-1 [Mail], 1/1/73–7/25/74"), Nixon Papers.

71. For example, Brown to President, June 17, 1969, Ex White House Central Files, Subject Files, WH (White House Administration), Box 10, "Ex 4-1 (Mail), 5/1/69–8/14/69, 1 of 2"; Brown to President, July 15, 1969, White House Central Files, Subject Files, WH (White House Administration), Box 10, "Ex 4-1 (Mail), 5/1/69–8/14/69, 2 of 2," Nixon Papers.

72. Haldeman to Brown, January 27, 1969, White House Central Files, Subject Files, WH (White House Administration), Box 15, "Ex WH 4-1-1 (Mail Reports), Begin 6/30/69, 1 of 2"; Price to Brown, December 31, 1970, White House Central Files, Subject Files, WH (White House Administration), Box 10, "Ex WH 4-1 (Mail), 2/14/70–12/31/70, 3 of 3"; Price to President, March 26,1971, White House Central Files, Subject Files, WH (White House Administration), Box 11, "Ex WH 4-1 (Mail), 3/1/71–3/31/71," Nixon Papers.

73. Haldeman relayed Nixon's unhappiness in a February 18, 1971, memo to Ray Price and Dick Moore, White House Special Files, Staff Member and Office Files, Dwight L. Chapin, Box 18, "Memoranda from Mr. Haldeman: January 1971 through February 1971," Nixon Papers.

74. Price's submissions can be found in, e.g., White House Central Files, Subject Files, WH, Box 11, "Ex WH 4-1 (Mail) 3/1/71–3/31/71," and Box 12, "Ex WH 4-1 (Mail) 9/1/71–9/17/71, 2 of 2," Nixon Papers.

75. President to Haldeman, June 21, 1971, White House Special Files, President's Personal File, Box 3, "Memoranda from the President, 1969–74," Nixon Papers.

76. For example, *Haldeman Diaries* CD-ROM, August 9, 1971, and February 6, 1973.

77. Klein to Ehrlichman, June 28, 1969, White House Central Files, Subject Files, WH, Box 10, "Ex WH 4-1 (Mail) 5/1/69–8/14/69, 1 of 2," Nixon Papers.

78. Klein to President, July 15, 1969, White House Central Files, Subject Files, WH, Box 10, "Ex WH 4-1 (Mail) 5/1/69–8/14/69, 1 of 2," Nixon Papers.

79. Magruder to Haldeman, February 24, 1971, White House Central Files, Subject Files, WH, Box 10, "Ex WH 4-1-1 (Mail) 1/1/71– 2/28/71," Nixon Papers.

80. For example, Clawson to Elliott, September 22, 1972, attaching "report on our recent merchandizing of Presidential letters"; Elliott via Price to President, October 3, 1972, "re: Anecdotal Material from Correspondence"; White House Central Files, Subject Files, WH, Box 9, Exec WH 4 (Office Management), "1/1/71–12/11/72, 2 of 2," Nixon Papers.

81. For example, Snyder to Higby, May 20, 1971, White House Special Files, Staff Member and Office Files, Charles W. Colson, Box 8, "Larry Higby," Folder 1, Nixon Papers.

82. Colson to Haldeman, March 23, 1971, White House Special Files, Staff Member and Office Files, Charles W. Colson, Box 2, "H. R. H. Memos—1971 Jan.–June 1971 [3 of 3]," Nixon Papers.

83. Klein to President, March 11, 1971, Office of the Staff Secretary, Administrative Files [Courier Files], White House Special Files, Staff Member and Office Files, Box 35, "March 13, 1971 to the President by Courier to Key Biscayne," Nixon Papers.

84. Michael Smith to Raymond Price, February 12, 1971, White House Central Files,

Subject Files, WH, Box 1, "Ex WH 4-1-1 (Mail Reports), 1/1/71–12/30/72, 1 of 3," Nixon Papers.

85. Ambrose, *Nixon,* 248.

86. See "January 1971," White House Special Files, Staff Member and Office Files, Buchanan, Chronological Files, Box 1, Folder 9, Nixon Papers.

87. Ambrose, *Nixon,* 248.

88. President to Ziegler and Haldeman, April 14, 1972 [transcript of dictation], White House Special Files, President's Personal File, Box 3, "Memoranda from the President, 1969–74," "Memos—April 1972," 1, Nixon Papers.

89. For example, *Haldeman Diaries* CD-ROM, August 29, 1969, October 7, 1969, October 18, 1969.

90. Ibid., February 28, 1972. See also February 29, March 5, and March 7, 1972, on Buchanan and the "negative approach" of the "News Summary" to coverage of the China visit. As the 1972 election approached, Nixon also directed Haldeman to ensure that works by columnists John Osborne and Hugh Sidey were excluded from the "News Summary" for several months, "regardless of what they write. . . . What they will be doing is to try to write those things which will get under our skin and their criticism force us to do things we should not do or to quit doing things we are doing" (President to Ziegler and Haldeman, April 14, 1972 [transcript of dictation], White House Special Files, President's Personal File, Box 3, "Memoranda from the President, 1969–74," "Memos—April 1972," 2, Nixon Papers.

91. Ambrose, *Nixon,* 409.

92. Fred W. Friendly, quoted in Maltese, *Spin Control,* 49.

93. Cf. Herbert G. Klein, *Making It Perfectly Clear* (Garden City, N.Y.: Doubleday, 1980), 197; Ambrose, *Nixon,* 248–49, 409–12; "HGK 1969—Memos to the President," White House Special Files, Staff Member and Office Files, Box 3, Nixon Papers.

94. For example, Allin to Haldeman, January 22, 1971, White House Special Files, Staff Member and Office Files, Patrick J. Buchanan, Box 1, "January 1971," Nixon Papers.

95. For example, Allin to Butterfield, March 22, 1971, White House Special Files, Staff Member and Office Files, Patrick J. Buchanan, Box 1, "March 1971," Nixon Papers.

96. An illustration can be found in Allin to Haldeman (cc: Magruder, Khachigian, Odle), December 4, 1970, White House Special Files, Staff Member and Office Files, Khachigian, Box 2, "Memos to Khachigian from White House Staff [1970–72]," Folder 2, Nixon Papers.

97. For example, Strachan to Odle, September 14, 1970, White House Special Files, Staff Member and Office Files, Gordon Strachan, Box 2, "Chronological File—September 1970," Nixon Papers.

98. Michael Baruch Grossman and Martha Joynt Kumar, *Portraying the President: The White House and the News Media* (Baltimore: Johns Hopkins University Press, 1981), 103; Ambrose has referred to this as "governing through notes" (*Nixon,* 410). Haldeman noted that when Nixon became "all of a sudden enamored with the use of the Dictaphone," he began "spewing out memos by the carload, plus about double the volume of news summary marginal notes" (*Haldeman Diaries* CD-ROM, September 23, 1969).

99. *Haldeman Diaries* CD-ROM, September 30, 1969.

100. On the early organization and operation of the Office of Communications, see, e.g., Maltese, *Spin Control,* 32–44, 244.

101. Ibid., 40.

102. As early as February 1969, President Nixon wrote to Ehrlichman asking for "progress reports on a continual basis" on the letters to the editor project (President to Ehrlichman,

February 5, 1969, White House Special Files, President's Personal File, Box 1, "Memos—February 1969," Nixon Papers).

103. See, e.g., Kenneth E. Collier, *Between the Branches: The White House Office of Legislative Affairs* (Pittsburgh: University of Pittsburgh Press, 1997), 128; Maltese, *Spin Control,* 37.

104. Haldeman's bracketed note, *Haldeman Diaries* CD-ROM, February 4, 1969.

105. President to Ehrlichman, January 25, 1969, White House Special Files, President's Personal File, Box 1, "Memos—January 1969," Folder 2, Nixon Papers.

106. For example, 5 o'clock agenda, April 8, 1969, White House Central Files, Subject Files, WH , Box 21, "Ex WH 7 Staff Meetings, Beginning 7/31/69," Nixon Papers.

107. President to Ehrlichman, April 10, 1969, White House Special Files, President's Personal File, Box 1, "Memos—April 1969," Nixon Papers.

108. See President to Haldeman, September 22, 1969, White House Central Files, Subject Files, WH, Box 22, "Ex WH 7 Staff Meetings, 8/1/69–12/31/69," Nixon Papers.

109. Chapin to Haldeman, September 24, 1969, White House Central Files, Subject Files, WH, Box 22, "Ex WH 7 Staff Meetings, 8/1/69–12/31/69," Nixon Papers.

110. Magruder, *An American Life,* 91. Cf. Chapin to Haldeman, October 15, 1969, White House Special Files, Staff Member and Office Files, Dwight L. Chapin, Box 8, "Chronological: Chapin—October 1969," Nixon Papers. An example of the product of the P.O. Group is the elaborate "game plan" on inflation, which was to be "handled as the nation's number one domestic problem." See News Planning Agenda, January 28, 1970, White House Central Files, Subject Files, WH, Box 22, "Ex WH 7 Staff Meetings, 1/1/70–8/31/70," Nixon Papers. Haldeman started the Presidential Objectives Planning Group in October 1969; see, e.g., Harry S. Dent, White House Special Files, Staff Member and Office Files, Box 11, "1969 Presidential Objectives Planning Group," Nixon Papers.

111. Chapin to Magruder, November 19, 1969, White House Special Files, Staff Member and Office Files, Dwight L. Chapin, Box 8, "Chronological: Chapin—November 1969," Nixon Papers.

112. *Haldeman Diaries* CD-ROM, January 7, 1970.

113. Magruder, *An American Life,* 105.

114. Klein, *Making It Perfectly Clear,* 199.

115. See, e.g., Box 12, "Chronological File—September 1970," and Box 12, "Republican National Committee Letters to Editor Project," in Gordon Strachan, White House Special Files, Staff Member and Office Files, Box 2, Nixon Papers.

116. See, e.g., Maltese, *Spin Control,* 71ff.; Magruder for Staff Secretary, January 9, 1971, White House Special Files, Staff Member and Office Files, Gordon Strachan, Box 1, "Action Memos," and Box 7, "Mailing Material—General Information," Nixon Papers; Magruder, *An American Life,* chap. 5.

117. Maltese, *Spin Control,* 70.

118. Magruder, *An American Life,* 129. The task force was cochaired by Bryce Harlow, director of the White House Office of Congressional Relations, and Deputy Attorney General Richard Kleindienst; other members included White House staffers Charles Colson and Lyn Nofziger, Justice Department officials William Rehnquist and John Dean, and U.S. Senators Howard Baker and Robert Dole.

119. Magruder contended that these two events in particular had serious implications for internal White House dynamics. Carswell's defeat "caused all hell to break loose" (*An American Life,* 131), and the evidently successful effort to persuade a majority of Americans to

view the Cambodian invasion as a "success" made the staff "too confident that we could manipulate public opinion in a hard line, rally-round-the-flag way" (ibid., 139).

120. *Haldeman Diaries* CD-ROM, April 4, 1970; see also April 6, 1970.

121. Haldeman to Colson, May 26, 1970, cc: Chapin, Magruder, Keogh, White House Special Files, Staff Member and Office Files, Charles W. Colson, Box 2, "HRH Memos 1969–70 (complete) [3 of 3]," Nixon Papers.

122. William Safire, *Before the Fall: An Inside View of the Pre-Watergate White House* (Garden City, N.Y.: Doubleday, 1975), 486. See also, e.g., Haldeman notes, *Haldeman Diaries* CD-ROM, February 23, 1970.

123. For example, Magruder, *An American Life,* 137–39, 157–59, and passim.

124. See Maltese, *Spin Control,* 85, citing interviews with both Colson and William Rhatican, who worked under Klein and Colson. These views are supported by Nixon's evident interest in Colson as the director of communications; see *Haldeman Diaries* CD-ROM, December 19, 1970.

125. See, e.g., *Haldeman Diaries* CD-ROM, December 18, 19, 24, 1970; February 25, 1971.

126. Maltese, *Spin Control,* 87–88. See also Howard to Colson, May 28, 1971, White House Special Files, Staff Member and Office Files, Charles W. Colson, Box 2, "H. R. H. Memos—1971 Jan.–June 1971 [1 of 3]," Nixon Papers. Meanwhile, Klein was left with formal responsibility for media liaison and correspondence (Maltese, *Spin Control,* 87).

127. Colson to Howard, April 17, 1971, White House Special Files, Staff Member and Office Files, Charles W. Colson, Box 8, "Dick Howard [2 of 23]," Nixon Papers.

128. Only Klein's unit had its own wire service machines. Colson claimed that he and his staff required easy access to the machines, since "I have an urgent and immediate daily need for certain specific wire stories." Moreover, Colson contended that the communications office needed to continue its part in the "response" operation after major presidential speeches: monitoring the wire service machines for stories about the speeches and delivering them to Haldeman's office. See Colson to Klein, September 18, 1971, White House Special Files, Staff Member and Office Files, Charles W. Colson, Box 9, "Herb Klein," Nixon Papers. Klein's initial memo lodging specific complaints was withdrawn from the files. At about the same time, though, Maltese quotes a similar memo to Colson in which Klein charged that some Colson staffers had "issued orders" to Donna Kingswell (a communications staffer) that "ranged from acting as a personal messenger to countermanding my orders on particular projects" (*Spin Control,* 90).

129. Klein to Colson, November 5, 1971, White House Special Files, Staff Member and Office Files, Charles W. Colson, Box 3, "H. R. Haldeman June–Dec 1971 [1 of 3]," Nixon Papers.

130. Colson to Haldeman, November 9, 1971, White House Special Files, Staff Member and Office Files, Charles W. Colson, Box 3, "H. R. Haldeman June–Dec 1971 [1 of 3]," Nixon Papers (emphasis in the original).

131. Klein called Colson "one of the meanest people I ever knew" (Gerald S. Strober and Deborah Hart Strober, *Nixon: An Oral History of His Presidency* [New York: HarperCollins, 1994], 273). Margita White apparently threatened to quit if she were transferred from Klein's to Colson's unit (Maltese, *Spin Control,* 87).

132. Klein to Colson, November 5, 1971, White House Special Files, Staff Member and Office Files, Charles W. Colson, Box 3, "H. R. Haldeman June–Dec 1971 [1 of 3]," Nixon Papers.

133. Strober and Strober, *Nixon,* 73. Earlier, Klein told James Reichley that Colson tended to devise "all sorts of schemes for brow-beating the press" and that Klein had to devote considerable time to heading off Colson's worst ideas. Herbert Klein, January 6, 1978, James Reichley Interviews, Box 1 (Nixon White House Interviews), 4–5, Ford Presidential Library.

134. Safire, *Before the Fall,* 290.

135. Maltese, *Spin Control,* 93.

136. For example, Colson to Higby, March 22, 1971, April 5, 1971, April 8, 1971, June 15, 1971, September 23, 1971, "Larry Higby," Folder 1; Colson to Howard, May 7, 1971, May 17, 1971, "Dick Howard [2 of 2]," in White House Special Files, Staff Member and Office Files, Charles W. Colson, Box 8, Nixon Papers.

137. See, e.g., materials in "Bill Rhatican," White House Special Files, Staff Member and Office Files, Charles W. Colson, Box 10, Nixon Papers.

138. For example, Colson to Scali, September 4, 1971, White House Special Files, Staff Member and Office Files, Charles W. Colson, Box 11 "John Scali [2 of 2] [1971]," Nixon Papers. More generally, see Scali folders in ibid.

139. Colson to Barker, June 14, 1971, White House Special Files, Staff Member and Office Files, Charles W. Colson, Box 5, "Des Barker [1971]," Nixon Papers.

140. Colson to Barker, July 9, 1971, White House Special Files, Staff Member and Office Files, Charles W. Colson, Box 5, "Des Barker [1971]," Nixon Papers.

141. See Van Shumway folders in White House Special Files, Staff Member and Office Files, Charles W. Colson, Box 12, Nixon Papers.

142. Maltese, *Spin Control,* 103.

143. Cole to Morgan, cc: Safire, April 16, 1971, White House Special Files, Staff Member and Office Files, Charles W. Colson, Box 10, "Ed Morgan," Nixon Papers.

144. Evans to Colson, January 26, 1972, White House Special Files, Staff Member and Office Files, Charles W. Colson, Box 6, "Ken Cole [1972]," Nixon Papers.

145. See Cole handwritten response on Colson to Cole, January 28, 1972, and Colson to Cole (with Higby "bcc"), February 1, 1972, White House Special Files, Staff Member and Office Files, Charles W. Colson, Box 6, "Ken Cole [1972]," Nixon Papers.

146. Ehrlichman, *Witness to Power,* 79. See also Haldeman's notes about an angry staff meeting, with loud complaints about Colson from Ehrlichman and George Shultz (*Haldeman Diaries* CD-ROM, November 30, 1971).

147. Flanigan to President [draft, with Colson's suggested changes], July 15, 1971, and Colson to Flanigan, July 15, 1971, White House Special Files, Staff Member and Office Files, Charles W. Colson, Box 14, "Misc. Staff Memos 1970–1971 [3 of 8] [6/2/71–7/28/71]," Nixon Papers. Cf. Strober and Strober, *Nixon,* 100ff.

148. Colson to Moore, Safire, Price, Scali, Chapin, May 14, 1971, re: "Future Public Relations Activities," White House Special Files, Staff Member and Office Files, Charles W. Colson, Box 11, "Bill Safire [1971]," Nixon Papers.

149. Colson to Cole, January 31, 1972, and Colson to Higby, January 31, 1972, White House Special Files, Staff Member and Office Files, Charles W. Colson, Box 8, "Larry Higby," Folder 2, Nixon Papers. Colson also grew impatient with what he saw as the lack of cooperation from RNC staffers (e.g., Colson to Frank Leonard, June 7, 1972, in ibid.).

150. One could argue, of course, that Colson's "solution" was indeed structural. In effect, he called for structuring that produced decision closure and monitoring to ensure faithful implementation.

151. Malek to Haldeman [with Colson's handwritten comments], May 12, 1972, and

Colson to Haldeman, May 17, 1972, White House Special Files, Staff Member and Office Files, Charles W. Colson, Box 4, "H. R. H. Memos [1 of 3] [5/10/72–12/16/72]," Nixon Papers. Colson noted that his comments would not address either foreign policy or the "P.R. aspects of the P's image." Instead, he focused on approaches to publicizing and "selling" the administration's positions on, e.g., "New Populism," busing, "inflation/food prices," welfare, "drugs and crime," and the environment. As did many of his memos, this one ended with an analysis of major voting blocs for 1972, including "white ethnic, blue collar, new middle class, Catholics."

152. On these changes generally, see, e.g., Maltese, *Spin Control;* Klein, *Making It Perfectly Clear.*

153. Larry Speakes with Robert Pack, *Speaking Out: Inside the Reagan White House* (New York: Charles Scribner's Sons, 1988), 40ff.; Maltese, *Spin Control,* 104–8. For a fuller view of the activities of the "government as usual" group, see, e.g., Clawson to Haig, January 22, 1974, "Office of Communications Daily Report," White House Special Files, Staff Member and Office Files, Alexander Haig, Box 14, "Ken Clawson, Interstaff Communications, 1974," Nixon Papers.

154. Ziegler to Clawson, March 21, 1973, White House Central Files, Subject Files, WH, Box 14, "Ex WH 4-1 (Mail), 1/1/73–7/25/74," Nixon Papers.

155. Paul Brace and Barbara Hinckley, *Follow the Leader: Opinion Polls and the Modern Presidents* (New York: Basic Books, 1993); Paul Brace and Barbara Hinckley, "Presidential Activities from Truman through Reagan: Timing and Impact," *Journal of Politics* 55 (May 1993): 382–98.

156. Collier distinguishes among "three related public relations strategies" for building presidential support in Congress: "merchandising," "building public prestige," and targeting "special publics" (*Between the Branches,* 20–22). These also appear to apply to presidential outreach more generally. The Nixon administration's PR efforts seemingly included all three approaches. The first two are examined here; the third is postponed until chapter 4, which explores group outreach.

157. Ibid., 20.

158. Grossman and Kumar, *Portraying the President,* 105.

159. Colson to Barker, July 27, 1971, White House Special Files, Staff Member and Office Files, Charles W. Colson, Box 8, "Dick Howard [1 of 2]," Nixon Papers.

160. Colson to President, November 12, 1971, White House Special Files, Staff Member and Office Files, Charles W. Colson, Box 1, "Memorandums for the President [2 of 2]," Nixon Papers. See also materials on the late 1970 Economy Project in "Game Plans," White House Special Files, Staff Member and Office Files, Gordon Strachan, Box 6, Nixon Papers.

161. For example, Colson memo for President's file, August 25, 1971, "Memorandums for the President [2 of 2]," Box 1; Colson to Haldeman, August 9, 1971, "H. R. Haldeman June–Dec 1971 [2 of 3]," Box 3; White House Special Files, Staff Member and Office Files, Charles W. Colson, Nixon Papers. See also Ehrlichman, *Witness to Power,* 276.

162. Higby to Colson, March 11, 1971, White House Special Files, Staff Member and Office Files, Charles W. Colson, Box 8, "Larry Higby," Folder 1, Nixon Papers.

163. For example, Magruder to Higby, September 10, 1970, "52" Casualties, Gordon Strachan, Box 1; Colson to Haldeman, June 12, 1971, "H. R. H. Memos—1971 Jan.–June 1971 [1 of 3]," Charles W. Colson, Box 2; Colson to Scali, July 6, 1971, "John Scali [1 of 2] [1971]," Charles W. Colson, Box 11; White House Special Files, Staff Member and Office Files, Nixon Papers.

164. For instance, Heith contends that White House use of presidential popularity data "reached its height with Nixon" ("Polling for Policy," 88). The president sent senior staffers numerous notes with ideas about strategies for enhancing his image (White House Special Files, President's Personal File, Memoranda from the President: e.g., President to Ehrlichman, January 25, 1969, Box 1; President to Haldeman, March 2, 1970, Box 2; President to Haldeman, January 14, 1971, Box 3; President to Haldeman, March 27, 1972, Box 3; President to Haldeman, Ehrlichman, March 10, 1973, Box 4, Nixon Papers). Nixon also spent considerable time discussing the issue in his sessions with Haldeman (e.g., *Haldeman Diaries* CD-ROM, February 2, 1970, October 8, 1970, December 3, 1970, August 16, 1971).

165. Ehrlichman Alphabetical Subject File, Box 19, "Goals," Fiche 48.

166. Butterfield to Finch, Rumsfeld, Klein, Ziegler, Buchanan, Safire, Moore, Koch, Huebner, Shumway, February 6, 1971, White House Special Files, White House Central Files, Subject Files: Confidential Files, 1969–74, Box 52, "[CF] PR 7-1 [Granted] 1/1/71–12/31/72 [1971–74]," Nixon Papers.

167. See, e.g., Gwen E. Anderson Files, Box 27; James E. Connor Files, Box 14; Ford Presidential Library.

168. In the Robert T. Hartmann Files, see, e.g., "Issues," Box 12; Decision Making Information polls for February and April 1975, Boxes 30, 31, 32; "Presidential Survey Research Proposal," Folders 1 and 2, Box 34. See also Baroody to Hartmann, May 30, 1975, "Hartmann, Robt (2)," William J. Baroody, Box 22, White House Memoranda, Ford Presidential Library.

169. Gergen to Cheney, September 1, 1976; Halper to Gergen, Slight, October 5, 1976; Van Cleve to Gergen, n.d. [but reporting on a June 16, 1976, speech by George Gallup]; Gergen to Duval, September 20, 1976; in "Public Opinion Polls," David Gergen Files, Box 8, Ford Presidential Library.

170. Eisinger, "Illusion of Certainty," 271–72.

171. Ibid., 264–65. See, also, e.g., Baroody to Cheney, October 31, 1975, "Richard Cheney," Box 21, William J. Baroody, White House Memoranda, Ford Presidential Library.

172. On Chanock's responsibilities, see, e.g., Eisinger, "Illusion of Certainty," 265, 270; Heith, "Polling for Policy," 42–44. Cf. Chanock, oral history interview, December 2, 1976, 14–15, James F. C. Hyde and Stephen J. Wayne Oral History Collection, "Polls," Box 2, Foster O. Chanock Files; Ford Presidential Library.

173. See, e.g., Anderson to Slight, November 25, 1975, "President Ford Committee (2)," Robert T. Hartmann Files, Box 26; Slight to Morton, May 28, 1976, "Polls," Warren and White Files, Box 20, Ford Presidential Library. Citing the "lack of communication within the President Ford Committee and between it and the White House," Slight resigned in June 1976 (James M. Naughton, July 11, 1976, *New York Times,* in "President Ford Committee [5]," Robert T. Hartmann Files, Box 26). He returned to the White House to work under David Gergen in the Office of Communications.

174. Eisinger, "Illusion of Certainty," 301.

175. Heith, "Polling for Policy," 45.

176. Eisinger, "Illusion of Certainty," 272.

177. See Heith, "Polling for Policy," 45–46. Heith reports, e.g., that President Carter received 21.87 percent of all "polling memos" sent during his administration, by far the highest proportion (ibid., 46). An on-line search of the President's Daily Diary included Caddell on twenty-five separate days (http://gsu.edu:8765/query.html?col...2Bcaddell& qm=0&ql=a&st=1&nh=500&lk=1&rf=1, July 12, 2001).

178. Heith, "Polling for Policy," 47.

179. Ibid. Robert Beckel, who worked in the White House Office of Congressional Relations, criticized Caddell's questions and interpretations. In Beckel's view, "one of the most tragic mistakes" was that Carter accepted his pollster's assessment of the "national mood" in 1978–1979. See Robert Beckel, Miller Center interview, November 13, 1981, Carter Presidency Project, Vol. VII, Carter Presidential Library. In contrast, Gerald Rafshoon maintained that as director of communications, he did not "order up polls; Caddell knew what was needed" (Miller Center interview, April 8, 1983, Carter Presidency Project, Vol. XXI, 66, Carter Presidential Library).

180. Jody Powell, Miller Center interview, December 17–18, 1981, Carter Presidency Project, Vol. X, Carter Presidential Library.

181. Heith, "Presidential Polling," 389.

182. See Robert T. Hartmann Files, Boxes 30–32, Ford Presidential Library.

183. See Robert T. Hartmann Files, Box 33, Ford Presidential Library. Cf. Heith, "Presidential Polling," 398.

184. Heith, "Presidential Polling," 395.

185. Eisinger, "Illusion of Certainty," 267.

186. Draft presentation on the Office of Public Liaison to the Cabinet, n.d., William J. Baroody, 1974–77, Subject File, Box 10, "Public Liaison Office—General (1)," 7, Ford Presidential Library.

187. Byington and Sterlacci to Baroody, January 31, 1975, William J. Baroody, White House Memoranda, Box 23, "Knauer, Virginia (3)," Ford Presidential Library.

188. See Seasonwein to Aragon, December 12, 1977, Joseph W. Aragon Staff Offices Papers, Box 17, "Canal: Press, Media, Public Affairs 10/77–4/78," Carter Presidential Library.

189. Caddell to Jordan, December 20, 1977, Joseph W. Aragon Staff Offices Papers, Box 17, "Canal: Press, Media, Public Affairs 10/77–4/78," Carter Presidential Library.

190. See report on findings, February 1978, in "Committee of Americans for the Canal Treaties (COACT) 1/78–2/78," Joseph W. Aragon Staff Offices Papers, Box 18, "Canal: Press, Media, Public Affairs 10/77–4/78," Carter Presidential Library.

191. See, e.g., Caddell to Eizenstat, August 9, 1979, "Caddell, Pat, 7/77–3/80," Domestic Policy Staff: Eizenstat, CF, O/A #743, Box 1; Brzezinski to President, April 18, 1977, "[Administrative Memos to White House Staff] 3/77–7/78," Carter Presidential Papers, Staff Offices, OPL: Costanza, Box 1, Carter Presidential Library.

192. Caddell to President, March 1, 1980, Domestic Policy Staff: Eizenstat, CF O/A #743, Box 1, "Caddell, Pat, 7/77–3/80," Carter Presidential Library.

193. Rafshoon to President, June 14, 1977, Chief of Staff's Office, Hamilton Jordan's Files, Box 34, "Image," Carter Presidential Library.

194. See also Anne Wexler, Miller Center interview (including Michael Chanin, Richard Neustadt, John Ryor), February 12–13, 1981, Carter Presidency Project, Vol. I, 109, Carter Presidential Library; Hendrik Hertzberg, Miller Center interview (including Christopher Matthews, Achsah Nesmith, Gordon Stewart), December 3–4, 1981, Carter Presidency Project, Vol. VIII, 59ff., Carter Presidential Library. At the same time, one should not overstate the general influence of polls and Caddell on speeches. Speechwriting director Hertzberg noted that the writers did not base much of what they did on poll data. They "listened to Caddell," but mainly because they found him "interesting" and "enjoyable" (Hertzberg, Miller Center interview, 123).

195. Caddell to President, June 11, 1979, Domestic Policy Staff: Eizenstat, CF, O/A #743, Box 1, "Caddell, Pat, 7/77–3/80," Carter Presidential Library (emphasis in original).

196. Bertram Carp and David Rubenstein, Miller Center interview, March 6, 1982, Carter Presidency Project, Vol. XIV, 49, Carter Presidential Library.

197. Wexler, Miller Center interview, 109–10.

198. For example, Elliott to President via Staff Secretary, January 12, 1976, Robert T. Hartmann Papers, Box 170, "White House—Staff Secretary's Office," Ford Presidential Library.

199. For example, Hugh Carter to President, cc: Senior Staff, July 28, 1978, Staff Offices, OPL: Costanza, Box 1, "[Administrative Memos to White House Staff] 3/77–7/78," Carter Presidential Library.

200. Powell, Miller Center interview, 71.

201. Maltese, *Spin Control,* 119.

202. Talking Paper, n.d., re: Jim Holland (probably for Nessen), Ronald H. Nessen Files, Box 45, "Holland, Jim," Ford Presidential Library.

203. Maltese, *Spin Control,* 122.

204. Talking Paper, October 17, 1974, Ronald H. Nessen Papers, Box 139, "Gerald Warren (10/74–1/75)," Ford Presidential Library.

205. Maltese, *Spin Control,* 123.

206. See, e.g., Nessen to Jones through Hoopes, November 1, 1974, Ronald H. Nessen Files, Box 44, "Jerry Jones"; White to Nessen, September 19, 1975, "Media Requests/Scheduling"; White to Nessen, October 9, 1975, "Office of Communications—General"; White to Nessen, June 17, 1975, "Office of Communications—Organization (1)"; Margita E. White Papers, Box 1, Ford Presidential Library.

207. For example, Nessen to Jones through Hoopes, November 1, 1974, Ronald H. Nessen Files, Box 44, "Jerry Jones"; Warren to PIOs, November 29, 1974, Warren and White Files, Box 21, "Public Affairs Officers—Meetings (2)"; White to Warren, January 29, 1975; Randall Woods to White, September 5, 1975; White to Nessen, June 30, 1976; Margita E. White Papers, Box 1, Ford Presidential Library. Cf. Maltese, *Spin Control,* 127ff.

208. Maltese, *Spin Control,* 128.

209. White to Nessen, November 26, 1975, David Gergen Files, Box 1, "Advocate Program, Organization and Scheduling (1)," in Maltese, Spin Control, 131.

210. Maltese, *Spin Control,* 128. At the outset of the Ford administration, Assistant Press Secretary Paul Miltich supervised the "News Summary" (Aldo Beckman, October 31, 1974, *Chicago Tribune,* in "Warren, Jerry," Ronald H. Nessen Files, Box 45). The summary followed Warren to the new "public affairs" unit and then remained in the Office of Communications under both White (Shuman to Greener, September 1, 1975, Margita E. White Files, Box 1, "Office of Communications—Personnel [1]," Ford Presidential Library) and David Gergen (Gergen to Cheney, September 1, 1976, David Gergen Files, Box 3, "Office of Communication—Administration," Ford Presidential Library).

211. Maltese, *Spin Control,* 135.

212. Ibid.

213. Ibid. Cf. David Gergen, February 21, 1978, A. James Reichley Interview Transcripts, Box 1, Ford White House Interviews, Ford Presidential Library.

214. For more on Gergen's and Rhatican's convention activities, see, e.g., Maltese, *Spin Control,* 139–42.

215. Ibid., 145.

216. On the division of labor and organization of the Office of Communications under Gergen, see, e.g., "Office of Communications—Administration," Boxes 3, 6, David Gergen Files, Ford Presidential Library; Maltese, *Spin Control,* 132–48, 248.

217. Gergen, Duval, and Cavanaugh to Cheney, April 23, 1976, Jerry H. Jones Files, Box 19, "Communications," Ford Presidential Library.

218. Gergen to Cheney, "Communications Group," David Gergen Files, Box 6, "Office of Communications—Administration," Ford Presidential Library.

219. Maltese, *Spin Control,* 138; Gergen to Cheney, "Communications Group," David Gergen Files, Box 6, "Office of Communications—Administration," Ford Presidential Library. Maltese calls Gergen, Nessen, and Greener the "communications troika" of the campaign (*Spin Control,* 144).

220. Bonafede, October 9, 1976, *National Journal,* 1439, in "National Journal, October 1976," Agnes M. Waldron Files, Box 20, Ford Presidential Library. See also Grossman and Kumar, who quote a senior Ford official's estimate that "more than 60 percent of the political staff in the White House were used in promoting and publicizing the President" (*Portraying the President,* 83).

221. For example, Bario, in Powell, Miller Center interview, 35–36. For illustrations of the work of the office, see "Memoranda: Wurfel, Walt 6/2/77–8/29/77 [CF O/A 55]," Box 48, Jody Powell Files; see also "Memoranda: Media Liaison 1/11/78–6/27/78 [CF, O/A 160]"; "Memoranda: Media Liaison 7/18/78–12/4/78 [CF, O/A 160]"; "Memoranda: Media Liaison 1/22/79–5/30/79 [CF, O/A 519]"; "Memoranda: Media Liaison 10/1/79–12/20/79 [CF, O/A 519]"; Box 44, Jody Powell Files; and "Media Liaison Mailings . . . ," Folders 1–4, Domestic Policy Staff: Eizenstat, Box 234, Carter Presidential Library.

222. Jenkins to Watson, December 19, 1980, Jody Powell Files, Box 43, "Memoranda: Jenkins, Ray 1/2/80–12/31/80," Carter Presidential Library.

223. Maltese, *Spin Control,* 155.

224. Wurfel, "Dear Broadcasters," November 28, 1978, Jody Powell Files, Box 49, "Wurfel, Walt 8/1/78–12/19/78 [CF, O/A 160]," Carter Presidential Library.

225. Jenkins to Watson, December 19, 1980, Jody Powell Files, Box 43, "Memoranda: Jenkins, Ray 1/2/80–12/31/80," Carter Presidential Library.

226. Maltese, *Spin Control,* 151.

227. See, e.g., organizational chart attached to Goodwin to Press Office staff, April 13, 1978, Jody Powell Files, Box 45, "Memoranda: Misc. Press Office Staff 1/12/78–11/1/78 [CF, O/A 160]," Carter Presidential Library; Powell, Miller Center interview, 2–3.

228. Bario, in Powell, Miller Center interview, 6–7.

229. See Wurfel interview with John Anthony Maltese in Maltese, *Spin Control,* 151. The criticisms in the following memo are consistent with such a concern: Duka to Powell, Granum, October 27, 1977, Jody Powell Files, Box 41, "Memoranda: Duka, Walt 2/16/77–10/27/77 [CF, O/A 55]," Carter Presidential Library.

230. Kenneth E. Morris, *Jimmy Carter: American Moralist* (Athens: University of Georgia Press, 1996), 258–59. Cf. Burton I. Kaufman, *The Presidency of James Earl Carter, Jr.* (Lawrence: University Press of Kansas, 1993), chap. 7 and passim. On Carter's approval levels, see, e.g., George C. Edwards III with Alec M. Gallup, *Presidential Approval: A Sourcebook* (Baltimore: Johns Hopkins University Press, 1990), 80.

231. Gerald Rafshoon, Miller Center interview, April 8, 1983, Carter Presidency Project, Vol. XXI, Carter Presidential Library; Rafshoon, exit interview, September 12, 1979 (downloaded from Carter Library website July 12, 2001).

232. Rafshoon, exit interview, 4.

233. Ibid.

234. Rafshoon to Senior Staff, October 12, 1978, Rafshoon Papers (Schneiders Papers), Box 28, "Memoranda from Jerry Rafshoon—September 1978," Carter Presidential Library; Rafshoon, exit interview, 4.

235. Rafshoon to Senior Staff, July 31, 1978, Jody Powell Files, Box 46, "Memoranda: Rafshoon, Jerry 5/18/78–8/25/78 [CF, O/A 160]," Carter Presidential Library.

236. Rafshoon, exit interview, 6.

237. Ibid., 4, 7.

238. Rafshoon, Miller Center interview, 6. See, e.g., Rafshoon to President, July 20, 1978, "Thematics at Press Conferences," Rafshoon Papers (Schneiders Papers), Box 28, "Memoranda from Jerry Rafshoon—July 1978," Carter Presidential Library.

239. Rafshoon, exit interview, 8.

240. Rafshoon, Miller Center interview, 27.

241. Maltese, *Spin Control*, 166.

242. Rafshoon, exit interview, 4.

243. Wurfel to Schneiders, August 7, 1978, Jody Powell Files, Box 49, "Wurfel, Walt 8/1/78–12/19/78 [CF, O/A 160]," Carter Presidential Library.

244. Rafshoon, Miller Center interview, 14, 15.

245. See, e.g., "Defense Authorization Veto" (multiple folders), Box 2; "Civil Service Reform," Box 1; "Energy strategy," Box 2; "SALT" (multiple folders), Box 6; Rafshoon Papers, Carter Presidential Library. On Office of Communications activities related to SALT II, see also Maltese, *Spin Control*, 171–75.

246. Rafshoon, Miller Center interview, 18.

247. Schneiders drafted "talking points" for an early meeting of Rafshoon and Wexler in which the deputy director argued that although the goals of the two operations were the same, the means were "entirely different": Wexler is "wholesale," working with interest group representatives; Rafshoon is "retail." Wexler aimed at making Carter successful in Congress and hence popular; Rafshoon wanted to make the president popular and thus successful. Schneiders also urged Rafshoon to promise that he would always keep Wexler informed of communications activities and expected a similar response. See Schneiders to Rafshoon, July 10, 1978, Rafshoon Papers, Box 7, "Wexler's Group," Carter Presidential Library.

248. Maltese, *Spin Control*, 177.

249. Richard J. Tofel, a Harvard student and former press office intern, used this label in a paper that Ray Jenkins, a special assistant to the president for press relations, attached to a memo to Jack Watson (Jenkins to Watson, December 19, 1980, Jody Powell Files, Box 43, "Memoranda: Jenkins, Ray 1/2/80–12/31/80," Carter Presidential Library). Jenkins joined the White House staff in August 1979.

250. Al McDonald, Miller Center interview (including Michael Rowny), March 13–14, 1981, Carter Presidency Project, Vol. II, 97, Carter Presidential Library.

251. Wexler, Miller Center interview, 89.

252. See, e.g., Maltese, *Spin Control*, 170, quoting an interview with Patricia Bario.

253. Both Bario's and Powell's comments appear in Powell, Miller Center interview, 16–17.

254. Maltese, *Spin Control*, 155.

255. Dale Leibach, in Powell, Miller Center interview, 16.

256. See Heith, "Presidential Polling."

257. See, e.g., Martha Joynt Kumar, "The Office of the Press Secretary," *Presidential Studies Quarterly* 31 (June 2001): 296–322; Martha Joynt Kumar, "The Office of Communications," *Presidential Studies Quarterly* 31 (December 2001): 609–34.

258. See, e.g., Karen M. Hult, "Strengthening Presidential Decision-Making Capacity," *Presidential Studies Quarterly* 30 (March 2000): 27–46.

4. INTEREST GROUP OUTREACH

1. Charles E. Walcott and Karen M. Hult, *Governing the White House: From Hoover through LBJ* (Lawrence: University Press of Kansas, 1995), 118–34. Market structuring permits "decisions to emerge from the largely undirected interplay of individuals, groups, and subunits. Explicit questions of value or direction are never collectively raised. . . . The attainment of any . . . common objective is a by-product of participants' pursuit of their own interests." See Karen M. Hult and Charles E. Walcott, *Governing Public Organizations: Politics, Structures, and Institutional Design* (Pacific Grove, Calif.: Brooks/Cole, 1990), 47–48.

2. Joseph A. Pika, "Opening Doors for Kindred Souls: The White House Office of Public Liaison," in *Interest Group Politics,* 3d ed., ed. Allan J. Cigler and Burdett A. Loomis (Washington, D.C.: CQ Press, 1991), 228.

3. Ibid.

4. For example, Chapin to Haldeman, April 25, 1969, White House Special Files, Staff Member and Office Files, Dwight L. Chapin, Box 7, "Chronological—Chapin—March April 1969 [1 of 2],"; Chapin to Wilkinson, June 6, 1969, and Chapin to Woods, July 7, 1969, ibid., Box 8, "Chronological—D. Chapin—July 1969 [2 of 2]," Nixon Papers.

5. E.g., Charles W. Colson, exit interview with Jack Nesbitt and Susan Yowell, January 12, 1973, 12; Haldeman to Flanigan, December 15, 1969, White House Special Files, Staff Member and Office Files, Charles W. Colson, Box 1, "HRH Memos 1969–70 (complete) [1 of 3]"; ibid., Box 7, "Peter Flanigan," Nixon Papers.

6. Buchanan to Laura Genero, White House Special Files, Staff Member and Office Files, Patrick B. Buchanan, Box 1, "June 1971"; Colson to Haldeman, n.d. [mid to late December 1970], White House Special Files, Staff Member and Office Files, Charles W. Colson, Box 4, "HRH Memos [3 of 3] [12/19/70–6/30/71]," Nixon Papers.

7. For example, Colson to Haldeman, n.d. [December 1970], White House Special Files, Staff Member and Office Files, Charles W. Colson, Box 4, "HRH Memos [3 of 3] [12/19/70–6/30/71]"; Cole to Ehrlichman, May 19, 1971, attached to Cole to Ehrlichman, October 4, 1971, Subject Files: Confidential Files, 1969–74, White House Central Files, White House Special Files, Box 46, II, "[CF] PL Political Affairs, 9/1/71–4/30/72 [1971–74]," Nixon Papers.

8. Bradley H. Patterson Jr., exit interview with Terry W. Good, September 10, 1974, 2, Nixon Papers.

9. For example, Colson to Bell, August 12, 1971, White House Special Files, Staff Member and Office Files, Charles W. Colson, Box 5, "George Bell 1970–71 [1 of 3]," Nixon Papers.

10. Colson to Howard, August 10, 1971, White House Special Files, Staff Member and Office Files, Charles W. Colson, Box 8, "Dick Howard, [1 of 2]," Nixon Papers.

11. *Haldeman Diaries* CD-ROM, Haldeman insert, February 23, 1970.

12. Ibid.

13. See, e.g., handwritten memo, n.d. [1970 or 1971], prepared for the new staff secretary. White House Special Files, Staff Member and Office Files, Office of the Staff Secretary, Box 150, "Staff Secretary Move," Nixon Papers. "In particular [Colson] is heading up our efforts to gain the support of Labor Leaders and the rank and file."

14. For example, September 8, 1972, meeting with Joe DeSilva, Secretary-Treasurer, Local 770; September 23, 1972, meeting with Thomas Gleason, President of the International Longshoremen's Association; October 19, 1972, meeting with Paul Hall, Seafarers International Union of North America, White House Special Files, Staff Member and Office Files, Charles W. Colson, Box 1, "Memorandums for the President [1 of 2]," Nixon Papers.

15. For example, Colson to Haldeman, December 5, 1969, White House Special Files, Staff Member and Office Files, Charles W. Colson, Box 1, "HRH Memos 1969–70 (complete) [1 of 3]"; Colson to Shultz, August 30, October 8, October 19, November 8, 1971; January 17, April 18, 1972, ibid., Box 11, "Geo Shultz [1971]," "Geo Shultz [1972]," Nixon Papers. See personnel recommendations and "clearance" in ibid., Box 8, "Dick Howard," Nixon Papers.

16. Nixon to Colson, March 8, 1971, White House Special Files, Staff Member and Office Files, Charles W. Colson, Box 1, "Memorandums for the President [2 of 2]," Nixon Papers.

17. Ibid.

18. For example, Colson to Haldeman, December 5, 1970, White House Special Files, Staff Member and Office Files, Charles W. Colson, Box 1, "HRH Memos 1969–70 (complete) [1 of 3]"; Colson to Haldeman, "Labor and the Economic Issue," August 19, 1971, ibid., Box 14, "White House Strategy Memos"; Colson to Shultz, October 28, 1971, ibid., Box 11, "George Shultz [1971]"; Colson to Staff Secretary, July 14, 1972, ibid., Box 9, "Bruce Kehrli—Staff Secretary [1 of 2]," Nixon Papers. In return for Lovestone's intelligence, Colson "shared classified FBI and other government files . . . about radicals in the unions" (Melvin Small, *The Presidency of Richard Nixon* [Lawrence: University Press of Kansas, 1999], 246).

19. For example, Colson to Shultz, October 28, 1971, White House Special Files, Staff Member and Office Files, Charles W. Colson, Box 11, "George Shultz [1971]"; Colson to Haldeman, October 6, 1970, ibid., Box 1, "HRH Memos 1969–70 (complete) [2 of 3]," Nixon Papers. See also Dean J. Kotlowski, *Nixon's Civil Rights: Politics, Principle, and Policy* (Cambridge: Harvard University Press, 2001).

20. John H. Kessel, *Presidential Campaign Politics: Coalition Strategies and Citizen Response*, 2d ed. (Homewood, Ill.: Dorsey, 1984), 147.

21. Colson to Haldeman, December 22, 1970, White House Special Files, Staff Member and Office Files, Charles W. Colson, Box 3, "HRH Memos 1969–70 (complete) [1 of 3]," Nixon Papers.

22. Colson to President, November 19, 1970, White House Special Files, Staff Member and Office Files, Charles W. Colson, Box 1, "Memorandums for the President [2 of 2]," Nixon Papers.

23. For example, Colson to President, December 5, 1970, White House Special Files, Staff Member and Office Files, Charles W. Colson, Box 1, "Memorandums for the President [2 of 2]"; Bell to Haldeman, June 3, 1970, ibid., Box 2, "HRH Memos 1969–70 (complete) [3 of 3]," Nixon Papers. See also Kotlowski, *Nixon's Civil Rights.*

24. See, e.g., Kotlowski, *Nixon's Civil Rights,* 112ff., 231. Although calling him a "bigot and a crass opportunist," Kotlowski notes as well that "Colson's right-wing position on civil rights stemmed from electoral considerations, the need to woo blue-collar voters, not laissez-faire principles" (112).

25. See, e.g., exchanges of memos between Colson and H. R. Haldeman, in "Ex WH 4 Office Management, 1/1/70–12/31/70," three folders, numerous dates, White House Central Files, Subject Files, WH (White House Administration), Box 8; Richard Nixon to H. R. Haldeman, "Memos—March 1970," "Memos—February 1971," "Memos—June 1972," "Memos—August 1972"; "Memoranda from the President, 1969–1974," White House Special Files, President's Personal File, Boxes 2–4, Nixon Papers.

26. For example, Colson to Bell, December 30, 1971, White House Special Files, Staff Member and Office Files, Charles W. Colson, Box 5, "George Bell 1970–71 [1 of 3]"; Bell to Colson, January 27, 1972, ibid., Box 1, "Memorandums for the President [1 of 2]"; Colson exit interview, 1973, 9, Nixon Papers.

27. Bell to Colson, July 28, 1971, White House Special Files, Staff Member and Office Files, Charles W. Colson, Box 1, "Memorandums for the President [2 of 2]," Nixon Papers.

28. On Bell's involvement in establishing and nurturing contacts with religious organizations, see, e.g., Colson to Haldeman, n.d. [response to November 30, 1970, memo from Haldeman], White House Special Files, Staff Member and Office Files, Charles W. Colson, Box 4, "H. R. H. Memos [3 of 3] [12/19/70–6/30/71]"; Krogh to Bell, cc: Colson, March 29, 1971, ibid., Box 5, "George Bell 1970–71 [2 of 3]," Nixon Papers. On his contact with senior citizen groups, see, e.g., Bell to Colson, May 17, 1971, ibid., Box 2, "H. R. H. Memos—1971 Jan.–June 1971 [1 of 3]," Nixon Papers.

29. Colson memo for President's File, August 25, 1971, White House Special Files, Staff Member and Office Files, Charles W. Colson, Box 1, "Memorandums for the President [1 of 2]," Nixon Papers.

30. Ibid.

31. Colson to Bell, August 3, 1970, White House Special Files, Staff Member and Office Files, Charles W. Colson, Box 5, "George Bell 1970–71 [3 of 3]," Nixon Papers.

32. See, e.g., Colson to Bell memos in White House Special Files, Staff Member and Office Files, Charles W. Colson, Box 5, "George Bell 1970–71 [3 of 3]," Nixon Papers.

33. Henry Cashen interview, October 11, 1977, James Reichley Interviews, Box 1, Nixon White House Interviews, Ford Presidential Library.

34. See, e.g., Burstein (vice president of a contracting company) to Cashen, June 21, 1971, thanking him for his assistance, in White House Special Files, Staff Member and Office Files, Charles W. Colson, Box 6, "Henry Cashen [1 of 2]," Nixon Papers.

35. Colson exit interview, 1973, 9. See also Colson to President, July 28, 1971, White House Special Files, Staff Member and Office Files, Charles W. Colson, Box 1, "Memorandums for the President [2 of 2]," Nixon Papers.

36. For example, Colson to Malek, March 7, 1971, White House Special Files, Staff Member and Office Files, Charles W. Colson, Box 10, "Fred Malek/Don Kingsley"; Colson to Haldeman, February 10, 1972, ibid., Box 4, "HRH Memos [2 of 3] [7/1/71–5/2/72]"; President to Haldeman, June 12, 1972, White House Special Files, President's Personal File, "Memoranda from the President, 1969–74," Box 4, "Memos—June 1972," Nixon Papers.

37. Colson to Cashen, June 14, 1971, White House Special Files, Staff Member and Office Files, Charles W. Colson, Box 6, "Henry Cashen [2 of 2]," Nixon Papers.

38. For example, Colson to Haldeman, November 6, 1970, "HRH Memos 1969 (com-

plete) [2 of 3]"; Cashen to Rumsfeld, August 12, 1971, "H. R. Haldeman June–Dec 1971 [1 of 3]"; White House Special Files, Staff Member and Office Files, Charles W. Colson, Box 1, Nixon Papers.

39. Pika, "Opening Doors for Kindred Souls," 288.

40. See, e.g., Colson to Howard, August 2, 1971, January 5, 1972, June 15, 1972, White House Special Files, Staff Member and Office Files, Charles W. Colson, Box 8, "Dick Howard," Nixon Papers.

41. Colson in particular harshly criticized the RNC effort. In mid-1971, he complained about the resources the RNC was devoting to ethnic liaison, noting that "this is the time when we should be sending organizational people and field people in to cultivate ethnic groups . . . gathering intelligence and working with us on strategy" (Colson to Haldeman, May 6, 1971, White House Special Files, Staff Member and Office Files, Charles W. Colson, Box 2, "HRH Memos—1971 Jan.–June 1971 [2 of 3]," Nixon Papers). Later, he expressed concern about the committee's emphasis on attempting to "[build the] long term image and credibility of the RNC" while paying less attention to the 1972 presidential election. Colson did not believe that the person in charge of the "ethnic operation" at the committee, Lazlo Pasztor, was effective. See memos in "Larry Higby," Folder 1, White House Special Files, Staff Member and Office Files, Charles W. Colson, Box 8. In addition, Colson aides noted useful activities to be undertaken by the "ethnic operation" at the CRP. See, e.g., Howard to Chapin, January 21, 1972, Subject Files: Confidential Files, 1969–74, White House Special Files, White House Central Files, Box 51, "[CF] PR-7 [Engagements—Appts—Interviews] 9/1/71–[6/5/74] [1971–74]," Nixon Papers.

42. "From Garbage Collector to Ph.D.: Dr. Balzano President's Assistant," *Sons of Italy Times,* in "News Summary," n.d. [UPI news feed April 17, 1972], White House Special Files, Staff Member and Office Files, Charles W. Colson, Box 5, "Mike Balzano," Nixon Papers.

43. Colson to Balzano, April 10, 1972, White House Special Files, Staff Member and Office Files, Charles W. Colson, Box 5, "Mike Balzano," Nixon Papers.

44. Colson, exit interview, 35.

45. For example, Colson to Higby, April 14, 1972, White House Special Files, Staff Member and Office Files, Charles W. Colson, Box 8, "Larry Higby," Folder 2, Nixon Papers.

46. See, e.g., Colson to Staff Secretary, July 14, 1972, White House Special Files, Staff Member and Office Files, Charles W. Colson, Box 9, "Bruce Kehrli—Staff Secretary [1 of 2]," Nixon Papers.

47. See Colson to Malek, January 5, 1972, White House Special Files, Staff Member and Office Files, Charles W. Colson, Box 10, "Fred Malek/Dan Kingsley," Nixon Papers. Evidently, Marumoto was also supposed to supervise Carlos Conde of Herb Klein's staff "in increasing [the] flow of materials in Spanish-speaking media."

48. Colson, exit interview, 9.

49. At least at the outset, Evans and McLane sought to divide their responsibilities for the aging, with the former handling more "political" matters (e.g., serving as liaison with organizations for the aging, monitoring appointments, coordinating speeches) and the latter dealing with more "substantive matters" (e.g., working to "assure White House support for policies that will aid in winning the elderly vote"). Evans remained "skeptical" about the division. See Evans to Colson, January 13, 1972, White House Special Files, Staff Member and Office Files, Charles W. Colson, Box 6, "Ken Cole [1972]," Nixon Papers. See also Colson, interview, 9, 12.

50. See Colson to Malek, January 5, 1972, White House Special Files, Staff Member and

Office Files, Charles W. Colson, Box 10, "Fred Malek/Dan Kingsley," Nixon Papers. On Hallett's previous assignment, see, e.g., Colson to Malek, December 14, 1971, ibid., "Fred Malek [2 of 2]."

51. Pika, "Opening Doors for Kindred Souls," 288–89. The only mention of such groups in the *Haldeman Diaries* is Tell It to Hanoi, representatives of which met with the president for a photo session on December 5, 1969.

52. See, e.g., Finch to Haldeman, January 15, 1973, White House Special Files, Staff Member and Office Files, Office of the Staff Secretary, Box 188, "Armstrong staff [#3]," Nixon Papers.

53. Kotlowski, *Nixon's Civil Rights,* 141. Small notes that "the value of government 'set-aside' contracts for minority businesses rose from $8 million in 1969 to $243 million in 1972" (*Presidency of Richard Nixon,* 174).

54. Kotlowski, *Nixon's Civil Rights,* 177.

55. Ibid., 115, 178, and passim.

56. On Brown's involvement in group liaison during the reelection period, see, e.g., Horton to Cole and Colson, January 27, 1972, attachment: "Issue/Constituent Group Assignments," White House Special Files, Staff Member and Office Files, Charles W. Colson, Box 3, "H. R. Haldeman January 1972 [4 of 4]," Nixon Papers. On charges of efforts to influence the contracting process, see Kotlowski, *Nixon's Civil Rights,* 147–48.

57. For example, Horton to Colson, August 26, 1971, White House Special Files, Staff Member and Office Files, Charles W. Colson, Box 14, "Misc Staff Memos 1970–1971 [2 of 8] [7/29/71–10/29/71]," Nixon Papers.

58. Stanley Scott [no recipient, but part of December 1972 job description exercise], White House Special Files, Staff Member and Office Files, Office of the Staff Secretary, Box 162, "White House Staff Member Office Files, 1972 #3," Nixon Papers.

59. The two did collaborate (along with several other blacks in the administration) on a lengthy analysis of how African Americans might be approached during the 1972 reelection campaign. See "The Black Vote in 1972," presumably directed to President Nixon, received in White House Special Files, September 29, 1971, in Subject Files: Confidential Files, 1969–74, White House Special Files, White House Central Files, Box 46, "[CF] PL Political Affairs, 9/1/71–4/30/72 [1971–74]," Nixon Papers.

60. Scott to Haig, August 17, 1973, "U.S. Aid in African Famine," White House Special Files, Staff Member and Office Files, Alexander M. Haig, 1970–74, Box 4, "Misc [2 of 2]," Nixon Papers.

61. Parker to Secretary of State Kissinger, October 1, 1973, White House Special Files, Staff Member and Office Files, Alexander M. Haig 1970–74, Box 8, "Dave Parker, Interstaff Communications, 1973," Nixon Papers.

62. Kehrli to Harlow, Timmons, Malek, Korologos, Friedersdorf, Ebner, October 27, 1973, White House Central Files, Subject Files: White House Administration, Box 1, Tab C: "Counsellors and Staff," "Ex WH 1 Budget 1/1/73–7/19/74," Nixon Papers.

63. Kehrli to Haig, January 18, 1974, White House Special Files, Staff Member and Office Files, Office of the Staff Secretary, Box 192, "WHPO [#3],"Nixon Papers.

64. Garment to Steve Horn (vice chair of the U.S. Committee on Civil Rights), June 14, 1973, White House Central Files, Staff Member and Office Files, Anne L. Armstrong, Box 30, "White House and Civil Rights," Nixon Papers.

65. For example, Colson response to Haldeman memo (November 30, 1970), n.d., White

House Special Files, Staff Member and Office Files, Charles W. Colson, Box 4, "HRH Memos [3 of 3] [12/19/70–6/30/71]," Nixon Papers.

66. Kotlowski, *Nixon's Civil Rights*, 176ff. Cf. *Haldeman Diaries* CD-ROM, July 18, 1970.

67. Kotlowski, *Nixon's Civil Rights*, 112.

68. For example, Haldeman to Finch, September 8, 1970, White House Special Files, Staff Member and Office Files, Dwight L. Chapin, Box 18, Nixon Papers. See also Kotlowski, *Nixon's Civil Rights*, chap. 8.

69. Kotlowski, *Nixon's Civil Rights*, 230.

70. Ibid., 231. The quoted words are Peter Flanigan's, reacting to Leonard Garment's draft response to the report; Haldeman "scrawled" his agreement and "shelved the idea" (ibid.; Haldeman handwritten comment on Flanigan to Haldeman, February 16, 1970, White House Special Files, Haldeman Files, Box 209, Nixon Papers).

71. Kotlowski, *Nixon's Civil Rights*, 231.

72. For example, Horton to Cole and Colson, January 27, 1972, attachment: "Issue/Constituent Group Assignments," White House Special Files, Staff Member and Office Files, Charles W. Colson, Box 3, "H. R. Haldeman January 1972 [4 of 4]," Nixon Papers.

73. Kotlowski, *Nixon's Civil Rights*, 240. The order, which the secretary of labor signed on December 1, 1971, "defined women as an 'affected class' and directed firms with federal contracts exceeding $50,000 to submit written plans, with goals and timetables, for recruiting them" (243).

74. See, e.g., White House Central Files, Staff Member and Office Files, Anne L. Armstrong, Box 8, "Meetings, Armstrong Staff"; Kehrli to Haldeman, January 23, 1973, White House Special Files, Staff Member and Office Files, Office of the Staff Secretary, Box 188, "Armstrong Staff [#3]," Nixon Papers.

75. Armstrong to Kehrli, March 28, 1974, White House Central Files, Staff Member and Office Files, Anne L. Armstrong, Box 12, "[Chron File—March 1974]," Nixon Papers.

76. AP article by Frances Lewine, May 14, 1974, in White House Special Files, Staff Member and Office Files, Office of the Staff Secretary, Box 130, "Personnel Matters (Wimer) [2]," Nixon Papers.

77. For example, Armstrong to Stan Ebner, July 30, 1973, White House Central Files, Staff Member and Office Files, Anne L. Armstrong, Box 11, "[Chron File—July 1973]," Nixon Papers.

78. For example, Hirschberg to Armstrong, January 17, 1974, White House Central Files, Staff Member and Office Files, Anne L. Armstrong, Box 12, "[Chron File—January 1974]"; Lindh to Armstrong, July 3, 1974, ibid., "Chron File July 1–15, 1974]," Nixon Papers.

79. Garment to Steve Horn (vice chair of the U.S. Committee on Civil Rights), June 14, 1973, White House Central Files, Staff Member and Office Files, Anne L. Armstrong, Box 30, "White House and Civil Rights," Nixon Papers.

80. Smith to Armstrong, October 29, 1973 [draft letter from Armstrong to Haig], "Nola [Smith] [Re: Personnel]," White House Central Files, Staff Member and Office Files, Anne L. Armstrong, Box 10, Nixon Papers.

81. Draft, n.d., "Speech Material—Pat [Lindh]," White House Central Files, Staff Member and Office Files, Anne L. Armstrong, Box 24, Nixon Papers.

82. See, e.g., Nola Smith to Hirschberg, Ruckelshaus, December 19, 1973, White House Central Files, Staff Member and Office Files, Anne L. Armstrong, Box 11, "Chron File—

December 1973"; Lindh to Senator Brock, ibid., Box 12, "Chron File—Aug 1–24 [1974]," Nixon Papers.

83. Yedlowski to J. Jones, June 28, 1974, "[Chron File—June 1974]"; Yedlowski to Bryan Barrett, July 10, 1974, "[Chron File—July 1–15, 1974]," White House Central Files, Staff Member and Office Files, Anne L. Armstrong, Box 12, Nixon Papers.

84. For example, Slight to Armstrong, August 2, 1974, White House Central Files, Staff Member and Office Files, Anne L. Armstrong, Box 7, "Central Files—Nixon Papers. Miscellaneous Correspondence [and staff memos]," Nixon Papers.

85. Ibid.

86. Slight to Armstrong, August 1, 1974, White House Central Files, Staff Member and Office Files, Anne L. Armstrong, Box 7, "Central Files—Nixon Papers. Miscellaneous Correspondence [and staff memos]," Nixon Papers.

87. Patterson, exit interview, 21. Klein aide Carlos Conde expressed similarly positive views; Conde to Armstrong, March 15, 1973, White House Central Files, Staff Member and Office Files, Anne L. Armstrong, Box 1, "(ALA) C," Nixon Papers.

88. Smith to Armstrong, October 29, 1973 (Smith drafted a letter for Armstrong to send to Haig, outlining her several frustrations with Jerry Jones's personnel office), White House Central Files, Staff Member and Office Files, Anne L. Armstrong, Box 10, "Nola [Smith] [Re: Personnel]," Nixon Papers.

89. Kehrli to Haig, February 19, 1974, quoting an earlier Haig memo, White House Special Files, Staff Member and Office Files, David Hoopes, Box 10, "White House Health Unit—Women," Nixon Papers. In this memo, Kehrli recommended that they reconsider and set aside time in the morning when the unit would be open to women, when the men were not using it. Haig agreed, and it was done.

90. Colson to Bell, April 5, 1971, White House Special Files, Staff Member and Office Files, Charles W. Colson, Box 5, "George Bell 1970–71 [2 of 3]," Nixon Papers.

91. Cashen to Colson, March 26, 1971, White House Special Files, Staff Member and Office Files, Charles W. Colson, Box 6, "Henry Cashen [2 of 2]," Nixon Papers.

92. Krogh to Colson, October 5, 1971, and Colson to Krogh, October 7, 1971, White House Special Files, Staff Member and Office Files, Charles W. Colson, Box 9, "Bud Krogh," Nixon Papers.

93. For example, Colson to Cashen, September 10, 1970, "Henry Cashen Files [2 of 2]"; March 9, 1972, "Ken Cole [1972]"; White House Special Files, Staff Member and Office Files, Charles W. Colson, Box 6, Nixon Papers.

94. Hullin to Ehrlichman, April 18, 1970, report on April 13 domestic affairs meeting [of the DC staff], WH (White House Administration), White House Central Files, Subject Files, Box 22, "Ex. WH 7 (Staff Meetings) 1/1/70–8/31/70," Nixon Papers.

95. Cole and Colson to Ehrlichman and Haldeman, cc: Chapin, March 6, 1970, White House Special Files, Staff Member and Office Files, Charles W. Colson, Box 1, "HRH Memos 1969–70 (complete) [1 of 3]," Nixon Papers.

96. Ibid.

97. Cole to Ehrlichman, May 19, 1971, attachment to Cole to Ehrlichman, October 4, 1971, Subject Files: Confidential Files 1969–74, White House Special Files, White House Central Files, Box 46, "[CF] PL Political affairs, 9/1/71–4/30/72 [1971–74]," Nixon Papers.

98. Cole to Ehrlichman, October 4, 1971, Subject Files: Confidential Files 1969–74, White House Special Files, White House Central Files, Box 46, "[CF] PL Political affairs, 9/1/71–4/30/72 [1971–74]," Nixon Papers.

99. Quotes are from Charles W. Colson, oral history interview with Frederick J. Graboske, June 15, 1988, Nixon Papers.

100. Colson to Weinberger, June 6, 1972, White House Special Files, Staff Member and Office Files, Charles W. Colson, Box 12, "Cap Weinberger," Nixon Papers.

101. For example, Cashen to Colson, January 21, 1972, "Weekly summary on matters with which I am currently involved," White House Special Files, Staff Member and Office Files, Charles W. Colson, Box 6, "Memos for Henry Cashen [1972]," Nixon Papers.

102. Colson to Rhatican, Cohen, May 30, 1972, White House Special Files, Staff Member and Office Files, Charles W. Colson, Box 10, "Bill Rhatican," Nixon Papers.

103. Cf. Kenneth E. Collier, *Between the Branches: The White House Office of Legislative Affairs* (Pittsburgh: University of Pittsburgh Press, 1997), 129.

104. Ibid., 115.

105. Colson to Timmons, December 17, 1970, White House Special Files, Staff Member and Office Files, Charles W. Colson, Box 14, "Misc Staff Memos 1970–1971 [6 of 8] [9/1/70–12/31/70]," Nixon Papers. Colson made sure to "bcc" Larry Higby, noting, "I'm beginning to sound more and more like H. Klein every day—in fact, I'm getting worried."

106. Collier, *Between the Branches,* 115.

107. Colson, exit interview, 12.

108. See, e.g., ibid., 13–14.

109. For example, Whelihan to Ziegler, March 19, 1973, White House Special Files, Staff Member and Office Files, Ronald Ziegler, Box 1, "Basic Reorganization of Press Office [1 of 3]," Nixon Papers.

110. Kehrli to Harlow, Timmons, Malek, Korologos, Friedersdorf, Ebner, October 27, 1973, White House Central Files, Subject Files: White House Administration, Box 1, "Ex WH 1 Budget 1/1/73–7/19/74," Nixon Papers.

111. Kehrli to Haig, January 19, 1974, Tab B, White House Special Files, Staff Member and Office Files, Alexander M. Haig 1970–74, Box 15, "Bruce Kehrli [2 of 2]," "Interstaff Communications, 1974," Nixon Papers. Although Colson no longer directed the group liaison operation, he did not formally leave the White House for private law practice (and later, prison on Watergate-related charges) until March 1973.

112. Baroody to Haig, May 7, 1973, White House Special Files, Staff Member and Office Files, Ronald Ziegler, Box 1, "Basic Reorganization of the Press Office [3 of 3]," Nixon Papers.

113. Ibid.

114. Ibid.

115. See, e.g., "Baroody Staff [#1]," White House Special Files, Staff Member and Office Files, Office of the Staff Secretary, Box 188, Nixon Papers.

116. Martha Angle, "Impeachment Lobby," *Washington Star-News,* December 7, 1973, attached to Harlow to Shultz, Armstrong, Garment, Stein, Bennett, Laird, Baroody, Timmons, Flanigan, Cole, White House Special Files, Staff Member and Office Files, Alexander M. Haig 1970–74, Box 11, "Bryce Harlow," "Interstaff Communications, 1973," Nixon Papers.

117. Kehrli to Haig, January 29, 1974, White House Special Files, Staff Member and Office Files, Alexander M. Haig, Box 15, "Bruce Kehrli [2 of 2]," "Interstaff Communications, 1974," Nixon Papers.

118. Flanigan, Baroody to President, May 17, 1974, White House Special Files, Staff Member and Office Files, Office of Staff Secretary, Administrative Files [Courier Files], Box 41, "May 18, 1974 Courier to Key Biscayne, FL." See also Baroody to the President,

March 15, 1974. Subject Files: Confidential Files, 1969–74, White House Special Files, White House Central Files, Box 12, "[CF] FG 1 The President, 1973 on [1971–74] (1 of 2)," Nixon Papers.

119. John Robert Greene, *The Presidency of Gerald R. Ford* (Lawrence: University Press of Kansas, 1995), 61.

120. Baroody, interview, February 6, 1985, William A. Syers Papers, Files, 1985—Interviews, Box 1, Ford Presidential Library.

121. Quoted on undated charts, evidently for a cabinet presentation on OPL, in "Public Liaison Office—Concepts," William J. Baroody, 1974–77 Subject File, Box 10, Ford Presidential Library.

122. See, e.g., UPI, "Aide Selling Ford as Right for Job," *Houston Post,* May 18, 1975, in "Congratulations from Baroody," William J. Baroody, 1974–75 Subject File, Box 5, Ford Presidential Library.

123. For example, "New Communications Link with Government," *Association Management,* November 1974, 47, in "Public Liaison Office—General (2)," William J. Baroody, 1974–77 Subject File, Box 10; Baroody, Warren to Rumsfeld, May 7, 1975; "Analysis of Present White House Office," December 7, 1976, White House Study Project, Report Number 1, Ford Presidential Library.

124. "New Communications Link with Government," November 1974.

125. Fact sheet, December 18, 1974, "Office—Organization," Robert T. Hartmann Files, Box 13; "Finding Aid," John O. Marsh, Ford Presidential Library.

126. A. James Reichley, *Conservatives in an Age of Change: The Nixon and Ford Administrations* (Washington, D.C.: Brookings Institution, 1981), 312–13.

127. For example, Baroody, interview, 1985; Pika, "Opening Doors for Kindred Souls," 290; memos in "Consumer Protection Agency—Administration Alternative Plan (2)," John O. Marsh, General Subject File, Box 10; UPI, "Aide Selling Ford as Right for Job," *Houston Post,* May 18, 1975, in "Congratulations from Baroody," William J. Baroody, 1974–77 Subject File, Box 5, Ford Presidential Library.

128. Baroody, interview, 1985.

129. Jeff Wood, " 'Baroody Briefings' Bringing Executives Inside Information," *Potomac Pulse,* December 16, 1975, in "Public Liaison Office—General (4)," William J. Baroody, 1974–77 Subject File, Box 10, Ford Presidential Library.

130. "New Communications Link with Government," November 1974. See also Baroody to C. Langhorne Washburne (assistant secretary for tourism), March 13, 1975, William J. Baroody, 1974–77 Subject File, Box 4, "Chrono File, 8/74–7/75 (2)," Ford Presidential Library.

131. Baroody, Warren to Rumsfeld, May 7, 1975, William J. Baroody, 1974–77 Subject File, Box 10, "Public Liaison Office—General (4)"; see also Marguerite McAuliffe to Baroody, November 6, 1974, William J. Baroody, 1974–77 Subject File, Box 4, "Chrono File, 8/74–7/75 (1)"; William J. Baroody, WH Memoranda, Box 24, "Marrs, Theodore (1)," Ford Presidential Library.

132. See, e.g., Baroody to Rumsfeld, handwritten reply to Rumsfeld's November 2, 1974, memo, "Rumsfeld, Donald," William J. Baroody, WH Memoranda, Box 25; "Valis, Wayne," William J. Baroody, WH Memoranda, Box 26, Ford Presidential Library.

133. For example, Lindh via Baroody to Cannon, May 1, 1975, "Cannon, James"; Lindh to Baroody, December 19, 1975, "Cheney, Richard"; William J. Baroody, WH Memoranda, Box 21, Ford Presidential Library.

134. Baroody, Warren to Rumsfeld, May 17, 1975, "Public Liaison Office—General (4)," William J. Baroody, 1974–77 Subject File, Box 10, Ford Presidential Library.

135. On DeBaca's efforts, see, e.g., "DeBaca, Fernando," William J. Baroody, WH Memoranda, Box 21, Ford Presidential Library.

136. For example, Griffin to Buchen, August 14, 1974, "Transition—Presidential Meetings (3)," Philip Buchen Files, General Subject File, Box 63, Ford Presidential Library.

137. Cannon to Buchen, June 8, 1976, "Personnel—General," Philip Buchen Files, General Subject File, Box 42; David H. Lissy, oral history interview with Stephen J. Wayne, November 30, 1976, in James F. C. Hyde and Stephen J. Wayne Oral History Collection, 3, Ford Presidential Library.

138. Brannon to Gergen, August 6, 1976, "Office of Communication—Administration," David Gergen Files, Box 3, Ford Presidential Library.

139. Anna Chennault to President Ford, February 8, 1975, "Gwen Anderson," William J. Baroody, White House Memoranda, Box 21, Ford Presidential Library.

140. Greene, *Presidency of Ford,* 19; Joseph Lelyveld, "Former Prof Holds 'Seminars' for President and His Top Advisers," *New York Times,* October 6, 1975, in "Newspaper Clippings (2)," William J. Baroody, 1974–77 Subject File, Box 9, Ford Presidential Library. At first, Goldwin worked as a detailee in the editorial office; later, he appeared on organizational charts for the Domestic Council staff.

141. See, e.g., Phil D. Helmig, Atlantic/Richfield to Jones, November 26, 1975; Jones to Cheney, December 18, 1975; Jerry H. Jones Files, Box 20, Ford Presidential Library.

142. For example, Wolthuis through Friedersdorf to Kendall, Loen, O'Donnell, Leppert, Bennett, March 7, 1975, "Congressional Relations Office (2)," John O. Marsh, General Subject File, Box 10, Ford Presidential Library.

143. For example, Baroody to Friedersdorf, January 10, 1975, "Knauer, Virginia (3)," William J. Baroody, White House Memoranda, Box 23, Ford Presidential Library.

144. Baroody to Seidman, December 12, 1974, "Seidman, L. William," William J. Baroody, White House Memoranda, Box 26; Baroody to Simon, Seidman, October 2, 1974, "Cabinet—Treasury (1)"; Baroody to Mary Brooks (director of the Bureau of the Mint), November 18, 1974, "Cabinet—Treasury (2)"; Baroody to Simon, May 28, 1975, "Cabinet—Treasury (3)"; William J. Baroody, 1974–77 Subject File, Box 4, Ford Presidential Library.

145. For example, Baroody to Cannon, May 15, June 6, June 30, 1975, "Cannon, James," William J. Baroody, White House Memoranda, Box 21, Ford Presidential Library.

146. See materials in "Scowcroft, Brent," William J. Baroody, White House Memoranda, Box 26, Ford Presidential Library.

147. For example, Scowcroft to Baroody, August 15, 1976, "Scowcroft, Brent," William J. Baroody, White House Memoranda, Box 26, Ford Presidential Library. In the memo, Scowcroft commented on the possible problems associated with OPL staffer Kuropas participating on the president's behalf in two Croatian American–sponsored bicentennial events.

148. Baroody, "Memorandum for Discussion [on] Presidential Leadership on Consumer Issues," January 22, 1975, "Agency for Consumer Advocacy (1)," William J. Baroody, 1974–77 Subject File, Box 1, Ford Presidential Library.

149. Byington to Seidman, March 24, 1975, "Consumer Protection Agency—Legislation," John O. Marsh, General Subject File, Box 10, Ford Presidential Library.

150. The OPL draft was circulated by the staff secretary on March 24, 1975. Rourke transmitted Cannon's revisions to Marsh, noting that Cannon "did not like the Baroody shop letter either. He has completely redone it and, in my opinion, it is a far better product" (Rourke

to Marsh, March 25, 1975, "Consumer Protection Agency—Administration Alternative Plan [1]," John O. Marsh, General Subject File, Box 10, Ford Presidential Library). Marsh sent this version to Cheney, Connor, Lynn, O'Neill, and Rumsfeld on March 25, 1975.

151. J. Jones to Cannon (cc: Rumsfeld, Baroody, Lynn, Seidman, Marsh, Lazarus), April 15, 1975, "Consumer Protection Agency—Administration Alternative Plan (2)," John O. Marsh, General Subject File, Box 10, Ford Presidential Library.

152. Baroody via Marsh to the President, n.d., "Agency for Consumer Advocacy (1)," William J. Baroody, 1974–77 Subject File, Box 1, Ford Presidential Library.

153. Knauer through Baroody to the President, June 23, 1975, "Knauer, Virginia (5)," William J. Baroody, White House Memoranda, Box 23, Ford Presidential Library.

154. Knauer to Baroody, September 8, 1976, "Knauer, Virginia (7)," William J. Baroody, White House Memoranda, Box 23; "Consumer Representation Plans Fail to Silence Agency Advocates," *National Journal,* March 27, 1976, 402–6, in "Consumer Protection Agency—Administration Alternative Plan (2)," John O. Marsh, General Subject File, Box 10, Ford Presidential Library.

155. Baroody to Nessen, January 12, 1976, "Nessen, Ron (2)," William J. Baroody, White House Memoranda, Box 24, Ford Presidential Library.

156. "Consumer Representation Plans Fail," *National Journal,* March 27, 1976, 402.

157. Pika, "Opening Doors for Kindred Souls," 29.

158. See, e.g., Bertram Carp, interview with Carp and David Rubenstein, Miller Center interview, March 6, 1982, Carter Presidency Project, Vol. XIV, 61, Carter Presidential Library; Michael Baruch Grossman and Martha Joynt Kumar, *Portraying the President: The White House and the News Media* (Baltimore: Johns Hopkins University Press, 1981), 114; Kenneth E. Morris, *Jimmy Carter: American Moralist* (Athens: University of Georgia Press, 1996); Pika, "Opening Doors for Kindred Souls," 29–30.

159. Ronnie Feit to All OPL Staff, February 2, 1977, "Memos, 2/77–6/77," Carter Presidential Papers: Staff Offices, OPL: Costanza, Box 14, Carter Presidential Library.

160. Memo, n.d. (although evidently mid-1977, for use by the presidential reorganization team), "Memos, 2/77–6/77," Staff Offices, OPL: Costanza, Box 14, Carter Presidential Library.

161. Robert Nastanovich, March 22, 1977, minutes of March 16, 1977, staff meeting, "[Office of Public Liaison Staff Meetings], 3/77–3/78," Staff Offices, OPL: Costanza, Box 31, Carter Presidential Library; Karen DeWitt, "Midge Costanza: The President's 'Window on the Nation,'" *Washington Post,* April 26, 1977, B1.

162. DeWitt, "Midge Costanza," B1.

163. Feit to OPL staff, February 9, 1977, "Memos, 2/77–6/77," Staff Offices, OPL: Costanza, Box 14, Carter Presidential Library.

164. For example, Costanza to the President, March 1, 1977, "Memos, 1/77–3/77," Staff Offices, OPL: Costanza, Box 14, Carter Presidential Library.

165. DeWitt, "Midge Costanza," B1.

166. Ronnie Feit served in this role early in the administration. See, e.g., Feit to All OPL Staff, February 2, 1977; Feit to OPL staff, February 9, 1977; and Feit to Costanza, February 14, 1977; all in "Memos, 2/77–6/77," Carter Presidential Papers: Staff Offices, OPL: Costanza, Box 14, Carter Presidential Library. By March 1977, Robert A. Nastanovich had become deputy assistant for public liaison and began directing the office's actual operation. In November, Seymour Wishman took over, staying until Anne Wexler arrived in April 1978. Wishman in particular tried to establish and enforce procedures within OPL; see, e.g., staff

meeting minutes, November 9, 1977, "Staff Meeting Minutes 3/77–10/77," Staff Offices, OPL: Costanza, Box 14; "Office of Public Liaison: Daily Routine, 11/77–12/77," Staff Offices, OPL: Costanza, Box 30, Carter Presidential Library.

167. Wales to OPL staff, March 31, 1977, "Memos, 2/77–6/77," Staff Offices, OPL: Costanza, Box 14, Carter Presidential Library.

168. For example, Ed Smith to Nastanovich, June 14, 1977, "[Office of Public Liaison] Activity Reports, 5/77–6/77"; Smith to Nastanovich, July 14, 1977, "[Office of Public Liaison] Activity Reports, 7/77–8/77"; Staff Offices, OPL: Costanza, Box 30, Carter Presidential Library.

169. Costanza to OPL staff, April 25, 1977, "Memos, 2/77–6/77," Staff Offices, OPL: Costanza, Box 14, Carter Presidential Library.

170. Nastanovich to OPL staff, April 7, 1977, "Memos, 2/77–6/77," Staff Offices, OPL: Costanza, Box 14; cf. "Issues Assignments," January 12, 1978, "[Office of Public Liaison Staff Meetings], 3/77–3/78," Staff Offices, OPL: Costanza, Box 31, Carter Presidential Library.

171. Nastanovich to OPL staff, April 7, 1977, "Memos, 2/77–6/77," Staff Offices, OPL: Costanza, Box 14, Carter Presidential Library.

172. Staff meeting notes, October 25, 1977, "Office of Public Liaison: Daily Activities Calendar, 10/77–1/78," Staff Offices, OPL: Costanza, Box 30, Carter Presidential Library.

173. Ibid.

174. "Issues Assignments," January 12, 1978, "[Office of Public Liaison Staff Meetings], 3/77–3/78," Staff Offices, OPL: Costanza, Box 31, Carter Presidential Library.

175. For example, Reiman to Costanza, February 14, 1977, "[Office of Public Liaison] Activity Reports, 1/77–2/77," Staff Offices, OPL: Costanza, Box 29; Reiman via Nastanovich to Costanza, April 12, 1977; Selig through Nastanovich to Costanza, April 11, 1977, "[Office of Public Liaison] Activity Reports, 4/77–5/77," Staff Offices, OPL: Costanza, Box 30, Carter Presidential Library.

176. For example, Staff meeting notes, October 25, 1977, "Office of Public Liaison: Daily Activities Calendar, 10/77–1/78," Staff Offices, OPL: Costanza, Box 30; January 12, 1978, "Issues Assignments," Staff Offices, OPL: Costanza, Box 31, Carter Presidential Library.

177. Nastanovich, minutes from March 16, 1977, staff meeting, "[Office of Public Liaison Staff Meetings], 3/77–3/78," Staff Offices, OPL: Costanza, Box 31, Carter Presidential Library.

178. Nastanovich to OPL staff, April 7, 1977, "Memos 2/77–6/77," Staff Offices, OPL: Costanza, Box 14; January 12, 1978, "Issues Assignments," Staff Offices, OPL: Costanza, Box 31, Carter Presidential Library.

179. Helen S. Silver, "Dr. Joyce Starr—Spokeswoman for Soviet Jewry at the White House," *Cleveland Jewish News,* June 5, 1978, 16, in "Starr, Joyce 10/76–9/78," Joseph W. Aragon Staff Offices Papers, Box 12. On Starr's activities more generally, see also "Middle East Issues—Jewish Community Concerns" [Folders 1–4], Domestic Policy Staff: Eizenstat, Box 235, Carter Presidential Library.

180. See "Middle East Issues—Jewish Community Concerns" [Folders 1–4], Domestic Policy Staff: Eizenstat, Box 235, Carter Presidential Library. Folder 3, e.g., contains information on United Nations action relevant to the Middle East and congressional activity on Soviet Jews.

181. For example, Starr to Lipshutz and Eizenstat, October 3, 1977, "Middle East Issues— Jewish Community Concerns [4]," Domestic Policy Staff: Eizenstat, Box 235; Starr to

Eizenstat, Aragon, Lipshutz, May 23, 1978; Starr to Lipshutz, Eizenstat, June 18, 1978; Starr to Lipshutz, Eizenstat, Aragon, Sanders, September 14, 1978; "Starr, Joyce, 10/76–9/78," Joseph W. Aragon Staff Offices Papers, Box 12, Carter Presidential Library.

182. Jordan to senior staff, April 20, 1977, "[Administrative Memos to White House Staff] 3/77–7/78," OPL: Costanza, Box 1; Peterson to [OPL] Staff, May 18, 1977, "Memos, 2/77–6/77," Staff Offices, OPL: Costanza, Box 14; Peterson to Costanza, October 11, 1977, "[Office of Public Liaison] Activity Reports, 8/77–9/77," Staff Offices, OPL: Costanza. Box 30, Carter Presidential Library.

183. For example, Reiman through Nastanovich to Costanza, July 11, 1977, "[Office of Public Liaison] Activity Reports, 7/77–8/77," Staff Offices, OPL: Costanza, Box 30, Carter Presidential Library. Selig evidently informed Wurfel about past administrations' use of such a group (Selig through Nastanovich to Costanza, June 13, 1977, "[Office of Public Liaison] Activity Reports, 5/77–6/77," Staff Offices, OPL: Costanza, Box 30, Carter Presidential Library).

184. Peterson through Nastanovich to Costanza, August 23, 1977, "[Office of Public Liaison] Activity Reports, 8/77–9/77," Staff Offices, OPL: Costanza, Box 30, Carter Presidential Library.

185. Ibid.

186. Selig through Nastanovich to Costanza, June 2, 1977, "[Office of Public Liaison] Activity Reports, 5/77–6/77," Staff Offices, OPL: Costanza, Box 30, Carter Presidential Library.

187. For example, on Latin American affairs and Hispanics and on the Middle East and Jewish groups, Starr via Nastanovich to Costanza, April 11, 1977, "[Office of Public Liaison] Activity Reports, 2/77–4/77," Staff Offices, OPL: Costanza, Box 29; on the issue of amnesty, Costanza to Vice President, Aaron, Lazarus, McKenna, and others, February 9, 1977, "[Staff Memos] 2/77–4/77," Staff Offices, OPL: Costanza, Box 4, Carter Presidential Library.

188. On OPL attendance at DPS meetings, see, e.g., April 10 and 19, 1977, "Staff Meeting Minutes 3/77–10/77 [Nastanovich notes]," Staff Offices, OPL: Costanza, Box 14. On the DPS presence at sessions with business groups, see, e.g., Selig through Nastanovich to Costanza, April 11, 1977, "[Office of Public Liaison] Activity Reports 4/77–5/77," OPL: Costanza, Box 30, 2; with veterans' organizations, Reiman via Nastanovich to Costanza, ibid.; with consumer groups, February 12, 1977, "Consumer Agency 6/77–12/77 [2]," DPS: Eizenstat, Box 172, Carter Presidential Library.

189. Reiman via Nastanovich to Costanza, June 2, 1977, and Wales via Nastanovich to Costanza, June 9, 1977, "[Office of Public Liaison] Activity Reports, 5/77–6/77," Staff Offices, OPL: Costanza, Box 30, Carter Presidential Library.

190. Wiesman minutes of staff meeting, December 8, 1977, "[Office of Public Liaison] Staff Meetings 3/77–3/78," OPL: Costanza, Box 31, Carter Presidential Library.

191. Haft through Nastanovich to Costanza, April 7, 1977, Staff Offices, OPL: Costanza, Box 31; cf. Frank Moore, Miller Center interview (including William Cable, Dan Tate, Robert Thomson), September 18–19, 1981, Carter Presidency Project, Vol. IV, Carter Presidential Library.

192. Haft through Nastanovich to Costanza, April 7, 1977, "Office Procedure, 2/77–11/77," Staff Offices, OPL: Costanza, Box 31, Carter Presidential Library.

193. On Starr's (and other OPL aides') involvement with hospital cost containment, see, e.g., the reports for July 1977 in "[Office of Public Liaison] Activity Reports, 7/77–8/77,"

OPL: Costanza, Box 30, Carter Presidential Library. For Wales's involvement with consumer protection, see, e.g., Wales via Nastanovich to Costanza, June 9, 1977, "[Office of Public Liaison] Activity Reports, 5/77–6/77"; staff meeting notes, October 27, 1977, "Office of Public Liaison: Daily Activities Calendar, 10/77–1/78," ibid.

194. See, e.g., Reiman through Nastanovich to Costanza, August 12, 23, 29 and September 27, 1977; Selig via Nastanovich to Costanza, September 12, 1977, "[Office of Public Liaison] Activity Reports, 8/77–9/77," OPL: Costanza, Box 30, Carter Presidential Library. See also Selig and Reiman to Aragon, Butler, September 30, 1977; Selig, Reiman via Costanza to Aragon, Butler, October 5, 1977, "Committee of Americans for the Canal Treaties (COACT) 9/77–12/77," Joseph W. Aragon Staff Offices Papers, Box 18, Carter Presidential Library.

195. For example, "Office of Public Liaison: Daily Activities Calendar, 10/77–1/78," OPL: Costanza, Box 30, Carter Presidential Library.

196. Marc Rosen, n.d., "Major Talking Points in OPL Staff Meeting 10/6/77," "Office of Public Liaison: Daily Activities Calendar, 10/77–1/78," OPL: Costanza, Box 30, Carter Presidential Library.

197. Doug Colton to A. D. Frazier Jr., March 26, 1977, "Executive Office of the President [Reorganization] Study 1/27/77 [CF/OA 61]," Richard Harden Papers, Box 12, Carter Presidential Library.

198. Costanza to Senior Staff, March 14, 1977, "[Staff Memos] 2/77–4/77," OPL: Costanza, Box 14, Carter Presidential Library.

199. See, e.g., Lazarus to Eizenstat, February 2, 1977, "Consumer Affairs—General"; memos in "Consumer Agency 6/77–12/77 [1]"; Domestic Policy Staff: Eizenstat, Box 176, Carter Presidential Library.

200. See, e.g., Martha M. Mitchell, "Finding Aid," Carter Presidential Library; President's schedule, May 18, July 8, 1977, "[Schedules: President Carter and Costanza] 3/77–10/77," OPL: Costanza, Box 14; "List of White House Contacts by Constituency," n.d. [probably late 1978], "Constituent Contacts, 7/6/77–1/12/80," Staff Offices, Special Advisor to the President—Moses, Box 5, Carter Presidential Library.

201. Starr requested and received tutoring in Spanish, for which the White House paid. See Starr to Hugh Carter, February 11, 1977, "Costanza, Midge [CF/OA 374]," Hugh Carter Files, Box 22, Carter Presidential Library.

202. Aragon's responses to a questionnaire for the EOP reorganization study, n.d., "[Aragon, Joe—Job Assessment] Executive Office of the President (EOP) 1977," Joseph W. Aragon Staff Offices Papers, Box 1. Cf. Frank del Olmo, "Aragon—He's No In-house Chicano," *Los Angeles Times*, May 2, 1977, in "Newsclippings 1/77–10/77," Joseph W. Aragon Staff Offices Papers, Box 9, Carter Presidential Library.

203. See, e.g., memos in "Hispanic Appointees 8/77–9/78," "Hispanic Caucus [of Congress] 2/78–9/78," "Hispanic News Editors/Media 10/77–8/78," Box 6; "Memos: Interoffice Incoming 1/77–10/77," Box 8; Aragon to Vice President, October 19, 1977, "Canal Briefings: Hispanic Organizations 9/77–4/78," Box 17; Joseph W. Aragon Staff Offices Papers, Carter Presidential Library.

204. A summary of activities and personnel in the counsel's office listed "Hispanic liaison" as one of Apodaca's responsibilities (July 24, 1979, Staff Offices, Counsel—Cutler, Box 52); on Sanchez-Dirks, see materials in "Ruth Sanchez-Dirks: Hispanic Detailee, 6/77–10/77," OPL: Costanza, Box 33, Carter Presidential Library.

205. DeWitt, "Midge Costanza," B1.

206. For example, Costanza to Vice President, Aaron, Lazarus, McKenna, February 9, 1977; Haft to Rubenstein, McKenna, Holbrooke, Holloway, Hunter, Giuliani, Jordan, Boydid, Gilliuat, February 12, 1977, in "[Staff Memos] 2/77–4/77," Staff Offices, OPL: Costanza, Box 14, Carter Presidential Library.

207. DeWitt, "Midge Costanza," B1. OCR aide Robert Beckel recalled that when members of Congress needed to be persuaded on particular pieces of legislation, Costanza "was in the middle of left-handed Nicaraguan refugees or something" (Miller Center interview, November 13, 1981, Carter Presidency Project, Vol. VII, 13, Carter Presidential Library).

208. See, e.g., Judy Bachrach, "Midge Costanza: The View from the Ground Floor," *Washington Post,* July 26, 1978, B1; "White House Women Draft Abortion Memo," *Washington Post,* August 4, 1977, A22; Jordan to President, n.d. [probably late July 1977], "Costanza, Midge," Chief of Staff's Office, Hamilton Jordan Files, Box 34, Carter Presidential Library.

209. Bachrach, "Midge Costanza," B1. Cf. Susan Wood, "The Weddington Way," *Washington Post Magazine,* February 11, 1979, 6.

210. Judy Mann, "The Abzug Affair: A White House Signal," *Washington Post,* January 17, 1979, C1.

211. Bachrach noted, "The single, unattached, unmarried, undefined Midge . . . might be galling to what one administration woman calls 'that Southern Boy Network that sent Midge to the basement' " ("Midge Costanza," B1).

212. See, e.g., Bachrach, "Midge Costanza," B1; Edward Walsh, "White House Staff Changes Involve Wexler," *Washington Post,* April 19, 1978.

213. "Finding Aid," Office of Public Liaison. See also Beckel, Miller Center interview, 13.

214. For example, David S. Broder, "Kraft to Be Carter's Campaign Chief," *Washington Post,* August 11, 1979, A1.

215. Anne Wexler, Miller Center interview (including Michael Chanin, Richard Neustadt, John Ryor), February 12–13, 1981, Carter Presidency Project, Vol. I, 34, Carter Presidential Library.

216. Aronson moved from the speechwriting unit to Hamilton Jordan's office, where he assisted Landon Butler with outreach to labor organizations. See, e.g., Proposed Plan, Jordan Office, as of January 28, 1980, Hugh Carter Files, Box 38, "Jordan, Hamilton/Office— 1980"; n.d. [early 1980], Office of the Assistant to the President for Women's Affairs (Sarah Weddington), Box 90, "Special Constituencies," "PSB File," Carter Presidential Library. The 1980 *White House Directory* (Washington, D.C.: National Journal Group) listed Aronson as "Deputy Assistant for Labor Liaison."

217. Cruikshank resigned in May 1980, and he was replaced by Harold L. Sheppard. Sheppard continued much of Cruikshank's work, speaking around the country and working on policy issues affecting senior citizens with other domestic policy staffers, OMB, and several executive branch departments. Like Cruikshank, he was lodged in the Domestic Policy Staff. See Staff Offices, Domestic Policy Staff, Aging (Cruikshank) and Aging (Sheppard), Carter Presidential Library.

218. Wexler, Miller Center interview, 34–35.

219. See, e.g., papers in Office of the Assistant to the President for Women's Affairs (Sarah Weddington), Boxes 12, 18, 38, 56, 60; Wood, "The Weddington Way."

220. In late 1978 and early 1979, friction between the White House and the President's National Advisory Committee for Women increased over the latter's public opposition to the administration's budgetary policies, especially proposed increases in defense spending and cuts in social welfare. On January 12, Carter fired Bella Abzug, the cochair of the com-

mittee, which prompted the resignations of more than half its members. Weddington's involvement in both Abzug's dismissal and White House decision making more generally provoked considerable controversy among feminist and other women's groups. See, e.g., Bill Peterson, "Women's Issues Seem Likely to Haunt Carter in 1980," *Washington Post,* January 14, 1979, A3; Wood, "The Weddington Way."

221. Even so, Weddington's external "success" was constrained both by the administration's focus on equal opportunities and by growing antifeminist sentiment. Hartmann contends that there was an important "divergence between the Carter administration's perception of the women's movement and what that movement had actually become." Carter and his staff generally overlooked the increasing emphasis on a "much wider range of issues that testified to the complexity of women's disadvantaged position and to the vast diversity of needs and interests among women." At the same time, "feminists . . . tended to exaggerate both the power of their movement and the reach of the president's influence." See Susan M. Hartmann, "Feminism, Public Policy, and the Carter Administration," in *The Carter Presidency: Policy Choices in the Post–New Deal Era,* ed. Gary M. Fink and Hugh Davis Graham (Lawrence: University Press of Kansas, 1998), 225. Cf. Burton I. Kaufman, *The Presidency of James Earl Carter, Jr.* (Lawrence: University Press of Kansas, 1993), 110–12.

222. Sanders to Jordan, February 8, 1979, "1/15/79–6/18/79," Senior Advisor to the President—Sanders, Box 1, Carter Presidential Library.

223. See, e.g., memos in "8/2/78–11/2/78," "1/15/79–6/18/79," "8/20/79–10/9/79," Senior Advisor to the President—Sanders, Box 1, Carter Presidential Library.

224. See, e.g., materials in "Inter-Office Memos, 8/5/80–9/22/80," Box 7, and "Watson, Jack, 9/25/78–7/15/80," Box 16, Staff Offices, Special Advisor to the President—Moses, Carter Presidential Library.

225. The "godfather" phrase was coined by Eddie Williams of the Joint Center for Political Studies. It appeared in the headline and text of a newspaper article on Martin (Jacqueline Trescott, *Washington Post,* October 10, 1978, in "Martin, Louis—Biographical Clippings," Staff Offices, Louis Martin, Special Assistant to the President, Box 57, Carter Presidential Library).

226. Ibid. Although she was not formally asked to resign, Mitchell soon left the White House to join the Small Business Administration; at the same time, 1,200 "individual petitions" reportedly were sent to the White House on her behalf by a "national hook-up" of black women who contended that she had been treated unfairly. See Theresa Humphrey, *The Afro-American,* September 12–26, 1978, in "Mitchell, Bunny [O/A 6475]," Staff Offices, Louis Martin, Special Assistant to the President, Box 67, Carter Presidential Library.

227. Edward Walsh and Susanna McBee, "Key Black Aide Leaving Staff of White House," *Washington Post,* May 4, 1978, in "Martin, Louis—Biographical Clippings," Staff Offices, Louis Martin, Special Assistant to the President, Box 57, Carter Presidential Library. O'Reilly contends that "nowhere was the organized civil rights community's disappointment more apparent than on the contentious question of affirmative action." The president's "awkward attempt to support affirmative action while condemning quotas" pleased almost no one and, in O'Reilly's view, marked the beginning of the slide to ultimate electoral defeat in 1980. See Kenneth O'Reilly, *Nixon's Piano: Presidents and Racial Politics from Washington to Clinton* (New York: Free Press, 1995), 344–45ff.

228. See Martin to Jordan, July 23, 1979, "Administrative Procedures [6]"; Martin to Watson, November 12, 1980, "Administrative Procedures [5]," Staff Offices, Louis Martin, Special Assistant to the President, Box 1, Carter Presidential Library.

229. For example, Martin to Phil Larsen, May 7, 1980; Martin to Watson, November 11, 1980, "Administrative Procedures [5]," Staff Offices, Louis Martin, Special Assistant to the President, Box 1, Carter Presidential Library. Cf. "Using the Mail," *National Journal,* April 5, 1980, in "Tapia Paul R., 11/28/79–4/5/80," White House Office of Hispanic Affairs— Torres, Box 35, Carter Presidential Library.

230. Martin to Watson, November 11, 1980, "Administrative Procedures [5]," Box 1. Cf. Martin to Lipshutz, October 27, 1978, "Federal Judges [1]," Box 39; Zuniga to Martin, April 20, 1979, "Internal Memos"; and Martin to Belford, May 29, 1980, "Interoffice Materials [1]," Box 46. All materials are in Staff Offices, Louis Martin, Special Assistant to the President, Carter Presidential Library.

231. See, e.g., Zuniga to Baux, November 9, 1978, "Chronology 1978," Box 19; Zuniga to Martin, November 28, 1978, "Zuniga, Karen [1]," Box 110, Staff Offices, Louis Martin, Special Assistant to the President, Carter Presidential Library.

232. Zuniga to "Dear _____," September 27, 1978, Box 6; Martin/Zuniga to black appointees, November 13, 1978, and Zuniga to Martin, November 15, 1978, Box 19, in Staff Offices, Louis Martin, Special Assistant to the President, Carter Presidential Library.

233. Martin to Jordan, July 23, 1979, "Administrative Procedures [6]," Staff Offices, Louis Martin, Special Assistant to the President, Box 1. Cf. text of Carter memo to Heads of Executive Departments and Agencies, Re: Black Colleges, n.d., Staff Offices, Louis Martin, Special Assistant to the President, Box 14, "Brown v. Board—Reception [O/A 9509] [1]," Carter Presidential Library.

234. Martin to Jordan, July 23, 1979, "Administrative Procedures [6]," Staff Offices, Louis Martin, Special Assistant to the President, Box 1, Carter Presidential Library.

235. Miller resume, in "Miller, I. Ray, Jr.," Staff Offices, Louis Martin, Special Assistant to the President, Box 59, Carter Presidential Library.

236. See Martin to Eizenstat, n.d. [early 1979], Malson to Martin, April 23, 1979, and other materials in "Media Task Force," Staff Offices, Louis Martin, Special Assistant to the President, Box 59, Carter Presidential Library.

237. For example, Roger Langley, "Hispanics Bitter after Meeting at the White House," *Express,* June 4, 1978, in "Hispanics [Correspondence] 1/78–6/78"; Henry B. Gonzales, May 24, 1978, "Hispanic Caucus [of Congress] 2/78–9/78," Joseph W. Aragon Staff Offices Papers, Box 6, Carter Presidential Library.

238. See, e.g., materials in "Colon, Gil: Office of Hispanic Affairs," Box 16; Torres to President, December 12, 1980, "Summary of Major Accomplishments [Memorandum to the President], 12/12/80," 5, Box 34; "News on Hispanic Affairs," vol. 1, no. 1, January 1980, in White House Office of Hispanic Affairs—Torres, Box 16, Carter Presidential Library.

239. "Using the Mail," *National Journal,* April 5, 1980, in "Tapia Paul R., 11/28/79– 4/5/80," Box 35, White House Office of Hispanic Affairs—Torres, Carter Presidential Library.

240. See, e.g., material in "Cuban/U.S. Issues [Briefing Book] [4/8/80–5/22/80]," Box 17; Torres, Tapia to Vice President, June 27, 1980, "Briefings, 1/8/80–6/27/80," Box 13; Torres to President, December 12, 1980, 4, "Summary of Major Accomplishments [Memorandum to the President], 12/12/80," Box 34, White House Office of Hispanic Affairs—Torres, Carter Presidential Library.

241. See, e.g., Torres to President, December 12, 1980, 3, "Summary of Major Accomplishments [Memorandum to the President], 12/12/80," Box 34; "Finding Aid," White House

Office of Hispanic Affairs—Torres; materials in "[White House Consultation on Farm Workers, 7/21/80–9/29/80]," Box 3, White House Office of Hispanic Affairs—Cruz, Carter Presidential Library.

242. "Finding Aid," White House Office of Hispanic Affairs—Torres, Carter Presidential Library.

243. Ibid.

244. For example, Colon to Torres, November 23, 1979, "Budget/Hispanic Affairs, 10/2/79–10/17/80," Box 13; Colon to Torres, "Hispanic Affairs Public Relations Material—Goals and Objectives, 1/22/80–2/27/80," Box 20, White House Office of Hispanic Affairs—Torres, Carter Presidential Library.

245. See, e.g., materials in "[White House Consultation on Farm Workers, 7/21/80–9/29/80]," Box 3, White House Office of Hispanic Affairs—Cruz, Carter Presidential Library.

246. See briefing material for a January 31, 1980, meeting including U.S. Attorney General Benjamin Civiletti, union leader Gilbert Padilla, Torres, and LULAC (League of United Latin American Citizens) officials, in "Tapia to Torres Memoranda, 12/13/79–9/5/80," Box 9, White House Office of Hispanic Affairs—Tapia, Carter Presidential Library.

247. See "Tapia to Torres Memoranda, 12/13/79–9/5/80," Box 9, White House Office of Hispanic Affairs—Tapia, Carter Presidential Library.

248. "Personnel Justification: Office of Anne Wexler," 1979, "Justification of Personnel, 8/9," Hugh Carter Files, Box 38, 2–3, Carter Presidential Library.

249. Geoffrey Godsell, "Why Can't They Be Like the Rest of Us?" *Christian Science Monitor,* January 6, 1981, 12. Cf. Stephen Aiello, "A Message from Dr. Stephen Aiello," in "The White House Office of Ethnic Affairs News," June 1980, in "Senior Staff Memos, Red Tag V. I. [very important], 1/8/80–6/30/80," White House Office of Hispanic Affairs—Torres, Box 33, Carter Presidential Library.

250. For example, Godsell, "Why Can't They Be," 12.

251. For example, when Polish workers struck in 1980, the Carter administration distanced itself from the situation, calling it a "domestic issue" that the Polish people and their government needed to resolve. Aiello was sent to a Chicago rally to reassure disappointed Polish Americans, who were worried about possible Soviet intervention. See, e.g., Joseph Treaster, "Strikes Making Polish-Americans Proud, but Anxious," *New York Times,* August 24, 1980, sec. 1, pt. 1, 22.

252. For example, Esteban Torres, in the White House Office of Hispanic Affairs, and Sarah Weddington, in charge of liaison with women, kept each other informed of their activities. They also worked together on matters involving minority women. See, e.g., material in "Weddington, Sarah, 8/30/79–3/19/80," White House Office of Hispanic Affairs—Torres, Box 36, Carter Presidential Library.

253. Wales to Public Liaison Committee, September 14, 1978, "Appointments—Past [1] [O/A 6475]," Staff Offices, Louis Martin, Special Assistant to the President, Box 5, Carter Presidential Library.

254. Wexler and Kraft to Distribution List, November 9, 1978, agenda for November 16 meeting, "Appointments—Past [2] [O/A 6475]," Staff Offices, Louis Martin, Special Assistant to the President, Box 5, Carter Presidential Library.

255. For example, Minutes of Public Liaison Committee, January 31, 1979, "1/15/79–6/18/79," Staff Offices, Senior Advisor to the President—Sanders, Box 1, Carter Presidential Library.

256. Wexler to Aiello, Burnett, Carp, Rubenstein, Cruikshank, Dobelle, Kahn, Jenkins, Maddox, Martin, McDonald, Peterson, Sanborn, Tarr-Whelan, Torres, Watson, Weddington, February 13, 1980, "Senior Staff Memos, Red Tag V. I. [very important], 1/9/80–6/30/80," White House Office of Hispanic Affairs—Torres, Box 33, Carter Presidential Library.

257. The effort continued until after the November 1980 election. Available evidence indicates that compliance was relatively poor, especially at the start, from within the White House. See "PSB File," "Weekly Status Report Departmental Speaking Engagement Calendars," Office of the Assistant to the President for Women's Affairs (Sarah Weddington), Box 92, Carter Presidential Library.

258. Pika, "Opening Doors for Kindred Souls," 191.

259. Indeed, Kumar notes: "Of the fourteen directors serving from 1977 to the end of the Clinton administration, a man served for only a part of one year in the twenty-year period [David Demarest in the first Bush administration]." See Martha Joynt Kumar, "The Office of Communications," *Presidential Studies Quarterly* 31 (December 2001): 629–30. The administration of George W. Bush has continued the practice, at the outset naming Lezlee Westine the director of OPL.

260. Lois Romano, "Women and the Narrow Corridors: At the White House, Frustrations Linger over the Lack of Access and Recognition," *Washington Post,* February 4, 1986, D1.

261. Pika, "Opening Doors for Kindred Souls," 292. On public liaison structuring in the Reagan and first Bush administrations, see, e.g., the semiannual issues of *Capital Source* (Washington, D.C.: National Journal Group), which list units and staffers in the White House Office.

262. Joseph A. Pika, "Reaching Out to Organized Interests: Public Liaison in the Modern White House," in *The Presidency Reconsidered,* ed. Richard W. Waterman (Itasca, Ill.: F. E. Peacock, 1993), 154.

263. Mark A. Peterson, "Clinton and Organized Interests: Splitting Friends, Unifying Enemies," in *The Clinton Legacy,* ed. Colin Campbell and Bert A. Rockman (New York: Chatham House, 2000), 154. From mid-1994 until the end of the first term (while Leon Panetta was chief of staff), OPL formally reported to the Office of the Deputy Chief of Staff for Policy and Political Affairs.

264. Peter H. Stone, "Lobbying Friends, after All," *National Journal,* October 22, 1994.

265. See, e.g., Nuestro Pueblo, "Round Tables Focus on Women's Issues," *New Orleans Times-Picayune,* April 4, 1996, 3A1; Mary Leonard, "Bush Liaison Courts Support of Women's Office Following Clinton Approach," *Boston Globe,* December 21, 2001, A5; Associated Press, "White House Closes Office on Women's Issues," *St. Louis Post-Dispatch,* March 29, 2001, A10; Virginia Sapiro and David T. Canon, "Race, Gender, and the Clinton Presidency," in *The Clinton Legacy,* ed. Colin Campbell and Bert A. Rockman (New York: Chatham House, 2000); 1993–2000 issues of *Capital Source* (Washington, D.C.: National Journal Group). Burrell contends that the unit's creation was part of a White House response to the fact that 54 percent of those who voted in 1992 but not in 1994 were women; see Barbara Burrell, "The Clintons and Gender Politics," in *The Postmodern Presidency: Bill Clinton's Legacy in U.S. Politics,* ed. Steven E. Schier (Pittsburgh: University of Pittsburgh Press, 2000), 241.

266. "Ben Johnson Named to Head Clinton's Race Initiative Office at White House," *Jet,* March 1, 1999, 6. See also *U.S. Government Manual,* 1999–2000, 2000–2001; *Capital*

Source, spring 1999, fall 1999; Ken Herman, "Bush Will Keep Race Relations, AIDS Offices Open," *Atlanta Constitution,* February 8, 2001, 13A; Sapiro and Canon, "Race, Gender, and the Clinton Presidency," 194.

267. Peterson, "Clinton and Organized Interests," 165.

268. See, e.g., Carl M. Cannon, James A. Barnes, Alexis Simendinger, Bruce Stokes, David Baumann, Marilyn Werber Serafini, and Jason Ellenburg, "The White House Profiles," *National Journal,* June 23, 2001; Herman, "Bush Will Keep Race Relations, AIDS Offices Open"; Leonard, "Bush Liaison Courts Support of Women's Office," A5.

269. Dana Milbank, "Karl Rove: Adding to His To-Do List," *Washington Post,* June 25, 2002, A17.

270. For example, Herman, "Bush Will Keep Race Relations, AIDS Offices Open"; Leonard, "Bush Liaison Courts Support of Women's Office"; Associated Press, "White House Closes Office on Women's Issues."

5. WHITE HOUSE COUNSEL

1. For example, Jeremy Rabkin, "White House Lawyering: Law, Ethics, and Political Judgments," in *Government Lawyers: The Federal Legal Bureaucracy and Presidential Politics,* ed. Cornell W. Clayton (Lawrence: University Press of Kansas, 1995), 110–11.

2. See Charles E. Walcott and Karen M. Hult, *Governing the White House: From Hoover through LBJ* (Lawrence: University Press of Kansas, 1995), 40–41, 110.

3. Gerald D. Morgan and Edward A. McCabe to Philip Buchen, October 2, 1974, "Office Organization and Functions (1)," Philip Buchen Files, Counsel's Office Files, Box 100, Ford Presidential Library, 2. Cf. Chapman to Garment, July 20, 1973, ibid.

4. Shirley Anne Warshaw, *The Domestic Presidency: Policy Making in the White House* (Boston: Allyn and Bacon, 1997), 37–38. In January 1970, Arthur Burns became chairman of the Federal Reserve Board.

5. Rabkin, "White House Lawyering," 112. By April 1971, Richard Moore (who initially worked under Charles Colson) also had the title of special counsel; Chotiner left the White House in early 1971.

6. David Young, quoted in Gerald S. Strober and Deborah Hart Strober, *Nixon: An Oral History of His Presidency* (New York: HarperCollins, 1994), 70.

7. See, e.g., David O. Stewart, "The President's Lawyer," *ABA Journal* 72 (April 1, 1986): 59; David Wilson, quoted in Strober and Strober, *Nixon,* 78; Rabkin, "White House Lawyering," 111.

8. John Dean, quoted in Strober and Strober, *Nixon,* 78. See also John Ehrlichman, *Witness to Power: The Nixon Years* (New York: Simon and Schuster, 1982), 84ff.

9. For example, Deputy Counsel (and later counsel under Ronald Reagan) Fred Fielding labeled Dean "very ambitious," and personnel aide and later Staff Secretary Jerry Jones called him "extremely ambitious." See Strober and Strober, *Nixon,* 280–81.

10. John W. Dean III, *Blind Ambition* (New York: Pocket Books, 1976), 28.

11. Ibid.

12. Stewart, "The President's Lawyer," 60.

13. Rabkin, "White House Lawyering," 114.

14. Ibid.

15. Dean to Haldeman, Ehrlichman, January 27, 1971, White House Staff Files, Staff Member and Office Files, John W. Dean III, Box 1, "JWD Chron File Jan 1971," Nixon Papers.

16. For example, Dean to the President, "Demonstration Status Report—May 4, 5 p.m.," May 4, 1971, White House Special Files, Staff Member and Office Files, John W. Dean III, Box 2, "JWD Chron File May 1971," Nixon Papers.

17. Draft memo, Dean to Haldeman, August 2, 1971, White House Special Files, Staff Member and Office Files, Box 3, "JWD Chron File August 1971," Nixon Papers.

18. See, e.g., Fielding to Colson (bcc: Dean), January 18, 1971, Box 1, "JWD Chron File Jan 1971"; Dean to Colson, May 12, 1971, and Dean to Colson, May 17, 1971, Box 2, "JWD Chron File May 1971"; Dean to Colson, December 27, 1971, Box 4, "JWD Chron File December 1971," White House Special Files, Staff Member and Office Files, John W. Dean III, Nixon Papers.

19. For example, Dean to Magruder, October 1, 1970; Dean to Nofziger (cc: Magruder), October 1, 1970, White House Special Files, Staff Member and Office Files, John W. Dean III, Box 1, "JWD Chron File Oct–Nov 1970," Nixon Papers.

20. Dean to Krogh, October 6, 1970, "JWD Chron File Oct–Nov 1970"; Dean to Ehrlichman, "PR Re Crime Fight," January 21, 1971, "JWD Chron File Jan 1971," White House Special Files, Staff Member and Office Files, John W. Dean III, Box 1, Nixon Papers.

21. Dean to President, October 19, 1970, White House Special Files, Staff Member and Office Files, John W. Dean III, Box 1, "JWD Chron File Oct–Nov 1970," Nixon Papers.

22. See, e.g., Dean to Peter Flanigan, January 27, 1971, Box 1, "JWD Chron File Jan 1971"; Arthur Fergensen to Fielding [which Dean passed on to Al Haig of the NSC staff] on the hearings before the Senate Foreign Relations Committee on war powers legislation on July 27–29, 1971, August 2, 1971, Box 3, "JWD Chron File August 1971." Both memos are in White House Special Files, Staff Member and Office Files, John W. Dean III, Nixon Papers.

23. See, e.g., Dean to Haldeman, October 29, 1972, "Proposed Activities through November 1972," White House Special Files, Staff Member and Office Files, John W. Dean III, Box 53, "Office [of Counsel to the President] Activities"; "Exhibit" of "Responsibility Assignments," attached to "Office of Counsel to the President: Organization and Responsibilities," "Discussion draft," November 3, 1971, ibid.; Dean to Wilson, February 19, 1971, and February 5, 1971, White House Special Files, Staff Member and Office Files, John W. Dean III, Box 1, "JWD Chron File Feb 1971," Nixon Papers.

24. "Exhibit" of "Responsibility Assignments," attached to "Office of Counsel to the President: Organization and Responsibilities," "Discussion draft," November 3, 1971, Box 53, "Office [of Counsel to the President] Activities"; Dean to Caulfield, December 3, 1970, Box 1, "JWD Chron File Dec 1970"; Caulfield to Dean, January 11, 1971, Box 1, "JWD Chron File Jan 1971"; Fielding to Caulfield, May 28, 1971, Box 2, "JWD Chron File May 1971." All are in White House Special Files, Staff Member and Office Files, John W. Dean III, Nixon Papers. See also handwritten memo, n.d. [1970 or 1971], prepared for a new staff secretary, in White House Special Files, Staff Member Office Files, Office of the Staff Secretary, Box 150, "Staff Secretary Move," Nixon Papers.

25. Dean to Haldeman, October 29, 1972, "Proposed Activities through November 1972," White House Special Files, Staff Member and Office Files, John W. Dean III, Box 53, "Office [of Counsel to the President] Activities," Nixon Papers. See also "Exhibit" of "Responsibility Assignments," attached to "Office of Counsel to the President: Organization and Responsibilities," "Discussion draft," November 3, 1971, ibid.

26. Haldeman handwritten comments on Dean to Haldeman, October 29, 1972, "Proposed Activities through November 1972," White House Special Files, Staff Member and Office Files, John W. Dean III, Box 53, "Office [of Counsel to the President] Activities," Nixon Papers.

27. "Office of Counsel to the President: Organization and Responsibilities," "Discussion draft," November 3, 1971; much the same information and language appear in Malek to Dean, November 8, 1971, White House Special Files, Staff Member and Office Files, John W. Dean III, Box 53, "Office [of Counsel to the President] Activities," Nixon Papers.

28. On possible protests during the Republican convention, see, e.g., Dean to Haldeman, July 6 and July 20, 1972, and on protests during the Democratic convention, see, e.g., Dean to Haldeman, July 7, 1972, White House Special Files, Staff Member and Office Files, John W. Dean III, Box 5, "Chrono July 1972," Nixon Papers.

29. Dean to Haldeman, December 1, 1972, White House Special Files, Staff Member and Office Files, John W. Dean III, Box 53, "Office [of Counsel to the President] Activities," Nixon Papers.

30. Leonard Garment, *Crazy Rhythm* (New York: Times Books, 1997), 252–53.

31. Ibid., 255.

32. Ibid., 266.

33. Ibid., 264.

34. See, e.g., ibid., 264–92 and passim.

35. Ibid., 291.

36. Ibid., 291ff.; see also lists of individuals in "Office of Counsel to the President" and "Office of Special Counsel to the President," White House Special Files, Staff Member and Office Files, Office of the Staff Secretary, Box 166 "White House Office Budget File [1 of 2]," Nixon Papers.

37. By early 1973, the counsel's office continued to perform routine work, but many of the associated memos were from Fielding. See, e.g., the chronological files for March and April 1973, White House Special Files, Staff Member and Office Files, John W. Dean III, Box 7, Nixon Papers.

38. On staff efforts, see, e.g., "Bill Timmons," White House Special Files, Staff Member and Office Files, Alexander M. Haig, Box 10—November, "Interstaff Communications, 1973"; Shepard to Haig, November 13, 1973, "Ken Cole (Domestic Council)," White House Special Files, Staff Member and Office Files, Alexander M. Haig, Box 9—November, "Interstaff Communications, 1973," Nixon Papers.

39. John R. Greene, *The Presidency of Gerald R. Ford* (Lawrence: University Press of Kansas, 1995), chap. 2; see also folders on, e.g., "Transition—Personnel Issues," "Transition—Policy Issues," and "Transition—Presidential Meetings," in Philip Buchen Files, General Subject Files, Box 63, Ford Presidential Library.

40. See, e.g., Ed McCabe, "Notes on White House Counsel under DDE"; Jerry Morgan, Ed McCabe, August 30, 1974, "Proposed Initial Organization—White House Legal Office"; Morgan and McCabe to Buchen, "Functions to Be Performed by the Office of Counsel to the President," October 2, 1974, "Office Organization and Functions (1)," Philip Buchen Files, Counsel's Office Files, Box 100, Ford Presidential Library.

41. Buchen, interview with William A. Syers, March 13, 1985, 7, Ford Presidential Library.

42. While he was in the White House, Areeda evidently did little to push for a return to an Eisenhower-era counsel's office. Among his tasks was reviewing the unit's contact with

federal regulatory agencies, whether there should be White House supervision of litigation that affected White House interests, and whether the Office of Telecommunications Policy should remain in the EOP (McCabe to Buchen, October 3, 1974, "Office Organization and Functions [1]," Philip Buchen Files, Counsel's Office Files, Box 100, Ford Presidential Library). Moreover, Warshaw notes that Areeda was Donald Rumsfeld's initial candidate for director of the Domestic Council staff and was placed in the counsel's office "waiting . . . to move into the domestic policy job." When James Cannon, an aide to Nelson Rockefeller, became head of the DC staff, Areeda left government. See Warshaw, *Domestic Presidency*, 68.

43. See, e.g., Chapman to Buchen, August 29, 1974, "Office Organization and Functions (1)"; Buzhardt to Buchen, September 25, 1974, "Office Organization and Functions (2)," Philip Buchen Files, Counsel's Office Files, Box 100, Ford Presidential Library.

44. Buchen to Jerry Jones, December 13, 1974, "Office Organization and Functions (2)," Philip Buchen File, Counsel's Office Files, Box 100, Ford Presidential Library.

45. See, e.g., McCabe to Buchen, October 3, 1974, "Office Organization and Functions (1)"; Lazarus to Buchen, Hills, n.d. [probably September 1975], "Office Organization and Functions (3)," Philip Buchen Files, Counsel's Office Files, Box 100; Buchen to President, October 27, 1975, "Staff—Hills, Roderick (2)," Philip Buchen Files, Counsel's Office Files, Box 101, Ford Presidential Library.

46. See, e.g., Buchen to Connor, June 27, 1975, "Staff—General (1)"; September 4, 1975, "Office Organization and Functions (3)," 3, Philip Buchen Files, Counsel's Office Files, Box 100, Ford Presidential Library.

47. McCabe to Buchen, October 3, 1974, "Office Organization and Functions (1)"; Lazarus to Buchen, Hills, n.d. [probably September 1975], "Assignments" and "Counsel's Office Professional Staff," "Office Organization and Functions (3)," 1–3, Philip Buchen Files, Counsel's Office Files, Box 100, Ford Presidential Library.

48. McCabe to Buchen, October 3, 1974, "Office Organization and Functions (1)," 1–3; Casselman to Buchen, July 31, 1975, "Staff—Casselman, William (2)," 3, Philip Buchen Files, Counsel's Office Files, Box 100, Ford Presidential Library.

49. Casselman to Buchen, July 31, 1975, "Staff—Casselman, William (2)," 3, Philip Buchen Files, Counsel's Office Files, Box 100, Ford Presidential Library. Although Casselman's formal title was counsel, he worked under both Buchen and the deputy counsel.

50. Lazarus to Buchen, Hills, n.d. [probably September 1975], "Assignments" and "Counsel's Office Professional Staff," "Office Organization and Functions (3)," 8; Casselman to Buchen, July 31, 1975, "Staff—Casselman, William (2)," 3, Philip Buchen Files, Counsel's Office Files, Box 100, Ford Presidential Library.

51. For example, Hills to Buchen, August 4, 1975, "Staff—Casselman, William (2)," Philip Buchen Files, Counsel's Office Files, Box 100; "Staff—Kilberg, Barbara," Philip Buchen Files, Counsel's Office Files, Box 101; Bobbie Greene Kilberg, Counsel's Transition Book, Boxes 18, 19, Ford Presidential Library.

52. Buchen to Ford, August 6, 1975, "Staff—Casselman, William (2)," Philip Buchen Files, Counsel's Office Files, Box 100, Ford Presidential Library.

53. Buchen to Jones, April 2, 1975, and Marsh to Buchen, July 11, 1975, "Staff—Wilderotter, James," Box 101; Lazarus to Buchen, Hills, n.d. [probably September 1975], "Assignments" and "Counsel's Office Professional Staff," "Office Organization and Functions (3)," 8, Philip Buchen Files, Counsel's Office Files, Box 100, Ford Presidential Library.

54. Lazarus to Buchen, Hills, n.d. [probably September 1975], "Assignments" and

"Counsel's Office Professional Staff," "Office Organization and Functions (3)," 8, Philip Buchen Files, Counsel's Office Files, Box 100, Ford Presidential Library.

55. See "White House—Senior Staff Meetings," Philip Buchen Files, General Subject File, Box 67, Ford Presidential Library.

56. For example, "Bobbie" to "Phil," June 12, 1976, "Staff—Kilberg, Barbara," Philip Buchen Files, Counsel's Office Files, Box 101, Ford Presidential Library.

57. Buchen to President, October 27, 1975, "Staff—Hills, Roderick (2)," Philip Buchen Files, Counsel's Office Files, Box 101, Ford Presidential Library.

58. Gorog to Hills, September 15, 1975, "Staff—Chapman, Dudley H.," Philip Buchen Files, Counsel's Office Files, Box 100, Ford Presidential Library.

59. Buchen, interview, 6.

60. See, e.g., Robert J. Lipshutz, exit interview with Marie Allen, September 29, 1979, Carter Presidential Library.

61. Ibid., 8.

62. This staff of five attorneys did not change during Counsel Lipshutz's two years. See, e.g., Lipshutz to McKenna, March 11, 1977, "Reorganization—Executive Office of the President, 2/4/77 [CF O/A 422]," Box 140; July 24, 1979, "Personnel of Counsel's Office" [evidently for Cutler as he was taking over as counsel], Box 52, Staff Offices, White House Counsel, Carter Presidential Library.

63. Lipshutz to Jordan, Powell, Eizenstat, Watson, Moore, Costanza, December 17, 1977, "Budget, White House, 11-12-77 [CF, O/A 435]," Box 5, Staff Offices, White House Counsel, Carter Presidential Library.

64. On the varying tasks performed by members of the counsel staff, see, e.g., July 24, 1979, "Activities of Counsel's Office" and "Personnel of Counsel's Office" [evidently for Cutler as he was taking over as counsel], Box 52; Huron, memo for the file, December 2, 1977, "Costanza, Midge, 4/77–8/78 [CF, O/A 119]," Box 11; Lipshutz to McKenna, March 11, 1977, "Reorganization—Executive Office of the President, 2/4/77 [CF O/A 422]," Box 140; Staff Offices, White House Counsel, Carter Presidential Library. See also Lipshutz, exit interview.

65. Lloyd Cutler, Miller Center interview, October 23, 1982, Carter Presidency Project, Vol. XVIII, 3, Carter Presidential Library.

66. For instance, Lipshutz, exit interview, 16–17.

67. Ibid.

68. For example, ibid., 14.

69. Lipshutz, interview with Martha Joynt Kumar, White House Interview Program, Washington, D.C., September 1, 1999; quoted in MaryAnne Borrelli, Karen Hult, and Nancy Kassop, "The White House Counsel's Office," *Presidential Studies Quarterly* 31 (December 2001): 566.

70. Michael P. Strine, "Counsels to the President: The Rise of Organizational Competition," in *Government Lawyers: The Federal Legal Bureaucracy and Presidential Politics,* ed. Cornell W. Clayton (Lawrence: University Press of Kansas, 1995), 268–69.

71. Lipshutz, exit interview, 15–16; cf. Rabkin, "White House Lawyering," 115–16.

72. Rabkin, "White House Lawyering," 115–17.

73. Cutler, interview with Martha Joynt Kumar (with Nancy Kassop), White House Interview Program, Washington, D.C., July 8, 1999; quoted in Borrelli, Hult, and Kassop, "White House Counsel's Office," 574.

74. Lloyd Cutler, exit interview with Marie Allen, March 2, 1981, 4, Carter Presidential Library. Cutler stayed with his law firm during this task.

75. Ibid., 5.

76. See, e.g., Cutler, Miller Center interview, 3.

77. Dick Kirschten, "Watergate Survivor Fielding Guards against Abuses of White House Power," *National Journal* 14 (February 13, 1982); http://www.lexis.com/universe/docum... lzV&_md5=4a7a71d82212ebe5cfaa2b4aa07ccf3; June 4, 2000.

78. Ibid.

79. Cutler, interview with Kumar, quoted in Borrelli, Hult, and Kassop, "White House Counsel's Office," 574. Cf. Cutler, Miller Center interview, 3. Kirschten included Clifford in his list of active counsels.

80. Lloyd C. Cutler, "The Role of Counsel to the President of the United States," address to the New York City Bar Association, April 14, 1980, in *The Record of the Association of the Bar of the City of New York* 35 (November 1980): 472.

81. See, e.g., ibid., 473–75; Cutler, exit interview, 6–13.

82. Cutler, exit interview, 16ff.

83. See, e.g., Naftali Bendavid, "Cutler's Task: Mixing Politics, Fealty, and Law: White House Counsel's Job Has No 'Handbook,'" *Legal Times* 16 (March 14, 1994); Cutler, exit interview, 1981; Cutler, interview with Kumar, quoted in Borrelli, Hult, and Kassop, "White House Counsel's Office," 581.

84. Cutler, "Role of Counsel to the President," 472.

85. For example, Cardozo and Huron to Cutler, October 24, 1979, "Judges, 5/78–12/79"; Huron to Cutler, January 17, 1980, Cardozo to Cutler, January 28, 1980, "Judges, 1–5/80," Staff Offices, White House Counsel: Cutler, Box 96, Carter Presidential Library.

86. See, e.g., Cutler to Brzezinski, March 27, 1980, Staff Offices, White House Counsel: Cutler, Box 52, Carter Presidential Library.

87. See, e.g., Bobbitt to Cutler, February 20, 1980; Onek to Cutler, March 10, 1980; Cutler to Civiletti, June 25, 1980; Onek to Cutler, July 14, 1980, Staff Offices, White House Counsel: Cutler, Box 97, "Legislative Veto, 10/79–11/80," Carter Presidential Library.

88. Mark Rozell, "Executive Privilege in the Carter Administration: The 'Open' Presidency and Secrecy Policy," *Presidential Studies Quarterly* 27 (spring 1997): 280.

89. See, e.g., Strine, "Counsels to the President," 272.

90. Borrelli, Hult, and Kassop, "White House Counsel's Office," 561–84.

91. Cutler, interview by Kumar, quoted in ibid., 581.

6. CONGRESSIONAL RELATIONS

1. See Charles E. Walcott and Karen M. Hult, *Governing the White House: From Hoover through LBJ* (Lawrence: University Press of Kansas, 1995), chap. 2; Kenneth E. Collier, *Between the Branches: The White House Office of Legislative Affairs* (Pittsburgh: University of Pittsburgh Press, 1997), chaps. 2–4.

2. As Collier observed, "although there have been some changes since in the name of the office and the titles of the positions, this organization became the model for future administrations" (*Between the Branches*, 61).

3. Quoted in ibid., 112.

4. Tom Korologos, interview with A. James Reichley, 1, A. James Reichley Interviews, Box 1, "Nixon White House Interviews," Ford Presidential Library.

5. Collier, *Between the Branches*, 112.

6. Max Friedersdorf to H. R. Haldeman, November 13, 1972, White House Special Files, Staff Member and Office Files, Office of the Staff Secretary, Box 162, "WH Staff Member Office Files, 1972, #1," Nixon Papers. Friedersdorf went on to note that "it has been suggested that the White House put a man into each agency and department to reinforce the President's will." That, he argued, might be the "only solution." Apparently, the problem varied by department. Congressional aide Fred Weber noted that when he worked on the Hill for the Labor Department early in Nixon's first term, the White House was calling all the signals for the legislative team (interview with A. James Reichley, October 17, 1977, 3, A. James Reichley Interviews, Box 1, "Nixon White House Interviews," Ford Presidential Library). By contrast, Senate aide Tom Korologos characterized the HUD congressional-relations office in 1970 as "the worst in all creation" (White House Central Files, Subject Files, Federal Government [FG], Ex FG 31, Box 4, "The Congress of the United States [2 of 3] [June 1969–July 1970," Nixon Papers). Still, Korologos, in an interview with Reichley, noted that department liaison people could be very helpful, especially at the committee level (A. James Reichley Interviews, August 31, 1977, Ford Presidential Library).

7. Wallace Johnson to H. R. Haldeman, November 15, 1972, White House Staff Files, Staff Member and Office Files, Office of the Staff Secretary, Box 162, "WH Staff Member Office Files, 1972, #1," Nixon Papers. Johnson's colleague Dick Cook agreed, arguing in a memo to Haldeman that most department and agency legislative offices were not competent. Cook to Haldeman, November 16, 1972, ibid.

8. See Charles E. Walcott and Karen M. Hult, "White House Staff Size: Explanations and Implications," *Presidential Studies Quarterly* 29 (1999): 646–48; Collier, *Between the Branches,* 112.

9. William Casselman, interview with A. James Reichley, October 28, 1977, 1–2, A. James Reichley Interviews, Box 1, "Nixon White House Interviews," Ford Presidential Library.

10. Kenneth BeLieu, interview with A. James Reichley, September 13, 1977, 1, A. James Reichley Interviews, Box 1, "Nixon White House Interviews," Ford Presidential Library.

11. Vernon C. Loen, interview with Stephen Wayne, November 18, 1976, 5, James F. C. Hyde and Stephen J. Wayne Oral History Collection, Ford Presidential Library.

12. Bryce Harlow, interview with A. James Reichley, November 3, 1977, 4, A. James Reichley Interviews, Box 1, "Nixon White House Interviews," Ford Presidential Library.

13. Collier, *Between the Branches,* 117.

14. Ibid., 111.

15. Loen, interview, 2–3.

16. BeLieu, interview, 3.

17. Ibid.

18. Collier, *Between the Branches,* 115.

19. Eugene Cowen, interview with A. James Reichley, October 5, 1977, 4, A. James Reichley Interviews, Box 1, "Nixon White House Interviews," Ford Presidential Library.

20. William Timmons, interview with A. James Reichley, November 29, 1977, 5, A. James Reichley Interviews, Box 1, "Nixon White House Interviews," Ford Presidential Library.

21. Pat O'Donnell, interview with William A. Syers, July 3, 1985, 3, Syers Papers, Box 1, "1985—Interviews," Ford Presidential Library. O'Donnell described an occasion when he and Timmons's top assistant, Max Friedersdorf, were flying with Nixon and other staffers on a plane that landed in Friedersdorf's Indiana hometown. A large sign proclaimed, "Wel-

come Home Max Friedersdorf." Nixon leaned over to Ehrlichman and asked, "Who the heck is Max Friedersdorf?"

22. See Walcott and Hult, *Governing the White House,* especially 49–51. The problem was particularly acute in the Johnson administration.

23. H. R. Haldeman to Herbert Klein, July 17, 1969, White House Special Files, Staff Member and Office Files, Herbert Klein, Box 1, "H. R. Haldeman I [2 of 3]," Nixon Papers. In a handwritten note, Haldeman urged that the matter be brought up at the next staff meeting. A month later, Staff Secretary John Brown sent a memo to the White House staff asking them to send copies of all "non-personal" correspondence with members of Congress to Harlow's office: "I think this procedure is being followed in most instances, but I am sure it is not being followed in all instances." White House Central Files, Subject Files, WH (White House Administration), Box 10, "Ex WH 4-1 (Mail) 8/15/69–9/30/69," Nixon Papers.

24. Lamar Alexander to Tom Whitehead, January 26, 1970, White House Special Files, Subject Files, General Government [FG], Ex FG 31, "The Congress of the United States [5 of 14] [January–April 1970]," Nixon Papers. Around the same time, Al Haig, then Henry Kissinger's deputy, apologized to Timmons for a Kissinger breakfast with members of Congress that had been scheduled without notifying Timmons (Alexander Haig to William Timmons, March 7, 1970, White House Central Files, Subject Files, Federal Government [FG], Ex FG 31, Box 2, "The Congress of the United States [5 of 14], January–April 1970," Nixon Papers).

25. Clark MacGregor to White House staff, November 10, 1971, White House Central Files, Subject Files, Federal Government (FG), Ex FG 31, Box 2, "The Congress of the United States [10 of 13] [September 1971–February 1972]," Nixon Papers.

26. William Timmons to Alexander Haig, May 12, 1973, White House Special Files, Staff Member and Office Files, Alexander M. Haig, Box 40, "Haig Memoranda—1973," Nixon Papers. Timmons indicated that this was a serious, ongoing irritation in his interview with Reichley.

27. Tony McDonald to Charles Colson, May 15, 1972, White House Special Files, Staff Member and Office Files, Charles W. Colson, Box 13, "Miscellaneous Memos [3 of 4] [4/12/72–4/21/72]," Nixon Papers.

28. Anonymous [probably Ken Cole] to Ehrlichman, October 9, 1970, White House Central Files, Subject Files, Federal Government (FG), Ex FG 31, Box 2, "The Congress of the United States [7 of 14] [October–December 1970]," Nixon Papers.

29. Ibid.

30. See White House Central Files, Subject Flies, Federal Government (FG), Ex FG 31-1, "The Congress of the United States," Box 4, "Legislative Leadership meetings [1 of 18] [January–April 1969]," Nixon Papers.

31. Collier, *Between the Branches,* 121.

32. Ibid. OCR aide Richard Cook concurred, noting that Nixon was simply not a good lobbyist. Cook interview with A. James Reichley, September 16, 1977, 2, A. James Reichley Interviews, Box 1, "Nixon White House Interviews," Ford Presidential Library.

33. White House Central Files, Subject Files, Federal Government (FG), Ex FG 31, Box 2, "The Congress of the United States [9 of 14] [April–August 1971]," Nixon Papers.

34. BeLieu (interview, 2) stressed the absence of leaders such as Lyndon Johnson, Robert Kerr, or Richard Russell in the Senate. In the Nixon era, nobody could deliver blocks of

votes or results in committee in the old-fashioned way, which made negotiating with Congress far harder.

35. See Joseph A. Pika, "White House Boundary Roles: Marginal Men Amidst the Palace Guard," *Presidential Studies Quarterly* 16 (fall 1986): 700–15. Nixon liaison staffer Fred Weber supported this interpretation, noting that his efforts to represent the view of the Senate in White House discussions caused him to be asked which side he was on (Weber, interview, 3).

36. This analysis draws heavily on Collier, *Between the Branches,* 114–20.

37. Ibid., 115. See also Dom Bonafede and Andrew J. Glass, "White House Report: Nixon Deals Cautiously with Hostile Congress," *National Journal,* June 27, 1970, 1353.

38. Collier, *Between the Branches,* 118. Colson, brought to the White House to organize groups (partly in support of legislative initiatives), would likewise become an important point of access for some in Congress.

39. Cowen, interview, 1–2.

40. Carl Bernstein and Bob Woodward, "Strategy to Counter Impeachment Lacking, Nixon Staff Says," *Washington Post,* July 28, 1974.

41. Walcott and Hult, *Governing the White House,* 191–92.

42. Alexander Butterfield to Nixon, May 1, 1969, White House Special Files, Staff Member and Office Files, Alexander P. Butterfield, Box 1, "Alex Butterfield (May 1969)," Nixon Papers. BeLieu's initial reaction is noted in Butterfield, memo for the record, April 15, 1969, ibid., "Alex Butterfield (Apr 1969)."

43. Butterfield complained about this in a memo to Nixon, May 23, 1969, ibid.

44. Haldeman to Jeb Magruder, December 21, 1970, White House Special Files, Staff Member and Office Files, Gordon Strachan, Box 5, "Domestic Program," Nixon Papers.

45. Egil M. Krogh, interview with Terry W. Good and John R. Nesbitt, December 18, 1972, Exit Interviews, Nixon Presidential Materials, Nixon Papers.

46. Most of the administration's responses to congressional Watergate investigations were handled by the counsel's office and its special Watergate unit (see chapter 5).

47. Loen, interview, 22. Loen reported not only that the staff was overworked but also that it could not get telecopiers or decent typewriters.

48. William T. Kendall, interview with James F. C. Hyde Jr. and Stephen J. Wayne, September 30, 1975, Tape 1, 4, Hyde and Wayne Oral History Collection, Ford Presidential Library.

49. Loen, interview, 2–3.

50. Joe Jenckes, interview with William A. Syers, August 8, 1985, 2, Syers Papers, Box 1, "Files, 1985—Interviews," Ford Presidential Library.

51. Kendall, interview, 6.

52. Jenckes, interview, 5.

53. Loen, interview, 13. Ordinarily, DC staffers limited themselves to briefing the liaison staff on policy issues. In Loen's account, OMB staff, albeit more influential, did not try to deal directly with Congress (14).

54. This, as OCR staffer Patrick Rowland noted, was not much different from any other appeal for a vote (interview with William A. Syers, June 27, 1985, 2, Syers Papers, Box 1, "Files, 1985—Interviews," Ford Presidential Library).

55. Ibid., 3.

56. Kendall, interview, 15.

57. Loen, interview, 9.

58. Kendall, interview, 16.

59. Charles Leppert, interview with William A. Syers, July 10, 1985, 3, Syers Papers, Box 1, "Files, 1985—Interviews," Ford Presidential Library.

60. Bryce Harlow, interview with William A. Syers, July 27, 1985, 3, Syers Papers, Box 1, "Files, 1985—Interviews," Ford Presidential Library.

61. William T. Kendall, interview with William A. Syers, June 26, 1985, 2, Syers Papers, Box 1, "Files 1985—Interviews," Ford Presidential Library.

62. Frank Moore, Miller Center interview (including William Cable, Dan Tate, Robert Thomson), September 18–19, 1981, Carter Presidency Project, Vol. IV, 11, Carter Presidential Library.

63. Ibid., 20–21. Moore noted that Carter's staff was less extensive and powerful than Larry O'Brien's staff in the early 1960s.

64. Ibid., 4. Wilson went so far as to give Moore a folder containing all the memos he had written to President Johnson, organized by issue.

65. Collier, *Between the Branches,* 171. See also Eric L. Davis, "Legislative Liaison in the Carter Administration," *Political Science Quarterly* 94 (summer 1979): 287–301.

66. Thus, Collier is partially justified in arguing that "the Carter White House was the first to attempt to organize along issue lines" (*Between the Branches,* 171), although this is something of an overstatement.

67. William Cable, exit interview with Emily Soapes, 7, Presidential Papers Project, Carter Presidential Library. Cable's idea was to get away from the notion of liaison staff as "representative" of any particular region. Staffers also were assigned to concentrate on particular issues, especially in connection with administration task forces.

68. Ibid., 8.

69. Collier, *Between the Branches,* 166.

70. Robert Beckel, Miller Center interview, November 13, 1981, Carter Presidency Project, Vol. VII, 74, Carter Presidential Library.

71. Hamilton Jordan, Miller Center interview (including Landon Butler), November 6, 1981, Carter Presidency Project, Vol. VI, 36, Carter Presidential Library.

72. Ibid., 36–37.

73. Quoted in Collier, *Between the Branches,* 168.

74. Cable, exit interview, 2–3.

75. Moore to Management Committee, March 1, 1977, Richard Harden Papers, Box 18, "Legislative Projects Coordinator 2/3/77–3/24/78 [CF/OA 62]," Carter Presidential Library.

76. Richard Harden to Robert Russell and Les Francis, May 2, 1977, Richard Harden Papers, Box 18, "Legislative Projects Coordinator 2/3/77–3/24/78 [CF/OA 62]," Carter Presidential Library.

77. Les Francis to Frank Moore, June 13, 1977, Richard Harden Papers, Box 18, "Legislative Projects Coordinator 2/3/77–3/24/78 [CF/OA 62]," Carter Presidential Library.

78. Al McDonald, Miller Center interview (including Michael Rowny), March 13–14, 1981, Carter Presidency Project, Vol. II, 17, Carter Presidential Library.

79. Ibid., 50.

80. The workings of the Panama Canal task force are documented in the Joseph W. Aragon Staff Office Papers, Box 16, "Ratification of Panama Canal Treaties," Carter Presidential Library. Aragon, the White House liaison to the Hispanic community, was closely involved, along with congressional-relations staff and representatives from the State Depart-

ment, the Democratic National Committee, and an ad hoc, bipartisan citizens' committee. Actually, the use of special White House staff structures for policy initiatives goes back to Truman and Eisenhower (see Walcott and Hult, *Governing the White House,* chap. 9), but the Carter approach was innovative in bringing personnel from the departments and agencies into the effort.

81. See McDonald and Hugh Carter to Moore, December 18, 1979, Hugh Carter Files, Box 16, "Congressional Liaison—1979 [1]," Carter Presidential Library. The memo lists personnel for congressional liaison as well as detailees for the energy and budget task forces.

82. Beckel, Miller Center interview, 47.

83. Ibid.

84. Lloyd Cutler, Miller Center interview, October 23, 1982, Carter Presidency Project, Vol. XVIII, 28, Carter Presidential Library.

85. Ibid., 29.

86. Collier, *Between the Branches,* 181.

87. Ibid., 180.

88. For instance, in the early fall of 1978, Senator Paul Simon (D-Ill.) commented that the congressional liaison operation was "much improved, I think generally excellent." Stuart Eizenstat copy of notes from conversation with Simon, late August or early September 1978, Domestic Policy Staff: Eizenstat Files, Box 253, "Pollster Repts—Pub Opin [1]," Carter Presidential Library.

89. See, e.g., the analysis in Samuel Kernell, *Going Public,* 3d ed. (Washington, D.C.: Congressional Quarterly, 1997), chaps. 1–2.

7. STRUCTURING FOR POLICY PROCESSES

1. Terry M. Moe, "The Politicized Presidency," in *The New Direction in American Politics,* ed. John E. Chubb and Paul E. Peterson (Washington, D.C.: Brookings, 1985). See also Terry M. Moe and Scott A. Wilson, "Presidents and the Politics of Structure," *Law and Contemporary Problems* 57 (1994): 1–44. It is worth reiterating, however, that our view here is closer to what Rudalevige called a "contingent centralization" perspective. See Andrew Rudalevige, *Managing the President's Program: Presidential Leadership and Legislative Policy Formulation* (Princeton, N.J.: Princeton University Press, 2002).

2. Charles E. Walcott and Karen M. Hult, *Governing the White House: From Hoover through LBJ* (Lawrence: University Press of Kansas, 1995), 159–81, 261.

3. Christopher C. Shoemaker, *The NSC Staff: Counseling the Council* (Boulder, Colo.: Westview, 1991), 16.

4. Ibid., 17.

5. Carter's design for national security decision making was spelled out in Presidential Directive/NSC 2, dated January 20, 1977. See Shoemaker, *NSC Staff,* 49–57.

6. Shoemaker, *NSC Staff,* 50.

7. See Walcott and Hult, *Governing the White House,* 169–71.

8. Shoemaker, *NSC Staff,* 52–54. See also I. M. Destler, Leslie H. Gelb, and Anthony Lake, *Our Own Worst Enemy: The Unmaking of American Foreign Policy* (New York: Simon and Schuster, 1984), 223.

9. Shoemaker, *NSC Staff,* 54. See also Zbigniew Brzezinski, *Power and Principle* (New York: Farrar, Straus, Giroux, 1983), 59–66.

10. Karen M. Hult and Charles E. Walcott, "The Conundrum of Domestic Policy Making" (paper presented at the 1989 annual meeting of the American Political Science Association).

11. See Walcott and Hult, *Governing the White House,* 152–58.

12. The structure and personnel of Moynihan's staff are detailed in Shirley Anne Warshaw, *The Domestic Presidency: Policy Making in the White House* (Boston: Allyn and Bacon, 1997), 26–30.

13. Rowland Evans and Robert Novak, *Nixon in the White House: The Frustration of Power* (New York: Random House, 1971), 11, quoted in Richard P. Nathan, *The Administrative Presidency* (New York: Wiley, 1983), 33.

14. Allen J. Matusow, *Nixon's Economy: Booms, Busts, Dollars, and Votes* (Lawrence: University Press of Kansas, 1998), 11.

15. See Dan Rather and Gary Paul Gates, *The Palace Guard* (New York: Warner, 1975), 81–89. Burns, professorial and "ponderous" in manner, immediately lost ground to the witty and articulate Moynihan.

16. Warshaw, *Domestic Presidency,* 33.

17. Ibid., 32–34.

18. Stephen Hess reported that he and Moynihan accepted and trusted Ehrlichman, whom they regarded optimistically as something of a closet liberal. Stephen Hess, interview with A. James Reichley, October 21, 1977, Reichley Interviews, Box 1, "Nixon White House Interviews," Ford Presidential Library.

19. Rather and Gates (*Palace Guard,* 202–5) note that the Chappaquiddick incident, which temporarily removed Senator Edward Kennedy from the presidential calculus, made the left-flank protection provided by Moynihan less essential.

20. For a discussion of the precedents drawn on by the commission, see Warshaw, *Domestic Presidency,* 34–36.

21. For a full listing, see ibid., 40.

22. Nathan, *Administrative Presidency,* especially chaps. 2–3. An excellent example of Ehrlichman's struggle to control the bureaucracy is found in Lamb and Twombley's study of the efforts to rein in HUD Secretary George Romney. See Charles M. Lamb and Jim Twombley, "Presidential Influence and Centralization: The Case of Nixon and Romney," *Politics and Policy* 29 (March 2001): 91–119.

23. Like the staff of the National Security Council, Domestic Council staffers were technically on the Executive Office, not the White House Office, payroll. Only the councils' heads, Ehrlichman and Henry Kissinger, were on the White House rolls.

24. These groups are described by Warshaw, *Domestic Presidency,* 44–55, and Nathan, *Administrative Presidency,* 34–38.

25. Nathan, *Administrative Presidency,* 35.

26. Ibid., 37.

27. Ibid., 38.

28. Roy L. Ash, oral history interview with Raymond H. Geselbracht and Frederick J. Graboske, January 13, 1988, 22–23, Nixon Papers.

29. Ibid., 52.

30. Warshaw, *Domestic Presidency,* 49.

31. Robert Wood, "When Government Works," *Public Interest* (winter 1970), quoted in Nathan, *Administrative Presidency,* 41.

32. See Warshaw, *Domestic Presidency,* 52.

33. Ash, oral history interview, 23.

34. Bradley H. Patterson Jr., exit interview with Terry W. Good, September 10, 1974, 2–6, Nixon Papers.

35. Brad Patterson, interview with A. James Reichley, November 11, 1977, 1–2, Reichley Interviews, Ford Presidential Library.

36. Lewis Engman, interview with A. James Reichley, February 17, 1978, 2, Reichley Interviews, Ford Presidential Library.

37. See Warshaw, *Domestic Presidency,* 58–60.

38. See Roger Porter, *The Economic Policy Board* (Cambridge: Cambridge University Press, 1980).

39. Ray Waldman, interview with A. James Reichley, January 11, 1978, 2, Reichley Interviews, Box 1, Ford Presidential Library.

40. This point was made by W. Allen Moore, interview with Stephen J. Wayne, in James F. C. Hyde and Stephen J. Wayne Oral History Collection, Part II, 29–30, Ford Presidential Library.

41. Warshaw, *Domestic Presidency,* 66.

42. Ibid., 67.

43. To an extent, this was both consistent with the NSC model and reasonable, in the sense that the DC staff was technically located in the EOP, not the White House Office.

44. Talking points for Rockefeller meeting with Ford, Marsh 1975, James Cannon Files, Box 69, "Domestic Council Organization," Ford Presidential Library, quoted in Warshaw, *Domestic Presidency,* 70–71.

45. Cheney to Rumsfeld, June 9, 1975, Michael Duval Files, Box 3, "Domestic Council Meeting," Ford Presidential Library, quoted in Warshaw, *Domestic Presidency,* 72.

46. Warshaw, *Domestic Presidency,* 75.

47. Ibid., 75–77.

48. Ash, oral history interview.

49. Warshaw, *Domestic Presidency,* 96.

50. Bertram Carp, Miller Center interview with Carp and David Rubenstein, March 6, 1982, Carter Presidency Project, Vol. XIV, 23, Carter Presidential Library.

51. Ibid.

52. Daniel E. Ponder, in *Good Advice: Information and Policy Making in the White House* (College Station: Texas A&M University Press, 2000), argues convincingly that the DPS served Carter well on the whole, although it struggled at times with policy disputes between departments.

53. This is an idea that was put to use during Ronald Reagan's first term and was a source of Chief of Staff James Baker's power, since his office staffed the clusters.

54. Warshaw, *Domestic Presidency,* 100.

55. See Donald L. Maggin, "How Carter Reorganized the EOP," *Management Review,* May 1978, Hugh Carter Files, "Reorganization [1]," Box 75, Carter Presidential Library.

56. Warshaw, *Domestic Presidency,* 104.

57. Ibid., 110.

58. Carter subcabinet member, quoted in Walter Williams, *Mismanaging America: The Rise of the Anti-analytic Presidency* (Lawrence: University Press of Kansas, 1990), 57.

59. Hamilton Jordan to Jimmy Carter, July 16, 1979, Hamilton Jordan's Files, Box 34, "[Image Analysis & Changes, 7/16/79]," Carter Presidential Library. Jordan's memo was a reaction to one from Caddell.

60. See Hult and Walcott, "The Conundrum."

61. Walcott and Hult, *Governing the White House,* 154–55.

62. Ibid., 155.

63. Kenneth I. Juster and Simon Lazarus, *Making Economic Policy: An Assessment of the National Economic Council* (Washington, D.C.: Brookings Institution Press, 1997), 14–15.

64. Ibid., 15.

65. Ibid., 15–16.

66. The most extensive account of the EPB is in Porter, *Economic Policy Board.*

67. This is the judgment of Williams, *Mismanaging America,* 51–53.

68. Porter, *Economic Policy Board,* 198.

69. Juster and Lazarus, *Making Economic Policy,* 17.

70. See Walcott and Hult, *Governing the White House,* 96–99. The key element in Roosevelt's efforts was the National Emergency Council, which could be considered an early prototype for DC-like structures.

71. The scope of Nixon's domestic accomplishments is only now being appreciated by historians. See, e.g., Melvin Small, *The Presidency of Richard Nixon* (Lawrence: University Press of Kansas, 1999); Joan Hoff, *Nixon Reconsidered* (New York: Basic Books, 1994), especially pt. I; and Iwan Morgan, *Nixon* (New York: Oxford University Press, 2002), especially chap. 4.

8. SPEECHWRITING

1. For elaboration of this point, see Karen M. Hult and Charles E. Walcott, "Policymakers and Wordsmiths: Writing for the President under Johnson and Nixon," *Polity* 30 (spring 1998): 465–87; Carol W. Gelderman, *All the President's Words: The Bully Pulpit and the Creation of the Virtual Presidency* (New York: Walker, 1997); Karen M. Hult and Charles E. Walcott, "Separating Rhetoric from Policy: Speechwriting under Gerald Ford and Jimmy Carter," *White House Studies* 1, no. 4 (2001): 463–78. Much of the analysis of the Nixon speechwriting process in this chapter is adapted from the first article cited.

2. An exception occurred under President Warren G. Harding, who employed on his staff a "literary clerk," Judson Welliver, to write speeches for him. Welliver is thus celebrated as the first White House speechwriter. Herbert Hoover also had an administrative assistant to write minor speeches, but he wrote major policy addresses himself. See Charles E. Walcott and Karen M. Hult, *Governing the White House: From Hoover through LBJ* (Lawrence: University Press of Kansas, 1995), 211–23.

3. See Hult and Walcott, "Policymakers and Wordsmiths."

4. Ibid.

5. The influence of the Johnson experience is difficult to establish with certainty because the Nixon transition documents are not yet available.

6. See Hult and Walcott, "Policymakers and Wordsmiths."

7. See White House Special Files, Staff Member and Office Files—Buchanan, Nixon Papers, for records of Buchanan's speechwriting work.

8. Haldeman Notes, February 10, 1970, Box 41, University Press of America Microfiche Collection.

9. Hult and Walcott, "Policymakers and Wordsmiths"; see also Haldeman Notes, August 13–14, 1971, Box 44; "Sunday, August 15 1971 Challenge of Peace Economic Speech," Pres-

ident's Speech Files, Box 68, Nixon Papers; William Safire, *Before the Fall: An Inside View of the Pre-Watergate White House* (Garden City, N.Y.: Doubleday, 1975), 509ff. On a few key occasions, the question of writers' awareness of policy did not arise because Nixon drafted the speeches himself. For example, he wrote the November 1969 "Silent Majority" speech, as well as the announcement of his trip to China.

10. Dwight Chapin to Stephen Bull, January 19, 1971, White House Special Files, Staff Member and Office Files—Buchanan, Box 3, "Chapin," Nixon Papers.

11. Safire, *Before the Fall,* 100. Cf. Herbert G. Klein, *Making It Perfectly Clear* (Garden City, N.Y.: Doubleday, 1980), 108.

12. "April 20, 1970 Vietnam Progress Report," Folders 1 and 2, President's Speech Files, Box 57, Nixon Papers.

13. John Ehrlichman, *Witness to Power: The Nixon Years* (New York: Simon and Schuster, 1982), 21.

14. See, e.g., Haldeman Notes, January 20, 1972, and April 18, 1972, Box 45.

15. See Charles Colson to Des Barker, Buchanan, Dwight Chapin, Ken Cole, Ken Clawson, Ehrlichman, Dick Moore, Dave Parker, Safire, John Scali, Bruce Whelihan, and Ron Ziegler, June 22, 1972, White House Special Files, Staff Member and Office Files—Buchanan, Box 5, "Colson—1972 (3 of 5)," Nixon Papers.

16. Klein, *Making It Perfectly Clear,* 129.

17. Haldeman Notes, July 28, 1969, Box 40. The president's dissatisfaction with the length and organization of his speeches can be seen in Haldeman Notes, February 9, 1970, Box 41, and June 30, 1971, Box 44.

18. See Raymond Price, *With Nixon* (New York: Viking, 1977).

19. On Nixon's growing isolation, see, e.g., John Osborne, *The Fifth Year of the Nixon Watch* (New York: Liveright, 1974), and John Osborne, *The Last Nixon Watch* (New York: Liveright, 1975). Examples of Nixon's variable involvement in drafting speeches can be seen in "November 7, 1973 Energy Speech," Box 89; "Wed, March 27, 1974, Republican Senate/House Dinner," Box 91, President's Speech Files, Nixon Papers.

20. Gergen to Haig, February 28, 1974, White House Staff Files, Staff Member and Office Files, Office of the Staff Secretary, Box 189, "Gergen Staff," Nixon Papers.

21. For a description of the Ford writing arrangements, see Hult and Walcott, "Separating Rhetoric from Policy." See also Robert T. Hartmann, *Palace Politics: An Inside Account of the Ford Years* (New York: McGraw-Hill, 1980), especially chaps. 7, 15, 16; Gelderman, *All the President's Words,* 63–194.

22. Hartmann, *Palace Politics,* 278. The number of words would eventually exceed three million in Ford's abbreviated administration.

23. John J. Casserly, *The Ford White House: The Diary of a Speechwriter* (Boulder: Colorado Associated University Press, 1977), 100.

24. Hartmann, *Palace Politics,* 343–45; Casserly, *Ford White House,* 49, 69.

25. On style, see Roderick P. Hart, *Verbal Style and the Presidency: A Computer-Based Analysis* (New York: Academic Press, 1984), 151. On content, see Pat Butler, interview with William A. Syers, 1985, William A. Syers Papers, "Files, 1985—Interviews," Ford Presidential Library; Casserly, *Ford White House,* 114, 154, 158.

26. See, e.g., Casserly, *Ford White House,* 201; Gelderman, *All the President's Words,* 121–27.

27. Robert Goldwin, interview with A. James Reichley, February 27, 1978, Reichley Transcripts, Box 1, "Ford White House Interviews," Ford Presidential Library.

28. Paul Theis, Memorandum to President Ford via Robert Hartmann, n.d., Ronald H. Nessen Files, Box 45, "Theis, Paul," Ford Presidential Library.

29. Butler, interview, 1.

30. Hartmann, *Palace Politics,* 384. Hart's computer-based rhetorical analysis similarly concluded that Ford's rhetoric was generally ineffective. Hart attributed the problem in part to the speechwriting process (*Verbal Style,* 167).

31. See Price, *With Nixon;* see also Safire, *Before the Fall.*

32. Casserly, *Ford White House,* 114. On major speeches, such as the 1976 State of the Union Address, the fighting could become far more severe. Hartmann (*Palace Politics,* 382–95) gives a detailed, if not unbiased, account.

33. Casserly, *Ford White House,* 144–45.

34. Ibid., 58, 177.

35. David Gergen, *Eyewitness to Power: The Essence of Leadership, Nixon to Clinton* (New York: Simon and Schuster, 2000).

36. Hartmann (*Palace Politics,* 393) had long complained of "wildcat" speechwriting done outside his shop by people like Gergen at the behest of the "praetorians."

37. Robert T. Hartmann, Memorandum to President Ford, circa March 1976, Robert T. Hartmann Files, Box 13, "Office—Organization," Ford Presidential Library.

38. Butler, interview, 3.

39. White House Study Project, December 7, 1976, "Analysis of Present White House Office, Counselor to the President (Hartmann)," Report No. 1, Ford Presidential Library.

40. Carter's writers normally had to draft about twenty-five speeches per week, although many of those were minor.

41. Hendrik Hertzberg, Miller Center interview (including Christopher Matthews, Achsah Nesmith, Gordon Stewart), December 3–4, 1981, Carter Presidency Project, Vol. VIII, Carter Presidential Library. Hertzberg was head of the writing staff after November 1978.

42. Jody Powell, Miller Center interview (including Patricia Bario, Al Friendly, Rex Granum, Dale Leibach, Claudia Townsend), December 17–18, 1981, Carter Presidency Project, Vol. X, Carter Presidential Library.

43. James Fallows, Memorandum to Jody Powell and Richard Harden, January 1, 1977, Domestic Policy Staff: Eizenstat Files, Box 253, "Personnel," Carter Presidential Library.

44. Fallows's successor shared his views completely. See Hertzberg, Miller Center interview, 112.

45. James Fallows, Memorandum to President Carter (and Carter reply), January 21, 1977, Jody Powell Files, Box 42, "Memoranda: Fallows, Jim 1/21/77–5/20/77," Carter Presidential Library.

46. Frank Moore, Miller Center interview (including William Cable, Dan Tate, Robert Thomson), September 18–19, 1981, Carter Presidency Project, Vol. IV, Carter Presidential Library.

47. James Fallows, Memorandum to President Carter (and Carter reply), January 21, 1977, Jody Powell Files, Box 42, "Memoranda: Fallows, Jim 1/21/77–5/20/77," Carter Presidential Library.

48. Caryl Conner, Memorandum to James Fallows, August 22, 1978, Staff Offices, Speechwriters Subject File, Box 29, "Speechwriting Organization, 8/78 JF," Carter Presidential Library.

49. Chris Matthews, in Hertzberg, Miller Center interview.

50. James Fallows, Memorandum to President Carter, February 1, 1978, Jody Powell Files, Box 42, "Memoranda: Granum, Rex 2/1/78–12/13/78," Carter Presidential Library.

51. Hendrik Hertzberg, Memorandum to Hamilton Jordan, August 20, 1979, Staff Offices, Speechwriters—Administrative File, Box 3, "Personnel, 12/31/77–6/9/80," Carter Presidential Library. Hart also partly blamed "too many hands" for what he considered Carter's lack of rhetorical success (*Verbal Style*, 193).

52. See James Fallows, "The Passionless Presidency: The Trouble with Jimmy Carter's Administration," *Atlantic Monthly* 243 (1979): 33–48. The dispute in this case was between Secretary of State Cyrus Vance and Brzezinski over what negotiating line to take toward the Soviet Union in the strategic arms limitation talks.

53. Achsah Nesmith, in Hertzberg, Miller Center interview, 133.

54. Hendrik Hertzberg, Memorandum to Hamilton Jordan, August 20, 1979, Staff Offices, Speechwriters—Administrative File, Box 3, "Personnel, 12/31/77–6/9/80," Carter Presidential Library.

55. Hendrik Hertzberg, Memorandum to Alonzo McDonald, February 18, 1980, Staff Offices, Speechwriters—Administrative File, Box 3, "Personnel, 12/30/77–6/9/80," Carter Presidential Library.

56. Ibid.

57. Peggy Noonan, *What I Saw at the Revolution: A Political Life in the Reagan Era* (New York: Random House, 1990), chap. 5. For a more positive spin on the first Reagan term, see Paul D. Erickson, *Reagan Speaks: The Making of an American Myth* (New York: New York University Press, 1985).

58. John Podhoretz, *Hell of a Ride: Backstage at the White House Follies, 1989–1993* (New York: Simon and Schuster, 1993). See also Lee Walczak, Richard Fly, and Douglas A. Harbrecht, "Howard Baker's Long, Hot Summer," *Business Week* 3 (August 1987), and Bernard Weinraub, "White House," *New York Times,* April 7, 1989.

59. Jeffrey H. Birnbaum, *Madhouse: The Private Turmoil of Working for the President* (New York: Random House, 1996), chap. 5.

9. ANALYSIS AND CONCLUSIONS

1. As the data on staff size reported by Hart show, however, the jump from Johnson to Nixon was actually less startling than has been supposed—depending on how one counts or whose figures one uses. See John Hart, *The Presidential Branch*, 2d ed. (Chatham, N.J.: Chatham House, 1995), 116. The figures we tend to credit most, mainly because they report detailees as well as formally budgeted staff, are reported in Charles E. Walcott and Karen M. Hult, "White House Staff Size: Explanations and Implications," *Presidential Studies Quarterly* 29 (September 1999): 638–56.

2. Walcott and Hult, "White House Staff Size," 641.

3. Hart, *Presidential Branch,* 124.

4. A major normative work on the White House in recent years is Martha Joynt Kumar and Terry Sullivan, eds., *White House World: Transitions, Organization, and Office Operations* (College Station: Texas A&M University Press, 2003). It is based on interviews with former White House officials going back to Nixon, but no further. Many are explicit in acknowledging that Nixon created the template for the modern White House. On the simi-

larities between the George W. Bush White House and those of his predecessors, see, e.g., Karen M. Hult, "The Bush White House in Comparative Perspective," in Fred I. Greenstein, ed., *The Presidency of George W. Bush: An Early Assessment* (Baltimore: Johns Hopkins University Press, 2003).

5. Charles E. Walcott and Karen M. Hult, *Governing the White House: From Hoover through LBJ* (Lawrence: University Press of Kansas, 1995).

6. Ibid., 248–50.

7. Ibid., 255–56.

8. Ibid., 256–57.

9. See Diane Heith, "One for All: Using Focus Groups and Opinion Polls in the George H. W. Bush White House," *Congress and the Presidency* 30 (spring 2003): 81–94.

10. Judson Welliver was the first White House staff speechwriter, dubbed a "literary clerk" in the Harding administration.

11. The best and most recent example is Kumar and Sullivan, *White House World.*

12. For an exception, see Matthew Dickinson, *Bitter Harvest: FDR, Presidential Power, and the Growth of the Executive Branch* (New York: Cambridge University Press, 1997).

13. See Charles Walcott and Karen M. Hult, "White House Organization as a Problem of Governance: The Eisenhower System," *Presidential Studies Quarterly* 24 (1994): 327–40.

14. For a similar argument about more contemporary presidencies, as well as possible prescriptions, see Karen M. Hult, "Strengthening Presidential Decision-Making Capacity," *Presidential Studies Quarterly* 30 (March 2000): 27–46.

15. In fact, Janis makes that argument. See Irving L. Janis, *Groupthink,* 2d ed. (Boston: Houghton Mifflin, 1982), chap. 9.

16. Cf. Paul A. Kowert, *Groupthink or Deadlock: When Do Leaders Learn from Their Advisors?* (Albany: State University of New York Press, 2002), 164.

17. For illustrations of the importance of orderly decision processes and effective means of reading the political and policy environments in foreign policy decision making, see John P. Burke and Fred I. Greenstein, with the collaboration of Larry Berman and Richard Immerman, *How Presidents Test Reality: Decisions on Vietnam, 1954 and 1965* (New York: Russell Sage, 1989), and Meena Bose, *Shaping and Signaling Presidential Policy: The National Security Decision Making of Eisenhower and Kennedy* (College Station: Texas A&M University Press, 1998). Both argue that the carefully structured (formally and informally) decision-making approach of the Eisenhower administration fared well substantively when compared with the looser arrangements favored by Johnson and Kennedy, respectively.

Index